Corel PHOTO-PAINT™ 7 PLUS
The Official Guide

Second Edition

About the Author...

 I hate biographies where you write about yourself in the third person, so I am writing this in first person. I have been in the computer industry a long time—a real long time. My first computer was water-cooled with an iron-core memory, and the input/output device was a teletype. In the 60s that was really high-tech, even before high-tech was a word.

I was a Corel user beginning in the heady days of version 2.0 when Dr. Cowpland used to answer technical questions. I have written every PHOTO-PAINT book there is, beginning with PHOTO-PAINT 5. I teach PHOTO-PAINT at Corel and Ventura seminars worldwide, as well as writing monthly articles about PHOTO-PAINT in *Corel Magazine,* Chris Dickman's *Corel DRAW Journal, TagLine* (a UK Ventura publication), and the *National Enquirer* (just kidding). I also occasionally write for *PC Computing*—and I would write for *Publish* magazine, but I don't own a Mac. I try to maintain an area on CorelNET (**www.Corelnet.com**) called Paint Shop. In my other life, I work as Senior Technical Support Engineer with one of the largest third-party support services in the country. I've even worked as a Windows 95 support engineer for Microsoft.

I have a lovely wife whom I've been married to these past 24 years, and we have two neat kids: Jonathan (21), who is a pre-med major at our local institute of higher learning, and Grace (16). I can be reached at **dhuss@prismnet.com**. Feel free to drop me a note and tell me what you like about the book or what you would like to see in the PHOTO-PAINT 8 book.

Corel PHOTO-PAINT™ 7 PLUS
The Official Guide

Second Edition

David Huss

Osborne **McGraw-Hill**

Berkeley   New York   St. Louis   San Francisco   Auckland
Bogotá   Hamburg   London   Madrid   Mexico City   Milan
Montreal   New Delhi   Panama City   Paris   São Paulo
Singapore   Sydney   Tokyo   Toronto

Osborne **McGraw-Hill**
2600 Tenth Street
Berkeley, California 94710
U.S.A.

For information on translations or book distributors outside the U.S.A., or to arrange bulk purchase discounts for sales promotions, premiums, or fundraisers, please contact Osborne/**McGraw-Hill** at the above address.

Corel PHOTO-PAINT™ 7 PLUS: The Official Guide

234567890 DOC 9987

ISBN 0-07-882321-8

Publisher: Brandon A. Nordin
Editor-in-Chief: Scott Rogers
Acquisitions Editor: Megg Bonar
Project Editor: Nancy McLaughlin
Associate Editor: Heidi Poulin
Technical Editor: Jennifer Campbell
Copy Editor: Gary Morris
Proofreaders: Karen Mead
Indexer: James Minkin
Editorial Assistant: Gordon Hurd
Computer Designer: Jani Beckwith
Illustrator: Lance Ravella
Color Insert: Leslee Bassin
Cover Design: Timm Sinclair
Quality Control Specialist: Joe Scuderi

This book is dedicated in loving memory to Grace Beckwith (1911-1996), because she was more of a Mother than an in-law. She will be missed.

CONTENTS AT A GLANCE

CONTENTS

HANDS-ON WORKSHOPS

Corel PHOTO-PAINT™ 7 PLUS: The Official Guide represent the latest in a series of books dedicated to the users of Corel software. This series provides both a solid grounding in product fundamentals and the knowledge necessary to master advanced features of the product. The author, along with the staff at Corel, has spent many hours working on the accuracy and scope of this book.

This edition provides an in-depth overview of Corel PHOTO-PAINT 7. New users, as well as those who have purchased upgrades, will find significant value in these pages. The hands-on exercises will help improve your ability to make excellent use of the exciting features of Corel PHOTO-PAINT. The book also reveals tips and tricks which have been developed over several versions of the software by the most experienced users, and includes a gallery of images created with Corel PHOTO-PAINT to illustrate the power of the product.

The Corel Press *Official Guide* series of books represents a giant step in the ability of Corel to disseminate information to users, through the help of Osborne/McGraw-Hill and the fine authors involved with the series. Congratulations to the team at Osborne on the creation of this excellent book!

DR. MICHAEL C. J. COWPLAND
PRESIDENT AND CEO
COREL CORPORATION

FOREWORD

This is the part of the book that few, if any, read. However, it still remains necessary to acknowledge and give heartfelt thanks to those who have helped make this book possible.

First and foremost, I thank my family, who had to give up their father and husband over the Christmas and New Year's holidays so that this book could go out on schedule. My family got to see a lot more of the back of my head than they ever thought they would.

Up Ottawa way (that's where Corel lives, in case you didn't know), I must thank Doug Chomyn, head of the PHOTO-PAINT development team, who endured thousands (OK, maybe hundreds) of seemingly endless questions about PHOTO-PAINT 7. I also must give a big old Texas thank you to David Garrett, of the Corel PHOTO-PAINT Quality Assurance department, who found answers to some of the oddest questions you could ever imagine. Other Corel folk that deserve mention include Kelly Greig, who managed the beta release along with her new family addition and didn't lose her sanity, and Claudia Schiffo and the rest of Corel technical documentation department, who have created the best *PHOTO-PAINT Users Manual* to date. (In fact, if they continue to improve the *Users Manual,* I may have to start writing books like *101 Things to Do with Your Commodore PET.*) Thanks also to Michael Bellefeuille, who had the unenviable job of overseeing the production of the *Manual...*and to Michelle Murphy, who did a lot of the work Michael was responsible for. Last but not least is Lucian Mustatea, who is more responsible for the existence of this PHOTO-PAINT 7 book than anyone realizes, including myself.

Thanks to all of my dear friends at Hewlett-Packard in the Greeley, Colorado area—including Sara Wilson (who owns me...don't ask...), Sandy Wakeman, and Jerry Day, who taught me more about scanners than he will ever know. Thanks.

Jennifer Campbell, of *Corel Magazine,* is the best technical editor a fella could ask for. When you are going through one of the hands-on Workshop exercises in this book, and it works just like it is supposed to, Jennifer is the one who deserves a lot of the credit. It is her job to make sure the gibberish I write is both understandable and accurate.

My thanks to my boss, Eli Ontiveroz, for his patience and flexibility with my erratic schedule during the creation of this book.

The Corel Press gang at Osborne McGraw-Hill deserves a big pat on the collective back for moving heaven and earth to get this book on the shelves and into the PHOTO-PAINT boxes as quickly as possible (Actually though, since

ACKNOWLEDGMENTS

Osborne is in the San Francisco Bay area, the moving earth part was easy.) Special thanks to Megg Bonar, who had as one of her first assignments at Osborne being my Acquisitions Editor—proving that no good deed goes unpunished. Thanks also to Gordon Hurd, who was able to discover the ultimate data encryption scheme using CC:Mail, which may be marketed next year as a file shredder. I would be remiss if I didn't mention Scott Rogers. So here goes: Scott Rogers. And to Daniela—It is really very simple: your car radio is not connected to the heater. Go ahead and turn on the heater. (You just can't change stations.)

My thanks to my close friends in the UK: Ed Brown, Anne Gray, and Dr. Kathy Lang, who tolerated my many missed deadlines during the writing of this book.

My thanks to all of you who also helped, but who in the frosty hours of the early morning, I've failed to remember. (This is like the tomb of the unknown contributor.)

Lastly, my daughter Grace (16) wanted to let you all know that she is still looking for Mr. Right.

CAUTION: *This book contains stuff that could be harmful to your non-computer literate status.*

So there you stand next to a multicolored wall of computer titles, wondering if this book is going to help you use PHOTO-PAINT or if it will become another dust collector on the shelf. Your puzzlement is understandable. After all, the word "idiot" or "dummy" doesn't appear anywhere in the title. By now you have looked at the color inserts and seen all of the images that YOU will create using the hands-on Workshop exercises in this book (as opposed to images that other people have produced), but perhaps you hear that still small voice in the background (not to be confused with the announcements of the half-price off sale in cookbooks) saying that you won't be able to do stuff like that. Let me assure you: you will.

Whenever you see this icon in the book, you'll know there's a Workshop exercise just ahead. Be sure and work through all of these nifty hands-on demonstrations! There's no surer path to becoming a comfortable, confident, creative PHOTO-SHOP graphics whiz than <u>practice, practice, practice</u>!

My "day job" (as in "don't give up your day job") involves talking to thousands of people every day (OK, dozens of people) who start off their conversations by telling me how stupid they are regarding their computers. These people are not stupid*. However, they have come to believe they are; convinced by a legion of techno-talking computer types—many of whom simply need to date more. In creating this book, I have worked with the following assumptions:

*Actually, I do recall one customer who, when asked what kind of computer he had, said that he wasn't sure but he thought it was electric. (Sigh.)

1. You have not received the Nobel Prize in any of the computer categories.

2. Your IQ is greater than that of mayonnaise.

3. You would like to learn how to use and enjoy a computer program other than *Doom* or *Duke-Nukem 3D*.

4. You do not have a four-year degree in graphic arts.

As often as possible, I have included explanations of the terms I use. I have also tried to go beyond just explaining what a tool in PHOTO-PAINT does—showing you how to use it and what to use it on.

My hope is that you will enjoy Corel PHOTO-PAINT as much as I have. You can leave comments, complaints, or any other feedback at my Internet address (**dhuss@prismnet.com**), or contact me on CompuServe (**76575,241**). I try and answer questions all the questions that are posted as time allows...but no promises. And please, only PHOTO-PAINT questions; any inquiries about raises, marriages, or winning lottery numbers should be directed to a live psychic hot-line. (Which brings up a question. If they really are psychics, why do I have to call them? Shouldn't they call me?)

Just remember, using PHOTO-PAINT isn't brain surgery; it's electronic finger painting without the mess. *Enjoy yourself.*

1

An Introduction to Corel PHOTO-PAINT 7

Y ou are about to begin an incredible journey into the world of photo-editing and digital wizardry. (Is it me, or does that last sentence sound like the preview for a new movie?) This world of photo-editing was once the exclusive domain of multimillion-dollar computer systems and dedicated graphic artists.

With Corel PHOTO-PAINT 7, you will quickly correct and produce images that can make your desktop projects dazzle. Photo-editing programs have traditionally been labor intensive. They required many hours of tedious effort in order to manipulate images (removing trees, adding people, changing sky color, and so on). PHOTO-PAINT 7 greatly simplifies this time-consuming process. Just as CorelDRAW enables you to achieve professional computer graphic effects with little effort, Corel PHOTO-PAINT 7 will allow you to reach that same professional level in the manipulation of photographs, paintings, and other bitmap images. The bottom line is that PHOTO-PAINT 7 is fun to work with, period. The fact that you can quickly produce professional results is a bonus. Next, Dave's genuine history of PHOTO-PAINT.

A Brief History of PHOTO-PAINT

Corel PHOTO-PAINT began its life as a software product called Photofinish, created by Z-Soft. It was introduced as Corel PHOTO-PAINT 3 in May 1992. It was then, at best, an interesting bitmap-editing package that was very similar to Microsoft PAINT, which Z-Soft also wrote.

When Corel PHOTO-PAINT 4 was released in May 1993, there were many improvements, and only a small amount of the original Z-Soft program remained in it. PHOTO-PAINT 4 had limitations in the size of the image files it could handle, and the absence of several other key features prevented it from being a first-class product. In fact, it resembled Microsoft PAINT on steroids.

PHOTO-PAINT 5, which Corel originally released in May 1994, showed marked improvement. There were many changes still in progress when the product had to ship. Those changes appeared when the maintenance release (E2) was shipped in September. PHOTO-PAINT 5 began to draw serious attention from the graphics community with its support of objects and layers and other features.

PHOTO-PAINT 6 entered the world of 32-bit applications, offering a robust set of photo-editing tools coupled with the power of a 32-bit architecture. If all this talk about 32-bit power is confusing, then—to borrow some terms from *Star Trek*—think of 32-bit power as warp drive and 16-bit as impulse power.

PHOTO-PAINT 7, which was released in November 1996, remains a 32-bit-only application that ranks among the best in the area of photo-editing applications. While retaining the general form and structure of PHOTO-PAINT 6, it provides greatly improved speed and functionality over the previous release.

For Corel PHOTO-PAINT 5 Users

PHOTO-PAINT 7 has changed substantially from the PAINT 5 release. Keyboard assignments, drop-down lists, filter names, mask and object methodology, and dialog boxes have all been modified to improve the product. Throughout the book I have attempted to leave notes like this to alert PHOTO-PAINT 5 users of specific changes.

NOTE: *PHOTO-PAINT 3 and 4 users, it's time to upgrade!*

Before We Get Started

One of the things that makes PHOTO-PAINT such a powerful package is that there are so many combinations of tools and functions available. Of course, this is also what makes PHOTO-PAINT confusing to the novice. If you are new to photo-editing programs, I have included a section in this book to help you understand the sometimes complex world of bitmap images. For the experienced Photoshop user, I have tried to associate Corel names with their equivalent Adobe Photoshop names wherever appropriate.

If you have worked with PHOTO-PAINT 5, you may be overwhelmed by the changes that have been made for releases 6 and 7. Truth is, when I first opened the beta version of PHOTO-PAINT 6 in early 1995, I wondered if I would ever get used to it. The good news is that the PHOTO-PAINT 7 interface has only minor differences. The exciting news is in the program itself—the changes that were made "under the hood." But I am getting ahead of myself. First, let me formally introduce you to PHOTO-PAINT 7.

PHOTO-PAINT 7: A Premier Photo-Editing Program

Corel PHOTO-PAINT 7 is first and foremost a photo- or image-editing program. It is in the same league as Adobe Photoshop, but it costs hundreds of dollars less. As a photo-editing program, it offers all of the features you should expect from a professional photo-editing package, and in several areas you can do more with PHOTO-PAINT 7 than with its main competitor. In case you are wondering why I mention Adobe Photoshop, it's because before PHOTO-PAINT came along, Adobe Photoshop was the unchallenged leader in digital photo-editing. Corel is, not so quietly, changing that.

One of the more useful tasks you can perform with PHOTO-PAINT 7 is to take a poorly composed, overexposed, scratchy photograph and make it look as if the photographer did a great job. Only you and PHOTO-PAINT 7 will know the truth. People today tend to get excited about all of the breathtaking, surrealistic effects they can achieve with photo-editing packages such as PHOTO-PAINT 7. I get excited, too, but it is the everyday work of making the images in our documents look as professional as possible, with the least amount of effort, that makes PHOTO-PAINT 7 such an important addition to your desktop publishing library.

Changing Reality (Virtually)

With PHOTO-PAINT 7 and this book, you will learn how simple it is to add people or objects to existing images. You can easily create things that don't exist, as shown in Figure 1-1, or, more commonly, remove unwanted objects like scratches, stains, or old boyfriends, as shown in Figure 1-2. You will even be able to change the way people look. I recently did a brochure for my church. The photo of one of the pastors had been taken several months and over 20 pounds ago. No problem. With PHOTO-PAINT 7, I took off those excess pounds in less than an hour—which is more than the pastor or the diet industry can do.

Altering people's appearance (removing blemishes, changing hair color, and so on) has been done by professionals for a long time. I knew a guy who was one of the kings of the airbrush (back in the predigital days), and was greatly appreciated by more than one playmate-of-the-month. Now, like my friend, you will be able to change the way people look. The only difference is that PHOTO-PAINT 7 doesn't require an airbrush, long hours, or years of experience.

What else can you do with PHOTO-PAINT 7? We have been talking up until now about changing existing images, but you can also create original images. If

With PHOTO-PAINT 7 you can quickly create a user-friendly program

FIGURE 1-1

Breaking up may be hard to do, as the song goes, but removing a boyfriend from a photograph is simple using PHOTO-PAINT 7

FIGURE 1-2

you're not an artist, do not feel excluded from this discussion. Like CorelDRAW, PHOTO-PAINT 7 lets you take clip art and assemble it to make exciting images. Corel has provided an assortment of objects that can be placed together to make a composite image. Using the PHOTO-PAINT filters and its powerful editing tools, you will quickly learn to create all kinds of original images, logos, and what-have-yous (and still maintain your I'm-not-an-artist standing). You can take the background from one photograph and place it seamlessly with another. Figure 1-3 shows how you can make an object stand out by replacing the background. Can you find the can of Coke? It's hidden under his paw—and I wouldn't want to fight him for it.

What's New in PHOTO-PAINT 7

Here is a list of the important features in PHOTO-PAINT 7.

PROPERTY BARS   Most of the common tool settings items now appear on Property bars, so users aren't overwhelmed by too many roll-ups. Put simply, the Property bar displays the most often used commands for whatever mode you select. If you are concerned that the roll-ups are gone, don't worry, they are still available.

Background
replacement
enhances
the subject

FIGURE 1-3

IMPROVED MEMORY MANAGEMENT   The completely new memory manager means that native PHOTO-PAINT 7 files load faster than ever. All aspects of memory handling have been significantly improved, which means it works faster and you get done sooner.

OBJECT TRANSFORMATIONS   A new transformation methodology significantly improves the rendering of objects when multiple transforms—rotations, resizes, scales, skews, distorts, and perspectives (new feature)—are performed.

UNLIMITED UNDO CAPABILITY   What more can I say? You are no longer limited to one of the real restrictions of programs of this nature—that of being able to undo only the last command. The Undo capability of PHOTO-PAINT 7 has many new options. You can now configure how many Undo levels are possible—if you have the memory.

NEW FILTERS   The new filters that have been added include

- **PhotoLab** This gives a large selection of automatic photographic color corrections (including converting color negatives to color positives).

- **Intellihance by Extensis** This program also provides powerful and automatic photographic image correction tools.

- **PhotoEdges by Auto F/x** These popular image edges treatments allow you to quickly give images produced in PHOTO-PAINT 7 a professional appearance.

- **MetaTools** Sample filters from the popular Kai Power Tools (KPT) 3.0 set of plug-in filters, are available in PHOTO-PAINT 7.

OBJECT MODES   PHOTO-PAINT 7 now offers three ways of constructing images with objects:

- **Normal** As in PHOTO-PAINT 6, image commands and transforms can be applied to any individually selected or grouped selection of objects, the background, or a masked selection.

- **Single** Image commands can be applied to one object (or the background) at a time.

- **Layer** All the features of Single mode plus the ability to "add to" (or extend) the currently selected object by applying image data (by painting, applying effects to the objects, pasting, and so on) to the area outside the object's original boundary. Also, you can create new, completely transparent objects. This is equivalent to placing a clear sheet over an existing image and applying paint and other effects to it. The image under the transparent layer shows how it would look if the changes were applied, but the removal of the transparent layer removes all of the changes.

IMPROVED TEXT EDITING AND HANDLING As with PHOTO-PAINT 5, you enter text directly on the image and the text becomes an object. With PAINT 6, when text is placed on an image, it also becomes an object but it retains its text attributes, which can be edited later. PHOTO-PAINT 7 offers control over character spacing (kerning) and line spacing (leading).

NEW DROP SHADOW COMMAND This allows you to automatically create a drop shadow for any object with the touch of a button.

NEW OBJECT TRANSPARENCY TOOL This tool lets you use interactive onscreen adjusters to change the transparency of an object. If you use Corel Xara, you will find this tool looks very familiar.

NEW IMAGE SPRAYER BRUSH This allows you to paint objects directly on the image area. Offering several preset files, it lets you paint with postage stamps, butterflies, leaves, or almost anything else you can imagine. In addition to the preset files included with the package, you can easily create your own custom files. If you use Fractal Design's Painter program, this tool will look very familiar. Remember that imitation is the sincerest form of flattery.

NEW OBJECT TRANSPARENCY BRUSH This allows you to adjust the transparency of an object relative to its original mask.

NEW SCISSORS MASK TOOL This hybrid of several mask tools follows edges in an image, automatically making the creation of complex masks much easier.

A Quick Tour of PHOTO-PAINT 7

I hope you are excited about some of the things that you will be able to do with this program. But before you run, you must learn to walk, and that walk begins with a quick tour of PHOTO-PAINT 7.

This chapter contains a lot of useful information, so I urge you to look through it. If you are a first-time user of PHOTO-PAINT, I recommend that you familiarize yourself with (don't memorize) the terms and concepts described in this chapter before you begin to use the program. Time invested here will pay off in later chapters.

Elements of the PHOTO-PAINT Screen

Figure 1-4 shows the Corel PHOTO-PAINT 7 main screen. Your screen may look quite different depending on how it is configured. (You'll learn about this in Chapter 3.) The following are the key elements that make up the PHOTO-PAINT screen:

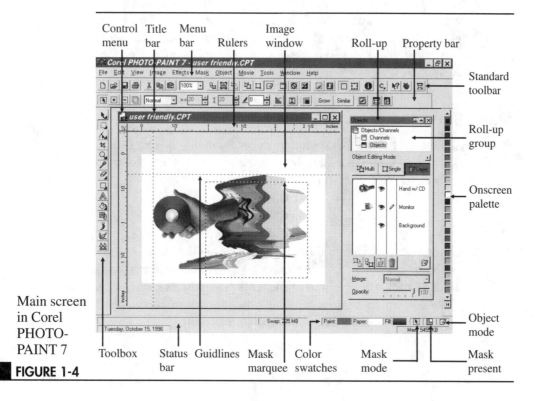

Main screen in Corel PHOTO-PAINT 7

FIGURE 1-4

Onscreen Color Palette

The onscreen color palette is used to select the Paint (foreground color used by the brushes), Paper (background), and Fill colors. These three terms—Paint, Paper, and Fill—are used throughout PHOTO-PAINT, so you should try to remember them. To choose a Paint color; that is, to change the color of a brush, click a color on the palette with the left mouse button. To choose a Fill color, click with the right mouse button. To select a Paper color, hold down the CTRL key and click the left mouse button.

 TIP: *If you don't enjoy memorizing mouse button/keyboard combinations, click and hold the right mouse button over the desired color. After two seconds release the mouse button and a pop-up menu appears allowing you to set the Paint, Paper, or Fill to that color.*

Control Menu

With Windows 95, the Control Menu went from an uninteresting square to a camera icon. Located on the left side of the Title bar, it still does most of the same things it did in Windows: displays commands to restore (if file is minimized), move, resize, minimize, maximize, and close windows. The control menu (Paper icon) for an image also provides image information.

Menu Bar

Press any menu heading in the Menu bar to access dialog boxes, submenus, and commands. Access is also available by depressing the ALT key followed by the highlighted or underlined letter in the command.

Title Bar

The application title or image title (image filename) is displayed in the Title bar. While it's nice to know the title, the important thing about the Title bar is the background. The background color of the Title bar indicates whether an image window is selected, which is important when you have several image files open and want to know which one you are about to apply an effect to.

Roll-ups

Roll-ups were designed to streamline operations using commands that are accessed repeatedly. They are opened through the Roll-ups command in the View menu on the Menu bar, through keyboard combinations, as listed in Table 1-1, or through the Roll-up toolbar if it is open. There have been several minor changes in this area. The Color Mask is no longer a roll-up, and the Navigator roll-up has been replaced with the new Pop-up Navigator, which is accessed by clicking the lower-right corner of a zoomed image. The newest addition to the roll-up family is the Scrapbook roll-up.

A roll-up provides access to controls for choosing and applying fills, outlines, text attributes, and other options. Roll-up windows contain many of the controls found in dialog boxes: command buttons, text boxes, drop-down list boxes, and so on. But unlike most dialog boxes, the roll-up window stays open after you apply the selected options. This lets you make adjustments and experiment with different options without having to continually reopen a dialog box.

When you are not using a roll-up, you can roll it up through its control menu (right-click on the Title bar and choose Arrange All), leaving just the Title bar visible. When you begin to accumulate a lot of roll-ups all over your screen, you can select Arrange All from the control menu, and they will all roll up and go into the corner nice and tidy. Or choose Close All and they will all disappear.

Rulers and Guidelines

Selecting Rulers from the View command in the Menu bar or the keyboard combination CTRL+R toggles the display of the rulers on the image. Rulers are

Roll-up	Keyboard Combination
Channels	CTRL+F9
Color	CTRL+F2
Nibs	CTRL+F11
Objects	CTRL+F7
Recorder	CTRL+F3
Scrapbook	CTRL+F12
Tool Settings	CTRL+F8

Keyboard Commands For Opening Roll-ups

TABLE 1-1

important in PHOTO-PAINT because they provide the only visual indicator of how large an image actually is. We will explore why this happens in Chapter 2. For now, be aware that it is possible for a photograph to completely fill the screen and yet be smaller than a postage stamp when you print it. That is why rulers are important.

Guidelines are new to PHOTO-PAINT 7 and provide a necessary alignment tool when setting up multiple objects in an image. Rulers, guidelines, and grids are explored in Chapter 4.

Toolbars

Toolbars were first introduced in PHOTO-PAINT 6 and are similar to the ribbon bar found in many other Windows applications. Buttons on the toolbars provide quick access to commonly used commands. All of the functions available on the toolbars can also be accessed through the Menu bar. The appearance of the Ribbon bar and the number of buttons visible are dependent on tool selection. With each release of Corel the number of roll-ups has increased, taking up more and more space on the display. The solution to this proliferation of roll-ups appears in PHOTO-PAINT 7 in the form of a new toolbar called the Property bar. As good as the Property bar is, we still use roll-ups. The toolbars shown in Figure 1-4 are the Standard toolbar and the Property bar.

In PHOTO-PAINT 5 there is a single ribbon bar; in PHOTO-PAINT 6 several more toolbars were added; and with PHOTO-PAINT 7, that single toolbar from PAINT 5 has returned and brought its entire family. There are now 17 toolbars in all (counting the Toolbox and the Property bar). If they were all open and floating at the same time, there would be no room for the image you need to work on. The good news is that only a few of them need to be open at any given moment. Right-clicking on the Toolbox brings up a menu where you can select or deselect from the list of 15 or more (you can add custom toolbars).

Image Window

This is the image-display window. The zoom factor of each image window is controlled independently by the Zoom command in View or by the Zoom control in the Ribbon bar. The default setting of Zoom—100 percent—is set in the Options section of the Tools menu. If you have a medium- to high-performance graphics board in your system, you can choose Best Fit. But for an accurate representation of the image on the screen, you should always use 100 percent.

TIP: *When you choose a zoom factor that is less or greater than 100 percent, the image may have a poor appearance. This is a result of the way the image is displayed by the graphics adapter under Windows 95 and does not reflect the actual image quality.*

Toolbox/Flyouts

The Toolbox contains all of the tools used for image editing. Many of the buttons in the Toolbox have flyouts to allow access to additional related tools. Most flyouts are identical to their toolbar. For example, compare the Mask flyout shown below with the Mask Tools toolbar that is placed along side of it.

Availability of a flyout is indicated by a tiny black arrow in the lower right-hand corner of the button. To open a flyout, you can click and hold the cursor on the button for more than a second or click directly on the black arrow. Clicking any tool in the flyout places the selected tool button at the head of the flyout.

Status Bar

The Status bar contains a wealth of information. By default, it is located at the bottom of the screen. Refer to Chapter 3 for information on how to customize the Status bar for your desktop needs.

Mask and Mode Icons

The mask icons are displayed in the Status bar. The three icons shown are the Mask Mode, Mask Present, and Object Mode icons. These icons are more important than you might imagine. You will sometimes try to apply an effect or use a brush stroke and either nothing will happen or what happens is not what you expected. More often than not, this is because you have a mask somewhere in the image that is preventing whatever it is that you are trying to do or you have the mask in something other than Normal mode. Make a habit of looking for the Mask icon when things don't work as planned.

Property Bar

A new feature with the release of PHOTO-PAINT 7, the Property bar is a great productivity enhancement. Most of the common tool settings items now appear on Property bars, relieving the screen from overcrowding by too many roll-ups. Put simply, the Property bar displays the most-often-used commands for whatever mode is selected by the user.

Standard Toolbar

The Standard toolbar is enabled by default. The first seven buttons are common Windows functions, and several new buttons have been added with the release of PHOTO-PAINT 7. The following table describes the more familiar buttons; the remaining buttons will be discussed in greater detail as we learn to use them.

Button	Function
New	Activates the Create A New Image dialog box for creating new image files.
Open	Activates the Open An Image dialog box to open existing files.
Save	Saves the currently selected image. This button is grayed out (unavailable) until the selected image has been modified.
Print	Allows printing of selected image.
Cut	Cuts (removes) the defined (masked) area and copies it to the clipboard.

Button	Function
Copy	Copies a defined (masked) area to the clipboard.
Paste as Object	Pastes (copies) the image in the clipboard into the selected image as an object. (Note: Unlike the Paste *command*, which gives you a choice of pasting as an object or as a new document, the Paste as Object *button* does not give you a choice.)
Zoom Level	Displays and controls the zoom level of the currently selected image.

Where to Find Help

Most users don't take advantage of the extensive help features built into products. I can't say for sure why they don't use them, but I can say that Corel has built a lot of help features into PHOTO-PAINT 7 that will answer many questions for you without the need to reference either this book or the manual that shipped with the product. Here is a brief summary of what and where they are.

Corel Tutor

It is hard to miss this one—it is one of six possible choices on the opening screen. Selecting Corel Tutor opens the Corel Tutor main menu, as shown here:

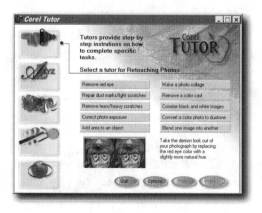

This is a step-by-step tutorial that teaches you how to use PHOTO-PAINT 7 to accomplish many tasks in photo-editing. Another way to launch the Corel Tutor is to click the Apple button on the Standard toolbar shown here. (Sorry to disappoint those of you who thought it launched the Macintosh version.)

 TIP: *If you cannot find some of the buttons mentioned in this section, there is a good chance their current setting is too large to fit on your display. To change the size of the buttons, select Toolbars... in the View menu and change the Button size slider so that all of the buttons in the Standard toolbar fit the display.*

Context Help

The button with the question mark and the arrow shown next to the Corel Tutor button in the preceding section, is the Context Help button. Clicking this button changes the cursor to an arrow with a question mark. It remains in this mode until clicked on a tool on the main screen. Clicking a tool brings up the context-sensitive help screen that explains the purpose of the item clicked.

What's This?

Placing the cursor anywhere on a tool or feature inside of a dialog box and clicking it with the right mouse button produces a small rectangle with the message "What's This?" This provides a brief description of the function selected. The trick to making it work is to click the "What's This?" message box with the left mouse button *after* you right-click the feature.

 TIP: *Don't forget to click the message box that contains the message "What's This?" to access the information.*

The Help Manual

Throughout the book I have included tips to direct you toward the more useful help files. These files provide all of the information that you would expect to find in the PHOTO-PAINT 7 reference manual. And speaking of which...

The manual that shipped with both the CorelDRAW 7 suite and the stand-alone version of PHOTO-PAINT 7 is an excellent reference. I am not just saying this because this is a Corel Press book. The crew that Corel assembled created a robust manual that is a vast improvement over the pathetic 48-page insert that was included with the original CorelDRAW 5 release.

Help on the Web

Several Internet sites provide answers to questions, including the Corel Web site, Chris Dickman's CorelNET (www.corelnet.com). Included at this site are back issues of *CorelDRAW Journal,* which contains monthly articles and step-by-step tutorials on using PHOTO-PAINT. Another useful site is the *Corel Magazine* home page (www.corelmag.com), which also has a wealth of back issues and other resources available. As Corel PHOTO-PAINT continues to increase in popularity, expect to see an even greater number of resources appearing.

Before finishing this chapter, we need to discuss some hardware requirements that are recommended for those about to venture into the land of PHOTO-PAINT 7.

Setting Up Your System—Do You Have What It Takes?

This is more than just a cute title. Corel PHOTO-PAINT 7 requires some substantial system resources in order to work properly. To make sure that you have sufficient system resources, it is necessary to spend a little time understanding what is "under the hood" with the system you already have. (Good news for you techno-wizards: If you already know everything about hardware, go directly to the next chapter.)

Hardware Considerations

The minimum requirement to run PHOTO-PAINT 7 is that you must have Windows 95 already installed and running. While the minimum hardware necessary to run Windows 95 is not insignificant, it is not sufficient for photo-editing. Let's consider some realistic system requirements for using PHOTO-PAINT 7.

RAM

According to Microsoft, it is possible to run Windows 95 on 4MB of RAM (lots of luck). The minimum amount of RAM that you should be using is 8MB, but even that's tight. According to all of the computer magazines, Windows 95 runs best with 16MB of RAM. They call it the "sweet spot." It is even said that increasing the amount of RAM above 16MB doesn't provide any significant boost in performance. While this is true for many Windows 95 applications, it is not true for programs that manipulate large bitmap images—like PHOTO-PAINT 7. If you can afford it, I recommend running with 32MB of RAM installed. I am running with 64MB RAM while working on this book. The reason for this large amount of RAM is because the price of RAM collapsed in the last half of 1996 and it was too good a deal to pass up. The performance increase you will realize with additional RAM greatly exceeds the dollar/benefit increase you will see with almost any other hardware purchase.

CPU

I recommend a 486 DX2/66 MHz as the very minimum system CPU for running PHOTO-PAINT 7. A Pentium (P5) 133 MHz is even better. The difference will be noticed mostly when applying the Effect filters. While working on this book, I am using the new Cyrix 686 P200 and it is really fast. How fast, you ask? I can actually finish a photo-editing project before I start. Now that's fast!

The Hard Disk

Your hard disk drive should have at least a 500MB capacity. If that figure gave you a start, take a look at your local computer superstore. In the early part of 1996, 1.2GByte drives were selling for $189 or less! So how big a drive do you need? After CorelDRAW 7 is loaded, you should have at least 50 to 100MB of free disk space remaining. Bitmap images take up a lot of space. So does Windows 95, for that matter. If you are going to be working on a lot of images and not constantly archiving them on tape or floppies, get yourself a drive large enough to handle the load. I am currently using a Seagate 4Gbyte and I have already filled up most of it. Scary isn't it?

That's all for this chapter and the first part. Next we will learn about digital images, resolution, and color. If you think pixels are mythical winged creatures that fly in the forest, you really need to read Chapter 2.

2

Understanding
Digital Images

As the field of digital imagery expands, many people are getting deeply involved with computer graphics with little or no background on the subject. While there are many books about graphics on the shelves today, most of them assume that you know the terminology and the technical material that serves as the foundation of computer graphics. The end result is frustration for the user. This chapter will help you fill in some of the gaps you might have in your graphics background.

Basic Terms in Digital Imaging

Before we dive into computer terms and acronyms, there is something you must first understand: There are many terms in the computer industry that are nonstandard, colloquial, or just plain dumb. This has led to one of my theorems regarding computer terminology: *The only thing that is universally accepted in the computer industry is that nothing is universally accepted in the computer industry.*

I don't expect the Pulitzer Prize for that one, but it goes a long way toward explaining why the computer industry uses so many different terms to describe the same thing. I am also a strong believer in using the terminology in common use, rather than the "technically correct" term. When it comes to communicating ideas, the popular or commonly used term is more important. In this book, I will always try to use the commonly used term (even if it isn't accurate) as well as the technically correct term. Here are a few terms we need to know something about.

Bitmap and Vector Images

When it comes to computer images there are two types: *bitmap* (also called *paint*) and *vector* (also called *freehand*). The following photograph of a jet is a typical example of a bitmap image. The image file is composed of millions of individual *pixels* (picture elements—discussed in the next section). Bitmap files tend to be much larger than their vector counterparts and resolution dependent (we will explore resolution dependency later in this chapter).

The jet from the CorelDRAW clip art collection that appears to be taking off from on top of the photograph is a vector image. The original clip art image contained no pixels and was composed of lines and fills. Vector images tend to be complex—meaning they may be composed of thousands of individual objects—and have much smaller image file sizes than their bitmap equivalents. The following illustration shows the complexity of the vector-based image as it appears (wireframe view) in CorelDRAW. Corel PHOTO-PAINT only works with bitmap images, so when a vector-based image file (like the jet) is loaded into Corel PHOTO-PAINT, it must first be converted, or *rasterized,* to a bitmap as it is loaded.

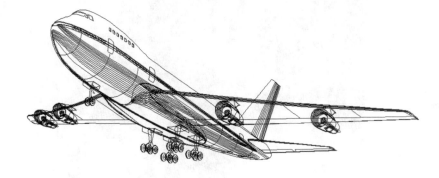

To work effectively with bitmap images, it is necessary to understand why they act differently than the object-based images in CorelDRAW. Let's begin by defining our terms.

Pixels

These are not elf-like creatures that fly through the forest at twilight. The term "pixel" is short for PIcture ELement. Bitmap images are composed of pixels. They are the individual squares that make up an image on a computer screen or on hard copy. One way to understand pixels is to think of a mural created with mosaic tiles. When you get close to a mural made of mosaic tiles, it looks like someone had a bad Lego day. This is because you are so close you are looking at individual tiles. But step away a few feet from the mosaic, and the individual tiles begin to lose their definition and visually merge. The tiles have not changed their size or number, yet the farther back you move, the better the image looks. Pixels in bitmaps work much the same way.

I have created a sample image, shown in Figure 2-1, to illustrate how pixels make up an image. The area surrounded by the white rectangle on the left has been zoomed in to 1600 percent and displayed on the right. It shows that as you zoom in on an image, the individual pixels begin to stand out more and the image they produce becomes less and less evident. Returning to our mosaic tile analogy, there are, of

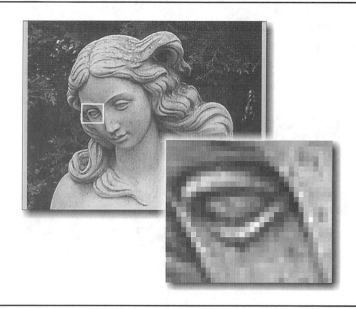

The pixels that compose the image become evident at a zoom factor of 1600 percent

FIGURE 2-1

course, major differences between pixels and mosaic tiles. Pixels come in a greater selection of decorator colors (more than 16.7 million, to be exact), and pixels don't weigh as much as tiles. However, mosaic tiles and pixels operate in the same way to produce an image.

Color Depth

What is *color depth*? It is the number of bits necessary to describe an individual pixel's color. If a color image has a depth of 4 bits, that means that there are 16 possible combinations of bits (2^4) to describe the color in each pixel. Another way to say it is there are 16 possible colors available, or the image has a 16-color palette. There are several different color depths available with PHOTO-PAINT. They are 1-bit (2 colors), 4-bit (16 colors), 8-bit (256 colors), 16-bit (65K colors), and 24-bit (16.7 million colors). There is also 32-bit color but it is used for prepress and essentially only represents 16.7 million colors using a different type of color model. The greater the color depth of an image, the more shades of color it contains, as shown in Table 2-1. The drawback is that as the color depth of an image changes, the file size changes, as shown in Table 2-2.

NOTE: *Corel PHOTO-PAINT does not support conversion of an image to 16-bit color depth.*

Color Depth	Type of Image	Color(s) Available
1-bit	Black-and-white	2 colors
8-bit	Grayscale	256 shades of gray
4-bit	Color	16 colors
8-bit	Color	256 colors
16-bit	Color, also called high color	65,000 colors
24-bit	Color, also called true color or RGB color	16.7 million colors
32-bit	Color, also called CMYK	16.7 million colors

Color Depth for the Various Image Types

TABLE 2-1

Color Depth	Size
32-bit (16.7 million)	793KB
24-bit (16.7 million)	632KB
8-bit (256 colors)	395KB
1-bit (2 colors)	28KB

File Size as a Function of Color Depth

TABLE 2-2

All image-file formats have some restrictions regarding the color depth that they can accommodate, so it becomes necessary to know what color depth you are working with in order to recognize what kinds of colors and other tools you can use with it.

If color depth is new to you, you may be wondering, Why do we have all of these different color depths? Why not make all of the images 24-bit and be done with it? There are many reasons for the different image types. One of the major factors of color depth is the physical size of the image file that each type produces. The greater the number of bits associated with each pixel (color depth), the larger the file size. If an image has a size of 20KB as a black-and-white (1-bit) image, it will take more than 480KB as a true-color (24-bit) image. If an 8 x 10 color photograph is scanned in at 600 dpi (don't ever do it!) at a color depth of 24-bit, the resulting 64MB+ file will probably not even fit in your system. Not to mention that every operation with this image will be measured in hours instead of seconds. There are other factors associated with the different color depths. Let's take a closer look at the various types of color depth used in the industry today.

Black-and-White Images

The term "black and white" has caused some confusion in the past because old movies and television shows are referred to as being in black and white. They are actually grayscale, not black and white. Don't try to educate anyone on this subject. Just remember that the old *Andy Griffith* and *Dick Van Dyke* shows are really in grayscale, not black and white.

In real black-and-white images, one bit of information is used per pixel to define its color. Because it has only one bit, it can only show one of two states, either black or white. The little pixel is turned either on or off. It doesn't get any simpler than this.

Black-and-white images are more common than you would imagine. The following illustration shows a black-and-white image that was scanned from a clip art book. It is common to associate this kind of image with Victorian woodcuts, but as you can see, there are contemporary examples of black and white as well.

A lot can be done with black-and-white images, which are also called *line art*. Users of Adobe programs may refer to them as bitmap images. This can be confusing since most photographic images are referred to as bitmaps. It is possible to use black and white (1-bit) to produce photographs that appear to be grayscale. It approximates the grayscale look by a process called *dithering*. Dithering can be thought of as pseudo-grayscale when it comes to black-and-white images. While dithering can simulate grayscale, quality suffers greatly when a dithered image is resized.

Four different types of black-and-white images can be produced with PHOTO-PAINT 7 by selecting Convert to in the Image menu and choosing Black and White (1-bit). To illustrate the differences between them, I have created a composite image in Figure 2-2 to show the results of each type of image. The original grayscale image that was converted is shown in Figure 2-3. I have displayed only one of the two possible diffusion methods since they appear nearly identical. The left panel of the image was converted to black and white using *error diffusion*, a dithering process that arranges the black-and-white pixels to appear to the viewer's eye as grayscale. Error diffusion is more complex than the other method, ordered diffusion. The difference in speed is almost unnoticeable on most Pentium computers.

WARNING: *While error diffusion dithering produces the best-looking results, it distorts the most when resizing.*

The middle panel was converted using the Line Art setting. This method measures the shade value of each pixel in the original image and converts it to either a black or a white dot. The *threshold value* determines whether it becomes black or white. Any value greater than the threshold becomes white; any below becomes

Result of converting an image to black and white using the Error diffusion (left), Line Art (middle), and Halftone (right) settings

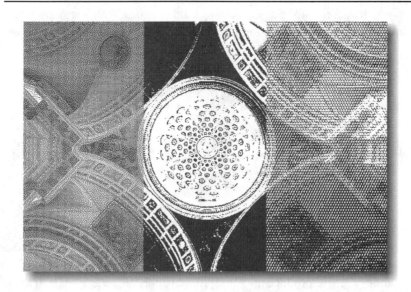

FIGURE 2-2

black. While the default value is set to the middle of the range (128 out of a possible 256), I changed the value of Threshold to 150 to get more of the detail in the dome.

The last panel in Figure 2-2 was created using the halftone screen. Halftones are discussed in greater detail in the section of this chapter dealing with resolution.

NOTE: *For more information about halftones, in PHOTO-PAINT, press the F1 key and select the Index tab. Type in* **Halftone types** *and click the Display button. Select Overview: Working with bitmaps and halftone screens.*

Grayscale Images

What we call black-and-white photos are in fact grayscale images. Photographs (color and grayscale) are *continuous tone* images, so called because the photo, unlike a digital image, isn't composed of square pixels but rather continuous areas of different colors or shades. To represent this information in a digital format requires dividing the image into pixels using eight bits of information for each pixel, producing 256 possible shades of gray. The shade of each pixel ranges from a value of white (0) to black (255). Grayscale is used for many other things besides "black-and-white" photos. When you learn about masks (beginning in Chapter 7), you will find out that most of the masks used in photo-editing are actually grayscale images. Figure 2-3 is the original grayscale image that has been converted to black and white in Figure 2-2.

4-Bit and 8-Bit Color

With the explosive growth of the Internet, 256-color (8-bit) images have become very popular. If you are using PHOTO-PAINT 7 to create images for the Web, you will be using them a lot. With the exception of some Windows and Web page icons, 4-bit color is rarely used, so we will devote most of this discussion to 8-bit or 256-color images. Referred to as *paletted* or *256-color,* an 8-bit color image can only have one of a possible 256 combinations of color assigned to each pixel. This isn't as limited as you might imagine.

When an image is converted to 8-bit, PHOTO-PAINT creates a reference palette to which all of the colors used in the image are assigned—hence the term "paletted." Many people are under the impression that 8-bit color is markedly inferior to 24-bit color. That used to be true, but the process of converting the image from 16- or 24-bit to 8-bit color has improved so dramatically that in many cases it is difficult, if not impossible, to tell the original image from the paletted one. We will explore some options that allow us to create vivid 256-color images from 24-bit color photographs in Chapter 5.

A grayscale image uses 256 shades to represent the continuous tone photograph

FIGURE 2-3

16-Bit Color (64K Color)

The 16-bit color depth reminds me of the EGA monitor standard. There was a brief time when the CGA standard wasn't enough. There is nothing worse than seeing a graphic computer game in CGA, and so EGA came next. It offered more colors and slightly better resolution than CGA. EGA was quickly replaced by VGA. In a way, 16-bit color (65K color) is like that. It came at a time when 24-bit color was just too expensive and 8-bit (256 color) wasn't enough. Most of the higher-performance cards now offer 24-bit color support and 16-bit is losing popularity.

Using 16 bits to define the color depth provides approximately 65,000 colors. This is enough for almost any color image. I have seen 16- and 24-bit images side by side, and it is almost impossible to tell them apart. All things being equal, most of the photo-editing public could work with 65K color from now until the Second Coming and never tell any difference. What are the advantages of 16-bit color? A lower-cost graphics card, and faster performance because you are moving one-third fewer bits. When will you use 16-bit color? Even though PHOTO-PAINT doesn't support 16K color, you may see it if you have a limited amount of video RAM on your display adapter card by increasing your resolution setting. Many times, the display adapter will change the display color depth from 24-bit to 16-bit.

 TIP: *If your display adapter is set to display 16-bit color, it does not affect the image quality, only the display of the image.*

24-Bit (True Color)

True-color images may use up to 16.7 million colors. They are so closely associated with the RGB color model that they are sometimes referred to as RGB 24-bit. (We will talk about color models later in this chapter.) RGB stands for Red-Green-Blue. Your monitor makes all of its colors by using combinations of these three colors. Your eye perceives color the same way: red, green, blue. The three colors that make up the RGB models each have eight bits assigned to them, allowing for 256 possible shades of each color. Your monitor creates colors by painting the images on the inside of your display with three electronic beams (called guns). Each color gun in the color monitor can display 256 possible shades of its color. The mixing together of three sets of 256 combinations produces a possible 16.7 million color combinations. While true color doesn't display every possible color, it gets pretty close. It is the model of choice for the desktop computer artist.

32-Bit Color

Look back at Table 2-1. Do you notice anything unusual about 32-bit color? Although the color depth increases by 25 percent, the number of colors remains the same. Why is that?

There are two answers, because there are two types of color depth that involve 32 bits. The first is more commonly seen on the Mac side of the world. When they say something is 32-bit, they are referring to a 24-bit RGB model with an additional 8-bit *alpha channel.* Apple reserved the alpha channel, but it has never specified a purpose for this data. Alpha channel has come to be used by most applications to pass grayscale mask information.

The other 32-bit type of color image expresses a CMYK (Cyan-Magenta-Yellow-blacK) model. (We will discuss the color models in more detail later in this chapter.)

NOTE: *Most of the graphic processors are advertising that they offer 32-bit, 64-bit, and now 128-bit graphic processor boards. This has nothing to do with color depth. It is a reference to the width of the data path. The wider the data path, the greater the amount of color data that can be moved, and therefore the faster the screens are redrawn.*

File Compression

Because bitmap image files tend to be very large, there is a need to use compression to conserve space on the hard drive. This compression is not related to any compression that you may already be using on your disk drive. Several compression schemes are either built into the file formats or are offered as an option when saving the file. Before we look at the individual file format, we need to know a few things about compression and its benefits and drawbacks. Compression is generally divided into two categories: lossey and non-lossey.

Lossey Compression

Lossey compression offers the greatest amount of compression, but at a price. As the name implies, some of the image quality is lost in the process. Lossey compression schemes can reduce very large files from several megabytes in size to only a few kilobytes. Most of the time the loss in quality is not apparent. The most popular example of lossey compression is the JPEG format. Another compression method that is becoming popular is Wavelet compression, which also supports 24-bit color. This file format stores bitmap information at very high compression levels.

 TIP: *Whenever you save an image using lossey compression, it is necessary to close and reopen the file to see the effect of the compression.*

Table 2-3 compares JPEG and Wavelet compression. The Best Quality value is the one chosen by Corel PHOTO-PAINT 7 when the Suppress filter dialog option is enabled. The Maximum Compression category is based on the maximum compression that produces a small amount of image degradation.

Non-Lossey Compression

Non-lossey compression has been around longer than lossey compression. It generally offers a significant amount of compression without any loss of image information (quality). Most of these compression schemes offer compression ratios between 2:1 and 4:1. The more popular versions of non-lossey compression found in Corel PHOTO-PAINT 7 are LZW and Packbits.

Image File Formats

Now that we have discussed the type of images that exist in a digital world, we need to understand some of the different ways these images can be saved. There are many different file formats for saving images. Each has its strong and weak points when it comes to storing different types of image files. Some formats cannot store more than 256 colors, some cannot be compressed, and others produce enormous files. Corel PHOTO-PAINT gives you a large assortment of file formats to choose from

Comparison of file compression results	Original File Size	Wavelet — Best Quality	Wavelet — Maximum Compression	JPEG — Best Quality	JPEG — Maximum Compression
	5.02MB	202KB	78KB	634KB	104KB

TABLE 2-3

when you save a file. If you are not familiar with the choices, this blessing of a wide assortment can become confusing. This section takes some of the mystery out of these formats with strange-sounding names.

Understanding File Formats

For some, the question will be, What is an image file format? The answer: An image file format defines a way of storing an image and any related information in a way that other programs can recognize and use. Each format has its own unique form, called a *file structure,* for saving the image pixels and other related file information such as resolution and color depth.

Each format is unique and is generally identified by its three-letter file extension. For example, the three-letter extension "CPT" on a filename identifies the file format as a Corel PHOTO-PAINT file. This extension is important because many programs use the three-character extension to identify the type of file import filter to select. If the wrong extension or a unique extension is used, it may be difficult, perhaps impossible, to import the image.

Corel PHOTO-PAINT is aware of the color depth of the image you are attempting to save and changes the selection of available file-format choices automatically. For example, if you have a 32-bit color image, the drop-down list will be reduced from the normal selection to the few file format choices that support 32-bit color.

Corel PHOTO-PAINT 7 has added several new file formats. The new Wavelet compression format represents an advance in image file compression. Corel PHOTO-PAINT 7 also introduces a new native CPT format that offers improved speed when loading the file.

Because there are dozens of file formats, it would be confusing to try to cover them all. Instead, we will look at the major ones supported by Corel PHOTO-PAINT and discuss a few of their strengths and limitations.

NOTE: *For more information about file formats, in PHOTO-PAINT, click the* <u>H</u>*elp menu, select* <u>T</u>*echnical Support, and click the Contents tab. Choose Import, export and OLE and click on List of Export File Formats. Locate the file format that you want more information on and either double-click on it or click on it and then click the display button.*

Going Native (CPT)

CPT is a native format of Corel PHOTO-PAINT. The term *native* means it is unique to the application. CPT (*Corel PHOTO-PAINT*) is the best format for your originals. Saving in a CPT format retains all of the unique PHOTO-PAINT information about the image being saved. Saving in other image formats results in the loss of this information.

The principle limitation of the CPT format is portability. To my knowledge, there are no non-Corel applications that can load an image saved as a CPT file. The image file can be saved as compressed (non-lossey). With the PHOTO-PAINT 7 release there are two possible CPT file formats available: Corel PHOTO-PAINT image (CPT) and Corel PHOTO-PAINT 6 image (CPT). Although they have the same file extensions, the native format of PHOTO-PAINT 7 (CPT) can only be read by PHOTO-PAINT 7. The new version of CPT loads significantly faster than images saved in the PHOTO-PAINT 6 image (CPT) format.

Windows Bitmap (BMP, DIB)

The native image format for Microsoft Paint is BMP (Windows Bitmap), which is included with every copy of Microsoft Windows and supported by nearly every Windows program. Corel PHOTO-PAINT supports BMP images up to 24-bit color (16.7 million colors). This is a popular format that decorates everyone's computer screen these days, but it does not offer compression and is generally used only for small image files (less than a few hundred kilobytes in size).

Graphics Interchange Format (GIF)

CompuServe licensed GIF (Graphics Interchange Format) a long time ago as a means of compressing images for use over their extensive online network. Many people think it originated with CompuServe. In fact, they bought the rights to use it from another company. GIF has become a very popular format, especially now that everyone is jumping on the Internet. As a way to send pictures over phone lines, it can't be beat. It has a major limitation of supporting only 8-bit (256-color) images. Corel PHOTO-PAINT does not offer an option to compress images saved as GIF files.

New to Corel PHOTO-PAINT is the ability to save GIF files in 89a and 87a format. These formats provide the capability to save a file with transparency and interlacing options, which is becoming increasingly important for creating Web graphics for use on the Internet.

Paintbrush (PCX)

PCX is one of the original file formats, created by Z-Soft for PC Paintbrush back when Noah was working on the ark. It is unquestionably one of the most popular image-file formats around, mainly because PC Paintbrush is the oldest painting program for the IBM PC. Corel PHOTO-PAINT supports PCX images up to 24-bit color. The only concern with using PCX images involves importing them into older applications. Because the PCX format has been around so long, there are many versions of PCX import filters around. It is possible, even likely, to find an older application that imports PCX files but cannot read the file exported by Corel PHOTO-PAINT.

Encapsulated PostScript (EPS—Supports 32-Bit)

PostScript is a page description language used by imagesetters and laser printers. This format is a favorite of your friendly neighborhood service bureau. Many people do not think about using the EPS format when working with Paint's bitmap images because of its association with vector-based drawings like CorelDRAW. Actually, EPS does work with bitmap images—for a price. By that I mean a bitmap image saved in the EPS format will be roughly three times as large as the same file saved in the TIFF format. So why use EPS? It was once the only way to place an image into CorelDRAW without the white background. This is no longer true; CorelDRAW can import CPT files with the object/layers intact. For more information, see Chapter 5. If you must send work to a service bureau, EPS may be the only format they will accept, especially for separations.

PICT

Although it is a problematic format, I am including PICT because Corel PHOTO-PAINT can import it. Apple developed PICT as the primary format for Macintosh graphics. Like PostScript, it is a page description language. This format has not been reliable for importing images into Corel, Pagemaker, and other programs. The rule with PICT is simple. If the image you are using is in PICT format, you have no choice but to import it as a PICT file and hope for the best. If you are saving an image so that it can be used on a Macintosh, use JPEG or TIFF. They are both excellent formats for the Mac and are much more dependable than PICT.

TARGA (TGA, TVA)

This format was originally created for TARGA display boards. If you haven't seen this image format before, it is probably because it is used by a small segment of the professional market that works with high-end color and video. In Corel PHOTO-PAINT, this file format supports up to 24-bit color. TARGA does not support 32-bit color (CMYK). TARGA does support 32-bit images—24-bit color with an 8-bit alpha channel, which can be used to retrieve mask information by Corel PHOTO-PAINT 6. Corel PHOTO-PAINT 5 cannot read the alpha channel information in TARGA file format. Many people believe that TARGA is technically superior to any other format on the marketplace. Others feel it is only good for multimedia, because it is a niche format that is not widely used. It is becoming popular with the growing 3D market because it can process all the information that a 3D image requires.

Tagged Image File Format (TIFF)

TIFF is probably the most popular full-color bitmap format around, supported by every PC and Mac paint program I have ever seen. TIFF is clearly the image format of choice. It is used as a default setting for every scanning program on the marketplace today.

You may have heard that there are many different versions of TIFF, which can conceivably cause some compatibility problems when moving images between programs. To date, the only problems I have experienced with TIFF files involved saving images as 24-bit color TIFF files and trying to read them on an application that doesn't offer 24-bit color support.

Corel PHOTO-PAINT supports all color-depth settings in TIFF, including 32-bit color (CMYK). However, don't save your images in 32-bit color unless it is specifically requested. Because 32-bit color (CMYK) is new, you may end up with a TIFF file that some older applications cannot read. Remember that 32-bit (CMYK) TIFF contains the same color information as 24-bit color TIFF.

Scitex CT Bitmap (SCT, CT)

Unless your service bureau specifically requests this file format, don't save in it. High-end commercial printers use Scitex computers to generate color separations of images and other documents. Corel PHOTO-PAINT can open images digitized with Scitex scanners and save the edited images to the Scitex CT (Continuous Tone) format. Because there are several restrictions regarding the transfer of images from the PC to a Scitex drive, you will probably want to consult with the person using the Scitex printer before saving to the CT format. It is possible that a TIFF or JPEG (compression) format is preferred. Scitex is only available when the image is in 32-bit color (CMYK).

Now that you understand a few terms, let's move on and learn about resolution.

Resolution—A Term with Too Many Definitions

Without an understanding of resolution and its effects, you may find yourself creating beautiful images that fill the entire display screen in PHOTO-PAINT yet appear to be smaller than postage stamps when you print them. Resolution is a misunderstood concept in desktop publishing, and the confusion is compounded by the fact that the term may have entirely different meanings depending on the device you are talking about. This chapter explains what resolution is and what it does for us in PHOTO-PAINT 7. The information about resolution that is discussed in this chapter applies to all image editing applications, not just PHOTO-PAINT.

Resolution and the Size of the Image

In a vector-based program we describe the size of an image in the popular unit of measure for the country or culture we live in. In the United States we refer to the standard letter-size page as being $8\frac{1}{2}$ x 11 inches. Image size in photo-editing programs is traditionally measured in pixels. The reason for using pixels is that the size of an image in pixels is fixed. So when I speak of an image being 1200 x 600 pixels, I know from experience approximately how big the image is. If we use a unit of measure other than pixels—say, inches—the dimensions of the printed image are dependent on the resolution of the image.

So What Is Resolution?

Resolution is the density of pixels per inch (ppi) that make up an image, and it is measured in dots per inch (dpi). In other words, it is a measure of how closely each pixel in an image is positioned to the one next to it.

Let's assume we have an image that is 300 pixels wide by 300 pixels high. So how big will the image be when I import it into CorelDRAW? This is a trick question. There is not enough information. Without knowing the resolution of the image, it is impossible to determine the size when it is imported into DRAW. If the resolution of this image is set to 300 pixels per inch, then the image dimensions are 1 x 1 inch when imported into CorelDRAW. If the resolution is *doubled* (set to 600 dpi), the image would be *half* the size, or .5 x .5 inch. If the resolution is *reduced by half* (150 dpi), the *image size doubles* to 2 x 2 inches. We can see that resolution exhibits an inverse relationship, which means that if one value increases, the other decreases. The physical size of an image in PHOTO-PAINT is most accurately expressed as the length (in pixels) of each side. Resolution tells you how many pixels are contained in each unit of measure.

To show the effect of changing resolution, I duplicated a photograph with PHOTO-PAINT, making four identical copies. Next I changed the resolution of (resampled) each of the copies so that I had four photographs at four different resolutions. Even though each of the images in Figure 2-4 is a different resolution, they appear the same size in PHOTO-PAINT. When all four files were imported into CorelDRAW, the results are as shown in Figure 2-5. Why do the photos appear to be the same size in Figure 2-4, you ask? Because the physical size of the images (in pixels) remained unchanged—only the resolution changed.

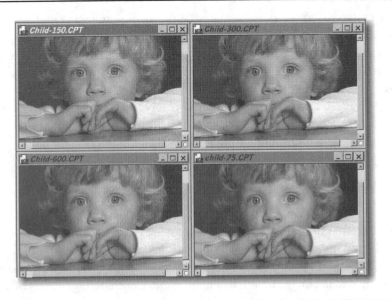

An identical photograph saved at four different resolutions displayed in PHOTO-PAINT

FIGURE 2-4

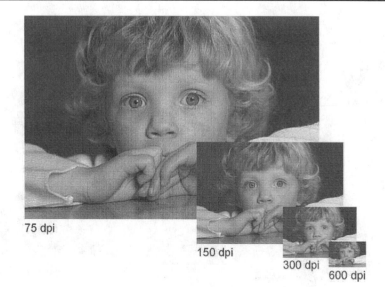

75 dpi

150 dpi

300 dpi

600 dpi

The same
four photos
are
imported
into
CorelDRAW

■ FIGURE 2-5

Screen Resolution

No matter what resolution you are using, Corel PHOTO-PAINT displays each pixel onscreen according to the zoom ratio. That is why all of the photos in Figure 2-4 appear to be the same size even though they are at different resolutions. At a zoom ratio of 100 percent, each image pixel is mapped to a single screen pixel. This is why the size of the image remains unchanged regardless of the image resolution. The display's zoom setting has no effect on the actual image file. If you are a little fuzzy on monitors and pixels, read on. If you know them cold, skip ahead to "Resolution and Printers."

When you bought your monitor and/or display card, you may have been bewildered by such terms as 640 x 480, 800 x 600, and so on. These figures refer to the number of screen pixels that the monitor can display horizontally and vertically. For example, let's say you have a plain vanilla VGA monitor. The standard resolution for this monitor is 640 pixels wide by 480 pixels high (640 x 480). In Figure 2-6, I have loaded a file that is 800 pixels wide by 533 pixels high. The image at 100 percent zoom is too large to fit into the screen of Corel PHOTO-PAINT. Figure 2-7 shows the same photograph with the screen resolution changed to 800 x 600 (also called Super VGA). The display area now contains a width of 800 pixels by a height of 600 pixels. Notice that the image appears smaller than in the previous figure, but

A photograph viewed at a screen resolution of 640 x 480 pixels, too large to fit into the screen

 FIGURE 2-6

it is still too large to fit into the screen area. The size of the photograph hasn't changed, but the screen (or display) resolution has. To make more pixels fit into the same physical screen dimensions, the actual pixels must be smaller. In Figure 2-6, the screen is 640 pixels wide. In Figure 2-7, the screen is 800 pixels wide, making the image smaller by comparison. The screen resolution in Figure 2-8 has again been changed, this time to 1024 x 768. Now all of the photo can be seen on the screen. Again, the photograph remains unchanged, only the screen resolution has increased. Screen or display resolution operates under the same principle we discussed in the previous paragraph. As the screen resolution increases, the image size decreases proportionally.

Many people have been surprised to discover that after spending a lot of money to get a high-resolution monitor and display card, their screen images only appear smaller rather than sharper. Now that you know the secret of the screen resolution game, have your friends buy you lunch and you can explain it to them, too.

Screen Setting Recommendations

With all of the exciting ads for high-resolution displays and graphics adapters, it is difficult not to get caught up in the fever to upgrade. If you have a 14- or 15-inch monitor, you should be using the VGA or Super VGA screen resolution setting on your graphics card. If you go for a higher resolution on a 14- or 15-inch display,

The same photograph viewed at 800 x 600 pixels (Super VGA)

FIGURE 2-7

even if your monitor supports it, your friends may start calling you Blinky, because you will be squinting all of the time to read the screen. Also, be cautious about

The photograph viewed at 1024 x 768 fits the screen

FIGURE 2-8

recommendations from the retail clerk/computer expert at your computer superstore. Remember that last week your "expert" might have been bagging groceries and may know less about computers than you do.

With the price of 17-inch displays dropping, more people are investing in a few extra inches on their display. Just because you have a 17-inch monitor does not mean you have a moral obligation to run it at the highest resolution that it and your display adapter will support. I use 800 x 600 or 1024 x 780 most of the time with my 17-inch monitor and it works very well. In fact the display adapter I am using only supports 24-bit color up to 800 x 600 without adding extra memory to the video card, so I cheated a little to make Figure 2-8 and viewed the image in 16-bit (also called high-color) mode.

Resolution and Printers

If this were a perfect world, image resolution would be the same as printer resolution (which is also measured in dpi). Then if we were printing to a 600-dpi printer in our perfect world, we would be using a 600-dpi-resolution image because each image pixel would occupy one printer dot. However, it is not a perfect world. First of all, pixels are square and printer dots are round. When we talk about printer resolution we are talking about the size of the smallest dot the printer can make. If you are using a 600-dpi laser printer, the size of the dot it produces is one-600th of an inch in diameter. The dot it creates is either on or off. There is either a black dot on the paper or there isn't. If we are displaying a grayscale photograph, we know that each pixel can be 1 of 256 possible shades. So how does the laser printer create shades of gray from black-and-white dots? Using halftones cells. What? Read on.

Creating Halftones

If I take an area on the paper and create a box that has a width of 10 dots and a height of 10 dots, it would have a capacity to fit 100 dots in it. If I were to place printer dots at every other possible point, it would only hold 50 printer dots. The result when printed on paper would appear to the eye as 50 percent gray. This is the principle behind the *halftone cell.* The halftone cell created by the laser printer is equivalent to the pixel—not exactly but close enough for the purposes of discussion. The number of halftone cells a laser printer can produce is a function of its *line frequency,* which some of us old-timers still refer to as *screen frequency.* Companies that produce advertisements to sell their printers to the consumer marketplace never discuss line frequency, expressed as lpi (lines per inch). And why not? Because, in this hyper-advertised computer marketplace, bigger is better (except for price). And which sounds better—a 600-dpi printer or a 153-lpi printer? The 153-lpi printer would have a resolution of around 1200 dpi. Names and numbers are everything in selling a product. This resolution specification hype adds general confusion to the scanner market as well. (We will learn more about scanners and scanning in Chapter 5.)

So what resolution should you use? I have included the values in Table 2-4 for use as general guidelines when setting up the resolution of an image in PHOTO-PAINT.

In the next section we will take a look at color to understand some basics of how it works and, more importantly, how to get what comes back from the printer to look like what we see on the display.

Basic Color Theory

Color is everywhere. Even black and white are colors (really). Color has the greatest and most immediate effect on the viewer of any factor in graphic design. Psychologists confirm that color has an enormous capacity for getting our attention.

Image Type	Final Output	Recommended Resolution
Black-and-white	Laser printer (600 dpi)	600 dpi
Black-and-white	Display screen	Convert black-and-white image to grayscale and use 72–96 dpi
Grayscale	Laser printer	150–200 dpi
Grayscale	Imagesetter	200–300 dpi
Grayscale	Display screen	72–96 dpi
Color	Color inkjet printer	100–150 dpi
Color	Imagesetter	150–200 dpi
Color	Display screen	72–96 dpi

Recommended Resolution Settings

TABLE 2-4

To use color effectively, we must have a basic understanding of it, both technically and aesthetically. Let's begin with the basics.

I knew I wasn't going to like high school physics the first day of class. We were asked to calculate the direction we would have to steer a rowboat up a fast-moving river in order to get to a pine tree on the other side. My answer was to row toward the pine tree. I got half credit. I mention this because, if you were looking for a detailed discussion on complex mathematics of color models, you won't find it here. If you are looking for information on setting up PHOTO-PAINT to work with different color models, check the index again. What you will find here is a nontechnical discussion of the basic concepts and terminology of color.

Knowing how color works in the natural world and how this "real-world" color operates in a computer will help you when dealing with the complexities of the aforementioned color models. It is going to be simple and I think you will find it interesting.

Why Is an Apple Red?

One of the first things they taught me in that physics class I didn't like was that without light there is no color. Pretty deep stuff. Light is radiant energy that moves in waves. Each color of light has a different wavelength (frequency). Here is the tricky part. As light radiates from its source and strikes an object, there are three things that can happen to the light waves. First they can bounce off of the object—that is, they are *reflected.* They can also be *absorbed* by the object. If you doubt that objects absorb light energy, place a piece of metal painted a dull black in a Dallas parking lot for a few hours on a sunny August day and then try to pick it up. Hot stuff! Lastly the light waves can go right through the object—technically speaking, they are *transmitted.* An example would be a sheet of glass. The light strikes the glass and goes through it.

Depending on the composition of the object, all of the light striking it may be reflected, absorbed, or transmitted. Realistically, it will be some combination of the three. Pure, or white, light contains all of the colors of the visible spectrum. When white light strikes a banana, the blue component of the light is absorbed and the red and green components are reflected. The banana appears yellow because red and green reflected light combine to create yellow. An apple absorbs the green and blue light and we see the red component reflected—making the apple appear red. I have included an extremely complex example of this principle in action in the illustration shown below. If an object absorbs all of the red, green, and blue components, it appears black. Conversely, if all of the colors are reflected, an object appears white. Reflection, absorption, and transmission are the guiding principles behind the two basic color models we are going to look at next.

Color Models

Color is made up of light components that, when combined in varying percentages, create separate and distinct colors. You also learned this in elementary school when the teacher had you take the blue poster paint and mix it with the yellow paint to make green. Mixing pigments on a palette is simple. Mixing colors on a computer is not. The rules that govern the mixing of computer colors change, depending on the color model being used.

Many color models are available in PHOTO-PAINT 7. They provide different ways to view and manipulate an image. Regardless of the one selected, they fall into one of two basic categories: *additive color* and *subtractive color.* Additive color (also known as RGB) is the system used by color monitors, scanners, photography, and the human eye. Subtractive color (also known as CMYK) is used in four-color publishing and printing. Let's take a closer look at both.

Additive Color (RGB)

This model is said to use the additive process because colors are produced by adding one or more colors to produce additional ones. RGB (Red-Green-Blue) involves transmitted light as the source of color. In the additive model, color is created by adding different amounts of red, green, and blue light.

Pure white light is composed of equal amounts of red, green, and blue. For the record, red, green, and blue are referred to as the *additive primary colors,* so called because when they are added (combined), they can produce all of the other colors in the visible spectrum.

Subtractive Color (CMYK)

The subtractive model is so named because colors are subtracted from white light to produce other colors. This model uses the secondary colors: cyan, magenta, and yellow. We have already learned this is called the CMYK model, because combining equal amounts of cyan, magenta, and yellow only produce black, in theory. When printed, they produce something closer to swamp mud than black; so, in order to create a vivid picture, black is added to compensate for the inability of the colors CMY to make a good black. In case you were wondering, K is used as the designator for the color black, since the letter "B" already designates the color blue.

CMYK is a printer's model, based on inks and dyes. It is the basis for almost all conventional color photography and commercial color printing. Cyan, magenta, and yellow dyes and inks simply transmit light better and are more chemically stable than red, green, and blue inks.

Describing Colors

If someone were to ask me to describe the color of my son's Jeep, it would be easy. It is black. The color of my wife's car is more difficult. Is it dark metallic green or deep forest green? The terms generally used to describe color are subjective. Even for simple classifications involving primary colors like red and blue it becomes difficult to describe the exact color. Is it deep sea blue or navy blue? In the world of color we need a way to accurately describe the *value* of color.

When creating or picking out a color in PHOTO-PAINT, you can specify the color either by defining values for its components or using a color matching system. When using the RGB model in PHOTO-PAINT (it is the default color model), color values are expressed in shades of RGB. The maximum number of shades that a color can contain is 256. For example, the value of red in an RGB model is defined as 255,0,0. In other words, the color contains the maximum amount (255) of the red component and a value of zero for the green and blue components. *Let me interject here that in PHOTO-PAINT you still pick colors from color palettes that contain recognizable colors like red, green, and blue. I didn't want you to think that you were going to have to sit with a calculator and figure out the value of puce.*

In CMYK, the component values are expressed as a percentage, so the maximum value of any color is 100. The color red in the CMYK model is 0,100,100,0. In other words, the color red is created by placing the maximum values of magenta and yellow with no cyan and no black.

2

Color Matching

While defining colors as either number of shades in the RGB or percentage of tint in CMYK is accurate, it is not practical. Given that we cannot assign names to the millions of shades of color that are possible, there needs to be a workable solution. The use of color matching systems like the Pantone™ Spot colors provides a solution. The designer and the printer have a book of print samples. The designer wants to use red in a two-color publication. He specifies that the second color is to be PANTONE Red 032 CV. The printer who gets the job looks up the formula in the Pantone book for the percentages of magenta and yellow to mix together and prints the first sample. She then compares the output with her book of print samples, called a *swatch book*. Most corporate accounts will use one of the popular color matching systems to specify the colors they want in their logos and ads. Color matching in the digital age is less then eight years old. It has come a long way in its short life and is now finding its way into the design of Internet Web sites. No longer restricted to four- and six-color printing, the color matching systems are dealing with the important issues of colors looking correct on the Internet too.

RGB Versus CMYK

Each color model represents a different viewpoint on the same subject. Each offers advantages and disadvantages. If you are a Corel PHOTO-PAINT user creating multimedia and Web pages or just printing to inkjet or color laser printers, knowing how to get what you need out of RGB will more than satisfy your requirements. If you must accurately translate color from the screen to the printed page, you must get more deeply involved in CMYK. That is all we are going to learn about these two color models in this chapter. There are some other terms to learn to help you work in PHOTO-PAINT, described in the following sections.

Hue, Saturation, and Brightness

The terms hue, saturation, and brightness (also called *luminosity*) are used throughout PHOTO-PAINT. *Hue* describes the individual colors—for example, a blue object can be said to have a blue hue. *Saturation* is technically the purity of the color. In practical terms it is the balance between neutral gray and the color. If an image has no saturation, it looks like a grayscale image. If the saturation is 100 percent, it may look unnatural, since the image's midtones, which the gray component emphasizes, are lost. *Brightness* is the amount of light reflecting from an object or how dark or light the image is.

Color Gamut

It may come as a surprise to you, but there are a lot more colors in the real world than photographic films or printing presses can re-create. The technical term for this range of colors is *gamut*. There are many gamuts—for monitors, scanners, photographic film, and printing processes. Each gamut represents the range of colors that can actually be displayed, captured, or reproduced by the appropriate device or process. The widest gamut is the human eye, which can see billions of colors. Further down on this visual food chain is the color computer monitor, which can display 16 million colors. Photographic film can only capture 10 to 15 thousand colors and a high-quality four-color printing process can reproduce from 5 to 6 thousand. We won't even discuss the limitations of color ink on newsprint.

Gamut curves are usually defined on a chart similar to the one shown in Figure 2-9. Even though this chart is shown in grayscale, gamut curves are usually shown in color to visually represent the color spectrum. The outer boundary of the chart represents all the colors that can be seen by the human eye. The areas within the gamut chart show what portion of the spectrum each device can either capture or reproduce.

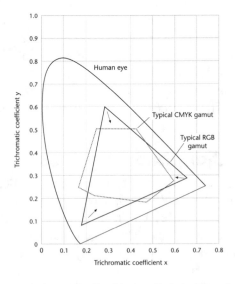

The gamut chart shows the range of colors that can be displayed or reproduced

Image used by permission of the Graphic Arts Technical Foundation (GATF).

FIGURE 2-9

From the previous descriptions it becomes apparent that there are some colors we can see but technology cannot reproduce. Corel PHOTO-PAINT includes a feature called the Gamut Alarm that visually displays the portions of an image that cannot be accurately reproduced. The determination of what colors cannot be reproduced is based on the output device selected.

Congratulations

If you have read through this chapter, you should have enough basic information to understand how the tools and commands in PHOTO-PAINT work. The diploma shown above is yours to keep and the good news is, there won't be a test. Now let's begin to work with PHOTO-PAINT 7. Were you thinking we weren't ever going to get to the actual program?

Setting Up Corel PHOTO-PAINT 7

As a larger-than-average person, I have come to discover that "one size fits all" is one of the great lies. I also know that the same is true when it comes to the default arrangement and settings of tools of any software application—this includes PHOTO-PAINT. That is why Corel allows many of the features to be moved, removed, and otherwise customized.

In this chapter you will learn how to customize your PHOTO-PAINT workspace so that it is both comfortable and productive. Corel has put a lot of features into PAINT that allow you, to quote a famous fast food chain, to "have it your way." There are literally several million combinations of tool settings possible, so we are not going to look at all of the configurable or customizable tools, just the commonly used ones.

Toolbars, Menus, and Keyboards

You can configure existing toolbars, menus, and keyboard commands as well as create new ones. PHOTO-PAINT comes with 17 toolbars installed. You can add, remove, and rearrange buttons on both existing and new custom toolbars. The same can be done with the commands that are available in the Menu Bar. Many of the default keyboard combinations can be altered, or new combinations can be made. While all three areas—toolbars, menus, and keyboard commands—offer unique benefits, one, the configurable toolbar, offers some of the greatest productivity advantages.

Toolbars

The toolbar buttons are configurable in both size and content. Our first step when we set up PHOTO-PAINT is to get them to the right size for the display. Then we can fiddle with them.

Selecting the Right Button Size

Because monitors come in all sizes from 9 inches to 23 inches, Corel has made the size of the buttons and therefore the size of the toolbars, configurable. One of the first steps in setting up PHOTO-PAINT 7 is to find the best fit for your monitor.

Every size of button except the smallest may cause a portion of the toolbar to drop off the end of a standard monitor. The rule for toolbar size is: The larger your display (physically), the larger the toolbar button settings can be—as long as the toolbar fits the screen. The quality of the icons on the buttons varies with size; the middle-sized buttons look the best.

Changing the Toolbar Size and Shape

From the View menu choose Toolbars. When the toolbar dialog box opens, click the Options button to display the Size section as shown next. (The actual dialog box does not have the wavy top; I created this effect with PHOTO-PAINT 7.) Move the Button slider to the desired size. Clicking the OK button in the dialog box applies the change to the toolbars. The Border slider increases or decreases the size of the border or bar that the buttons appear to sit on. Moving the slider all the way to the left means all button and no border; all the way to the right, and the border surrounding the buttons increases to its maximum.

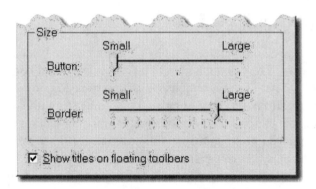

Selecting Toolbars That Are Displayed

If you choose to display all 17 of PHOTO-PAINT's standard toolbars, you won't be able to find the image. To make a toolbar visible, select Toolbars from the View menu and place a check by the desired toolbar. The first time you launch PHOTO-PAINT, there are three toolbars checked (visible): Standard, Property Bar, and Toolbox. Because toolbars take up screen space and the Property Bar provides much of the functionality of the other toolbars, I recommend that you initially keep only the default toolbars selected.

 TIP: *If you feel more comfortable with the Standard toolbar as it existed in PHOTO-PAINT 6, you can choose it in the Toolbar selection box.*

Placing the Toolbars

You can move the toolbar anywhere on the screen. By clicking on any part of the toolbar that doesn't have a button, you can drag it to any of the four sides of the window. When it gets close to a side, it will attach itself (dock) there. To make it a floating toolbar, move it away from the side.

 TIP: *Be careful when docking the toolbars. PHOTO-PAINT doesn't seem to mind if the toolbar you just docked is too long and some of the buttons go beyond the edge of the monitor, making them no longer visible.*

Customizing Toolbars

There are several ways to customize a toolbar. Here are some basic concepts about buttons and toolbars. Every command in PHOTO-PAINT has a button that can be placed on a toolbar. All of these buttons can be rearranged, moved to a different toolbar, or removed from a toolbar completely. To move a button, hold down the ALT key and drag the button to its new location. If you drag it off of the toolbar, the button will be removed. (See your reference manual for details on creating new toolbars.) I recommend that you spend some time working with PHOTO-PAINT 7 to get a feel for what arrangement will work best before you begin customizing.

If you are going to be doing the projects throughout this book, the following is a simple project that creates a custom toolbar to make the other projects in this book easier and get you used to creating/modifying toolbars.

Building Your Own Custom Toolbar

 The following procedure creates a custom toolbar. Before any customization can be done, you must open an image. I don't know why, but you must. The first step is to create an image that allows us access to the Customize command.

1. Open a new file (CTRL+N), click the OK button when the dialog box opens, and minimize the image by clicking the Minus button in the upper-right corner.

2. Select Customize from the Tools menu and click the Toolbars tab. The Customize dialog box shown here is divided into two areas: the Command categories (left) and Buttons (right).

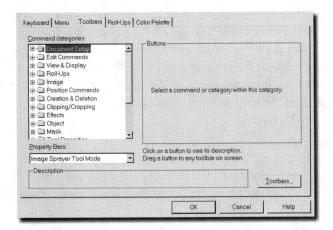

3. In the Command categories, locate Edit Commands and click the plus sign to the left of the Folder icon. This action opens a list of all of the Edit commands that are available in PHOTO-PAINT and displays all of the icons in the Buttons area. Scroll down the list until you find the Clear command, and click on it once. This action surrounds the Clear icon (looks like an "X") with a box as shown here:

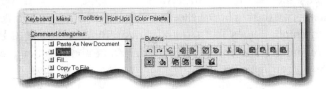

4. Click and drag the Clear button to the desktop. When you release it, it becomes a toolbar.

5. Repeat this procedure with the Fill button (also an Edit command). It isn't necessary to return to the Command categories side to select the button. Click the button that looks like a bucket (next to the Clear button), and drag it over to the new toolbar. When you release it, the Fill button will attach itself to the new toolbar. If the button ends up below the Clear button instead of on the side of it, grab the left or right of the toolbar with the cursor and make the toolbar wider.

6. Give the new toolbar a name by clicking the Toolbars button in the lower-right corner of the dialog box. This opens the Toolbar dialog box. Scroll down until you find the new toolbar, which is named Toolbar *x (x* is a number). Name the toolbar by clicking on the name with the right mouse button. From the secondary menu that opens up, select Rename. The name of the toolbar is highlighted. Change the name to Custom. Click the OK button.

You have created your first custom toolbar. To remove a toolbar that you made, or if you accidentally made an extra one or two doing the above exercise, select Toolbars from the View menu, select the toolbar, and click the Delete button.

Menus and Keyboard Commands

The arrangement of the menus work in a similar fashion to the toolbars. An example of rearranging the menu structure would be moving a command that is nested several levels deep to the top of the menu for easy access. Another time-saver is the ability to assign a command to a keyboard shortcut. PHOTO-PAINT comes with a large set of default keyboard combinations. The operation of customizing a keyboard combination is pretty much self-explanatory. Assigning a keyboard combination to a command allows you to execute commands quickly without the need to click a button or access the menu. The only disadvantage of using keyboard combinations is the need to memorize the keyboard shortcut. Also, remember that you cannot use existing reserved combinations like CTRL+S (Save). Refer to the PHOTO-PAINT user's manual or online help for detailed information about either the menu or keyboard command configurations.

Each of these methods—toolbars, menus, and keyboard commands—offers the PHOTO-PAINT user a wealth of productivity enhancements that can be applied to a specific project or to the program in general.

Making Your Preferences Known

The preference settings for PHOTO-PAINT 7 are located in the Tools menu and are called Options. The Options for PHOTO-PAINT are located on six different tabs. In this section I will explore most of the settings and offer some suggestions for selecting options. Please note that a few of the Options have changed location in the Plus release. If you have the original release of PHOTO-PAINT 7 that shipped with CorelDRAW 7, refer to your user's manual for the location. The first tab on the Options dialog box is called General.

General Tab

The General tab, shown next, contains many of the settings that determine how PHOTO-PAINT functions. The setting that determines what PHOTO-PAINT does when you launch it is found in the On Startup setting. By default, it is set to the Welcome screen, which is a new feature with this release of PHOTO-PAINT.

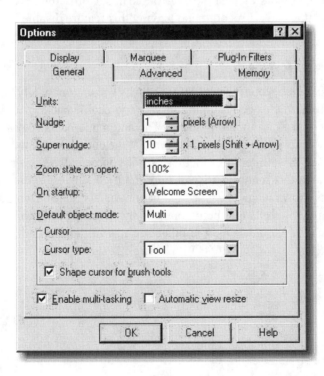

There are a few default settings in the General page that you should consider changing. I recommend keeping the Zoom state on open at 100 percent. If you have To Fit or some other zoom level selected, it will slow down the amount of time necessary to display an image after it is loaded.

An important setting in the Cursor section is the Shape cursor for brush tool checkbox. When enabled, this changes the cursor to the size and shape of a selected Brush tool. This is important since this feature allows you to see the size of your Brush tool. The only reason (that I am aware of) for not selecting this feature is that the cursor shape can slow down the Brush tool action if you have a slow system.

Near the bottom of the page is the Automatic view resize option. This changes the size of the image window automatically so that it always fits the current size of the image anytime you change the zoom level. As neat as this feature is, you may want to leave it unchecked when editing an image. This option keeps the edge of the image window tight to the edge of the image, which creates a problem as the cursor approaches the edge of the image window. The program thinks you want to take action on the image window size or placement on the workspace rather than on the image. This makes working near the edge of the image difficult. If you will be doing the projects in this book, I recommend leaving this feature disabled.

Advanced Tab

On the Advanced tab, you instruct PHOTO-PAINT to automatically back up the file you are working on at specific time intervals and enable backup copies of images to be produced when an image is saved. The automatic backup of an open image (Auto-save) sounds good, but keep in mind that the changes you make to the image will be saved at these intervals whether or not you actually want them to. If you choose to enable this feature (it is off by default), I suggest setting it to Save to checkpoint, as shown next. The Checkpoint command creates a temporary copy of an image. This avoids changes being made to the original file before you are ready to save them. You should leave the other settings in their default state until you become more familiar with PHOTO-PAINT.

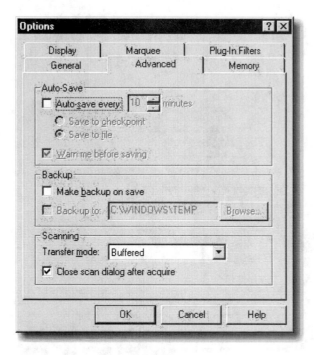

3

Memory Tab

The Memory tab, shown next, determines which and how much hard disk space is available for PHOTO-PAINT to save temporary files, and the allocation of the system memory for image editing and Undo lists and levels. The correct settings in this tab improve the performance of PHOTO-PAINT by adjusting the use of system resources to the way you work.

Because bitmap images require larger areas of memory than traditional Windows applications, PHOTO-PAINT uses space on your hard disk drive for temporary storage. This area is called a *swap disk*. If you have more than one hard disk drive, the program, by default, will select the first drive (alphabetically) as the primary swap disk and the second drive as the secondary swap disk regardless of the amount of available space on the drive. Check your settings to make sure that the drive with the greatest amount of available space is set as the primary swap drive. If one of the drives is slower than the other, select the fastest drive for the primary swap drive.

The Memory tab has settings to enable and disable the Undo and Undo list commands. This is an important feature. The traditional problem with a photo-editing package is the lack of multiple undo levels. With PHOTO-PAINT 7 you can determine how many undo levels you have. Before you decide to set the undo level to 99, be aware that each level of undo uses up system resources. Each undo level keeps a copy of the image at that level. Setting to a high level can consume a lot of swap disk space and ultimately slow down your system. I recommend keeping the undo level to less than 3. Another feature that has been improved in PHOTO-PAINT 7 is the Undo List. Enabling this feature will allow you to undo as far back as you choose. It does this by recording each command that is applied to an image and then reapplying the commands (minus the ones you wanted to undo) in a sequential manner. While it is slower than the normal Undo, it does not consume as many system resources as undo levels.

You can also determine the amount of RAM assigned to temporarily store images when you open and edit them. Allotting too much RAM for the images can result in slower performance of other Windows applications. I recommend leaving this setting at its default state.

NOTE: *Any change you make to the settings in the Memory tab requires restarting PHOTO-PAINT for the changes to take effect.*

Display and Marquee Tabs

Use these two tabs to change the colors, actions, and appearance of the marquees in PHOTO-PAINT. These settings are not intended to make the marquees more esthetically appealing, but to allow the adjustment of their colors and shapes for the types of images you are working on. For example, the Object marquee is blue, but against a blue background you cannot see it. Generally, these settings should be left in their default state unless the color of the image makes it difficult to see the marquees.

The feature I have requested since the release of PHOTO-PAINT 5 is the ability to disable the read-only warning when loading an image from a CD-ROM. Thank you, Lucian and Doug! Immediately uncheck this feature. When enabled, every time a photo-CD is opened you get a warning that it is a "read-only" file. It may not sound like much, but after you have loaded a couple of hundred photo-CD images, you will understand.

Plug-in Filters Tab

The use of the settings in this tab are discussed in Chapter 14 .

NOTE: *For more information about customization features, press the* F1 *function key and select the Content tab. Select Customizing the Work Area and click the Open button.*

Roll-ups

Unless this is your very first time working with Corel, you are already familiar with roll-ups. For those who have never heard of roll-ups, a *roll-up,* shown in Figure 3-1, is a dialog box that contains the sort of things most dialog boxes contain—command buttons, boxes, and so on. However, unlike most dialog boxes, roll-ups can stay open while you continue to work. If you need to maximize your workspace but wish to keep the roll-up open, roll it up by clicking the arrow in the Title Bar. This leaves just the Title Bar visible. Click the arrow again to unroll it.

 TIP: *A new feature with the Objects roll-up in PHOTO-PAINT 7 is the ability to stretch the roll-up by clicking and dragging either its top or bottom so more layers can be seen. This action only works if the Objects roll-up is not grouped with another roll-up.*

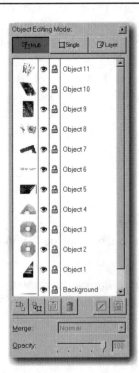

The Objects roll-up (extended) showing many of the objects in an image

FIGURE 3-1

Grouping Roll-ups

With the introduction of the Property Bar in PHOTO-PAINT 7, the need for many roll-ups to be on the screen has been reduced—but not eliminated. If you use roll-ups often, you may want to organize them into groups so they take up less space and are more easily accessible. Roll-ups can be grouped together so that a single roll-up gives you access to the commands of several roll-ups.

Because the roll-up groups support drag and drop, you can easily group and ungroup roll-ups as the need arises while working. To group together two roll-ups hold down the ALT key, and click and drag the Title Bar of one roll-up on top of the other. You can do the same thing with the right mouse button. That's all there is to it. The following illustration shows the two original roll-ups and the resulting roll-up group. You remove a roll-up from a group the same way you add it. See the user's manual for more details on roll-ups and their customization.

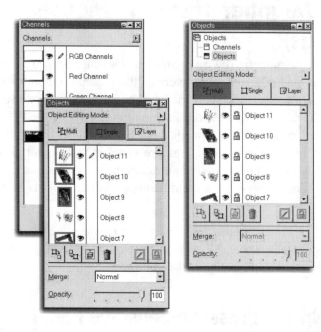

Onscreen Palette

The onscreen color palette first appears on the right side of the screen. Like the toolbars, it can be dragged and docked anywhere on the screen. You can change several of the color features by selecting Customize in the Tools menu and clicking on the Color Palette tab. From here you can configure the color wells and control how the right button on the mouse responds when clicking one of the color wells. I recommend keeping the default setting of Set fill color. It offers a quick and easy way to change fill colors.

 TIP: *When configuring the color palette, you may want to disable the Use 3D wells setting if you are experiencing sluggish performance from your display.*

The Pen Is Mightier Than the Mouse (Pen Settings)

If you are fortunate enough to own a digitizer tablet with a pressure-sensitive stylus, you can assign nine different parameters to the pressure output of the pen. The pressure-sensitive stylus responds to increases and decreases in pressure as the user presses it on the tablet. This pressure information is provided to PHOTO-PAINT, and the selected brush settings change with the pressure. If you do not have a pressure-sensitive stylus and tablet, I assure you that you do not need one to use PHOTO-PAINT. Even though I have an excellent Art Z II tablet courtesy of the Wacom Co., it is not necessary for completing any of the projects in this book.

 TIP: *A pressure-sensitive stylus is not a good substitute for a mouse. You will need to have both. All of the major manufacturers allow both the mouse and the stylus to be active at the same time.*

Setting Up the Pressure-Sensitive Pen

The Pressure Sensitive Pen Settings dialog box lets you control the relationship between the pressure you apply with the pen to the tablet, and the effect produced by brush tools. As you press down on a drawing tablet with the pen, the effect produced by such tools changes. For example, if you set the Size option to 25 percent and apply pressure to the tablet, the nib widens to a maximum of 25 percent just as a real paintbrush does as you apply more pressure.

From the Tools menu, select Pen Settings and the Pressure Sensitive Pen Settings dialog box opens, as shown next. The settings of this box determine which brush parameters change as a result of the pressure information provided by the pen.

3

Pressure Sensitive Pen Settings ? ✕

Selection	Value
☐ Size	100
☐ Opacity	0
☐ Softness	0
☐ Hue	0
☐ Saturation	0
☐ Brightness	0
☐ Texture	0
☐ Bleed	0
☐ Sustain Color	0

Pen Eraser:

Eraser Tool ▾

Settings: ▸

Wacom ARTZII ▾

Save Settings...

Apply   Close   Help

TIP: *The Pen Settings dialog box is unique in that it can remain open while using the pen, allowing you to change and test the various settings.*

Just because multiple settings can be applied doesn't mean you need to use all of them. For most photo-editing work, I don't even use the pressure information, since I only need the feel of a pen in my hand to finely control some touch-up work. I recommend that you start with the size setting, experimenting with it in a blank image area. To add one of the settings to the pen, you must click the checkbox, change the value, and click the Apply button.

NOTE: *For more information about setting up pressure-sensitive pen settings, select <u>Pen</u> Settings from the <u>Tools</u> menu. When the dialog box opens, click the Help button in the lower-right corner. There is a wealth of information about each of the settings.*

Setting Up Color Management on PHOTO-PAINT 7

The primary purpose of color management is to get the colors you expect from your output device. To make the colors on your screen match the colors you get from your printer, you must first set up the Corel Color Manager. If you used this tool in PHOTO-PAINT 5 or 6, you'll notice it has been greatly improved. If the thought of calibrating PHOTO-PAINT to its monitor, scanner, and printers sounds difficult and complex, you will soon find out it isn't.

Who Needs Corel Color Management?

There is a misconception about who should be using the Corel Color Manager. This is not a feature that should be tagged "For Professional Use Only." The truth is, it is designed to operate with both high-end equipment and inexpensive color printers to produce the best colors possible. So if you are thinking the Color Manager isn't for you because you only have an inexpensive color inkjet printer, you are wrong. However, if your printer is a color dot-matrix, you are right—Color Manager is not for you!

Why Colors May Not Look Right

If you work on a photograph of an apple and an orange, you want the scanned image on your monitor to look exactly as it did in the photograph. You expect to see accurate and clearly distinguished shades of red and orange both on the screen and from the printer. Before inexpensive color printers became available, color wasn't important. After all, it is difficult to determine shades of red and orange on a grayscale image. Now that so many users are printing in color, they are noticing that their apples are not quite red and their oranges seem to be less orange and more green. Why? Color management is only part of the answer. There are a number of factors affecting color.

3

Color Gamut

Chapter 2 introduced the concept of the color gamut. Any device that detects or produces color is limited to colors in its color gamut. For example, since the human eye can detect the color purple, it is within our gamut, whereas ultraviolet is beyond us. Typically, desktop devices can produce a far narrower range of color than the eye can detect, and since each device uses a different technique, color model, or set of inks, each has its own unique gamut. All you need understand about the gamut is that there are colors that are outside of the gamut for a device and therefore these colors cannot be reproduced.

Corel PHOTO-PAINT provides a visual indicator for colors that are outside of gamut called, appropriately, a *Gamut alarm.* The Gamut alarm is enabled by selecting Color correction from the View menu and single-clicking the name Gamut Alarm from the drop-down list that appears. Once the Gamut alarm is made active, any colors that cannot be reproduced by the printer will appear as a single shade of color. A word of caution about the information displayed by the Gamut alarm: An image may contain a large quantity of out-of-gamut colors and have the color still match the original. The Gamut alarm is only a visual indicator of colors that may not accurately reproduce.

 NOTE: *For more information about gamut alarms in PHOTO-PAINT, press the F1 function key and select the Index tab. Type in **Gamut** and select "Gamut alarm, changing the color of ". Click the Display button.*

Color Space

A *color space* is a geometric representation of gamut, containing all of the colors in a device's color gamut plotted as points on color models like RGB or L*A*B*. When different color spaces are "mapped" to the same model, it becomes easy to see where the capabilities of various devices differ.

To compensate for all of these device exceptions and limitations, use the Corel Color Manager, which acts as a mediator between your hardware and all of the Corel graphics applications on which you work. It uses the CIE standard to map the color spaces of individual devices into device profiles and uses these devices together to plot a common color space for your system. If you didn't understand that the important part is the result, all of your devices will speak the same color language—and more importantly—they will produce the same colors. In other words, your apples will not only be red, but on the monitor they will look like the photograph you scanned. Most important, the output of the printer will look like what you see on the monitor—mostly.

Setting Up the Color Manager

The Corel Color Manager is a separate application that can be launched directly from the Windows Explorer or from within PHOTO-PAINT. To launch it from within PHOTO-PAINT, select Color Manager from the Tools menu. The dialog box opens, as shown in Figure 3-2.

Setting the Color Manager is simple. From the dialog box, select profiles for your monitor, printer, and scanner (if you have one). To select a monitor, click the checkbox at the far right. Click the down arrow button in the monitor space to open a list of monitors. Select your monitor from the list. Be aware that if you choose to load the profiles from the CD-ROM (#1), it will take several minutes for the profiles to load. If your monitor is not on the list, see the help file or the user's manual for information about manually creating a profile for your monitor. Select your composite printer and scanner the same way.

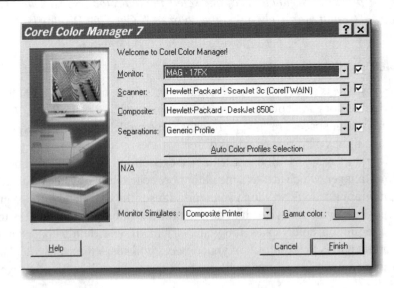

The Color
Manager
dialog box

FIGURE 3-2

TIP: *To get the most out of Color Manager, you should be using a 16- or 24-bit display adapter. While 256 color (also called paletted color) produces good results, it is difficult to get accurate color.*

Monitor Calibration

Of all of the devices in the Color Manager, it is the monitor that benefits most from manual calibration. This is because as the monitor ages, its color characteristics change. For example, my monitor has a gamma value of 1.8 in its specification, yet when I manually calibrated it, the gamma value was closer to 2.5. The difference in the accuracy on the screen colors was noticeable.

 TIP: *When calibrating a monitor, make sure it has been on for at least an hour and that your room lighting is close to what it will be when working on images.*

Printers

The *composite printer* is either the printer that you use to proof your work or your final output device or both. The *separations printer* is your final output device. It is called "separations" because in commercial printing, the process of splitting colors in a composite image to produce a number of separate grayscale images, one for each primary in the original, is referred to as *making separations*. For example, for a CMYK image, four separations must be made: one each of cyan, magenta, yellow, and black. If your final output device is a composite device (your inkjet qualifies), then you don't need to set up a separations printer. You should disable it by clicking the checkbox next to it.

Scanners

If the scanner selection is grayed out and you have a scanner, click the checkbox and select your scanner from the list. If you have an off-brand scanner without a TWAIN interface, don't waste your time looking for it in the selection list. The scanner needs to be set up in the Color Manager to use the Corel Scan Wizard. For more information on setting up scanners, check the online help and the user's manual.

TIP: *If you are using a grayscale scanner, you do not need a profile and should leave the scanner selection checkbox unchecked.*

Other Selections

A few more features of the dialog box in Figure 3-2 deserve mention. The Monitor Simulates setting can be set to either Composite Printer or Separations Printer. Depending on which printer it is set to, the Color Manager will attempt to display an accurate representation of the final output color. The Gamut color swatch allows you to change the color used to indicate areas on the image that are out of gamut. The only time you would need to change this setting is when you have colors in the image that are too close to the gamut warning color, making determination of the out-of-gamut areas difficult.

After selecting all of the devices, click the Finish button and a profile will be generated. In PHOTO-PAINT 5 and 6, you could generate multiple profiles and save them. This has changed in PHOTO-PAINT 7. If you are using more than one printer, either composite or separations, as your output device, you only need open the Color Manager, change the printer, and regenerate the profile. Unlike the previous versions of Color Manager, profiles are now generated very quickly.

Color Correction Command

After setting up the Color Manager, the next step is to set up the Color Correction command. It is found in the View menu, and it activates the settings you've selected in the Corel Color Manager, ensuring that the colors you see on your monitor match the capabilities of the other devices in your system. To accurately display color, it is necessary to change the Color correction setting located in the View menu, shown next, from the default setting of None to either Fast or Accurate. The Fast setting provides the fastest color calibrated display possible, while the Accurate setting is slower but more genuine. Visually, the only difference between the two settings you may encounter is some banding with the Fast setting. *Banding* in an image occurs when the colors or shades are sufficiently different to produce visual areas (bands) of color.

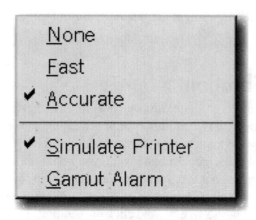

 TIP: *Only enable the Color Correction settings when you are in the final stages of your project. Both Fast and Accurate settings slow down the refresh of display adapters—even the really fast ones!*

Simulate Printer

The other two settings in the Color Correction menu are Simulate Printer, which is enabled automatically when Accurate is selected, and Gamut Alarm. The Simulate Printer uses the color profile for the printer selected (Composite or Separations) in the Monitors Simulates setting of Color Manager. It does not use the printer that is currently selected from the file menu.

Gamut Alarm

As mentioned previously, the Gamut Alarm setting alerts you to the colors in your image that are beyond the capabilities of your printer by displaying a single color in place of the out-of-gamut colors. As a point of clarity, just because a color or range of colors is out-of-gamut doesn't mean it won't print or even look correct. I have printed several test pages of images that contained more out-of-gamut than in-gamut colors, and the printed image looked almost exactly like the one displayed on the monitor. I recommend you treat Gamut Alarm as an indicator of *potential* color matching problems.

Screen Calibration

After you have set up the color, the last step is to confirm that the image on the screen is physically calibrated. It is very important to make sure that one inch in your image really corresponds to one inch in your printed image. This makes the size of your image displayed on the screen accurate when you select the Zoom 1:1 level.

It is a simple operation that only requires a ruler (preferably a clear plastic ruler). From the Tools menu, select Options or use CTRL+J. When the Options menu opens, choose the Display tab, shown next, and click the Calibrate rulers button. The screen is filled with a horizontal and a vertical ruler. Change the vertical and horizontal adjustments until the tick marks on the screen rulers match the ruler you hold on the screen. When it matches, click the OK button and close the Options dialog box.

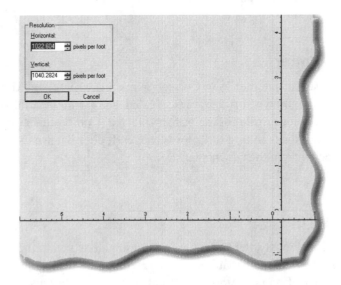

4

Basic Tools and Procedures

Corel PHOTO-PAINT 7 provides an assortment of tools to make working on images easier. For aligning and positioning objects in an image, rulers, grids, and guidelines are provided. While these tools are generally associated with vector-based (CorelDRAW) or page layout (Corel Ventura) programs, they can be used for tasks other than accurate positioning of graphic elements—for example, creating unusual backgrounds. The navigation tools help to quickly get around large images, while the Zoom tools provide the necessary magnification levels required to perform accurate retouching and other image manipulation. As capable as these tools are, the ones most appreciated are those that help undo our mistakes. Fortunately, Corel PHOTO-PAINT 7 offers a lot of ways to help even beyond the traditional last-action-only Undo command. Another necessity is the ability to save our images in a format that can be either archived or transported to another location. I will explore some of the potential pitfalls of file compression and other image management issues.

Rulers, Grids, and Guidelines

Rulers are important in PHOTO-PAINT because they provide one of the few visual indicators that show the physical dimensions of an image. The grids, which are nonprintable, serve as both an alignment tool for placing graphic elements in an image and a way to proportionally arrange them. The guidelines help, whether cropping an image or aligning elements in an image to a fixed point. With the Snap to Guidelines feature, guidelines can be used like the grids, but with the added advantage of being where they are needed rather than at the fixed intervals of the grids.

Rulers

In Chapter 2 you learned it is possible for a photograph to completely fill the screen, yet print smaller than a postage stamp. By displaying rulers on an image you can see the dimensions of the image in inches. Here is a quick exercise that demonstrates why rulers are so important.

A Ruler/Resample Demonstration

This demonstration is to familiarize you with the rulers and to visibly display the effects of changing the resolution of an image.

1. Open an image file (CTRL+O). From the Corel CD-ROM, select the file OBJECTS\TRANSPOR\BALLOON4.CPT.

2. Select <u>D</u>uplicate from the <u>I</u>mage menu, and when the dialog box opens, name the duplicate image COPY.

3. From the <u>W</u>indow menu, select Tile <u>V</u>ertically. Two identical copies now fill the screen as shown here.

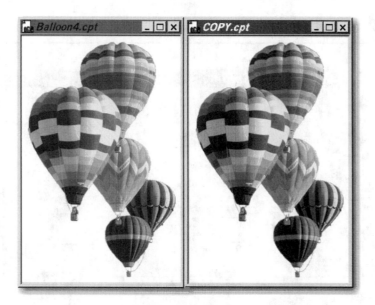

4. With COPY.CPT selected, choose Resam<u>p</u>le from the <u>I</u>mage menu. I will explain resampling further in Chapter 6. For now, you only need to know it can change the size of the image. When the Resample dialog box opens, check the Maintain original <u>s</u>ize checkbox. In the Resolution section, double-click the value for H<u>o</u>rizontal, change it from 300 to 75, and click the OK button.

5. With COPY.CPT still selected, display the rulers (CTRL+R) or select Rulers from the View menu. Click on the title bar of BRUSHES.CPT and display its rulers (CTRL+R).

6. The rulers on this file display in pixels. To change the rulers to inches, double-click the ruler to open the Grid & Ruler Setup dialog box, as shown in Figure 4-1, or select Grid and Ruler Setup from the Tools menu. Enable the Same units for Horizontal and Vertical rulers checkbox. In the Units section, click the down-pointing button in Horizontal and select inches. Click the OK button. Even though both images appear to be the same size, an examination of the rulers shows that they are not.

TIP: *The quickest way to open the Grid & Ruler Setup dialog box is to double-click either a ruler or a gridline on the image.*

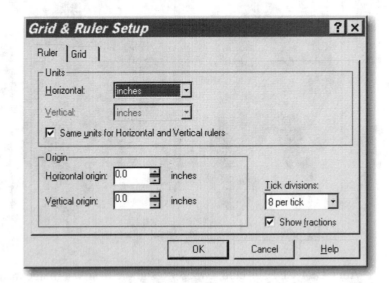

The Grid & Ruler Setup dialog box

FIGURE 4-1

7. To see the images in their actual size, make sure BALLOON.CPT is still selected (Title Bar is highlighted). In the Standard toolbar, change the Zoom Level from 100 percent to 1:1. Select COPY.CPT and change it to a Zoom level of 1:1. Shown next is the result of changing the resolution of both images when they are displayed using 1:1 zoom level.

The ruler normally uses the upper-left corner of the image window as its point of origin. To change this, click and drag the origin point to the new desired position. The origin point is where the two rulers intersect.

To read a ruler, move the cursor over the part of the image you want to measure. When the cursor is in the image, it produces dashed lines on the horizontal and vertical rulers to indicate the cursor position. To get a more accurate reading, increase the zoom level. The information displayed in the ruler will increase as a function of the zoom level as shown in Figure 4-2.

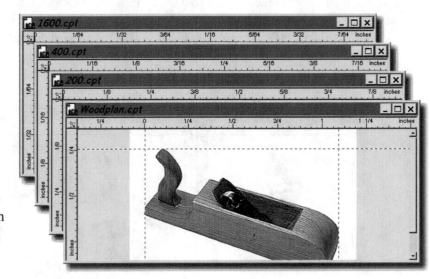

Ruler
markings
change with
the zoom
level
settings

FIGURE 4-2

Repositioning the Rulers

You can place a ruler anywhere on an image. There are times when placing the ruler at a different location allows you to more clearly see dimensions of a graphic element in the image.

To reposition either ruler, hold down the SHIFT key, click the ruler you want to move, and drag it to a new position. The ruler outline will appear as double-dashed lines as you move it.

To return either the horizontal or vertical ruler to the position of origin, hold down the SHIFT key and double-click it. If you need to move both rulers at once, hold down the SHIFT key and drag the intersection point of the two rulers. To return both at once, double-click at the intersection.

NOTE: *When you reposition and release a ruler the first time, the image may jump a short distance (the width of the ruler—five pixels). Click and drag the ruler and reposition it a second time, and the image will not jump.*

Grids

Grids are extremely useful for performing a variety of design functions in PHOTO-PAINT. You can align objects and masks to them as well when you work with objects and layers. In Chapter 13 you will discover that the grid works with the New Object command to make tracing paper.

Grid Properties

Grids are simple, so you don't need to spend a lot of time learning about them. Select Grid in the View menu to make the grid visible or invisible. From the Grid & Ruler Setup dialog box, you can change the frequency of the grid (number of grids per unit of measure) and other grid properties. An important property of the grid to remember is that it is nonprintable. Even though they appear on the display, the gridlines do not occupy space in the image. There may be occasions when you want to include the grid in the image. This can be done (as shown next), but only by using a screen capture program such as Corel CAPTURE and bringing the image into PHOTO-PAINT 7.

Guidelines

Guidelines are created by clicking the ruler with the left mouse button and dragging a guideline into the image. The guidelines can be either horizontal or vertical. For all practical purposes, you can make as many guidelines as you want. Double-clicking a guideline with the Object Picker tool opens the Guidelines Setup dialog box. While there are several different guideline settings that can be controlled with this dialog box, the one to remember is the Clear all button. This removes all of the guidelines you created with a single action. For more details on the settings for the guidelines, refer to either the online help or the PHOTO-PAINT 7 user's manual.

Rules About Rulers, Grids, and Guidelines

Here are some little-known facts about rulers, grids, and guidelines:

- When a file is saved and later reopened, it uses its last ruler and grid settings.

- The grid is not always visible when a file is opened, even if the grid was visible when the image was saved.

- The Show Grid and Snap-to-Grid modes are turned off when an image is first opened.

Zoom and Navigation Tools

The zoom tools of PHOTO-PAINT 7 provide several options for viewing and working on your image from as close up or as far away as necessary. Zoom tools magnify or decrease the size of your onscreen image without effecting the actual image size. You also have a wealth of navigational tools for moving to different locations in an image that is either too large or has a zoom level too high for the image to fit on the screen.

Working the Zoom Tools

You can change the zoom level several ways in PHOTO-PAINT. You can choose a preset zoom level from the drop-down list in the Standard toolbar, or you can enter a value into the Zoom Level box and press ENTER. The preset zoom levels can also be selected from the View menu.

In addition to the zoom level settings in the View menu, there are three other zoom settings: Zoom to fit, Zoom 100%, and Zoom 1:1.

Zoom to Fit

This option changes the zoom level so that the image fits into the current window. The keyboard shortcut is F4. This is very handy when you want to quickly see the entire image.

Zoom 100% and Zoom 1:1

The first time I saw these two commands in PHOTO-PAINT 6, I thought they did the same thing. I was wrong. Zoom 100% matches pixels in the image with screen pixels in the display. Zoom 1:1 should be called "display in actual size," since it changes the zoom level to display the image at its physical size.

Zoom 100% provides the most accurate possible representation of the image you are working on. I mention this because there are times when images in the display will appear to be degraded. This is often the result of the image being at some zoom level that is difficult for your video adapter to properly display. In the following image, a screen capture of the word "ZOOM" was made at zoom levels of 100 percent and 88 percent. The 100 percent zoom level text looks smooth, with no sign of the "jaggies," those irregular edges that primarily appear on the diagonal portions of an image. The 88 percent text below appears to be very ragged. The insert on the left of the image is a magnified portion of the first letters.

TIP: *Always use Zoom 100% to see the most accurate representation of an image in PHOTO-PAINT.*

The Zoom Tool

 The Zoom tool allows you to magnify or decrease the size of your onscreen image without effecting the actual image size. To use it, click on the Zoom tool and drag a rectangle around the area you want to zoom in on.

 TIP: *The quick way to activate the Zoom tool is to hold down the* Z *key while any other tool is selected. As long as the* Z *key is held, the tool remains a zoom tool.*

Right Mouse Button Zoom Feature

The Zoom Tool Settings roll-up, accessed by double-clicking the Zoom button in the Toolbox, contains a single checkbox for enabling or disabling the right mouse button as a means of zooming out on an image. If the checkbox is disabled, you can still zoom out by holding down SHIFT while clicking the image.

The Hand Tool

 If you zoom in enough so that the entire image is no longer visible, you can move around the image by clicking the scroll bars that appear at the sides and bottom of the image window. An easier method is to use the Hand tool and drag the image. As you click and drag the image, it moves inside the window. While you can select the Hand tool from the Zoom tool flyout, the quick way is to hold down the H key. The cursor turns into a hand as long as the key is held down.

Navigator Pop-up

New to PHOTO-PAINT 7 is the Navigator pop-up. This easy-to-use image navigation tool is available whenever the entire image no longer fits in its window. Placing the cursor on the icon in the lower-right corner of the image (where the scroll bars meet) and holding down the left mouse button displays the Navigator pop-up, as shown next. The Navigator remains open as long as the button is held. The cursor moves the rectangular box in the Navigator, and as the box moves, the image moves. Releasing the mouse button closes the Navigator.

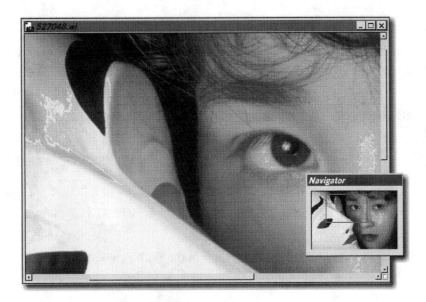

Tools for Correcting Mistakes

Corel PHOTO-PAINT 7 has more ways to undo mistakes than any previous version. One of the frustrations considered normal for users of photo-editing programs was that the Undo feature only allowed the last action to be undone. That has all changed in PHOTO-PAINT 7. Besides having as many undo levels as your memory resources will allow, the Undo list actually works very fast—and correctly in this release. Another innovation I consider the ultimate undo tool: Clone from Saved.

Tools in this genre fall into two overlapping categories: those like the Eraser that remove portions of the image as the tool is dragged over them; and those that remove previous actions.

The Eraser Tool

 Found on the Undo Tool flyout (Toolbox) and on the Undo toolbar, the Eraser tool is as simple as it gets. The Eraser tool changes the color value of pixels in the image with the Paper (background) color as it is dragged over them. This makes it look like that portion of the image is erased, though nothing actually is. New with PHOTO-PAINT 7, the Eraser tool now has a soft edge that makes the erased area less jagged.

The Local Undo Tool

Also located on the Undo Tool flyout (Toolbox) and the Undo toolbar, the Local Undo tool allows the selective removal of the last action that was applied to the image.

Something for You to Try with the Undo Tool

While the Undo tool works fine at removing portions of the last applied actions, it can also be used to create some interesting effects. This demonstration will quickly show you how to create something unusual.

1. Load PHOTOS\PORTRAIT\527048.WI on the Corel CD as shown in Figure 4-3.

2. Select Image, Resample and enter 5 in the Width value box (units of measurement should be inches). Click OK.

Original
photograph
from Corel
CD

FIGURE 4-3

3. Select <u>F</u>ill from the <u>E</u>dit menu, opening the Edit Fill & Transparency dialog box. Click the Bitmap fill button (looks like a checkerboard), and click the Edit button. From the Bitmap Fill dialog box, click the Load button. From the Corel CD-ROM, locate the file \TILES\ WOOD\LARGE\WOOD071.CPT. Click Open. Click OK and click the next OK button. The fill covers the entire image as shown in Figure 4-4.

4. From the Eraser flyout on the Toolbox, select the Local Undo tool. In the Property bar, change the brush shape to a square and the nib size of the brush to 76 (pixels).

5. Position the brush so that it removes the portions of the image illustrated in Figure 4-5. Holding down the CTRL key *after* clicking the mouse button constrains the Local Undo brush action to the vertical (or the horizontal).

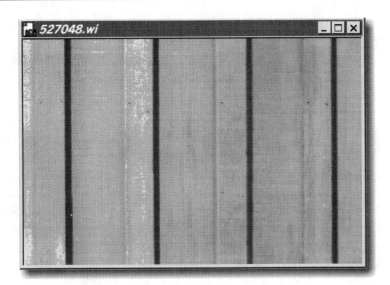

Entire
image
covered
with bitmap
fill

FIGURE 4-4

Part of
the fill
selectively
removed
by Local
Undo tool

FIGURE 4-5

The Checkpoint Command

The Checkpoint command, located in the Edit menu, is one of the most frequently used commands when photo-editing. It lets you save a temporary copy of the current image that you can return to anytime.

 TIP: *When doing any kind of work on an image, you should get in the habit of automatically selecting the Checkpoint command each time you begin to experiment with different effects and techniques.*

The temporary file created by the checkpoint command is closed when the image file is closed or when exiting PHOTO-PAINT (whether you planned to exit the program or it crashes). To return to the image saved by Checkpoint, select the Restore to Checkpoint command located in the Edit menu.

The Undo and Redo List—
Try It, You'll Like It!

The Undo List is essentially a command recorder that frees you to experiment by providing a way to remove one or more actions. If you make a change to an image that doesn't come out the way you thought it would, you can undo the change, undo a series of changes, or even redo the changes you have just undone.

The Undo List command found in the Edit menu opens a dialog box, shown here, that lists each action you have performed in chronological order and allows you to choose which one to start with. This command, and all those following it, will be undone. It accomplishes the Undo action by starting at the beginning of the Undo List and replaying the list.

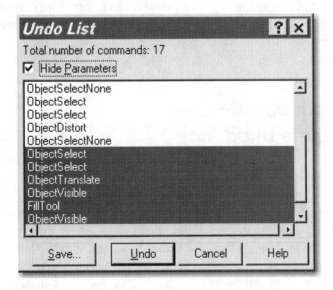

This list continues to grow until the file is saved, or the Checkpoint command is enabled. At that time the list is cleared. The more actions that are on the list, the longer it will take your system to replay the entire list without the commands you removed, and the greater possibility that it may not replay perfectly. Don't let this scare you. If you haven't used the Undo List because you didn't like earlier versions of it, I strongly recommend you try it in PHOTO-PAINT 7. You will be impressed—I guarantee it. So what happens to the commands that are removed? They go to the Redo list, of course.

 TIP: *Select the Hide Parameters in the Undo List dialog box feature to remove all of the clutter that follows the command names.*

The Redo List dialog box lists the names of the operations performed on an image that were reversed using the Undo List command. The command works in the same way as the Undo List except it replays the commands that were removed.

With all that the Undo List does, it also functions as a true command recorder. Whenever the Undo List is active, you can save the list as a file for Corel Script. This means you can replay the list of commands.

Clone from Saved— The Ultimate Undo Tool

 The Clone from Saved tool allows you to selectively restore a portion of an image to its previously saved version. I will explore Clone tools in depth in Chapter 11, but for now, I'll discuss this single area of the Clone tools. Clone from Saved is actually a brush tool that uses the contents of the last saved version of an image as the source and paints it onto the same portion of the current image. There are two basic presets (called Types). They are Eraser and Light Eraser (fewer calories). To operate Clone from Saved, click the Clone tool button at the bottom of the Toolbox. Open the Tool Settings roll-up (see Figure 4-6) by double-clicking the Clone tool button or using the keyboard combination CTRL+F8. You can change the brush nib size and other parameters (transparency, soft edge, etc.) in the Tool Settings roll-up or in the Property bar. Any part of the image you brush with the Clone tool is restored to the last saved version of the image.

 NOTE: *If you resampled an image since you opened it, the Clone from Saved tool will not work because the original and the current resampled images are no longer the same size.*

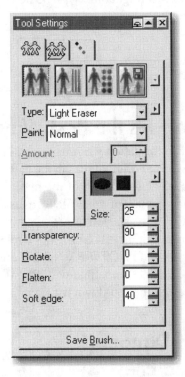

The Tool
Settings
roll-up

FIGURE 4-6

Making the Most of Image File Management

The opening and closing of image files in PHOTO-PAINT 7 is similar in operation to most Windows 95 applications, so I will not spend time explaining these procedures. If you need detailed information about this subject, you'll find it in both the PHOTO-PAINT 7 user's manual and the online help. Here are some recommendations about managing your image files in PHOTO-PAINT 7.

Resampling and Cropping

If you are opening very large images to be resampled or cropped, you should consider selecting this option when opening the file. Corel PHOTO-PAINT 7 offers the ability to crop or resample the image during the loading process. This saves a lot of system resources that might otherwise be tied up opening a very large image; having to either resample or crop it.

NOTE: *The Resample option available when opening files can only reduce file size—it cannot increase it.*

Going Native—It's the Best Way

Although some of this information was mentioned in Chapter 2, it bears repeating. You should always save your original files in the native CPT format. When an image is saved in PHOTO-PAINT format, all of the masks, objects, and layers are saved with it. The same cannot be said of other file formats. Pay special attention to which of the two available CPT formats you use. The native format of PHOTO-PAINT 7 cannot be read by any previous PHOTO-PAINT release. If you will need to open the file with older versions of PHOTO-PAINT or CorelDRAW, you should consider saving in the CPT file that is compatible with PHOTO-PAINT 6. This is indicated in the Files of Type selection drop-down list.

Wonders and Dangers of Compressed Files

With your original safely saved as a CPT file, you can use the Save As command in the File menu to save the file in a different format suitable for archiving or distributing on the Internet. Compressed files have been around for some time. Corel PHOTO-PAINT offers several compression schemes for its files, including CPT files. The types of compression fall into two general categories, *lossless* and *lossy*. These categories are also referred to as nondestructive and destructive compression, which should give you some hint about why you save an image in the CPT format before compressing it.

Lossless Compression

With lossless compression (Packbits, LZW), the compressing and decompressing processes are not destructive to the image. The compressed image is identical to the original image. While nondestructive, its compression ratio is usually only 2:1. This is why lossless compression is used for graphics files that are being archived or those going to the service bureau where the need for quality and accuracy is great. It is not a practical solution for the Internet.

Lossy Compression

During the process of compressing the graphic with lossy compression, some of the image information is forever lost. If you choose high-quality compression, very little of the image information detected by the human eye is lost; however, the greater the amount of compression, the poorer the resulting image quality. The most commonly used lossy compression is JPEG. Other lossy compression formats include the Photo-CD (PCD) format and the new Wavelet format included in PHOTO-PAINT 7, which is increasingly popular on the Internet as it is supported by more and more Web sites.

Compression Comparison

A picture is still worth 1000 words (50 if it is compressed). Figure 4-7 shows a photograph and a compressed version of it. The uncompressed size of this image is 540KB. Using the Wavelet compression (WI) at its best setting of 1 reduces the image size to 114KB. The Wavelet Compressed Bitmap (WI) option is located in the Save an Image to Disk dialog box. Wavelet compression has a quality range of 1 to 100; a setting of 1 offers the best image and least compression, and a setting of 100 produces a very small but nearly unrecognizable image. With Wavelet compression, you can use settings up to 40 or 50 without any really noticeable image degradation. At a setting of 40, our 540KB file is reduced to a mere 16KB.

Using the highest quality JPEG setting of 2 compresses the image to 203KB. JPEG compression offers a quality factor range of 2 to 255. You can use a setting in the range of 140-160 without noticeable image loss. The same image compressed using this setting produces a 27KB file.

Regardless of the compression type you select or the settings you use, you must close and reopen the image before you can accurately see the result of compression. Figure 4-7A shows what the photograph looked like after it was saved at the maximum compression using JPEG. Figure 4-7B shows that same file after it was closed and reopened.

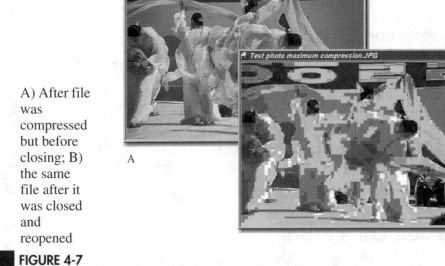

A) After file was compressed but before closing; B) the same file after it was closed and reopened

FIGURE 4-7

Compression Considerations

The hazard of using compression formats is from either applying too much compression when initially saving the image or continually opening, changing, and saving using a lossy compression format. I have already discussed the problems of applying too much compression. Many users do not know that every time a lossy compressed image is opened, changed, and saved, more of the image quality is lost. The best way to make changes is to open the CPT original and then save the changed file both as a CPT and as a JPEG.

Closing Thoughts

I have covered a broad range of PHOTO-PAINT tools. While I realize that some of them may seem about as interesting as 40 pounds of wet fertilizer, they make the day-to-day job of working with PHOTO-PAINT easier and more productive. Now that you know how to use the tools to handle an image, in the next chapter you'll learn how to get images into PHOTO-PAINT from a wide variety of sources.

5

The Ins, Outs, and Abouts of PHOTO-PAINT

U nless you have a digital camera or a video frame grabber, or you are an artist doing all of your original work on the computer, you will have to find some way to get the source images that you need into the computer. Corel provides many ways to bring images into and out of PHOTO-PAINT. While the scanner is the primary way we get photographic images into PHOTO-PAINT, there are also CorelCAPTURE, Photo-CDs, and a wide variety of import and export functions that allow you to move images between PAINT and other Windows applications. In this chapter we will look at these methods and how to use them.

Scanners, Scanning, and CorelSCAN

The most commonly used device to input photos, line art, or hand-drawn pictures into a computer is a scanner. Several programs within CorelDRAW support scanners. You need to use a scanner, either yours or one at a service bureau, to bring existing photos and artwork into PHOTO-PAINT. A *scanner* is a device that captures an image and converts it into a digital pixel map for computer processing. Think of it as a camera and a photocopier combined and connected to a computer. Like a camera, most scanners capture an image with depth (grayscale or color), whereas a copier records only black and white. As with a copier, the object being scanned is usually placed on a glass plate (the copyboard), where it is scanned. The image, however, is not captured on film or reproduced on paper; but rather is stored in a computer file, where it can be opened with Corel PHOTO-PAINT and manipulated to the limits of one's imagination and work schedule.

Three Ways to Bring Scans into PHOTO-PAINT 7

Corel provides three different paths for moving images from a scanner directly into PHOTO-PAINT.

- **The Corel TWAIN driver for your brand and model of scanner (if it is available)**   The Corel TWAIN interface provides access to some of the scanner's automatic features such as auto-exposure. Figure 5-1 shows the Corel TWAIN interface for a Hewlett-Packard ScanJet. Four different sets of scanner controls are available through the four tabs near the top of the dialog box. The exact contents of the Corel TWAIN driver varies depending on the scanner being used.

- **The TWAIN driver provided with your scanner**   Figure 5-2 shows the TWAIN interface provided by Hewlett-Packard for their ScanJet scanner. TWAIN interfaces provided by scanner manufacturers range in functionality from the bare essentials to very sophisticated interfaces like the HP DeskScan software, which provides many presets and automatic scanning functions. Both of these methods of scanning into PHOTO-PAINT were and are available in both PHOTO-PAINT 5 and 6.

- **CorelSCAN**   New to PHOTO-PAINT 7, CorelSCAN automates many of the operations that can be done on a scanner. The opening screen is shown in Figure 5-3. We will discuss the three methods as we learn how to scan.

The Corel TWAIN interface— one of three ways to scan images into PHOTO-PAINT 7

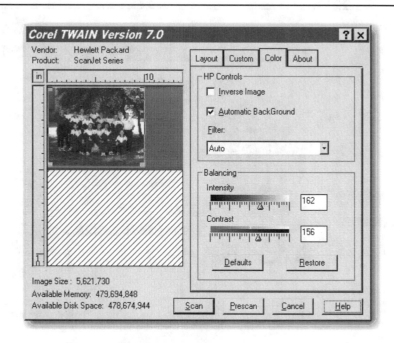

FIGURE 5-1

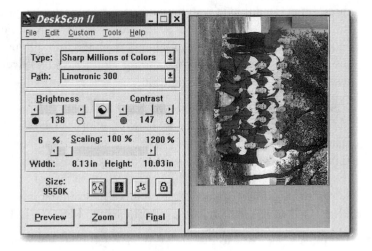

DeskScan
II—an
automated
TWAIN
interface
provided
with HP
scanners

FIGURE 5-2

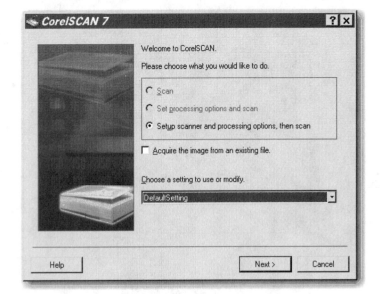

CorelSCAN—
the new
automated
scanning
system in
PHOTO-
PAINT 7

FIGURE 5-3

The Story of TWAIN (Not Mark)

Not so long ago, it was the responsibility of every company that wrote paint (bitmap) programs to provide the software programs necessary to communicate with the scanner. However, every scanner spoke its own language, so to speak, and the result was that unless you owned one of the more popular scanners, you could not access the scanner from within your paint or drawing program. Most of the time, it was necessary to run a separate scanning program (provided with your scanner) to scan in an image. After the image was scanned, you could load it into your favorite paint or OCR program. That may seem like a lot of work, and let me assure you, it was.

Then one day all of the scanner people got together and said, "Let us all make our scanners speak one language." (Sort of a Tower of Babel in reverse.) So they came up with an interface specification called TWAIN.

Why is the interface specification called TWAIN? This is one of those mysteries that might puzzle computer historians for decades to come. I have never received a straight answer to the question, only intriguing possibilities. My favorite explanation is credited to Aldus (now Adobe) Corporation. They say TWAIN means "SpecificaTion Without An Interesting Name." Logitech, one of the driving forces behind the specification gives a different answer: "It was a unique interface that brings together two entities, application and input devices, in a meeting of the 'twain.'"

Whatever the origin of the name, the TWAIN interface allows Corel PHOTO-PAINT (or any other program that supports TWAIN) to talk to the scanner directly through a common interface, and for that we should all be thankful.

5

Setting Up to Scan

The first step in initially setting up the system is to ensure that your scanner's TWAIN drivers are installed. The default installation for PHOTO-PAINT 7 does not install any scanner drivers. If you have already installed the software that came with your scanner, you probably have the necessary TWAIN driver installed. To determine what TWAIN drivers are installed, choose Acquire Image from the File menu. This action opens a drop-down list. Choosing Select Source opens the Select Source dialog box as shown here.

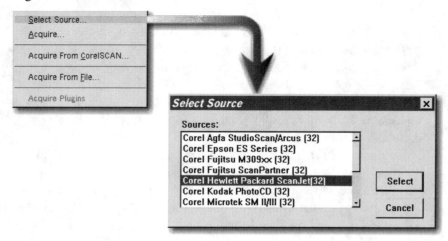

All of the installed TWAIN drivers in Windows 95 are on this list. If your scanner does not appear, its TWAIN driver is not installed. If the list is empty, you cannot use any scanner until one is installed. To install a TWAIN driver, either run the software that came with your scanner or run Corel Setup again, choose Custom install, and select your scanner.

 NOTE: *Some older scanners do not have TWAIN support and cannot be used to scan directly into PHOTO-PAINT.*

Scanning

To scan an image using either the Corel or the scanner's TWAIN drivers, choose Acquire Image from the File menu and choose Acquire. Depending on which driver you select, either the Corel TWAIN driver (Figure 5-1) or your own scanner's dialog box will appear. You can also run CorelSCAN either as a stand-alone application or from within PHOTO-PAINT 7 by choosing Acquire Image from the File menu and selecting Acquire from CorelSCAN. This opens the beginning dialog box shown in Figure 5-3. CorelSCAN is a wizard style of operation that uses whichever of the two TWAIN drivers you desire. The first time you use CorelSCAN, it will run a series of tests to determine whether it can use the Corel TWAIN driver or whether it must use your scanner's TWAIN driver.

CorelSCAN scans an image at the maximum resolution of the scanner and saves it as a raw image. From there, any processing that is requested by the user (red-eye removal, image enhancement, and so on) is applied to a copy of that raw image to produce the final output. When the image is finished, you have the option to save the original raw scan or to discard it.

CorelSCAN does not require the user to understand the scanning process. It asks you a series of questions regarding the source material being scanned, such as, Is it a black-and-white photo? a picture from a magazine? and so on. Next, it asks what processing you want done—red-eye removal or image enhancement, for example—and where the final output of the scan is going to be used, for example, multimedia or laser printer. These answers help you determine how CorelSCAN will set up and process the scan. When using CorelSCAN, you should be aware that selecting "high quality art" will cause the image to be scanned at the highest optical resolution of the scanner using 24-bit color for the "raw" scan. This can take a long time and result in very large image files. I recommend that you change the value of CorelSCAN's recommended resolution from the maximum to one no larger than 200 dpi.

The automated features offered by CorelSCAN include dust and scratch removal, image enhancement, rotation, red-eye removal, and cropping. There are others, depending on the image type you choose to process. While all of these features can be accomplished in PHOTO-PAINT 7, CorelSCAN provides a wizard-like approach for scanning that you may find desirable. Regardless of which approach you take, you will end up with an image in PHOTO-PAINT 7—which was our original goal.

 NOTE: *For more information about CorelSCAN, when the screen shown in Figure 5-1 appears, click the Help button. You will find a wealth of information there on CorelSCAN and its features.*

Some Basics About Scanning

Scanning is not difficult—we aren't talking brain surgery here. It is simply knowing a little and working a little to extract the most out of a printed image. Over the last few years, the price of desktop scanners has dropped while the performance has increased dramatically, resulting in more and more people owning and using them. Sadly, many users, including graphics professionals, do not understand some of the basics necessary to get the best quality image from a scanner into Corel PHOTO-PAINT and out to a printer.

A Trick Question

During a recent 51-city Corel WordPerfect roadshow, I had the opportunity to ask literally hundreds of attendees the following question: *"If you are going to print a photograph on a 600 dots per inch (dpi) laser printer, at what resolution should you scan the image for the best output?"* More than half answered they would use a resolution of 600. Was that your answer? If so, read on. If you answered with any resolution from 100 to 150 dpi you are correct. Take two compliments out of petty cash. For some of you this may be review, but even if you knew the correct answer, I hope that in reading this part of the chapter, you may either learn something new or remember something you once knew.

Scanning and Resolution...Making It Work for You

It seems logical that the resolution of a scan should be the same, or nearly the same, as that of the printer. The problem is that when we talk about the resolution of the scanner in dots per inch (dpi), we are not talking about the same dots per inch used when describing printer resolution. In Chapter 2 we learned about pixels. Scanners scan pixels, which are square, and printers makes dots, which are round. The resolution of the scanner is measured in dots per inch, which is incorrect because its resolution is more accurately described in samples per inch. Each sample represents a pixel.

The resolution of the printer dot is measured in dots per inch. The resolution of the printer determines the size of the dot it makes. For example, each dot made by a 600 dpi printer is 1/600 of an inch in diameter. These printer dots only come in two flavors: black and white. To produce the 256 shades of gray that exist between black and white on a printer, these tiny dots are grouped together to form halftone cells. For example, let's assume for the sake of illustration that each halftone cell made by our printer is 10 x 10 dots in size. Each halftone cell can hold a maximum of 100 dots. To print the shade 50 percent gray, the printer turns on half of the dots in each halftone cell and leaves half off. This gives the appearance to the eye of being 50 percent gray.

When we talk about scanner resolution, we are actually talking about samples per inch. Each sample of a scan at 600 dpi is 1/600-of-an-inch square (remember that pixels are square). Unlike the printer's dot, which can have only two possible values, each scanner pixel can have one of 256 possible values (for simplicity we are assuming grayscale). The relationship between scanner pixels and printer dots is shown in the photograph taken during a conversation between the two of them, as shown here.

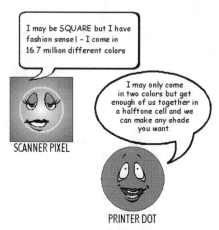

At this point we can see that a scanned pixel is much more like a printer halftone cell than the original printer dot. So how do you determine how many halftone cells per inch your printer is capable of producing? If you look in the back of your printer manual, you won't find a setting for halftone cells per inch, but you may (I emphasize the *may* part) find a setting for either screen or line frequency. Line frequency is measured in lines per inch (lpi). An old rule of thumb for scanning used to be: Scan at twice the line frequency of the final output device. This rule has become pretty outdated. You should scan at roughly 1.5 times the line frequency of your final output device.

There is some serious math we could use to calculate the ideal resolution to match the scan to the output device, but there is a simpler way. The following sections give some basic recommended resolutions and tips for scanning different types of images. These recommendations are compiled from information provided by various scanner manufacturers and service bureau operators.

Scanning Text and Line Drawings in PHOTO-PAINT 7

Text and line drawings are truly black-and-white images. They are also called *line art* and *bi-level images*; Adobe refers to them as *bitmap images*. Regardless of what you call them, either a white dot or a black dot is scanned and then printed. We encounter these all the time. When you receive a logo or letterhead to scan, it is invariably line art. Unlike continuous-tone images (like photographs), which have smooth transitions, changes in line art are abrupt, which produces a sharp edge. It is because of this sharp edge that this type of image is most often scanned using the following rule:

> Scan line art and text with a resolution equal to the maximum resolution (in dpi) of the final output device, up to but not more than the scanner's maximum optical resolution, and apply sharpening with the scanner (if possible).

There is another way to scan line art into PHOTO-PAINT that deserves consideration. Sometimes the original has many fine lines that tend to plug up when scanned. Rather than scanning the image as line art, scan it as a grayscale image with sharpening. Then use the Threshold command located under Transform in the Image menu to remove any light gray background that appears as a result of the color of the paper the original was printed on.

Figure 5-4A shows an old woodcut printed on a poor grade of paper that was scanned as line art at 635 dpi without sharpening. There are a lot of fine lines in the feathers in the lower-left corner and around the eyes that have gone to solid black, thus losing detail. Figure 5-4B is the same image but with sharpening applied during the scan. The sharpening brings out more detail in the feathers. In Figure 5-4C the bird is scanned as a grayscale image with sharpening. In this scan, we have much more of the image detail, but the paper the original was printed on creates a background that is a light shade of gray. The way to remove the background is to apply the Threshold filter to convert everything below a specified threshold to white. After applying Threshold, we have an image that looks like a black-and-white image (Figure 5-4D) but with more image detail. The operation of the Threshold filter is discussed in Chapter 24.

A word of caution when you scan at the maximum resolution of your scanner: You may find it causes problems with the RIP (raster image processors) when you are outputting to an imagesetter. RIPs seem much more sensitive to the high resolution of these images than they are to the image size. It is not uncommon for the RIP to output a 20MB grayscale image with a resolution of 200 dpi with no problems and have it throw a hairball when it gets a 1000 dpi image, even if it is a small one.

A) Image scanned as line art at 635 dpi; B) as line art at 635 dpi with sharpening; C) as grayscale at 200 dpi with sharpening; D) light gray background removed from the image in C with Threshold filter

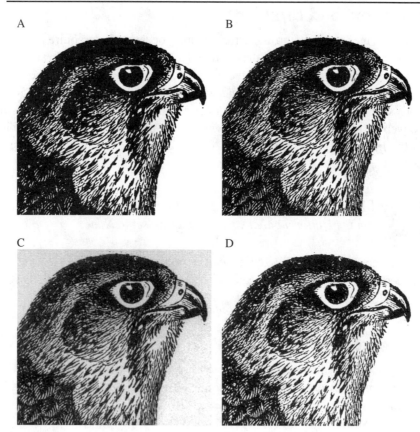

 FIGURE 5-4

 TIP: *Black-and-white bitmap images seem to print much faster if the art is at the same resolution as the imagesetter itself. I am told this is because the imagesetter doesn't have to rescale the work, so the image gets sent right through.*

Line art and text are the only things that should be scanned at the maximum resolution of the scanner. Because the color depth value of each pixel is binary (either on or off), the file sizes do not become extremely large. If you scan this type of image at a lower resolution, you will discover that it produces jaggies like the ones you saw in Chapter 4.

Color Text and Drawings

These images present a problem for scanning because they require high-resolution scanning with the addition of the overhead associated with color. In such a case, file sizes become as large as the federal deficit in a big hurry. There are several work-arounds to this. If your scanner supports it, scan the image in at 256 colors. If your scanner can only do 24-bit color, scan the image into PHOTO-PAINT and convert it to 256 colors using the Convert To command and the Paletted (8-bit) option in the Image menu. Converting the file to 256 colors reduces its file size by 66 percent.

TIP: *When converting to 256 colors, choose the Optimized palette, not the Uniform palette. Keep dithering set to None.*

You could use CorelTRACE to convert color text and drawing to a vector image, or scan these images as black-and-white and replace the black in PHOTO-PAINT with colors similar to the original.

Photographs

Continuous-tone images (such as photographs) can be color or black and white. This type of image is less detailed and requires lower resolution than line art. The rule for this is simple: *Scan photographs at 100-200 dpi.*

Some variations to this rule are as follows:

- For 300-dpi laser printers, scanning at 100 dpi is usually sufficient.

- For 600-dpi lasers, scan at 150 dpi.

- For imagesetters (including high-resolution lasers that produce camera-ready art), scan at 200 dpi.

Why You Shouldn't Scan at Excessively High Resolutions

Even after going through all of the explanations about the best settings to get a good scan, some still believe that scanning at a higher than necessary resolution somehow gives their image extra detail or makes it look sharper. In fact, doing this rarely improves image quality and produces very large file sizes. Remember that each time resolution is doubled, the file size quadruples. Large image files take a long time to process, and time is money at your local neighborhood service bureau. Also, scanning at a resolution higher than the output device can reproduce tends to cause detail in the shadow area to be lost, and if the resolution is high enough and the image small enough, the final result may actually be a blurry picture. Let's move on to some other scanning-related commands and issues.

The Deskew Command

After scanning an image, if you notice it is crooked, lift the lid on the scanner, straighten the image, and scan it again. Sounds simple, right? You would be amazed at how many users will accept a crooked scan and not do that simple step. Don't be one of them. If you receive a scan with a crooked image, you can straighten it in PHOTO-PAINT using the Deskew command located in the Image menu. According to Corel: "The Deskew command places imperfectly positioned images squarely in the image area." The description is for the most part accurate, but it is missing some critical information. The Deskew command actually works *only* on four-sided images that have a white (256,256,256) background—it ignores all other background colors. It not only deskews the image, but also crops the image based on the white border. The deskewing action works well and causes little to no distortion of the original image. This filter has no user-definable settings.

Figure 5-5 is an image of a little girl named Brianna that I deliberately placed on the scanner crookedly. The background (created by the scanner cover) is not white, so when the Deskew command is applied, nothing happens. In Figure 5-6, a mask was created so the background and border of the photograph could be given a white fill. With the white background in place, the Deskew command now works as shown in Figure 5-7. Remember to use white. This command doesn't work with any other color, not even a slightly off-white.

Removing Dust, Scratches, and Other Debris

When you apply sharpening to an image, all of the dust and other small artifacts in the image make themselves known. They have always been there—they just blend into the image until sharpening is applied. I want to warn you not to fall into the trap of spending hours removing specks of dust and debris from a scanned image with PHOTO-PAINT when they could have been prevented in the first place by either dusting the original photograph with a fine-hair brush, cleaning the glass on the scanner with some glass cleaner before scanning, or both. If the dust and debris are

Scan of a
crooked
photograph

FIGURE 5-5

Background
and border
replaced
with white

FIGURE 5-6

The image
straightened
and cropped
by the
Deskew
command

FIGURE 5-7

part of the image you have scanned, you may need to use the Dust and Scratch filter, which is discussed in Chapter 16. The best dust and scratch filter on the market today is your favorite brand of glass cleaner. Keep a bottle of it along with a roll of paper towels (officially, a soft cloth) and a can of compressed air (which I recommend over the fine camel-hair brush) near your scanner at all times. If you feel the glass on your flatbed scanner is clean and doesn't need this attention, try this test. Lift the lid and start a scan. Look at the glass from the side as the light moves. Surprised?

So much for scanning. There are times when we need to get our image directly from the computer screen. This type of application is found mostly in technical documentation, including this book. For this purpose, Corel included CorelCAPTURE.

Using CorelCAPTURE 7

CorelCAPTURE 7, which has improved with each release of CorelDRAW, is one program I probably use as much as I use PHOTO-PAINT 7. Every image in this book, with the exception of the screen shots of this program, was captured in one way or another by CAPTURE 7.

CAPTURE 7 works with any image that can be displayed on your monitor. The images don't even have to be in Corel. The operation of CAPTURE 7 is very simple. After launching the program, you define what keystroke or keyboard combination activates it, what portion of the screen will be captured, and where the captured image will be put. It can't get much simpler than that. In the following sections we will share some tips on using this program more effectively and also look at a few of the more commonly used areas of the CAPTURE dialog box. For details on the operation of any part not discussed, I recommend either the CorelCAPTURE section of the user's manual or the online help screen.

Setting Up CAPTURE

The first time you go to use CAPTURE, you might be in for a mild surprise like I was when I first looked for it. It wasn't there. Ever since the program appeared in the CorelDRAW suite, it has always been automatically loaded with the typical installation. Not any longer. If you didn't do a custom installation, CAPTURE 7 wasn't loaded. You can still load by running Setup again, selecting Custom, and choosing CAPTURE. It is located under the category Graphic Utilities. That is also where you will find it after it is installed. When you finally locate it and launch it, the Activation page of the CAPTURE dialog box appears and you are ready to use the program.

The Activation Page

From the Activation page you can pick the hot key you want to use for activation of the program. By default, it should be set to the function key F7. You can also set the delay for activation from this page. The delay feature is necessary when you have a "shy" function. That is my term for a part of a program you are attempting to capture that disappears the instant you hit the CAPTURE activation key. An example of this would be the

Pop-up Navigator. By using the delay, you can activate the CAPTURE program with the hotkey, open the "shy" portion, and then wait for the capture to occur. The other options are self-explanatory.

The Source Page

You can specify which part of the image you want to capture on the Source page. Here are some tips I learned while working with this page. If you need to capture a mask or other software marquee, use Full Screen. If you use anything less, only part of the marquee is captured. The best way to capture an image window, dialog box, and so on, is to use the Menu or control setting. If the Include border option is selected, the Title Bar on the image

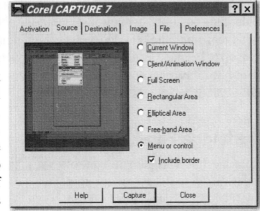

window will be included. The Elliptical Area and Rectangular Area features do not have a constrain key, so you must create your circle and square capture areas by using a steady hand on the mouse and your calibrated eyeball. If you use any setting that captures an area that is nonrectangular, the resulting capture will be in a rectangular image area.

The Destination Page

On the Destination page you choose where to send the screen capture you create. Since I must make a lot of screen captures for books and articles, I save the image to the clipboard and then use the New from clipboard command in the File menu in PHOTO-PAINT to make it into an image. The only caveat is to remember that the clipboard can only hold one object at a time. More than once, I have saved a screen

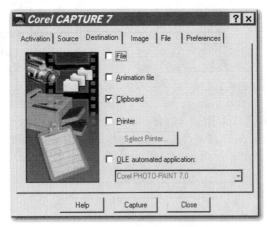

capture in the clipboard and then, before unloading it in PHOTO-PAINT, proceeded to copy some text to the clipboard while in another application, thus wiping out my screen shot. Other than this small consideration, the clipboard works best for me.

Another option worth discussing is the File setting, which creates a file containing the capture each time the hot key is selected. The type of file it creates is determined by the settings in the File page. If you don't have Use automatic naming set in the File page, the CAPTURE program will overwrite the same file each time you hit the hot key, just like the clipboard. While I personally have rarely used them, you can also select setting the capture to a printer of your choice or even set it up to be made available to an OLE application. The Animation file setting can be used to create an animated file. Once you begin recording the animation, use SHIFT+ESC to stop the capture process.

The Image Page

From the Image page, you control the parameters of the image that CAPTURE produces. It has been designed so that you can pick the ultimate destination of the screen shot, and CAPTURE provides a recommended resolution. For multimedia and the Web, you should be using the Screen setting. A very helpful feature on this page is the Resizing section, which is activated with the Resample captured option.

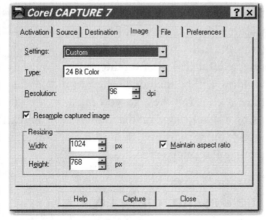

Throughout this book I have included screen shots of the toolbars and buttons. These images are, by their nature, very tiny. You can capture them at screen resolution and increase their size using the Resample command or set the Resizing option for the size you want the final image to be. Figure 5-8 displays on the left a screen capture of the Mask Brush tool taken using the preset Screen setting in CAPTURE and then resampled (made larger) in PHOTO-PAINT 7 to the needed size. On the right is an image captured using the resizing section set to the desired size, which results in a much sharper image. I have found the same to be true when

An image resampled after capture (left) and resized during capture (right)

FIGURE 5-8

enlarging existing screen shots of vector images (such as toolbars and line art). To show an enlargement of a specific area in an image, I use the zoom setting on the display to get the best combination of zoom and image quality, capture it, and save the captured image.

The File Page

You can select what type of files you want to create on the File page. If you don't have File or Animation selected in the Destination page, this page will have no effect. Just a few notes of interest. The default file format is JPEG. I recommend not using this lossey compression format for images that you may later want to modify for reasons explained in detail in both Chapters 2 and 3. The Select Capture Directory button is important since

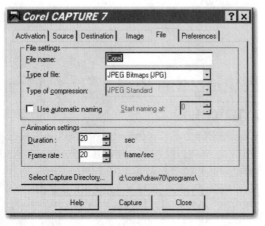

it determines where your files are going to be placed when they are created. The default location is an obscure area deep within the CorelDRAW program files. If you are recording a sequence of events, the Use Automatic Naming feature is handy and will, with each capture, create another file with a sequential numbered name beginning with the first number you place in the Start Naming At setting.

The Preferences Page

The only item of note on the Preferences page is the Capture cursor feature, which is enabled by default. This doesn't actually capture the cursor, but places a cursor arrow on the captured image in the location of the cursor position. This means that if you have some fancy cursor, or one of PHOTO-PAINT 7's many cursors, that you wish to capture, it cannot be done. So where did I get the cursors that appear in this book? Corel provided the bitmap files for me to use in this book.

This was probably more information about CAPTURE than you really wanted to know, so let's move on to loading Photo-CDs.

Photo-CDs

Developed by Kodak as a consumer file format, the Photo-CD was a failure. Later it became popular as a method of distributing photographic images and has since become a common form of exchange for such images. Corel Corporation is the world's largest supplier of images on Photo-CDs, although there are none in the CorelDRAW 7 release. Ironic, isn't it? Corel PHOTO-PAINT 7 provides several color correction methods for use with Photo-CDs, which we will look at briefly in this section.

Picking the Right Size When Opening a Photo-CD

When a Photo-CD is initially opened, the dialog box displays the Image tab as shown in Figure 5-9. If color correction is not desired, the only choices that must be made are the size of the image and the color selection. The size choices and their size in pixels are Wallet (192 x 128), Snapshot (384 x 256), Standard (768 x 512), Large (1536 x 1024), and Poster (3072 x 2048). The available color selections are 16.7 million (24-bit), 256 colors (8-bit), and 256 grayscale. After you have the size and color, click the OK button to load the image.

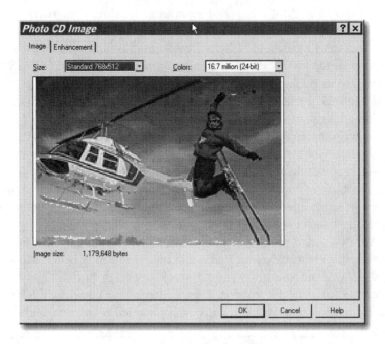

The
Photo-CD
dialog box

FIGURE 5-9

 TIP: *Larger file sizes require large amounts of system memory, take longer to load and to apply effects, and require more disk space for storage. Therefore, always try to pick a size and color depth that are sufficient for your application.*

Applying Color Correction When Opening Photo-CDs

If you want to apply color correction, click on the Enhancement tab, which opens the color-correction page of the dialog box. This is a great color-correction system that makes some of the not-so-great Photo-CDs on the market look much better. Either of the color-correction systems provided will correct the color of the image before you load it into Corel PHOTO-PAINT. Any correction applied at this stage of the process is superior to any correction that might be applied after the image is in Corel PHOTO-PAINT.

Selecting the Enhancement tab on the Photo-CD dialog box and selecting Gamut CD opens the Photo-CD Enhancement dialog box for the Gamut CD color-correction system, as shown in Figure 5-10. This color correction system is only available if you select 24-bit color images. This dialog box allows you to correct the color of the image before you import it into Corel PHOTO-PAINT. You select neutral colors (black, white, and grays) in the image, and then the software maps these neutral colors to adjust the dynamic range of the image. This color correction is within the gamut system, so it doesn't go beyond the capability (gamut) of color printing. Gamut, in short, is a system that knows what colors can or cannot be printed by Standard Web Offset Process (SWOP). Colors that cannot be printed are referred to as being "outside of gamut." The Gamut CD correction system ensures that all of the colors in the Photo-CD are within gamut. The best part is that the Gamut CD color correction almost always improves the overall appearance of the image, even if you don't need the color correction for printing purposes.

After you learn how to use it, if you apply it every time you bring in an older or poor-quality Photo-CD, your Photo-CD image will look better. Most of the newer Photo-CDs from the good digital stock agencies have already applied color correction, making this enhancement unnecessary. I have several old Photo-CD images that had black backgrounds until I applied correction, and they turned out

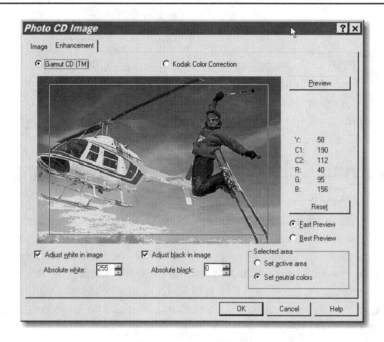

The Gamut CD Color correction system provides automatic color correction for Photo-CDs

FIGURE 5-10

not to be black backgrounds after all. In one, a night shot of a wolf, the "black background" turned out to contain a forest that had appeared to be mud before the correction was applied.

Exploring the Gamut CD Color Controls

The following options are available using the Gamut CD Color-Correction system.

Color-Correction Methods

Gamut CD   This color-correction method uses gamut mapping to enhance the color fidelity and tonal ranges of the CD image. *Gamut mapping* is a system that ensures that colors in a computer image are reproducible by a printer. Of the two methods, I have had the greatest success with this one.

Kodak Color Correction   The Kodak Color Correction method allows you to alter color tints and adjust brightness and saturation, as well as adjust the level of contrast. The Kodak system, while excellent, is not automatic, making it more complicated to use.

Setting the Active Area Using Gamut CD

Generally, the default area should be used. If you need to change the Selected area, choose the Set active area option and click and drag the mouse to specify an active area within the image in the view field. This ensures Gamut CD will base its color correction on the area of the photo that you are going to use and helps cut out any black borders left over from the original scan that would interfere with accurate correction.

Set the Set Neutral colors option by clicking on pure whites, blacks, and grays within the active area, which leaves a small "x" on the preview image in most displays. The more samples that are selected, the better the color correction.

- **Adjust White in Image**   Choose this option if you have good white elements in the photo. If you do not have a white, disable this option, since the gamut mapping will over-brighten your picture as it maps the lightest elements of your picture to white. This option will assist Gamut CD in enhancing the tonal range of your image and removing color cast. If your white is not pure white, you may wish to lower the 255 setting in the number box to the right.

- **Adjust Black in Image**   Choose this option if you have good black elements in the photo. If the image does not have blacks, disable this option, as the gamut mapping will darken your picture as it maps the darkest elements of your picture to black. This option will assist Gamut CD in enhancing the tonal range of your image and removing color cast. If your black is not pure black, you may wish to raise the setting in the number box to the right from 0.

- **Color Swatch and Values**   This option displays the YCC and RGB color value of the currently selected color from the image as the cursor is moved around the image in the preview window. The color swatch displays the color that is being assessed.

- **YCC**   The YCC color system is the color model of the Photo-CD. The Y represents the luminance or grayscale values of the image, and C represents the color chrominance values. The YCC color space is similar to the way television broadcast color is transmitted. The YCC values are of little help in setting up the Gamut CD system.

- **RGB**   RGB represents the values of the Red, Green, and Blue color components in the image. It is the RGB information that is of the greatest help in establishing the neutral colors of the image.

- **Fast Preview option**   This option displays the effect the Gamut CD settings you have chosen will have on the image. The first time you preview, you may wonder why it is called "Fast Preview." Click the Preview button to find out.

- **Best Preview**   If you click Best Preview, bring a book. This option displays the effect the Gamut CD settings you have chosen will have on the image. This method will be more accurate than Fast Preview but will take longer to build. Actually, several of the people who wrote the Corel PHOTO-PAINT program think it is faster to just click the OK button to see the color correction. If you do that, you will lose your sample settings. Use the Fast Preview instead. If you are paid by the hour and need to milk the job for some more time, you will love Best Preview.

Using Gamut CD Color Correction

 This is all great, but how do I use it? That was my question to the people at Corel when I was writing the Corel PHOTO-PAINT 5 manual. Their answer surprised me:

They hadn't used it that much themselves. I shouldn't have been surprised that these folks work their brains out writing code for PAINT and have little time for loading and correcting their favorite Photo-CDs. Since that time, they and I have learned a lot about using Gamut CD. So here is Dave's handy-dandy method for using the Gamut CD Color Correction System, based on lots of practice and a little too much coffee.

The principle of this system is that you select the neutral colors (white, black, and gray) in an image. The Gamut CD system uses those colors for its gamut mapping to enhance the color fidelity and tonal ranges of the image, ensuring that the colors in a computer image can be reproduced by a printer.

1. **Open the Photo-CD image**   When the Photo-CD dialog box opens, pick the size and color desired.

2. **Click the Enhancement tab**   Ensure that the Gamut CD button is enabled. I highly recommend using the default Selected area, which is shown by the light-colored rectangle on the image in the preview window. If you needed to change the Active area, click the Set active area button and drag a rectangle in the preview window that includes the portion of the image you wish to be included in the color-correction calculations.

3. **Click on the whitest white spot you can find**   Don't trust your eyes on this one. Watch the Color swatch on the right side of the dialog box as you move the cursor over the white area. Specifically, watch the numbers by R, G, and B. The whitest white will produce the highest numbers in RGB. This is basic color theory. Pure white reads 256 on each of the RGB channels. Make several of these white samples. The more you make, the more accurate the color correction will be. Don't lose your mind here— three or four samples are sufficient.

4. **Click on the blackest black you can locate in the active area**   "Active area" is the key phrase here—do not click on the black border. The idea with these samples is to establish the dynamic color range of the image, so shooting some of the black off of the negative border will throw the correction off. You pick the black the same way you pick the white, by the numbers. In this case, you are looking for the lowest numbers in the RGB values.

5. **Find a good middle-of-the-road gray if there is one (optional)**   This is used to set the midtones, and finding a gray can be very subjective. Use the numbers again. In this case you are looking for RGB numbers around

the 128 value (blue will be a little higher). Most grays are in the 180-185 region. If you use a gray, the result will be shifted toward the warmer colors.

6. **Select the Fast Preview option and click the Preview button**   On a good 24-bit color monitor, the difference can be very impressive. If you like the results, click the OK button. If not, reset the color correction by clicking the Reset button and start over again.

Notes on the Gamut CD Color-Correction System

Here are some pointers on using Gamut CD.

- There isn't a specific order to enter the neutral colors. The computer sorts it all out.

- If there isn't a good black (RGB less than 90) or a good white (RGB greater than 220), don't use them, and uncheck the respective Adjust White In Image or Adjust Black In Image checkbox.

- If you don't like the results of the preview, click Reset and choose the color samples again. The image will appear the same, but the color values will be correct.

- If the preview is too dark, try increasing the value in the Black In Image value box. If the preview is too light, try decreasing the value in the White In Image value box.

The Kodak Color-Correction System

This color-correction method, which is selected by enabling the Kodak Color Correction button in the Enhancement page, opens the dialog box shown in Figure 5-11. The Kodak system allows you to alter color tints, and adjust brightness and color saturation, as well as adjust the level of contrast.

This is not an automatic system like the Gamut Image Enhancement System. You can control the tints of the three primary colors, red, blue, and green (RGB); Brightness; and Saturation (the amount of color in the image). There are several adjustments in the dialog box that are unique to Photo-CD images. The effects of changing any of these settings do not appear in the preview window until the Preview

The Kodak color-correction system's wide assortment of manual color-correction tools

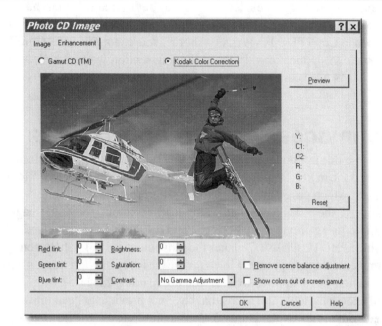

FIGURE 5-11

button is clicked. There is no automatic preview. The controls for this dialog box are as follows.

- **Contrast** This allows you to adjust contrast by choosing preset amounts from a drop-down list.

- **Remove scene balance adjustment** Enabling this button removes the Scene Balance Adjustment, which is made by the photo-finisher at the time the original image was scanned and preserved on the Photo-CD disc. You should remove this if the image looks lifeless or dull. It may result in some areas of the image blowing out (bright spots becoming large white areas).

- **Show colors out of screen gamut** If the changes you've made are too extreme, the preview will display out-of-gamut pixels as pure red or pure blue. Colors that are out of gamut cannot be printed accurately, and it is important for critical prepress work for all colors to be within gamut boundaries.

Color correction takes time. If you have images that have not been color-corrected, it is worth the time spent trying to apply correction at this stage rather than in Corel PHOTO-PAINT. Another source for images is CorelDRAW and other Windows applications. In the following section we will look at some of the different ways we can move an image between these programs.

Moving Images Between Applications

Just because this is a book on PHOTO-PAINT doesn't mean that I think everything should be done in PHOTO-PAINT. In fact, the opposite is true. Get into the practice of deciding which program(s) to use on a project *before* you begin.

Many of the rules you may have learned about moving images between applications using previous versions of PHOTO-PAINT have changed. This is good news, since PHOTO-PAINT 7 makes the movement of images between applications very simple. In this section we will cover the basics of moving images between both Corel and non-Corel applications. If you are reading this book from front to back, you will encounter tools and terms that have not previously been introduced. I have included some brief explanations and cross-references so that you won't get too confused.

PAINT to DRAW with Objects

Since most people ask how to move an image they have created in PHOTO-PAINT 7 to DRAW, we will cover it first. In previous releases, this was a little complicated, but now it is very simple. For those of you who have CorelDRAW 7, I have included a simple hands-on project.

Viewing PHOTO-PAINT Images in CorelDRAW 7

This is an easy exercise for viewing a PHOTO-PAINT 7 image in DRAW.

1. In CorelDRAW, create a new image. Select the Rectangle tool, and holding down the CTRL key, make a five-inch square.

2. Select the Fountain fill tool from the Fill Tool flyout, and when the Fountain Fill dialog box opens (shown in the following illustration), click

the down-pointing arrow at the right of the Presets value box and select Circular - Blue 02. Click the OK button.

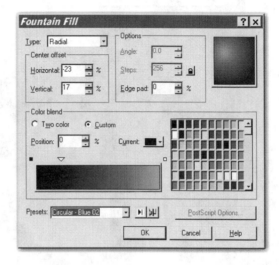

3. Select the Object picker tool at the top of the Toolbox, and from the File menu, choose Import (CTRL+I). When the Import dialog box opens, locate the file FISH02.CPT in the \OBJECTS\FISH folder of the CD-ROM containing the Objects. The result appears in Figure 5-12.

4. To remove the white rectangle, you must first ungroup the fish from it. With the fish object still selected, click the Ungroup button in the Property Bar.

5. Click somewhere on the rectangle to deselect the two objects, and then click on the fish again. This time, only the top object is selected. Click the TAB key to change the object selected to the white background and click the DEL (Delete) key. The result is shown in Figure 5-13.

6. Close the file and don't save any changes.

CorelDRAW Import Considerations

In the previous hands-on session, we imported a PHOTO-PAINT image that contained an object. An *object* is a bitmap image that floats above the background. The image actually contained two objects, the background and the fish. CorelDRAW treats the objects in PHOTO-PAINT files just like regular objects in DRAW, even though it is a bitmap and not a vector drawing. If the image has no objects, CorelDRAW imports the entire image as a bitmap image.

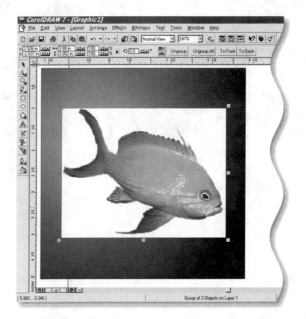

The fish
imported
with a white
background

FIGURE 5-12

The fish
without the
white
background
object

FIGURE 5-13

5

PAINT (Without Objects) into DRAW

It isn't necessary to have objects in a PHOTO-PAINT image for the subject to be clipped to the boundary of the image. In PHOTO-PAINT, the subject of the image that you want to bring into DRAW can be defined by a mask. A *mask* is a layer over the entire image that is used to define areas in the image. For more information on masks, see Chapter 7. The mask marquee appears in Figure 5-14 as a black-and-white dotted line that surrounds the flower.

To save the image so the flower will be clipped to the masked area, select Save As in the File menu and save the image as an Encapsulated PostScript (EPS) file. You will first receive a warning that any objects in the image will be merged. After clicking OK, the Export Dialog box opens as shown in Figure 5-15.

EPS Export Dialog Box

The Image Header section allows you define what the bitmap file of the file looks like. This header file is used for placement of the image in another application. This is why an EPS image may sometimes look very poor because you are not actually looking at the image but at the low-resolution header file.

The Clipping section is available if either a mask or path is present in the image. When the Save feature is enabled, it saves the contents of the mask marquee on the image in the EPS file. The program converts the mask to a path before saving, so the process may take some time, depending on how complicated the mask is. The sections of the image that are outside the mask marquee are still in the image but will not be visible, nor will they print, when you use the EPS file in another application. You can still see those sections if you open the image in Corel PHOTO-PAINT.

To delete the sections that are outside the mask marquee, enable the Crop Image To Path/Mask When Saving option at the bottom of this dialog box.

The edge of
the image
defined by
the mask
marquee

FIGURE 5-14

From DRAW, select Import from the File menu, opening the Import dialog box shown in Figure 5-16. The key to bringing in only the area inside the mask is to choose PostScript Interpreted (PS, PRN, EPS) in the Files of type portion of the dialog box. The resulting image is shown in Figure 5-17. In Figure 5-18, I have shown what happens when you import the files using either the All Files (*.*) or the EPS Files of type setting.

PAINT to Other Applications

Sometimes you will want to save a file for use in a non-Corel application. To make an image so that only the area within the mask appears in the final output, you need to follow the procedure for creating an EPS file in PAINT (without objects) into DRAW. The difference is that most non-Corel applications do not have an option for importing files called PostScript Interpreted. When you import the EPS image, it may not display properly on the screen, meaning the white rectangle may remain, but will not be printed as long as you print it on a PostScript output device.

Getting images from DRAW into PAINT

Getting an image from DRAW into PAINT involves a process called *rasterization* (see the adjoining box). The Corel image, or the portion of the image, that you want to bring into PAINT is saved as a Corel CDR (vector) file. Unlike DRAW, the CDR

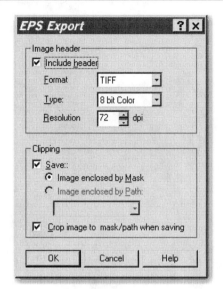

The EPS
Export
dialog box

FIGURE 5-15

file is not imported into PAINT—there is no Import command in PAINT—but is
opened just like a PAINT file, with one exception. Opening any vector file opens

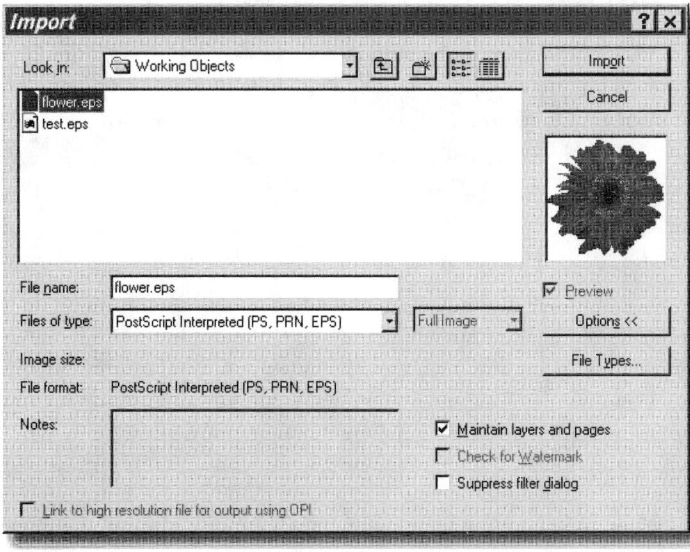

The DRAW
7 Import
dialog box

FIGURE 5-16

Result of
importing
an EPS
image as
PostScript
Interpreted

FIGURE 5-17

the Import Into Bitmap dialog box as shown in Figure 5-19. Select the settings and
it will take a few moments to rasterize the image. After the image is loaded, it will
be necessary to mask the area of the image you want and convert it to an object.

Rasterization and Dithering

When we go from Corel DRAW to PHOTO-PAINT (or any other bitmap
application), it is necessary to convert the vector (or line) format into
bitmap (or paint) format. This process is called *rasterization.* How the
rasterization is accomplished determines how faithfully the image we
import into Corel PHOTO-PAINT is reproduced.

When a color in the original image cannot be produced precisely
(either because of display or color mode limitations), the computer
does its best to make an approximation of the color through a process
called *dithering.* With dithering, the computer changes the colors of
adjacent pixels so that to the viewer they approximate the desired
color. Dithering is accomplished by mathematically averaging the
color values of adjacent pixels. The use of dithering can also affect the
process of getting an image from CorelDRAW to PHOTO-PAINT.

Import Into Bitmap Dialog Box

Use the Import Into Bitmap dialog box, shown in Figure 5-19, to specify how you want to rasterize the CDR or other vector-based image. Many users are intimidated by all the choices that are available to them in this dialog box. Never fear; after you read this section, they will begin to make sense.

Color

This imports the CorelDRAW file as shades of gray or color. The greater the number of colors, the larger the exported file and the better the image will appear. Figure 5-20 shows the results of importing a musical symbol in DRAW and importing the image into PAINT at several different numbers of shades and dithering. All of the images were imported using Super-sampling (when available as an option).

Dithered

This dithers the colors and gray shades of the DRAW file. Dithering is only available when you have selected a Color setting of 256 shades or less of color (it is disabled in grayscale). If the image contains fountain fills or color blends, dithering can cause obvious banding in the exported bitmap. Here are some guidelines to help you decide whether to dither the bitmap:

- If you are importing 16 or 256 colors or grays, use dithering.

- If you intend to scale this bitmap in PHOTO-PAINT, dithering is not recommended.

Size

This specifies the dimensions of the exported bitmap. Choose one of the preset sizes from the list box or choose Custom and type the dimensions in the Width and Height boxes.

By default, the size of the image in CorelDRAW is used. I recommend the default setting of 1 to 1. Smaller bitmaps (with lower resolution) or larger bitmaps (with higher resolution) can be created by scaling the image up or down in CorelDRAW prior to exporting.

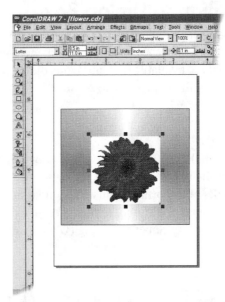

The same
image as
Figure 17,
imported as
an EPS file

FIGURE 5-18

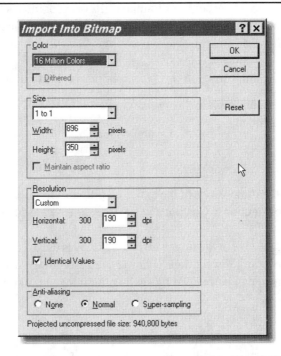

The Import
Into Bitmap
dialog box

FIGURE 5-19

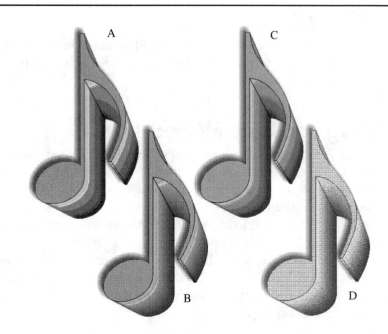

A) 256 colors without dithering; B) grayscale; C) 256 colors with dithering; D) black and white with dithering

FIGURE 5-20

 NOTE: *If you choose one of the preset sizes from the list box, the dimensions you choose may not be proportional to the bitmap's original aspect ratio. The exported bitmap will distort unless you place an empty border around your bitmap with the same ratio as the preset. For example, in DRAW 7, create a rectangle around your image 6.4 x 4.8 inches if you are exporting at 640 x 480. Then assign No Fill and No Outline to the rectangle. Now the aspect ratio of the image will be maintained when you export.*

Resolution

This specifies the resolution (in dots per inch) for bitmaps exported at a size of 1 to 1. Choose one of the preset resolutions from the list box, or choose Custom and type the resolution in the DPI box.

 NOTE: *As resolution increases, so does the size of the export file and the time required to print the image.*

Anti-Aliasing

There are three choices for Anti-aliasing. Anti-aliasing produces smoother bitmap rasterization. By default, it is set to Normal. Super-sampling is a method that takes longer but produces superior results.

The Drag-and-Drop Method

Another way to move an image from one application to another is *drag and drop*. This method is limited to screen resolution if there isn't an existing image in PHOTO-PAINT 7 that is open. Screen resolution for a standard VGA monitor is 96 pixels per inch. However, images that are dragged between Corel applications are at a resolution of 72 dpi. If you drag a CorelDRAW object into a 300-dpi image, its resolution will be 300 dpi. It is not resolution that restricts the quality of the drag-and-drop method. The noticeable loss in image quality results when fountain fills and color blends are rasterized. Regardless of the resolution, fountain fills and blends are dithered. Generally, restrictions that apply to drag and drop apply to interapplication clipboard operations.

When to Use Drag and Drop

One of the big advantages of using the drag-and-drop method is the speed at which it operates. Without going into the technical details of how rasterization is accomplished with drag and drop, let's simply say that it is not the best choice for importing images that have fountain fills or a large number of colors, like color photographs.

So what good is drag and drop? Multimedia applications are, by design, generally limited to screen resolution, making them an ideal candidate. Drag and drop is an excellent way to import items with solid or no colors, such as symbols or items with a limited number of diagonal lines. (Diagonal lines are a particular obstacle to any form of rasterization.)

Using Drag and Drop

If you do decide that drag and drop is the best choice for your project, you should follow these guidelines:

- Both applications must be open. This means that neither one can be reduced to a little icon in the Task Bar.

- PHOTO-PAINT does not need to have an image area open. If an existing image is not open, a new image will be created.

- To drag an image from CorelDRAW, you must click on it and drag it into the PAINT application. When the cursor is over the paint application, the icon will turn into an arrow-rectangle icon.

 TIP: *When dragging an image into PAINT, be patient. It sometimes takes longer than you might expect for the cursor to change into the arrow-rectangle icon. As Radar would say in* M.A.S.H: *"Wait for it."*

- When you let go of the left mouse button, two things happen:

  - The image is rasterized and placed into PAINT. If there was not an existing image file open, the object dragged into PAINT is rasterized at 72 dpi. If there is an existing image, it is rasterized at the resolution of the image.

  - The image in CorelDRAW disappears. To restore the image that was dragged kicking and screaming out of CorelDRAW, just click anywhere in the CorelDRAW window (which makes it active again) and select *s* from the Edit menu or click the CTRL+Z key.

 TIP: *To prevent an object from being deleted in CorelDRAW when it is dragged into another application, hold down the* CTRL *key when you click and drag, and a copy of the object will be dragged into the other application.*

Using PAINT and DRAW Together Effectively

You may want to use PHOTO-PAINT to enhance bitmap images and then bring them back into DRAW for adding text. An exception to this rule is if you need to apply special effects to the text. The reason for placing text in DRAW is that the resulting output text will be much sharper. When text is created in PAINT, the text is a bitmap image that is resolution-dependent. In other words, the text is no longer text but a bitmap picture of the text. It is fixed to the same resolution of the image it is placed in. This means that text placed in PAINT will be the resolution of the image. If it is 300 dpi (dots per inch), then the text will be a bitmap image that is 300 dpi regardless of whether it is printed to a 300-dpi laser printer or a 2450-dpi imagesetter. Text in a program like DRAW is resolution-independent. Any text that is placed in DRAW remains as text. At printing time, DRAW sends the font information to the output device, allowing it be printed at the maximum resolution of the device. If it is output to a 2450-dpi imagesetter, then the resolution of the text will be 2450 dpi. The result is sharper text.

Using OLE

It is a widely advertised fact that the entire Corel line of products, beginning with DRAW 4, supports OLE 2.0 (Object Linking and Embedding). Corel PHOTO-PAINT 7 and Corel DRAW 7 now both support in-place editing. OLE is a powerful interapplication program that is routinely demonstrated by dragging an image from one application and dropping it into another. OLE has been given a lot of hype by Microsoft and the press. On paper, OLE looks great; in practice, it carries a lot of overhead.

In-place editing means that when you place a PHOTO-PAINT image into a word-processing application like Microsoft Word, you can actually open PHOTO-PAINT inside of Word by right-clicking on the image. By copying the image to the clipboard and then using the Paste Special command in the Edit menu of Word or other OLE-compliant application, you can right-click the image and PHOTO-PAINT will open up within Word. For the average PHOTO-PAINT user, this isn't a big issue. Because of the resources needed for photo-editing in PHOTO-PAINT, I cannot recommend using OLE's in-place editing unless you have a really powerful system with lots of memory. Even then, I am not sure what the great advantage would be. I guess this means I will get a lump of coal in my stocking from Santa Bill Gates this Christmas. Enough said about OLE.

Closing Thoughts

We have covered a lot of material in this chapter, which I hope will help you use both Corel and non-Corel applications together to make some incredible projects.

6

Controlling Image Size, Direction, or Format

J ust as images don't always come in the proper size, they also don't always come in the desired orientation. When you are laying out a newsletter, for instance, it seems that when you get the images you want, they are inevitably facing the wrong direction. You usually want them facing inward if they are on the outside edge, and facing outward if they are on the inside edge. (I know you knew that; I just thought I would throw it in.) Corel PHOTO-PAINT offers a collection of commands to allow the image to be reoriented, resized, and reformatted quickly and easily.

The Duplicate Command

This command was introduced in Corel PHOTO-PAINT 6. In Corel PHOTO-PAINT 5 all of the commands in the Image menu produced changed copies of the image while leaving the original intact. Since many people complained that this created many unnecessary copies of the image cluttering up the main screen, Corel changed the commands so they did not produce duplicates.

The Duplicate command produces a new file that is a copy of the original image. When you select Duplicate in the Image menu, a dialog box opens. You have two decisions to make. First, you enter a name for the duplicate file or accept the name generated by Corel PHOTO-PAINT. Second, you must decide whether to use the Merge Objects with Background option, if it's available. If you don't know what objects are, don't be concerned; they are explored later in the book. For now, objects are bitmap images that float on top of the picture. The Merge Objects with Background option gives you the choice of making the duplicate image with all of the objects as they are in the original or with all of the objects merged into the background. Once they are merged, they are no longer objects.

The Duplicate command becomes important when you must produce several copies of a file to create an effect, as we will soon see.

Note for Corel PHOTO-PAINT 5 Users

There is a Duplicate command in Corel PHOTO-PAINT 5 as well. It is located in the Window menu. That Duplicate command does not make a new file; it produces only a temporary copy of a file. Any changes made to it are reflected on the original. Each application of Duplicate command in Corel PHOTO-PAINT 7 creates a separate file, leaving intact the file it was duplicated from.

The Image Flip and Rotate Commands

In their headlong rush to get to the fancy effects, many users ignore the Flip and Rotate commands in the Image menu. These are more useful than you might think.

The Flip Command

This command is pretty much self-explanatory. Accessed through the Image menu, it makes either a vertical or horizontal mirrored copy of the original image. To use the Flip command, select Flip from the Image menu. A flyout appears, showing the two choices: Horizontally and Vertically. Clicking either of these executes the command, producing a copy of the image with the selected effect.

 TIP: *Before using the Flip command, examine the image carefully to make sure it doesn't contain any text. More than once I have seen ads of nationally recognized sports figures holding footballs or basketballs on which the text was backwards.*

Now, if these commands seem pointless to you, you are not using your imagination. Remember, the best tool in Corel PHOTO-PAINT is located between your ears.

The AIR SHOW image in Figure 6-1 began with the single jet you see next.

With the help of the Duplicate command, a second copy of the entire image was made. The Flip Horizontal command was used to make a horizontal copy of the original. The Paper Size command was used to double the width of the original. The original was copied to the clipboard and pasted as a new object into the duplicate. The text and shadows were created with the Text tool.

The Rotate Command

Rotate offers the ability to rotate the entire image. Again, this may not seem like much, but there are many things you can do with this little command.

This banner began as a photograph of a single jet

FIGURE 6-1

Let's say you are laying out a sports magazine. You have a story about the play-offs that needs a graphic to introduce it. Everybody uses the picture of the arena packed with screaming fans and sweaty players. You want something different. You find what you want in a stock photo.

It's great, but it's a vertical photo—and you wanted something to cover several columns. No problem with the Rotate command. Choosing the Rotate command from the Image menu, you can select 90° Clockwise.

That operation took less than two minutes. You meet your deadline, your editor is happy with you. Of course, if you had had more time (10 minutes) and had already

6

learned how to create and rotate objects, you could have created the graphic shown in Figure 6-2. I only included this to show you some of the things that can be done with PHOTO-PAINT 7.

By using the Rotate command and a little imagination, you can create excellent banners for magazines, brochures, and so on.

Rotating an Image

To rotate an image, choose Rotate in the Image menu. A flyout appears with the available choices. Selecting <u>C</u>ustom from the drop-down list opens the Custom Rotate dialog box.

NOTE: *If the original image has objects, they will all become visible in the rotated copy. They will not be merged. This includes the hidden objects. (If you are bewildered by those last few sentences, it will become clearer when you get to Chapter 13, which is all about objects.)*

Rotating
objects
gives us
even more
creative
freedom

FIGURE 6-2

The Custom Rotate Dialog Box

The Custom Rotate dialog box enables you to rotate the current image by a specified amount. A new image is created from the results of the rotation. The variables are as follows:

Variable	Function
Angle	Lets you specify the amount of the rotation. (Enter it in whole numbers; note that the dialog box does not compute decimal numbers, but it accepts decimal numbers without giving any indication that it isn't using them.)
Direction	Determines the direction of rotation. Click the Clockwise or Counter-clockwise buttons.
Maintain Original Image Size	Fixes the image's height and width dimensions. The rotated image is cropped at the image boundaries. If this is left unselected, the dimensions of the image are automatically calculated (adjusted) to fit the edges of the rotated image.
Anti-Aliasing	Reduces "jaggies" on rotated images.

Next we will learn how to make images the correct size for use in other programs.

Manipulating the Image by Resizing

Resizing an image is a common practice in word-processing and page-layout programs. There is more to resizing than you might first imagine.

Why You Shouldn't Resize or Crop an Image in Other Applications

Many page-layout programs like Corel VENTURA, Pagemaker, and Quark offer graphic cropping and resizing as part of the program. They are usually fine for very minor image adjustments, but for any significant changes, you should open the files in Corel PHOTO-PAINT and make the changes there. There are several reasons for doing so, as follows:

- If you crop a large image file in a word-processing or page-layout program, the file size remains unchanged. Even if you use only 5 percent of a 16MB image file, the entire file remains part of the document file. Large document files create problems with lengthy print times and difficulty in transport to a service bureau. If you crop that same 16MB file in Corel PHOTO-PAINT, it may become an 800KB file.

- Resizing bitmap files in these applications can cause image distortion, which often shows up as unwanted moiré patterns over the entire image.

There are many different ways to change the size of an image once it has been loaded into Corel PHOTO-PAINT. Most of the commands are found in the Image menu; they affect the entire image and cannot be applied to a portion of it.

How to Display Information about an Image

The Image Info window contains all of the information you could ever want to know about an image. Click the Corel PHOTO-PAINT icon in the upper-left corner of the currently selected file and select Info… from the drop-down menu.

Please note that the Image Info window is not a dialog box. Information is displayed but cannot be edited. Once opened, the Image Info window must be closed by clicking the OK button before any other actions occur.

Image-File Information (Bigger Is Not Better)

The Image Info window provides the following information:

Name:	Filename of the Selected Image File
Width:	Width in the units of measure selected by choosing Options in the Tools menu in the General page
Height:	Height in the units of measure selected by choosing Options in the Tools menu in the General page

Name:	Filename of the Selected Image File
X dpi:	Resolution (horizontal) in dots-per-inch
Y dpi:	Resolution (vertical) in dots-per-inch
Size in Memory:	Size of the uncompressed file
Original File Size:	Size of file after it is saved
Format:	Type of image file format, i.e., grayscale, 256 color, 24-bit color, etc.
Subformat:	Compression information
Type:	Color mode of image, e.g., grayscale
Objects:	Number of objects in an image (Corel PHOTO-PAINT format only)
Status:	Indicates if any changes have been made to the image since it was opened

You will find yourself using the Info command more than you may expect. Generally I use it to check the size of my image file before I save it.

Resizing the Image Window

Although this is not directly related to image resizing, a resizable window is essential for working with images. To resize the image window, move the cursor over the corner or sides of the image window until the cursor becomes a double-headed arrow. Click and drag the Image window until it is the desired size. The image remains unchanged and a gray border appears around the original image. It is very helpful to increase the image area size when working on an image close to the edge. When you are working with various Corel PHOTO-PAINT tools near the edge of the image, the program reacts when the cursor touches the Image window's border. Increasing the view area prevents the cursor from changing into a double-headed arrow any time the edge is approached.

 TIP: *For a quick resize of the image to see it better, grab the corner of the window and drag it until it is the size you desire, and then depress the Zoom to Fit (F4) key.*

Changing the Size of an Image

Images are rarely provided to you in the exact size that is required for your project. In the old days, when we needed to change the size of an image, we made a PMT (photomechanical transfer) of the image, which could then be reduced or enlarged. Fortunately, Corel PHOTO-PAINT provides several much simpler ways to change both the size and the surrounding working area of an image. There are several ways to change the size. They include *resampling* and *cropping* and their variations.

Resampling

This command makes the image larger or smaller by adding or subtracting pixels. You can also change the resolution of the image in this dialog box and thus affect the printed size without adding or subtracting pixels.

The Crop Tool

This acts like a traditional cropping tool. It allows you to define a specific area of an image and remove all of the area outside the defined area. In Corel PHOTO-PAINT 5, we did the same thing with the Rectangle Mask tool.

Changing Paper Size

This handy command uses a combination of resampling and cropping. The Paper Size command increases overall image size by increasing the size of the base image. It is as if you put a larger sheet of paper under the original. It can also be used to crop the image.

The Resample Command

The resolution and the dimensions of an image in Corel PHOTO-PAINT can be changed using the Resample command. One of the best aspects of the Resample command is that it can change the size of an image without the need for you to grab the old calculator to work out the math. Resampling should not be confused with the scaling features of CorelDRAW or other DTP programs like Pagemaker and Quark. These applications stretch or compress the bitmap images, often resulting in serious distortion. Resampling actually recreates the image, adding or subtracting pixels as required. Figure 6-3 shows the effects of resampling a photograph. The

A graphic
example of
the effects
of
Resampling
on a
photograph

FIGURE 6-3

6

original sample (left) was resampled at 200 and 800 percent. Don't let the quality of this image keep you from resampling; just remember that it does distort the image.

Figure 6-4 shows the effect of resampling on a bitmap graphic. In this case, it is the Info button that was captured with CorelCAPTURE 7. Because the bitmap graphic doesn't have the tonal range (number of shades) of the photograph in Figure 6-3, the effect is more apparent.

 TIP: *Be aware that adding or subtracting pixels from an image decreases the quality of an image. Having said that, resampling remains the best way to change the size of an existing image.*

Two Approaches to Resampling and Their Results

Resampling an image with Corel PHOTO-PAINT 7 falls into two general categories: fixed and variable resolution. Each changes the size of the printed image using a different method, and each has its own advantages and disadvantages.

Resampling
causes
greater
distortion in
images with
fewer shades

FIGURE 6-4

Fixed Resolution Resampling

With this method, the resolution of the image remains unchanged, while the dimensions are either increased or decreased. Wait! Didn't I explain in Chapter 2 that if the dimensions increased, the resolution had to decrease? I did. Because the resolution is fixed, Corel PHOTO-PAINT must either add or subtract pixels from the image to make it fit the new dimensions entered. When the space between the pixels increases, Corel PHOTO-PAINT creates more pixels to keep the resolution constant. When you resample, Corel PHOTO-PAINT goes through the entire image comparing pairs of adjacent pixels and creating pixels that represent the average tonal value. I told you that so you would know why your computer seems to take so long to resample an image.

Conversely, when the dimensions of the image decrease, Corel PHOTO-PAINT subtracts pixels from the image. This sounds ideal, doesn't it? Actually, you always lose some detail when you resample an image, regardless of whether you add or subtract pixels. There is no magic here. The greater the amount of resampling, the greater the amount of image degradation introduced.

If the Maintain Aspect box in the Resample dialog box is checked, any change made to one dimension will automatically change the other. By disabling Maintain Aspect, it is possible to change one value without causing the other to change.

Whenever you change the aspect ratio of an image, you introduce distortion. The distortion will be noticeable if the values entered vary too greatly from the original aspect ratio.

Another consideration when using the fixed resolution method is the increase in file size. The following table shows how quickly file sizes increase when a PHOTO-PAINT (300-dpi) file is increased in size using fixed resolution resampling.

100%	200%	300%	400%
1.01MB	4.03MB	9.82MB	17.23MB

Variable Resolution Resampling

The other resampling method is the one I generally use (when I must use one). Variable resolution resampling is accomplished by clicking the button labeled Maintain Original Size. By forcing PAINT to keep the file size (number of pixels) unchanged, the resolution is changed to fit the newly requested image size. You can safely allow the resolution to be reduced to 150 dpi for grayscale and 100-120 dpi for color images.

The advantages of this method are that the file size remains the same and the operation is instantaneous. The reason it happens so quickly is that the image is not physically altered. Only information in the file header is changed. The resolution information is maintained in the header of bitmap image files. When PAINT changes the resolution of an image, it only needs to change two sets of numbers in the file. The disadvantage to this method is the loss of image detail that results from the lower resolution. In most cases, if you keep the resolution at or above 100 dpi, you should be able to resize the image without any noticeable loss of image detail.

 TIP: *When Resampling by changing resolution, you cannot see any physical change in the displayed image while in Corel PHOTO-PAINT. This is because the program maps each pixel of the image to a pixel on the display regardless of the resolution setting. To see the effect, you must save the image and view it.*

Resample Dialog Box Options

Here is a list of the Resample dialog box controls and what they do. Not the most fascinating reading, but handy information when you need it.

Option	Description
Units	Lets you choose a unit of measurement from the drop-down list box.
Width/Height	Lets you enter a number or use the scroll arrows to choose a size (entered in units of measure), or enter a percentage in the % box. The dimensions of the image remain proportional to the original. Any value entered in one box will cause the other box to change proportionally if the Maintain Aspect checkbox is checked.
Horizontal/Vertical	Allows you to enter a resolution value or let PAINT select a value for you. Resolution is measured in dots-per-inch.
Process	Selects the process to convert. Choices are Anti-alias and Stretch/Truncate.
Anti-Alias	This is the best selection. It creates a smoother image by removing jagged edges from the original. This is done by averaging or interpolating pixels. It takes longer to process, but it is worth it.
Stretch/Truncate	Only use this if you have a very slow system or you need rough approximations. It creates a rough image by stretching duplicated pixels and eliminating overlapped pixels. This process is very fast and the results less than great.
Maintain Aspect Ratio	When this is checked, the dimension/resolution values of the image remain proportional to the original. If you enable Maintain Aspect Ratio, values in the Width/Height and Resolution boxes remain proportional to the original values. For example, if you increase the height by 50 percent, the width will be increased by 50 percent. The same is true of the Horizontal and Vertical resolutions. They remain equal, regardless of the values entered.

Option	Description
Maintain Original Size	When selected, this keeps the file size the same as the original, regardless of the values of resolution or Width/Height selected. This option is used to resample the image by changing the resolution. Changes in resolution are not reflected on the display, only when printed.
Original Image Size	Displays the size of the original image.
New Image Size	Displays the calculated size of the resampled version based on the values entered in the dialog box.
Reset	Returns all the values in the dialog box to the values of the original image when the Resample dialog box was opened.

6

Resample on Open

The Resample option that is available when an image is opened is identical to the Resample command, with one exception. The Resample command can increase or decrease the image size and its resolution, while the Resample option on Open an Image can only be used to decrease the image size.

Additional Notes on Using Resample

Always use anti-aliasing when resampling an image unless time and/or system resources are critically short. Stretch/Truncate should be used when you need to see a quick sample of how the resampled size will fit. When changing resolution, remember that resolution settings that are greater than the final output device can support will result in large image files that require extra printing time without improvement in output quality. Changes to the resolution do not affect the appearance of the image displayed in Corel PHOTO-PAINT because each image pixel is mapped to the display screen.

Cropping an Image

Cropping involves the removal of part of an image either to change its size or to enhance the composition of the subject matter. Cropping in Corel PHOTO-PAINT 5 is done with either a mask tool or the Paper Size command.

Using the Crop Tool

There are several ways to crop an image and the Crop tool offers several different ways to select what is cropped and what is not. The choices are:

- Crop to Selection
- Crop to Mask
- Crop to Border Color

CROP TO SELECTION After you select the Crop tool, you draw a rectangular bounding box that surrounds the subject and excludes the area you wish to crop. You can move the rectangle or size it using the handles that surround the box. Double-clicking inside the rectangle crops the image to the shape of the rectangle.

Instead of double-clicking the left mouse, you may click the right mouse button and the available options for the Crop tool appear. The Crop to Mask option is grayed out (not available) if there are no masks in the image. Selecting Crop to Selection crops the image, just as if you had double-clicked inside the rectangle.

CROP TO MASK This option operates like Crop to Selection except that it crops to a mask rather than to a rectangle created by the Crop tool. To crop an area, surround it with a mask. Select the Crop tool and right-click inside of the mask. Choose Crop to Mask.

Regardless of the type of mask you place on the image—circle, trapezoid, and so on—the Crop to Mask feature will calculate a rectangular area that will fit all of the points on the mask you have used. The final result will be a rectangular image. Here you see the original photograph with a circle mask on it.

Next you see the resulting crop. Notice that the photograph has only been cropped to the edges of the mask.

CROP TO BORDER COLOR   The Crop to Border command removes borders of a particular color from an image. An example would be the ugly black border that seems to surround so many of the photo-CDs. The idea is to select the color of the border using the Eyedropper tool and click the button, making the black border disappear. In theory, that is the way it should work. The problem with the command has nothing to do with Corel PHOTO-PAINT. It is that nearly all borders are irregular, and since all crops must be rectangular, the result is that pieces of the original border do not get cropped.

Crop to Border is a two-step process. After you select the Crop tool, you right-click on the image to be cropped and select Crop to Border from the pop-up menu. This opens the Crop Border Color dialog box.

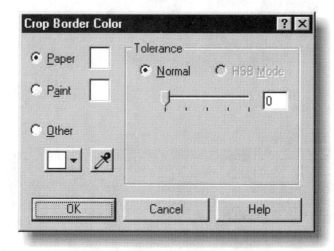

It is from the Crop Border Color dialog box that you select the color that will be used as the border color to be removed. The Crop Border Color dialog box lets you crop out the paper color, paint color, or a custom color you select from an image. The sensitivity of the cropping is controlled using the Normal or HSB Tolerance slider, which crops color based on similarities between adjacent pixels. These sliders control just how many shades of colors will be included in the cropping action.

A word of warning here. If the tolerance is set to zero, there is a chance that when you use the command, nothing will happen. Let me explain. Let's say you have a black border surrounding a photo-CD image. You choose Paint (foreground) color, since the border is black (the default color for Paint is black). The Tolerance is set to zero, meaning that only the Paint color will be selected. Nothing changes after you execute the command. What happened? Because the Tolerance was set to zero, only an exact match of the Paint color would be cropped. While the black on the border looked black, it was only a close approximation. As you go through the book, you will learn about shading and numerical color values. To crop to the color, you can increase the Tolerance (a setting from 5-10 will suffice). Don't go crazy and set the Tolerance to a large value of 100. When the Tolerance value gets large enough, it reaches a threshold that I call the avalanche point. When it is set this high, almost all colors in the image are included in the border color.

For border colors that are not black or white, I recommend you use the Eyedropper tool to select the color from the image to be cropped. Your chances of finding the right color in a standard palette are very slim. When using the Eyedropper tool to get a color match, remember that most border colors are not uniform and you will still need to increase the Tolerance if you are going to include the entire border. Corel PHOTO-PAINT offers you two Tolerance modes to choose from, Normal and HSB. Stay with Normal and don't worry about the HSB for the Crop to Border command.

Using the Paper Size Command

The second command in the Image menu is used to increase or decrease the size of the image area by creating a new image area in the specified size and placing the original image within it. It is called Paper Size because Corel refers to the background as paper. This command takes the original image and places it *unchanged* on larger or smaller paper (background). The new image (Paper) color is determined by Corel PHOTO-PAINT's Paper Color setting. If the paper size is decreased to a size smaller than the original image, the image is cropped. If the paper size is larger than the original image, it is placed on a paper based on the Placement selection made in the dialog box. Table 6-1 lists the Paper Size dialog box options.

Making a Poster with the Paper Size and Duplicate Commands

You will find that the Paper Size command in Corel PHOTO-PAINT is very useful for a variety of projects. In this hands-on exercise, we will create the background for a poster using the Paper Size, the Duplicate, and the Flip command.

1. Open the file PHOTOS\DESIGN\554026.WI. Select Resample from the Image menu and change the Width to 5 inches. Click the OK button.

2. Choose Duplicate from the Image menu and when the dialog box opens, name the duplicate file RIGHTEYE.CPT.

3. Select Flip, Horizontally, from the Image menu.

Option	Function
Width/Height	Lets you enter a value for the width and height of the paper.
Units	Lets you determine the units of measurement for width and height. The options are inches, millimeters, picas/points, points, centimeters, pixels, ciceros/didots.
Maintain Aspect Ratio	Ensures that the width and height values maintain their proportion to one another.
Placement	Lets you determine the placement of the image on the paper. The drop-down list box has the following options: Top Left, Top Center, Top Right, Center Left, Centered, Center Right, Bottom Left, Bottom Center, Bottom Right, and Custom. If you choose Custom, use the hand cursor in the Preview window to move the image to the correct location.
Preview Window	Displays the position of the image based on the values entered in the dialog box. The cursor changes to the Hand cursor if placed over the Preview window. The image can be moved with the Hand cursor to the desired position on the paper. If the image is moved with the Hand cursor, the placement is automatically Custom.

Paper Size
Dialog Box
Options

TABLE 6-1

4. Mask the entire image (CTRL+A) and copy it to the clipboard (CTRL+C). Minimize RIGHTEYE.CPT.

5. Select the original image and from the Image menu, choose Paper Size…. When the dialog box opens, uncheck the Maintain aspect ratio box. Change the Width value to 10 and select Center Left for Placement. Click the OK button. The resulting image is shown in Figure 6-5.

6. Click the Past as Object button on the toolbar, and the RIGHTEYE.CPT is pasted as an object.

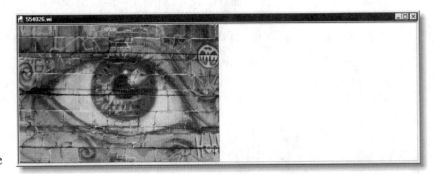

The Paper
Size
command
doubles the
width of the
image

FIGURE 6-5

6

7. Select <u>A</u>lign from the Object menu and set it to Vertically: C<u>e</u>nter;
Horizontally: <u>R</u>ight. Click the OK button. The image now fills the image
window. With the object still selected, move it to the left with the left
arrow key until the graffiti in the middle are on top of one another, as
shown in Figure 6-6.

8. Select Com<u>b</u>ine from the <u>O</u>bject menu and choose <u>O</u>bjects With Background.

The two
eyes are
overlapping,
but they
now appear
together in
the picture

FIGURE 6-6

9. Choose the Crop tool from the Toolbox. Place the cursor in the upper-left corner of the image, click and drag it to the lower-right corner of photograph. Do not include the white area on the right side. Click the right mouse button inside of the image and choose Crop to Selection.

10. This completes the background for the poster. Your image should look like Figure 6-6. Save the file under the name EYES.CPT. We will add the text in Chapter 13 and do the final effect on the eyes in Chapter 19.

Note for Corel PHOTO-PAINT 5 Users

Note that in PHOTO-PAINT 7, the Paper Size command no longer creates a duplicate image. Rather, it creates the new image and deletes the original.

Tips on Changing Paper Size

The Paper Size command can be used to crop an image precisely by changing the paper size to the desired value and selecting centered placement. By moving the image with the cursor, it is possible to place the image at the exact desired position on the new paper size. Paper size provides a method of placing an image on a larger background. You can make borders around an existing image. Try using Paper Size several times on the same image with complementary colors to make a quick border.

Image Conversion

Corel PHOTO-PAINT does not have an export command like the one found in CorelDRAW. It can, however, convert images in two ways: by saving files in a wide variety of formats (.EPS, .TIF, etc.), and by converting open images to different color modes (256-color, grayscale, etc.) using the Convert To command in the Image menu.

Converting color images to grayscale can save enormous amounts of disk space when producing graphics that will be printed in grayscale. Converting a 24-bit color image to grayscale reduces the image file to one-third of its original size. For example, if the original 24-bit color image is 1.1MB, converting it to grayscale will result in a file size of approximately 250-300KB.

Another use of this feature is viewing color images for pages that will be printed in grayscale. This book is an example of that type of work. All of the examples that are shown were originally color. I have learned that it is very important to convert the images to grayscale so I can see what they will look like when they appear in the book. Often, in previous books, I would find an excellent example to show an effect or technique, only to discover that the effect did not show up when printed in grayscale.

To Convert an Image

To convert an image, select Convert To in the Image menu. A drop-down list opens with the following choices:

Option	Function
Black and White (1-bit)	Converts the image to black and white (not to be confused with grayscale). This selection opens a menu with the following choices:
	Line Art: Produces an image containing only black and white pixels. A pixel is assigned either a black or a white value, depending on the grayscale value assigned to the pixel (1-256) and the threshold level setting in the Options box. There are no intermediate steps between the two extremes. No halftone is applied to the image.
	Ordered: Controls the appearance of images with pixel depths greater than that of the display device. Dithering is performed at a faster rate than error diffusion by approximating pixel values using fixed dot patterns.
	Error Diffusion: Controls the appearance of images with pixel depths greater than that of the display device. Provides the best results by calculating the value of each pixel using 256 shades of gray and spreading the calculation over several pixels.

Option	Function
	Half Tone: Produces a continuous tone image such as a black-and-white photograph using dots of various sizes. On laser printers that cannot print different-sized dots, the halftone is produced by printing different numbers of dots in a given area.
16 color (4-bit)	Converts the image to 16 colors.
Grayscale (8-bit)	Converts the image to grayscale.
Duotone	Converts a grayscale image into a duotone image.
256 Color (8-bit)	Opens the Convert To Paletted (8-bit) dialog box. Converts the image to 256 colors. (See additional discussion later in this chapter.)
RGB Color (24-bit)	Converts the image to 24-bit color (also called True-Color or 16.7 million color). It uses eight bits of data for each of the three channels of Red, Green, and Blue (RGB).
CMYK Color (32-bit)	Converts the image to 32-bit color. This is a 24-bit color image that is separated into four channels: Cyan, Magenta, Yellow, and Black (CMYK), which is the standard separation for four-color printing.

Duotones

PHOTO-PAINT offers the ability to create duotones, tritones, and quadtones. These are grayscale images printed using different colored inks, with each ink covering and reinforcing a particular range of the original grayscale image. The original purpose of duotones was to compensate for the fact that printing inks had a limited dynamic range when printing halftone images. When inks other than black or gray are used, duotones create incredible effects. The operation of this feature is discussed in Chapter 24.

Using the Convert To Command

Choose the desired format to which the image is to be converted. The current format of the selected image is grayed out. With a paletted image, for example, only the Duotone option is grayed out as an invalid choice because the image must be a grayscale to create a Duotone. Different paletted options are valid choices. The selection of a format begins the conversion process.

Note For Corel PHOTO-PAINT 5 Users

Remember that this process no longer creates a copy of the image being converted. If you convert an image from 24-bit color to grayscale, the original will be converted. If you do not want to change the original, then use the Save As command in the File menu to save the file under a new name before you convert it.

TIP: *Use the Convert To command when experimenting with different file formats. When I was making the screenshots for this book, I frequently converted images to grayscale to see what they would look like when printed. You can use the Undo command to revert to the original and try another color combination.*

Understanding Color Reduction

Before discussing the Convert To Paletted Image dialog box, we must understand some more basics of color images. When we reduce a color image from a palette of 16.7 million colors (24-bit) to a palette of 256 possible colors, something has to give. It is much like putting 16.7 millions pounds of flour in a 256-pound sack. Conversion is accomplished by using a color table. All 256-color graphic images contain information about how color is supposed to be mapped in a feature called a *color table*. This produces a 256-color image that is indexed to the color table. This type of file is also referred to as an *indexed color file*.

In a Super VGA World, Why Convert Images to Paletted (256 Colors)?

The answer is the Internet. The explosive growth of online services demands 256 colors. If you don't do a good job converting your image from 24-bit to 256 color, it can look terrible. Believe it or not, you can use some of the 256-color images in color publications and have them look as good as (or at least very close to) 24-bit quality.

 TIP: *Don't be too quick to dismiss the Paletted option because of previous bad experiences with a 256-color palette. Corel uses a proprietary 256-color palette that produces color that can be very close to 24-bit color but without the system overhead. (Image files in Paletted mode are two-thirds smaller than 24-bit files).*

The Convert To Paletted Image Dialog Box

This dialog box is opened by the selection of Paletted (8-bit) in the Convert To section of the Image menu. It allows you to choose the type of dithering and the palette type.

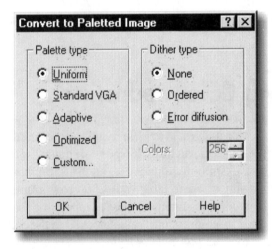

Dialog Box Options

Five buttons determine the palette type that is used to convert the image. The options are Uniform, Standard VGA, Adaptive, Optimized, and Custom.

UNIFORM PALETTE   When we convert an image to a Paletted image using a Uniform palette with no dithering (we will discuss dithering in a moment), the smooth transitions between different colors are lost, resulting in a posterized effect. Corel PHOTO-PAINT allows us to look at the palette that was created using the Color Table command in the Image menu. The Uniform palette spreads out the colors across the entire spectrum, regardless of the color content of the image. With the Uniform Palette, there are usually colors in the palette that don't exist in the image. Because it includes the entire spectrum in the palette regardless of the image content, Uniform is rarely a good choice for palette selection.

STANDARD VGA   Standard VGA provides the Standard VGA 16-Color Palette in the conversion process. While there are situations that may require the Standard VGA palette, remember that a 16-Color (4-bit) palette is very limited.

ADAPTIVE PALETTE   This palette is an improvement over the Uniform palette. It takes longer to process, but the results are well worth the extra time. This method takes the overall range of hues (colors) and approximates the necessary palette to accommodate the greatest range of colors in the 256-color palette.

OPTIMIZED PALETTE   This is the best of all the palettes. It is a proprietary method that produces a palette that is as close to the original color as possible. It doesn't take much longer to process than does the Adaptive palette, but the results are noticeably superior on most images. There is still some image degradation, but it is very slight. There is a visual difference between the color palettes produced by the Adaptive and the Optimized, although the appearance of the palette is of little consequence.

CUSTOM PALETTE   The Custom Palette allows you to pick all of the colors in the image. I cannot think of a single reason, other than for special effects, that you would ever want to use this option. The computer can do a far better job of creating a palette than any of us could ever hope to accomplish.

6

Dithering, or...What Do You Do with the Leftover Colors?

When we convert an image that has many thousands of colors down to 256 colors, we are sometimes forced to practice a little visual sleight of hand to make the loss of color less apparent. We do it through dithering. *Dithering* is the placement of adjacent pixels in a bitmap image to create a value that the human eye sees as a color that does not really exist. Yes, it is eye trickery, plain and simple. If the color doesn't exist, Paint creates a combination of adjacent colors to give an approximation of the missing color.

Three buttons determine the type of dithering performed when the image is converted: None, Ordered, and Error Diffusion.

None

The default is that no dithering is performed. This is the best choice if the image looks good without it. The colors in the image are limited to the 256 colors in the palette.

 TIP: *If you will need to resize the image later (e.g., for the Internet), you should definitely avoid dithering. Resizing an image with dithering produces moiré patterns, an interference in the patterns that make up the image.*

Ordered

Ordered dithering is performed at a faster rate, but the result is less attractive. It is also known as *pattern* dithering. Each pixel that is not in the available 256-color spectrum is evaluated and two palette colors are applied to the two adjacent pixels to give the appearance of the missing color. For example, if the missing color is green, one pixel would be made yellow and the other blue. Together in close proximity, they would appear to be green. Of the two dithering options, this is the least desirable.

Error Diffusion

This provides the best results, but is slower to process. It is the best of the two types of dithering. Error diffusion changes a color pixel whose value falls outside of the 256-color palette into an adjacent pixel's color. That pixel in turn replaces another pixel's color, and this continues until the last pixel is determined to be close enough to one of the colors in the palette. This type of dithering produces the softest transitions between the areas of color that would normally have harsh lines of color separation.

We have covered a lot of information in this chapter, and it is now time to move on and begin to learn about masks.

6

7

The School of Masks

Now that we have covered some of the basics of applying enhancements to the entire image, we need to understand how *masks* operate. I call this chapter "The School of Masks" because here you will learn many of the fundamentals and techniques necessary to create and control masks. It is the creation, manipulation, and transformation of masks and objects that form the foundation of any advanced work done in Corel PHOTO-PAINT. With that said, let us begin this chapter by introducing masks.

What Is a Mask?

The official Corel definition of a mask is "a defined area that covers part of an image or the entire image." Another way to say the same thing is that by using a mask, you can control exactly where on the image an effect will be applied. For example, Figure 7-1 shows a photograph of London. To change the background but leave the rest of the image unaffected, I need to make a mask that protects it from changes. With the

Original
photograph

FIGURE 7-1

help of a mask, London, which is not known for its mountains, becomes a charming little town in a canyon, as shown in Figure 7-2.

Here's an analogy. If you have ever painted a room in a house, you know that one of the most tedious jobs is painting around the window sills and baseboards. The objective is to get the paint on the wall but not on the surrounding area, so either you paint very carefully (and slowly) or you put masking tape over the area where you don't want the paint to go. In using the tape, you have created a mask.

Another example of a mask is a stencil. When a stencil is placed over an object and then painted, only the portion of the stencil that is cut out allows paint to be applied to the surface. Both stencils and masking tape are examples of masks.

Corel PHOTO-PAINT masks are much more versatile than a stencil or masking tape (and not as difficult to remove when you are done). The masks used in Corel PHOTO-PAINT enable you to control both where and, as you will learn in later chapters, how much of an effect is applied to an image.

NOTE: *For Photoshop users. So you won't be confused, a "mask" in PHOTO-PAINT is known as a "Selection" in Photoshop.*

7

Mountains added with the help of a mask

FIGURE 7-2

How Masks Are Created

Corel PHOTO-PAINT provides a variety of mask-creation and mask-selection tools. Figure 7-3 shows some of them. The newest addition to the family is the Property bar (not shown), which combines elements of all of the other toolbars. These tools, used in combination with their related commands, provide the Corel PHOTO-PAINT user with an almost limitless selection of masks.

Don't be concerned about the names of tools for the moment. We will examine each of these so that you can understand their functions and the best times to use them.

Two Groups of Masks

The mask tools shown in Figure 7-4 appear in PHOTO-PAINT 7 either as a flyout on the Toolbox or as a toolbar that can be opened separately. The masks that can be created with these tools can be divided into two basic groups: *regular* mask tools and *color-sensitive* mask tools. Regular masks are created by the user, who defines

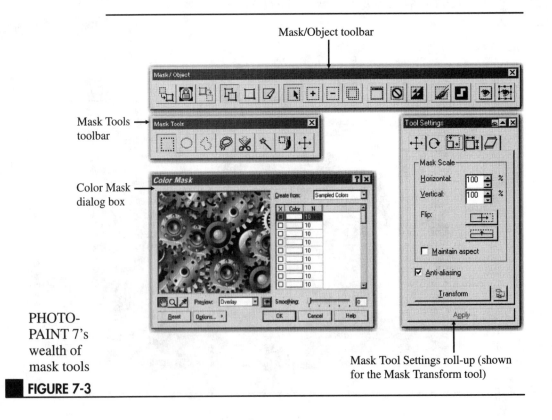

Mask/Object toolbar

Mask Tools toolbar

Color Mask dialog box

Mask Tool Settings roll-up (shown for the Mask Transform tool)

PHOTO-PAINT 7's wealth of mask tools

FIGURE 7-3

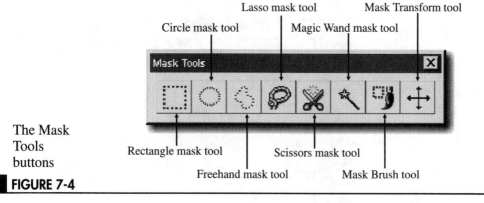

The Mask Tools buttons

FIGURE 7-4

their size and location within the image by using the mouse or other pointing device. The regular mask tools are the Rectangle, Circle, and Freehand mask tools. Unlike the regular mask, the boundaries of the color-sensitive masks are created by Corel PHOTO-PAINT based on information entered by the user in conjunction with the color values of the image. Color-sensitive mask tools are the Lasso, Scissors Mask, and Magic Wand. The remaining two buttons on the Mask Tools flyout are the Mask Brush tool and the Mask Transform tool, which is used to modify both the regular and color-sensitive masks.

Fundamentals of a Mask (Hands-on)

If you are unfamiliar with using masks, this hands-on exercise will lead you through the basic steps of creating and manipulating them. It will also introduce you to some of the properties of a normal mask.

1. Create a new file by clicking the New file button in the toolbar, and selecting <u>N</u>ew... from the <u>F</u>ile menu or using the keyboard combination (CTRL+N). This action opens the Create A New Image dialog box, as shown next. Change the settings in your dialog box so that they match those shown in the illustration and click the OK button. This produces a blank image window.

Create a New Image

Color mode:	24-Bit RGB Color	OK
Paper color:	RGB: 255,255,255	Cancel
		Help

Image size

Size: Custom

○ Portrait ○ Landscape

Width: 6.0 inches

Height: 6.0 inches

Resolution

Horizontal: 72 dpi

Vertical: 72 dpi

☑ Identical values

☐ Create a partial file

☐ Create a movie   Number of frames: 1

Image size: 364 KB

Memory available: 529443 KB

2. Select the Rectangle mask tool from the Toolbox. Place the cursor in the upper-left region of the image. Click and drag the mouse, creating a rectangle as the mouse is moved; then release the mouse button. You have created a regular mask. The size of the rectangle is not critical, but don't try to encompass the entire image. The boundary of the mask is indicated by a black-and-white marquee, described as "marching ants" because of the motion. If a marquee is not visible, check the Mask menu and see if Marquee Visible has a check mark beside it. If it doesn't, click it or use CTRL+H to toggle it on and off.

3. Select the Image Sprayer tool from the Toolbox. This is a new tool in PHOTO-PAINT 7. The Image Sprayer allows you to load one or more images, and then spray them across your image. The default image is the butterfly, but any image will work. Place the cursor on the image area, click the button, and drag it all over the image. Your result will look something like the image shown here:

4. Next, invert the mask either by clicking the Invert mask button in the Standard toolbar using the keyboard combination (CTRL+I) or by selecting Invert in the Mas<u>k</u> menu. This action makes everything that was protected by the mask unprotected and the area outside of the mask protected. The marquee indicates the invert action.

5. We will demonstrate the effect of inverting the mask using a new command in PHOTO-PAINT 7. Select <u>F</u>ill… from the <u>E</u>dit menu. When the Edit Fill & Transparency dialog box opens (Figure 7-5), click the Texture fill button (indicated by the white arrow) and click the OK button. The image floods the image area outside of the original mask with the currently selected texture, as shown in the following illustration. If you have a different texture selected than the one shown, it will not affect the tutorial.

6. Close the file by choosing <u>C</u>lose in the <u>F</u>ile menu. You do not need to save the file as we will not be using it again in this book.

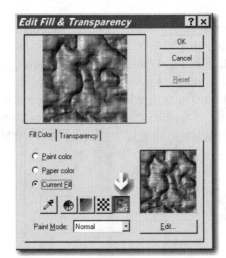

The Edit
Fill &
Transparency
dialog box

FIGURE 7-5

Properties of Masks

From the previous tutorial we learned a few things about masks. A mask restricts the application of effects to areas inside of the mask. For example, when we attempted to paint butterflies outside of the mask, nothing happened. The area outside of the mask as indicated by the marquee is protected. The area inside of the mask has no protection. Here is a summary of some basic mask properties:

- A mask "sits," or floats, on top of the original image.

- A mask can be loaded as an image.

- Since a mask is an image, masks can be saved separately from the image and loaded later as masks.

- An image can have only one mask.

- A mask can be retained when the image is saved as a Corel PHOTO-PAINT (CPT) image.

If all we could do with masks was make rectangles they would be pretty useless. We will learn more throughout this chapter about mask properties as we explore the mask tools that create them and how to use them.

Basic Mask-Creation Tools

We will start our exploration with the mask tools used to create regular masks. Unlike the color-sensitive mask tools, these tools allow us to define where the boundaries of the mask will be. All of the following mask tools are available either from the mask flyout in the Toolbox or from the Mask Tools toolbar.

Rectangle Mask Tool

This is the tool we already used in the previous tutorial. You will probably use this mask tool more than any other in the Toolbox. In case the name of the tool didn't give it away, it is used for making square and rectangular masks. A mask is made by clicking and holding down the left mouse button and dragging until the desired shape is achieved. Here is the part you didn't know. Holding down the SHIFT key produces a mask that increases or decreases proportionally from the center. If you hold down the CTRL key, it constrains the shape of the mask to a square.

Circle Mask Tool

 The Circle mask tool enables you to define oval or circular masks. This mask works just like the Rectangle mask tool except that holding down the CTRL key constrains the mask to a circle.

Mask Transform Tool

 This tool is not actually a mask tool but a mask modifier. All of the masks that can be created with the mask tools can be moved, scaled, rotated, skewed, have perspective applied—in other words, you can do just about anything you want to a mask with this tool.

When the Transform tool is selected, eight handles appear on the mask. Clicking inside of the mask changes the shape of the handles—each shape represents a different transform mode. Figure 7-6 shows the control handles associated with the different modes and functions. There are many ways to manipulate a mask using this tool, but its most common function is to move a mask on an image or to change the size (scale) of a mask. The other transform functions are mostly used when working with objects (see Chapter 13 for more details).

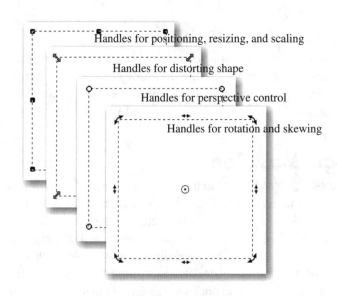

Mask
transformation
control
handles

FIGURE 7-6

NOTE: *For more information on Mask transformations, read Chapter 5 in the PHOTO-PAINT 7 manual. In PHOTO-PAINT 7, depress the F1 function key and select the Index tab. Type in* **Mask Transformations** *and click the Display button. For individual descriptions of the transform modes, click the How To button when the mask transformation description appears.*

Circle Masks, Mask Transforms, and Selections (Hands-on)

The following hands-on exercise uses the Circle mask and Mask Transform tools and introduces another aspect of working with masks: the *selection*. In this exercise we are going to use several of the mask tools to create and move the contents of a masked area from one part of an image to another.

1. Open the image \PHOTOS\DESIGN\554026.WI located on the Corel CD-ROM. After this image has finally opened (it takes a few moments for it to decompress), you will discover it is *huge*! We will change that in step 2.

2. From the Image menu, select Resample…. When the Resample dialog box appears, change the Image size Width from 16 to 5 inches as shown here. Click the OK button.

Resample		? X
Image size		
Width: 16.0	5 ▲▼ 31 ▲▼ %	inches ▼
Height: 10.7	3.33333 ▲▼ 31 ▲▼ %	inches
Resolution		**Process:**
Horizontal: 96	96 ▲▼ dpi	⦿ Anti-alias
Vertical: 96	96 ▲▼ dpi	○ Stretch/Truncate

☑ Maintain aspect ratio   Reset
☐ Maintain original size
Original image size: 4,718,592 bytes
New image size: 460,800 bytes

OK   Cancel   Help

3. Select the Circle mask tool from the Toolbox. Placing the cursor near the point shown by the arrow in Figure 7-7, hold down the CTRL key and drag a circle mask over the eye in the wall. It doesn't need to fit exactly. To try again, click the same spot. Each time you create a mask, it replaces the existing mask.

4. Select Checkpoint from the Edit menu. If at any point in the tutorial you take an action that cannot be corrected with the Undo command, select Restore to Checkpoint from the Edit menu.

5. Once you have the eyeball masked with the Circle mask tool still selected, place the cursor inside of the mask you just created. The cursor changes from the tool shape to an arrow. Now click inside of the mask and drag the entire mask up and a little to the right as shown in Figure 7-8. The contents of the mask moved with the mask and are now floating above the image. You have created a selection.

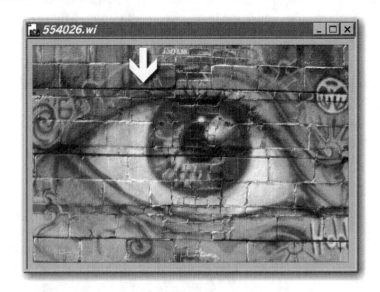

Arrow indicates starting point for Circle mask tool

FIGURE 7-7

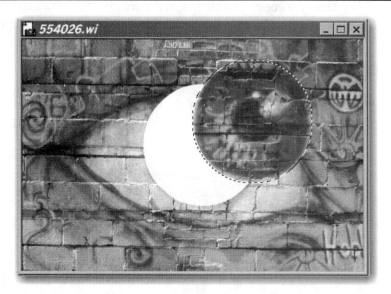

554026.wi

Contents of
the mask as
a selection

FIGURE 7-8

7

Selections

The bitmap image contained by the mask marquee is called a *selection* and is said to be *floating*. While it may appear that the mask removed the image and left the original color, actually, the area occupied by the mask has been replaced with the current Paper color. This action is like the Cut command of the clipboard. Dragging an existing mask with any of the mask tools (except the Mask Brush tool and the Mask Transform tool) create floating selections. The selections remain floating until you click the mask tool anywhere outside of the mask, select the Mask Transform tool, or choose Defloat from the Mask menu.

6. Click inside of the mask (selection) with the Circle mask tool again and drag it around the image. The contents of the selection (defined by the mask marquee) move with it; even if you move part of the selection off of the image, it may disappear, but it remains unchanged.

7. Now take the cursor and click it anywhere outside of the mask boundary. This will merge the contents of the selection into the image. Before you take any other actions, select Undo (CTRL+Z) and the selection is restored.

8. From the Mask flyout in the Toolbox, select the Mask Transform tool. This action will display a message, shown here, warning you that the contents of the selection will be merged into the image. Click the Yes button. The mask remains, but the contents of the selection are not part of the image.

9. Resize the mask by grabbing one of the handles and dragging it in or out. Click inside of the mask and move it anywhere within the image edge. Now drag it so part of the mask is beyond the edge of the image and bring it back again. The portion of the mask that went beyond the edge was removed, and the shape of the mask was permanently changed. In step 6 the mask did not change when you did this because it was a selection.

10. Select Restore to Checkpoint from the Edit menu and select the Circle mask tool.

11. Hold down the ALT key and drag the mask down and to the left as shown next. This action creates a selection but doesn't replace the original masked area with Paper color. Instead, a copy of the mask contents is placed in the selection.

12. Continue to hold down the ALT key and drag several more copies of the selection. Figure 7-9 shows the result of placing multiple copies throughout the image. It appears the "eyes" have it.

13. Now drag the selection off of the image and onto the PHOTO-PAINT main screen. Figure 7-10 shows the selection is removed from the image and it becomes a new image. The selection that was removed can be restored by ensuring the original image is active (look at the Title bar) and using Undo (CTRL+Z).

14. Close both of the images and don't save the changes when asked.

Properties of Mask and Selection

Let's review some of the properties we observed when using the mask tool in the previous tutorial. First, if you move an existing mask with a mask tool (except the Mask Brush or Mask Transform tool), it becomes a selection. If the ALT key is held down when the selection is created, the original image in the masked area remains; if not, it is replaced with the current paper color. A selection can be moved around an image, even beyond the edge of the image borders, and it will still maintain both its shape and contents. If a selection is dragged completely off of the image, it becomes a new image.

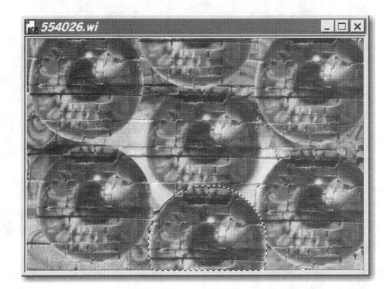

Using the
ALT key to
make many
copies of
our eye

FIGURE 7-9

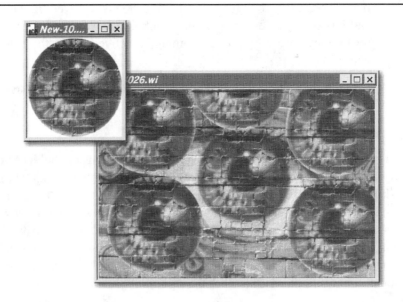

Making the
selection
into an
image

FIGURE 7-10

Freehand Mask Tool

For those of you familiar with Corel PHOTO-PAINT 5, the Freehand mask tool has changed considerably. It is now a combination of the Polygon Mask and the Freehand mask tool. Traditionally, a freehand-type tool is difficult to use with a mouse. By combining the two mask tools, it becomes possible to effectively mask irregularly shaped objects with a mouse with some degree of accuracy. The concept behind the operation of this tool is as follows: As long as the left mouse button is clicked and held down, it acts as a traditional freehand tool. Wherever the cursor is moved, the mask is applied. What makes this mask tool so effective is that, unlike the Freehand tool in Corel PHOTO-PAINT 5, when the mouse button is released, the mask does not immediately join its end points. Instead, the mask can be continued until all of the subject is masked. Then, by double-clicking the left mouse, the mask becomes complete. Here is a little exercise to familiarize you with the Freehand mask tool.

Emphasizing a Subject with the Freehand Mask Tool (Hands-on)

7

Many times in photo-editing, we need to emphasize a subject. One way to do that is by masking the background and slightly blurring it. This produces a false depth-of-field effect. In other words, the object that is not blurred appears closer to the viewer than the blurred portion. It is one of the many techniques we use to fool the eye of the viewer. In this exercise we will take a photograph of some native structures, produce a mask with the Freehand mask tool, and blur the background.

1. Open the file \PHOTOS\ARCHITCT\539000.WI on the Corel CD-ROM. Again this image is way too big, so we need to resample it. From the Image menu select Resample…. When the Resample dialog box appears, change the Image size Width from 15 to 6 inches. Click the OK button.

2. Select the Freehand mask tool from either the Mask Tool flyout or the Mask Tools toolbar, if it is visible.

3. Because we will be using the Freehand mask tool on the very edge of the photograph, I recommend that you make the image area larger than the photograph. Place the cursor on one of the four corners of the image window. The cursor will change to a two-headed arrow. Click and drag

the corner to enlarge it. Enlarging the window will prevent the mask tool
from interacting with the image window's border.

4. At the upper-left corner of the image, click the left mouse button. Now
   move the mouse down to the point shown by the arrows in Figure 7-11,
   and you will notice that a line is attached to the cursor. Next, continue in a
   counterclockwise direction, clicking at the arrows shown in the figure. As
   with so many things, the selection of points to place the mask involves
   personal taste and technique. I choose to do the larger jumps between the
   points so the blurring will not require the mask to closely follow the edge
   of the buildings. Continue to do this until you reach the upper-right
   corner. If you set a point in the wrong place, clicking the DEL key will
   remove it. Continuing to click the DEL key removes each successive point
   in the mask.

5. Double-click the mouse, and PHOTO-PAINT creates a straight line to the
   starting point to complete the mask. You have just completed a Freehand
   mask, which should look like Figure 7-11. I have highlighted the mask in
   the figure with white paint to make it stand out more in the book. Don't
   worry if your mask is a little inside or outside of the building. It isn't
   critical in this exercise.

Points on
the path for
creating a
Freehand
mask

FIGURE 7-11

6. Now that we have the background and some of the buildings masked, select Blur in the Effects menu. From the drop-down list that appears, choose Gaussian Blur…. When the Gaussian filter dialog box opens, ensure it is at a setting of 2 and click the OK button. The Blur filters and their use are explained in Chapter 15. The Gaussian blur makes the background appear slightly out of focus. The results are shown in Figure 7-12.

7. Close the file and do not save any changes.

Operational Points of the Freehand Mask Tool

The Freehand mask tool is very versatile for creating irregular masks. Unlike the Freehand tool in PHOTO-PAINT 5, this one does not complete its action when the mouse button is released but when the left mouse button is double-clicked.

■ Begin by clicking the left mouse button to anchor the starting point.

■ Move to the next point, and click there. When you click the mouse button, a line is drawn from the last point to the cursor. A closed polygon now exists between the two points (the anchor and the second point) and the cursor.

7

Gaussian
blur applied
to the image

FIGURE 7-12

- Move the cursor to continually reshape the polygon based on the points placed and the current cursor position.

- End by double-clicking a point that finishes the last line and completes the mask.

- When the shape you are masking is not composed of straight lines, you can either make many small increments of lines or click and hold the left mouse button and drag the cursor around the image area to be masked.

- If you accidentally place a point that is not where you want it to be, just use the DEL key to remove the last point on the mask. Each successive DEL continues to remove mask points until the starting point is reached.

- Holding down the CTRL key when placing points constrains the angle of the next point to 45-degree increments.

TIP: *Consider using the Freehand mask tool when creating a large and complicated mask, even if it doesn't have a single straight line in it.*

The Importance of Looking for the Mask Icon

Whenever a mask is created, one of four tiny icons appears in the lower-right corner of the main screen. This tells you that a mask is present on the image and what mode it is in. These tiny icons save you a great deal of frustration once you train yourself to look for them. As a rule, users do not look for icons placed almost off the screen. I am working on a 21-inch, high-resolution monitor, and the icon is small; finding it on a 14-inch screen must be even harder. *Make it a habit to look for the icon.*

If you have created a small mask or have zoomed in on a corner of the image and can't see the masked area, Corel PHOTO-PAINT will not allow any effect to be applied to the image (other than in the masked area). Here's the best part: when you attempt to apply an effect, PHOTO-PAINT will tell you that it completed the action, yet nothing will have been done. Talk about frustration!

Rule: If you are unable to apply an effect to an image, check first to see if the Mask icon is present. We will talk about the different mask modes later in the chapter. Even if you can't see the mask, the computer thinks the mask is there and will prevent you from applying any effect. Knowing this will save you time and money (for the cost of aspirin and tech-support calls).

Mask Modes

In the previous tutorials the creation of a mask caused any existing masks to be deleted. As we begin to work with more complex masks, this mode of operation, called *Normal,* prevents any modification of masks. As you may have guessed, there are other mask modes available in PHOTO-PAINT 7 that allow us to add to, subtract from, and otherwise modify to our heart's content any existing mask. The four mask modes are pretty much self-explanatory. They are: Normal, Additive, Subtractive, and Exclusive OR (XOR). OK, so maybe only three of the four modes are self-explanatory. Mask modes can be selected either from the Mode setting in the Mask menu, through keyboard combination, or through toolbar buttons. The mode of the currently selected mask tool is indicated by an icon displayed in the Status Bar and by the shape of the cursor. Figure 7-13 shows the mask mode buttons, their keyboard combinations, and the respective icon that appears in the Status Bar when the mode is active. We will be using these modes frequently throughout the book.

Get into the habit of checking the current mask mode before either making a mask or applying an effect. It is very easy to fall into a trap when the mask mode is left in a mode other than Normal. The mode that seems to cause the most difficulty when it remains active is the Subtractive mode. With indicators in the status bar and the cursor tool, it is easier to be aware of the mask mode.

7

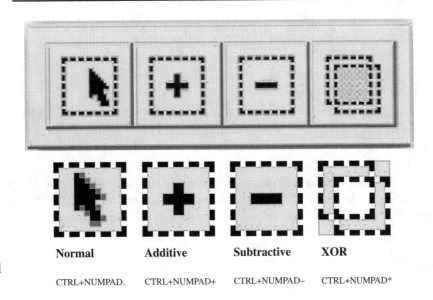

The mask mode buttons and their icons

Normal	Additive	Subtractive	XOR
CTRL+NUMPAD.	CTRL+NUMPAD+	CTRL+NUMPAD−	CTRL+NUMPAD*

FIGURE 7-13

TIP: *Is something not working as you expect? Check the mask mode first.*

Mask Brush Tool

 The ultimate mask cleanup and touch-up tool, the Mask Brush tool enables you to brush or paint an area to be masked. Unlike a regular brush tool that applies color to an image, the Mask Brush tool can be used to apply or remove a portion of a mask. The size and shape of the Mask Brush tool is set from the Property Bar or the Tool Settings roll-up. The roll-up is accessed through the Roll-ups in the View menu or by using CTRL+F8, which reflects the settings of the currently selected tool.

Color-Sensitive Masks

The previous mask tools made masks wherever we would drag the mouse. The following masks are color sensitive and create masks based on the color content of the image and the tolerance settings of the selected mask tool. This category allows you to create incredibly complex masks quickly—if you know how to use them. The color-sensitive masks are the Lasso Mask, Magic Wand, the Scissors mask tool, and the Color Mask. The Color Mask is the only mask tool not located on the Mask flyout. It is accessed through the Mask menu. It is explored in Chapter 8. Although the Scissors mask tool is the only new mask tool in PHOTO-PAINT 7, the other tools have been significantly improved in this release.

Lasso Mask Tool

 If you are an experienced Photoshop or PhotoStyler user, you might think you know what this tool does, but you're in for a surprise. The Lasso mask tool is a handy tool that unfortunately bears the same name as a different tool in both of the aforementioned programs.

The lasso metaphor is perfect for this tool. On a ranch, a lasso surrounds an object, and when you pull on the rope, the lasso closes until it fits tightly around the object. The Lasso tool works very much in the same way, but without the rope.

How the Lasso Mask Tool Works

The Lasso mask tool enables you to define a mask that is irregular in shape in much the same way as the Freehand tool. When the mouse button is released, the mask shrinks until it surrounds an area of colors that fall within the limits set by the Tolerance slider in the Tool Settings roll-up. The mask will contain the area surrounded by the Lasso mask tool. It is used when it is necessary to restrict the region where the mask is to be placed.

Whereas the Magic Wand Mask begins at the pixel starting point and *expands* until it reaches its limits, the Lasso Mask *shrinks* until it reaches its limits.

How to Use the Lasso Mask Tool

The Lasso mask tool operates much like the Freehand mask tool.

- Click and hold either mouse button to anchor the starting point for the mask.

- Still holding the mouse button, drag the cursor around the area to be masked. This causes a line to be drawn around the object. The pixel underneath the cursor when the line is started determines the starting color value.

- Continue to drag the cursor around the area until you are near the starting point.

- When the button is double-clicked, the computer will complete the line and compute the masked area.

Replacing a Background Using the Lasso Mask Tool (Project)

Here is a common application. The client wants to use a specific type of picture in a brochure. Unfortunately, the photograph you have been given has several problems. The plane is too small (relative to the size of the entire image), and the sky is a dull blue. Your solution? You could hire a photographer (big bucks) or enhance the photograph. Guess which one we are going to do in this exercise? You're right if you said "enhance the photograph." We'll be using the Lasso mask tool and a few other commands to mask the subject of the photograph and replace the background.

1. In the Open An Image dialog box, select the Crop command (located to the left of the Options button) to open the file \PHOTOS\AVIATION\ 601039.WI located on the Corel CD-ROM. If we resample this large photograph, the plane remains small, so we are instead cropping the plane during loading of the file, as shown here.

2. When the Crop Image dialog box opens, enter the settings shown in Figure 7-14 and click the OK button.

3. Select the Lasso mask tool from the Mask flyout or the Mask Tools toolbar, if it is open. Double-click the Lasso mask tool button. This action opens the

Tool Settings roll-up, shown in the next illustration, that is common for the color-sensitive masks (except for the color mask). The default value for this setting is 10; change it to 12. The setting of 12 tells Corel PHOTO-PAINT to compare pixels as the mask is shrinking, and to keep going until it reaches a pixel that is greater or less than 12 shades of the starting pixel value. It does this with all of the pixels in the enclosed area until it is finished. Anti-aliasing tells it to make the resulting mask smooth.

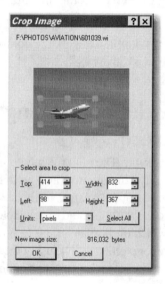

Cropping
the plane
instead of
resampling

FIGURE 7-14

Setting Color Tolerance

Setting color tolerance correctly determines how accurately the color-sensitive mask tools perform their job. The tolerance setting determines the range of effects for color-sensitive tools (and also fills). The higher the value, the more colors will be included in the operation. The are two methods of setting tolerance: Normal and HSB. The *Normal* method makes its selection based on the color similarity of *adjacent pixels* in the color mode of the image you are working with. The tolerance value you choose controls how discriminating the color selection will be. The *HSB* method creates its selection based on the similarity of hue, saturation, and brightness levels between adjacent pixels.

The key to finding the optimum tolerance method and setting is experimentation. You should begin by using the default setting (10) in Normal mode. If that setting doesn't include enough of the colors (shades if working with grayscale), increase the setting to include more. If the mask or fill that was produced took in too many colors from the image, decrease the setting. You will get better results if you make several small changes rather than large ones.

As you approach a setting that seems to work, keep a few points in mind. Zoom in and look carefully at where the boundary is being created. If the tolerance setting is too low, a portion of the background will remain in the form of a halo or edge glow. If it is too high, the mask will actually go inside of the subject area, causing a portion of the area you are attempting to mask to be lost. There will be times when the best setting will cause the inclusion of similar edge colors in isolated areas. If this happens, use the Mask Brush tool to remove them. It is easier than taking a lower tolerance and adjusting the entire mask.

HSB mode should be used when the color values in the area you are attempting to mask are too similar to the background. By using the HSB mode, you may be able to differentiate between areas that seem impossible in Normal mode. I recommend starting with different Saturation or Hue settings first, since the Normal mode uses values very similar to the Brightness setting. In Chapter 8 we will explore how to use channels to increase the capability of color-sensitive mask tools.

NOTE: *For more information about tolerance, in PHOTO-PAINT, depress the F1 function key and select the Index tab. Type in* **Tolerance** *and click the Display button. You will see an excellent and detailed explanation of how tolerance settings work.*

4. Since we want to mask the background (and not the jet), select the Subtractive mask mode. This means the final mask will be inverted.

5. Click the cursor at the arrowhead tip in the upper-left corner indicated by the arrow in Figure 7-15 to establish the starting (anchor) point. Now click around the jet at the points indicated by the arrows until you have surrounded it completely with a rectangle. Double-click the last point and the mask is created. Switch the mode back to Normal when the mask is completed.

6. To replace the background with something more dynamic, use the new Fill... command located in the Edit menu. Selecting it opens the Edit Fill & Transparency dialog box. Select the Fountain fill (second button) in the lower portion of the Fill Color tab and click the Edit button in the lower-right corner.

Arrows
display
points to
click mask
tool

FIGURE 7-15

7. When the Fountain Fill dialog box opens, click on the down-pointing arrow in Presets: in the lower-left corner and select Circular - Blue 01. After selecting the preset, change the other values in the dialog box to match those shown in Figure 7-16. Click the OK button and also click the OK button in the Edit Fill & Transparency dialog box. The result is shown in Figure 7-17.

8. Save the file as FEDEX.CPT. From the File menu select Save As.... We will be using it in a project in Chapter 20 to demonstrate the Lens Flare filter.

When the project is complete, the only decision that remains is how to send the finished project to the client—UPS comes to mind.

Scissors Mask Tool

The Mask Scissors tool is new in PHOTO-PAINT 7. Like a Lasso mask, it contracts around an image. Unlike the Lasso mask, it detects edges in your image—that is, the outline of the areas that are in contrasting color to their surroundings—and places the mask marquee along that edge as you are outlining the mask. Because the tool

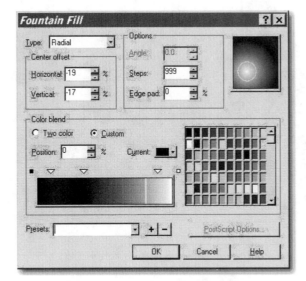

Fountain
Fill dialog
box

FIGURE 7-16

sometimes cannot tell where the outline of the subject is, the Mask Scissors tool can also be used to draw freehand segments by holding down the left mouse button.

The Tolerance settings, which are set in the Tool Settings roll-up or the Property bar, controls the sensitivity of the edge detection. A low tolerance setting means that edges do not need as much contrast to be detected as they do with a high tolerance.

The Radius, which is also set in the Tool Settings roll-up, is an invisible square (ranging from 10 to 999 pixels) that has dimensions equal to the value you type. This invisible square determines the area in which the automatic edge detection will work. When you move the cursor beyond the Radius you have defined, the Mask Scissors tool can no longer detect edges.

Magic Wand Mask Tool

The Magic Wand mask tool is used to create masks both quickly and automatically. Like the other color-sensitive mask tools, the ability of the Magic Wand to make an accurate mask is dependent upon the Tolerance settings in the Tool Settings roll-up and the actual color-value composition of the image. In other words, it takes a little

The finished photograph: a composite of a cropped original and a fountain fill

FIGURE 7-17

time to get the hang of using this tool correctly. However, once you do, it is very handy. The Magic Wand mask tool differs from the Lasso mask in that the Magic Wand mask expands from a starting point until all of the adjacent colors that meet the selection criteria are included where the Lasso contracts.

How the Magic Wand Mask Tool Performs Its Magic

Two simple facts about the Magic Wand tool are: (1) there is nothing magic about it, and (2) it is very simple to use once you understand the concept behind its operation. In theory, you simply click on the area that needs to be masked or the area that surrounds the area to be masked, and Corel PHOTO-PAINT does the rest. There are actually times when this will work as intended.

As with the Lasso mask tool, Corel PHOTO-PAINT treats the pixel under the cursor when it is clicked as the starting point. The program reads the color value of the pixel; then, using the limits entered in the Tolerance setting of the Tool Settings roll-up, it *expands* the mask pixel by pixel until it can no longer find pixels that are within the limits. For example, if the starting pixel has a hue value of 60 and the Tolerance value has been set to 50, the mask will continue to expand from its starting point until every adjacent pixel with a value between 10 (60 minus 50) and 110 (60 plus 50) has been included in the mask.

 TIP: *When using the Magic Wand mask tool, the most important decision to make is the choice of whether to mask the object or the area around the object. If the area to be masked is filled with a wide variety of colors or the colors in it have a wide tonal range, then look at the area surrounding it. Remember, it only takes one click of the button to invert the mask.*

Taking the Magic Wand Mask Tool for a Test Drive (Hands-on)

 Remember the photograph of London at the beginning of the chapter? In this hands-on exercise we will use the Magic Wand tool to do a simple background replacement like we did with the Lasso mask tool and the background.

1. Open the file \PHOTOS\LANDMARK\509075.WI on the Corel CD-ROM. Make sure the Open An Image dialog box is changed back from Crop to Full Image.

2. Again this image is way too big, so we need to resample it. From the Image menu select Resample…. When the Resample dialog box appears, change the Image size Width from about 15 to 6 inches. Click the OK button and the photograph of London appears as shown in Figure 7-1.

3. Select the Magic Wand tool from the Mask flyout in the Toolbox. Set the Mask mode to Additive. Double-click the Magic Wand button. When the Tool Settings roll-up appears, ensure that the Tolerance value is set to 10 and turn off anti-aliasing, which allows the mask to accurately follow the complex edges of the Parliament buildings.

4. Click anywhere on the sky in the upper part of the image and a partial mask appears to cover part of the sky. At this point we could click the parts of the sky that were previously out of range for the Tolerance setting, but there is another mask command that is useful here. In the Mask menu, select Grow. The mask completes the action and fills the entire background.

The Grow Command

The Grow command found in the Mask menu uses the current color tolerance to expand the mask. The mask expands until it reaches pixels that are dissimilar in color (by a value greater than the tolerance setting) to those located along the original mask marquee.

5. To place another photograph in the background, select Paste from File in the Edit menu. This action opens the Paste An Image From Disk dialog box, which, except for the title, is identical to the dialog box for opening an image. Change the method for opening the file from Full image to Resample. Click the Open button. From the Corel CD-ROM, select \PHOTOS\MOUNTAIN\392046.WI.

6. When the Resample dialog box opens, check the units of measure; if they are set to pixels, change them to inches. To make this photograph the same size as the original of London, we need to change the <u>W</u>idth value to 6 inches. Click the OK button. The resampling will take a little while. The mountain photograph is now floating (as an object) on top of the photograph of London, and only the mask from the original photograph can still be seen, as shown here.

7. Our next step is to clip the object using the mask. Select Clip Object to Mas<u>k</u>... from the <u>O</u>bject menu. The portion of the object that was outside of the mask is removed, resulting in the image shown in Figure 7-18. To see the image without the mask marquee, either turn off the marquee or click the Full Screen Preview (F9) key.

8. Hit the ESC key to return to the normal display. For now, save the file as LONDON.CPT using the Save <u>A</u>s command in the <u>F</u>ile menu.

Our image
of London
with a
different
background

FIGURE 7-18

Well, we have covered a lot of material in this chapter. If you have gone through each of the exercises, you have learned a lot about masks and how they work. In the next chapter we will learn more about these powerful tools.

8

Advanced Masks

This chapter begins with the all-important topic of mask management. You will then learn about using photographs as masks, the Color Mask, and several PHOTO-PAINT mask commands buried in the Mask menu that are real gems. You will also take a brief look at the Path Node edit tool.

Mask Management

All masks created in Corel PHOTO-PAINT can be saved and reloaded. This ability to save masks is essential because:

- Only one regular mask can be on an image at a time.

- Masks are valuable. If you spent several hours creating one, it is essential to have a copy.

- It is a great way to copy the same size image area out of several different images.

How Masks Are Saved with Images

There are two ways that masks can be saved, either *with* the image or *as* an image. Saving an image containing a regular mask in Corel PHOTO-PAINT format (.CPT) will automatically save the mask, too. In addition to Corel PHOTO-PAINT format, masks can be saved in TARGA (.TGA) and TIFF (.TIF) formats. They can also be saved as Alpha channel information in Photoshop's .PSD format.

The ability to save a mask apart from the image allows a mask created in one image to be loaded and applied to other images for special effects or accurate placement of objects. How another application uses the saved mask information depends on the application. For example, the mask information in a .TIF or .TGA file is interpreted by Photoshop as an Alpha channel.

Saving a Mask

Saving a mask is just like saving an image file. The mask does not have a unique file extension. In fact, you can save a mask in almost any graphics format you desire. After a mask has been created, it can be saved two ways: to disk, or in temporary storage in a channel. Use of the Mask channel is explained later in this chapter. The following procedure is for saving a mask to disk:

1. Select the mask with the Mask Transformation tool.

2. Choose <u>S</u>ave from the Mas<u>k</u> menu. At this point you have two choices: <u>S</u>ave to Disk and Save <u>A</u>s Channel. Select <u>S</u>ave to Disk and the Save a Mask to Disk dialog box opens.

3. Choose from the Save as Type list, name the mask, and click the Save button. The mask has been saved and can be recalled at a later time.

When naming masks, try to include the fact that the file is a mask as part of the name (e.g., Mask for Project 22.CPT or Tree mask.TIF). One of the benefits of using Windows 95 is the ability to assign 256-character filenames.

 TIP: *Do not use a unique extension such as .MSK for the mask. This three-character extension is used by Corel PHOTO-PAINT and most other Windows applications to determine the correct import filter to use. Although the mask can be saved in any bitmap format (e.g., .PCX, .TIF, .BMP, etc.), it is recommended that you save masks in Corel PHOTO-PAINT's native .CPT format.*

Loading a Mask

 The Load Mask function allows a wide variety of image file formats to be loaded as masks. Loading a mask into an image involves the following procedure:

1. Select the image to which the mask being loaded will be applied.

 TIP: *If you have several images open on your screen, make sure that the one you want to load the mask into is active. If you load the mask into another image, it will replace any existing mask in that image.*

2. Choose Load on the Mask menu and then Load from Disk. The Load A Mask From Disk dialog box opens.

3. Select the file to be used for a mask. The mask will be a black-and-white or a grayscale image. Click the Open button, and the mask will load into the image and the mask outline will appear on the image.

Loading a Photograph as a Mask

Any image file can be used for a mask. Using photographs or other non-mask files may give unpredictable, although not necessarily undesirable, results. A non-mask file is any image file that was not created using the mask tools in Corel PHOTO-PAINT.

Note for Corel PHOTO-PAINT 5 Users:

In Corel PHOTO-PAINT 5, the mask must be a one-bit (black-and-white) image file, while the Transparency mask is a grayscale image. Since the release of Corel PHOTO-PAINT 6, the two have been combined. The regular mask is now a grayscale image.

When loading a mask, it is important to be aware that Corel PHOTO-PAINT *will resize the mask to fit the image!* This used to be a problem in earlier versions of PHOTO-PAINT that required ensuring that the mask and the image were the same size. No more. Now it works great, and I will prove it in the next hands-on exercise.

Making the Lady in the Leaves

I stumbled upon this jewel when trying to come up with an easy exercise to show how to use a photograph for a mask. I call it "Lady in the Leaves." In it I will load the photograph as a mask. The photograph I am using is 15 inches wide, but PHOTO-PAINT will automatically resize it. Next I will invert the mask. Because a mask acts like a negative when we apply effects through it I must first invert positive images before applying any effects. Lastly, I will apply leaves from the new Image Sprayer tool to the masked image.

1. From the File menu, select New or use CTRL+N. Leave the Color mode at 24-bit color and the Paper color white. Change the image size to 6 × 4 inches at 96 dpi.

2. On the Mask menu, select Load and choose Load From Disk. Change Look in: to the drive with the Corel CD-ROM that contains the photos.

Locate and select the file \PHOTOS\PORTRAIT\527028.WI, and click the Open command. It will take a few moments to load the image because PHOTO-PAINT must resample the image to make it fit.

To see the mask, click the Mask Overlay button on the toolbar. Click it again to turn off the Mask Overlay. Click the Invert Mask button on the toolbar.

4. Click the Image Sprayer button in the Toolbox. Click the Load Image Sprayer List button located on the far left end of the Property bar. When the Load Image List dialog box opens, change to the CD-ROM drive and locate and select the file \IMGLISTS\MAPLE.CPT. Open the Tool Settings roll-up and change the <u>P</u>aint mode to Subtract.

5. On the <u>E</u>dit menu, select the Che<u>c</u>kpoint command. Place the cursor in the image and click one time at a point as shown next. Because the Image Sprayer applies its image randomly, yours will look different. If you don't like the leaf that was applied or where it was applied, use the Undo (CTRL+Z) to remove it. That's all there is to it. Continue clicking until you have an image you like. To clear the image and start over again, select Restore to Chec<u>k</u>point on the <u>E</u>dit menu. Figure 8-1 shows what my finished image looks like. Yours will be different—vive la différence!

The Lady in
the Leaves
is made
using a
photograph
for a mask

FIGURE 8-1

Removing a Mask

There are several ways to remove a mask. One of the quickest is to click the Remove Mask button on the toolbar. A mask must exist on the active image for the mask buttons on the toolbar to be available. The mask may also be removed by selecting Remove on the Mask menu, or by pressing the DEL key if the mask is selected. The mask is selected whenever the Mask Transform tool is selected. (The mask will have control handles on it.) If the mask is not selected, *the contents of the mask will be cleared when the DEL key is depressed*. Therefore, use the DEL key with caution.

Inverting a Mask

One of the more useful mask functions is the Invert Mask command. When a mask is created, the area inside the mask can be modified while the area outside the mask is protected. The Invert Mask command reverses the mask so that the area that was inside the mask now becomes protected and the area outside can be modified. The Invert Mask command can be accessed through the Mask menu, or by clicking the Invert Mask button, or with the keyboard combination CTRL+I.

Suggestions about Using the Invert Mask Command

Some masks are so complex it is difficult to determine what part of the image lies inside or outside of the mask. A quick way to check is to select the Mask Overlay button. The tinted area is protected; the lighter area is not. The Mask Overlay is a display function and does not affect the operation of PHOTO-PAINT.

Mask All

To mask the entire image, click the Select All button from the toolbar or choose the Select All command from the Mask menu. You can also double-click any of the basic Mask selection tools in the Toolbox: Rectangle, Circle, or Freehand. The mask will encompass the entire image inside of the image window. If the image is only partially visible because you have zoomed into an area, the entire image is still masked. In this situation, you will not be able to see the entire mask.

Mask Channel Operations

The Mask channel is a temporary mask storage area, and if you do any amount of work with masks, you have got to love this feature. You can temporarily store masks in mask channels by using the Channels roll-up. When you create a mask, Corel PHOTO-PAINT makes a copy of the current mask and stores it in a channel where you can access and reuse it in the image as many times as you wish. You can also save a mask channel to a file or open a previously saved channel into the current image.

Once saved in a channel, a mask can be selected and reused within an image. When you change a mask in an image, you can reflect the changes in the channel by clicking the Update Channel button in the roll-up. There are also commands for saving a mask channel to a separate file or opening a previously saved mask channel. With the exception of the current mask, the contents of the Mask channel are lost when an image is closed.

The Channels Roll-Up

The Channels roll-up can be opened several ways: by pressing CTRL+F9, selecting Channels from the View menu in Roll-Ups, or selecting the Channels Roll-Up button on the Property bar. The Channels roll-up provides several different command function buttons at the bottom of the roll-up. The Mask Channels section displays the Mask channels that are currently occupied. Figure 8-2 shows the Objects/Channels roll-up group with the Channels roll-up enabled. We will use Channels roll-up in a hands-on exercise later in this chapter.

Manipulating Masks

After a mask has been created, we often need to modify it. Corel has provided several mask manipulation tools to help us do this. Probably the most-often-used mask manipulation tool is the Feather Mask command.

The
Channels
roll-up

Channel to mask │ Delete current channel
Save mask to new channel │ Save to current channel

FIGURE 8-2

Feather Mask

Feathering a mask changes the transparency of the pixels located near the mask boundary. Any effect or command applied to the selection fades gradually as you get near the protected area. Feathering can be applied to a mask during or after its creation.

It is particularly useful if you want to apply an effect to the masked area but not the surrounding area. Feathering a mask makes the transition between the two areas gradual, therefore less noticeable.

When you select Feather from the Mask menu or click the Feather Mask button, a small dialog box opens that allows you to set the direction, amount, and type of feathering that is applied to the current mask.

The Width setting determines how wide the effect is to be applied to a mask edge. The Average Direction effectively applies a Gaussian Blur to all of the pixels directly inside and outside of the mask. This provides the smoothest mask of the choices. Selecting any other Direction enables a choice of two different Edges: Linear and Curved. In Figure 8-3 the Feather Mask command was applied to three identical masks using Average direction, Middle direction with Linear Edge, and Middle direction with Curved Edge settings. The masked area was filled with 100 percent black fill and zoomed to 300 percent. The Average mask (left) has the greatest amount of blurring. Linear (middle) has a tendency to produce points at perpendicular intersections of straight mask lines. The Curved feather (right) doesn't spread out as much as the other two, although the Width setting was the same.

Three different feather settings: a) Average direction; b) Middle with Linear; c) Middle with Curved

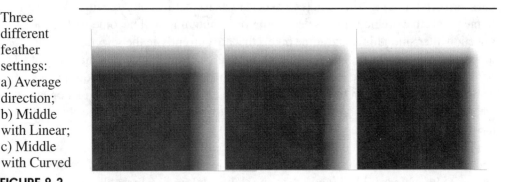

FIGURE 8-3

The Shape Category Mask Commands

Some of the other mask commands you may have occasion to work with are located in the Shape category in the Mask menu. These commands are Border, Remove Holes, Smooth, Threshold, Expand, and Reduce.

The Border Mask command subtracts a portion of an existing mask to produce a border whose width is determined by the setting in the Border dialog box that opens when this command is selected. It offers the option of three different Edges: Hard, Medium, and Soft. The resulting mask frames protect pixels in the image. Borders only move outward from the mask regardless of the Mask Mode setting. Be careful when applying this command to circles; it tends to degrade the general shape of the circle.

 TIP: *For a creative effect, try applying the Border command to a square or rectangle mask multiple times.*

Remove Holes is a real time-saver—sometimes. This command removes those nasty little mask fragments that tend to be left when using the color-sensitive masks. Unfortunately, it may also remove any isolated portions of masks that you may not want to remove. That said, when it works, it works great. It has no adjustable settings; it will either work or not work for your purposes. Keep the old faithful Undo command (CTRL+Z) handy and give it a try.

The Smooth Mask command creates a more fluid mask boundary by smoothing out sharp bends (jaggies) in the mask that occur when creating color-sensitive masks. Some pixels that are not in the selection before smoothing will become part of the selection after smoothing, and some pixels that are currently in the selection will no longer be included in it. The Smooth command can sometimes eliminate entire portions of a mask like the Remove Holes command. The amount of smoothing this command does depend on the Radius setting you enter in the dialog box that opens when selecting the command. Large values tend to completely change the shape of the mask.

The Threshold Mask command is the opposite of the Smooth command. When you have a mask that has too indefinite an edge, as in a feathered mask, this command makes it into a binary (black-and-white) mask by applying a Threshold function to it. If you do the hands-on exercises in Chapter 18, you will get to use this filter.

Oddly enough, this is one of my favorite filters in this category because it allows me to make the edges of masks more distinct. The only setting when using this mask command is the Level setting (1-255). With it you determine the point in the mask at which any grayscale value below the threshold becomes white and above it becomes black.

Expand and Reduce Mask commands do just what they say they do. Use them to make masks larger or smaller. Like the Border Mask command, these tend to degrade shapes if large values are used or they are applied multiple times.

Creating Distressed Text

 In this little hands-on exercise, you are going to create the illusion of text that was stenciled on a wooden crate. You will be using some tools that you may not be familiar with, but have no fear. Follow the directions and you will be fine.

1. Create a new image by selecting New from the File menu. The size is 4 × 4 inches at 96 dpi, and 24-bit color.

2. From the Edit menu, choose Fill. This action opens the Edit Fill & Transparency dialog box. Select the Bitmap Fill button (the one with the Checkerboard icon on it) and click the Edit button in the lower-right corner of the dialog box. When the Bitmap fill dialog box opens, click the Load button. From the Import dialog box, locate the file \TILES\WOOD\LARGE\WOOD07L.CPT on the CD-ROM. Click the Open button to select the file. Click the OK button to close the Bitmap Fill dialog box and OK to apply the fill.

3. Click the Text Tool button in the Toolbox. Click the image and type the word **DANGER**. Change the Font to Stencil at a size of 96. Part of the word will be off of the image area at this point. Click the Object Picker tool in the Toolbox and double-click it to open the Objects roll-up.

4. On the Object menu, select Rotate and choose Free, causing rotation handles to appear on the text. Holding down the constrain (CTRL) key, drag one of the corner handles until the text is at an angle of 45 degrees, as shown in Figure 8-4. Also, move the text so all of it is inside the image if necessary. Double-click on the text to apply the Transformation.

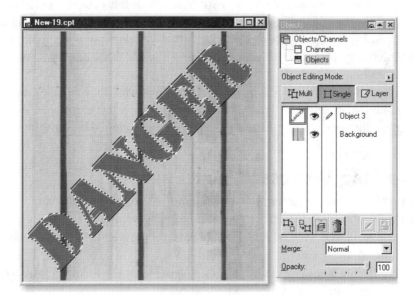

The rotated
text shown
with the
Objects
roll-up open
and mask
from
next step

FIGURE 8-4

5. Enable Preserve Image (CTRL+Q) if it is not already enabled. To check, open the Image menu and ensure there is a check mark by Preserve Image. Create a mask from the object (text) using CTRL+M. From the Object menu, select Delete. The text disappears leaving only the mask.

6. From the Mask menu, select Save and then Save As Channel. You will receive another dialog box asking you to name the Mask channel. Name it Original Mask. In the upper portion of the Objects roll-up, select Channels.

7. From the Mask menu, select Shape and then Expand. When the dialog box opens, enter a Width value of **4** (pixels). Click OK. Click the Paint On Mask button to see that the mask has become almost unreadable, as shown here. Click the Paint On Mask button again to return it to its normal mode. Now it's time for some mask magic.

8. From the Mas<u>k</u> menu, choose <u>M</u>ode, then XOR. This is the Exclusive OR mode of the Mask tool that, if you were honest, you had serious doubts it had any function whatsoever. From the Mas<u>k</u> menu, choose <u>L</u>oad and select Original Mask. Click the Paint On Mask button again and you will see we now have an outline of the text as shown here. Disable the Paint On Mask button.

9. Click the red color swatch in the onscreen palette to change the Paint Color to red. Select the Paint tool button in the Toolbox. Open the Tool Settings roll-up (CTRL+F8), and choose the Spray Can. Change the <u>T</u>ype to Power Sprayer. Change the <u>P</u>aint setting to Subtract. This will cause the <u>T</u>ype to change to Custom Spray Can as shown in Figure 8-5. If the Spray Can is not in the top four icons on your Tool Settings roll-up, click the small button to the right of the buttons and select it from the list that appears.

10. Drag the cursor over the masked area. When you are finished, turn off the Mask marquee by clicking the button. The Subtract <u>P</u>aint mode prevents the red from painting over the dark shadow areas which would have made it look unreal. Your finished image should look like Figure 8-6.

The Tool Settings roll-up for the Paint tools

FIGURE 8-5

The
completed
exercise
looks like
you really
painted it
on the wood

FIGURE 8-6

The Color Mask and Similar Command

The Color Mask has changed more with each new release of PHOTO-PAINT than any other tool in the program. All of this change has produced a lot of improvement. All of the color-sensitive masks I have discussed until now could only include colors that were connected to the original sampled color. With the Color Mask and the Similar command, pixels are selected based on their color content regardless of the position of those pixels in relation to the original sample point.

The Color Mask

Selecting the Color Mask, located in the Mask menu, opens a dialog box (Figure 8-7) that may at first look a little intimidating. Actually, the principle behind its operation is quite simple. Use the eyedropper to select colors in the image that you want masked. If you don't like the result of one of your color selections, remove the check mark from its box. Use one of the many preview options to determine how successful the selection process has been and click the OK button to create a mask.

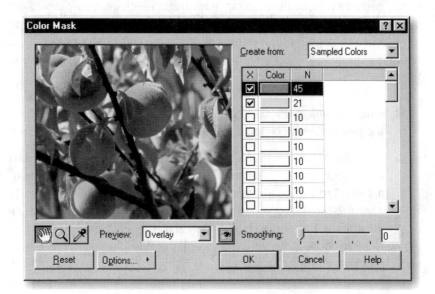

The Color
Mask
dialog box

FIGURE 8-7

If you used the Color Mask in a previous version of PHOTO-PAINT, you might find it a little confusing here, so I have included some handy tips to help you get up to speed quickly.

- The Color Mask is no longer a roll-up, so you must complete the selection of the mask and apply it before you can do any other operation.

- The Color Mask command no longer creates color masks. It creates regular masks. Color masks, which were a different type of mask in PHOTO-PAINT 5, no longer exist.

- You can save and load your Color Mask dialog box settings as a Color Mask.

Replacing a Background Using the Color Mask

Replacing a background in a complex image can take time, even with the Color Mask. The following exercise has only a few steps, but if you were to get this job ready for a client, it would take you longer than you might imagine. In this exercise we are going to replace the blue sky background with another photograph. I chose this image over a few others that had solid backgrounds because it is a rare day indeed when someone will give you a photograph of an outdoor subject shot against a solid background. The challenge will be to remove as much of the blue as possible from the edges of the leaves that are blurred in the background.

1. Open the image \PHOTOS\AGRICLTR\676028.WI. Select Resample in the Image menu, change the Width to 7 inches, and click the OK button.

2. From the Mask menu, select the Color Mask. When the dialog box opens, it will look like the one shown in Figure 8-7. If you have room on your display, I recommend positioning the Color Mask dialog box so you have access to the image you are working with, as shown in the following illustration. Select the Hand button and right-click in the preview window twice to zoom completely out. Click the Reset button to clear any previous settings.

3. Click the Eyedropper button and place it either in the preview window or on the image. As you move the eyedropper around, notice that the color

swatch in the Color column of the dialog box changes to reflect the color currently under the Eyedropper cursor. Click the image at a point in the upper-right area in the dark blue sky.

4. Click the Preview button (it looks like an eye), and the image in the preview shows masked (protected) areas in a red tint. The areas that are not protected are clear, allowing the original color to be viewed. Change the Tolerance value (the N column) to 40 (%) by clicking the number 10 and changing the value. Notice that the preview automatically updates the image. Now, portions of the leaves are included. You will correct this later.

5. Below the spot you originally sampled is the brightest blue in the image. Click on the next empty color in the column. If you don't change to the next color, the sample you are about to select will replace the first one. Select the Eyedropper again and click the area on the preview that contains the bright blue. Change its tolerance value to 30.

6. You have portions of the mask that are appearing on the leaves and the peaches. Move the Smoothing slider to the right until it reaches 75. This action should remove most of the tiny holes created by the Color Mask. Click the OK button.

7. Turn off the Mask marquee. To view the mask, use the Mask Overlay button. It is more accurate and much less disconcerting to watch. If the mask still needed some final touch-up work, you would do it at this point with the Mask Brush tool. Turn off the Mask overlay by clicking the Mask Overlay button again.

8. From the Edit menu, select Paste From File. When the Paste an Image from Disk dialog box opens, locate and select the file \PHOTOS\ MOUNTAIN\580000.WI. Change the Full Image option to Resample. Click the OK button. When the Resample dialog box opens, change the Units setting to Inches. Change the Width setting to 7.5 inches. Click OK. The photograph covers the image as shown in Figure 8-8.

9. From the Objects menu, choose Clip Object to Mask. The result is shown in Figure 8-9. If you are reading through this exercise, the difference in the backgrounds is much more apparent when viewing it in color. Close the file and don't save any changes when asked.

The mountain is placed as an object on the masked image of fruit trees

FIGURE 8-8

Removing Background Corona

If you did the previous exercise, there is still a faint blue corona surrounding the branches in the lower portions of the image. There will always be coronas like that on any portion of an image that has an indistinct edge. This is the part I told you would take time to correct. There are several ways to remove the background corona left by the color-sensitive mask tools.

If the corona has one dominant color (such as blue in the previous exercise), you can use the Color Replacer tool in the Eraser flyout of the Toolbox to remove it. Use the Eyedropper tool from the Toolbox to select the light blue from the corona as the Paint color and the dark from the background as the Paper color (CTRL+RIGHT CLICK). Double-click the Color Eraser Tool button to open its Tools Settings roll-up. From here, you can adjust the range of colors around the sample color that you want to replace. Set the range of colors to 40 and do a test sample to see if the results are satisfactory. Then you only need to brush over the corona with the Color Replacer tool. All of the colors in the corona that match the Paint colors are replaced with the

The image
with a new
background

FIGURE 8-9

8

Paper color. This method is time-consuming because the Color Replacer tool only changes one color at a time. Still, it is effective and is also one of the few uses I have found for this particular tool.

Another method to remove the background corona involves a different approach to applying the object. In step 8 of the previous exercise, before pasting the object from a file, copy the content of your mask (peaches) to the clipboard. Combine the Object (mountains) and then Paste the contents of the clipboard (peaches) as an object. This would make the peaches an object on top of the new background. We could then use the Feather command to remove the background corona. The disadvantage to this method is that the object begins to develop blurry edges if the amount of feathering necessary to remove the corona becomes too great.

The best method involves masking the image as we did in the exercise, copying the contents of the mask (peaches) to the clipboard and then pasting the peaches onto a new background. Then wherever the corona appears you can use the Clone From Saved Brush tool to restore the original background.

Color Mask Options

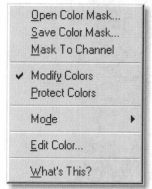

Clicking the Option button on the Color Mask dialog box opens a menu, shown here, containing many of the settings that determine how this mask tool operates.

You can save all of the settings as a Color Mask (.CMK) file, which can be opened and used at a later time. The Color Mask can also be saved to a mask channel through this option. If you choose to use this, remember that the Mask channel is a temporary storage area that disappears when the image is closed.

The default settings for the Color Mask tool are intended to create a mask in Modify Colors mode. In this mode, everything that is not selected is protected. The opposite, Protect Colors mode, is available as well.

The Mode option opens another menu, shown in this illustration, from which you can determine what criteria the Color mask uses to select its color. For many applications, the Normal setting (default) will do the job. HSB uses a combination of Hue, Saturation, and Brightness to make its selection of colors. You can also use the HSB components individually to determine which colors are selected.

Choosing Edit Color opens the Select Color dialog box, from which you can specify a particular color to select. For example, if you only wanted to select every place in the image that the color Pantone CV742 was used, this is where you would make the selection.

At the top of the Color Mask is the Create From drop-down list. This opens a large list of preset settings, shown here, that allows you to quickly select a type or range of colors or shades. Some of the selections are not what they appear to be. For example, the setting Blues does not select everything blue in an image; rather, it is set to the color Blue in the palette at a high value (50). If we had selected this as the starting point in the previous exercise, it would not have initially selected any colors in the sky. You can choose Blues and then change the blue that is used as the reference by clicking the sky with the Eyedropper tool.

Using the Color Mask More Productively

The following suggestions may help you when using the Color Mask.

If you are attempting to mask a narrow range of colors, like the blue in a sky, use multiple samples or take a single sample and increase the Tolerance setting for it. Many times when selecting a color or range of colors you end up with parts of the image selected that you didn't want selected. Rather than waste time trying to balance the color/tolerance settings to get the "perfect" mask, focus on getting the area selected that was the original objective. Any areas that are also included in the mask can be easily deleted with one of the mask tools after the mask is applied. It is always easier to remove a portion of a mask than to create one that has a ragged or irregular boundary.

When changing the color tolerance value, the preview window won't reflect the changes until you hit the ENTER key or click another color.

If you must edit photographs a lot to select and modify backgrounds, this tool will serve you well. If the background is very well-defined and noncontiguous, you may want to consider the Similar command, which happens to be the next subject.

Similar Command

The Similar and Grow commands in the Mask menu share a common selection process. Both use the color content of the pixels making up the marquee boundary as their reference (or starting) point. Both expand by comparing the reference value with the color value of adjacent pixels to see if they fall within the Color Tolerance value that was set in either the Tools Settings roll-up or the Property bar. All pixels that fall within that range are included; those outside the range are not. Where the two commands differ is in the adjacent part. The Grow command continues to grow until there are no more adjacent pixels. The Similar command continues to evaluate every pixel in the image.

The difficulty you may encounter with the operation of either of these commands happens when working with a mask boundary containing pixels with many different colors. All of the colors in the mask boundary (plus or minus the Color Tolerance setting) will be included. When you run into a situation like this, lower the Color Tolerance to a very low number or change from Normal to HSB.

8

Stroke Mask Command

This command is used to automatically apply brush strokes along a path defined by the mask. From the Stroke Mask dialog box, you can select any brush or effect tool. Any parameter that can be selected from the Tool Settings roll-up for a brush or effect tool can be selected and used with the Stroke command.

Applying the Stroke Command

In this hands-on exercise, you are going to create a small poster for a small organization that is trying to abolish the use of stamps. Your Mask Stroke command will make the job really simple.

1. Create a new image that is 4 × 4 inches at 96 dpi, 24-bit color, with white Paper color.

2. From the Tools menu, select Grid & Ruler Setup. Select Show Grid and Snap to Grid. Change the Spacing to .5 in both Horizontal and Vertical. Click OK.

3. Select the Circle Mask tool from the Toolbox. Starting at a point that is two squares in and down from the upper-left corner, click and drag a 4 × 4 circle.

4. From the Mask menu, select Stroke Mask. When the Choose Stroke Position dialog box opens, leave it at Middle of the Mask border and click OK.

5. When the Stroke Mask dialog box opens, click the Other tab. Click the Edit button. When the Image Sprayer Tool dialog box opens, click the Load button and select Stamps. Click Open. Click OK to close the Image Sprayer dialog box and OK again to apply it. It will take a few moments depending on the speed of your computer. Figure 8-10 shows the results I got. Yours will be different because the Image Sprayer applies its stamps randomly.

6. Remove the mask by clicking the Remove Mask button. Turn off Snap to Grid by pressing CTRL+Y, and from the View menu, uncheck Grid.

7. With the Paint color set to Black, click the Text tool in the Toolbox. Change the Font to Stencil, the size to 72, and the Interline spacing to 82. Click the image and enter the text **STAMP OUT STAMPS**. Click the

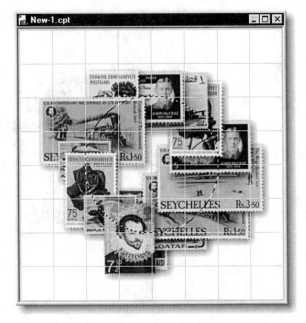

The stamps
applied with
the Stroke
Mask
command

FIGURE 8-10

8

Object Picker button in the Toolbox. Open the Align dialog box
(CTRL+SHIFT+A) and select Align to Center of Page. Click OK. The
problem now is that the black text blends in with the stamps, as shown
in Figure 8-11.

8. Click the white color swatch in the onscreen palette. Open the Objects
   roll-up (CTRL+F7). Ensure the Preserve Image button is enabled. Select
   Create from Object (CTRL+M). Your text is now masked. Click the Lock
   icon next to the text in the Objects roll-up to lock it. The text will
   become deselected.

9. From the Mask menu, select Stroke Mask. When the Choose Stroke
   Position dialog box opens, leave it at Middle of the Mask border and
   click OK.

10. When the Stroke Mask dialog box opens, select the Airbrush tool from
    the Brush tab and choose the Medium Cover as shown in Figure 8-12.
    Click the OK button. The final result is shown in Figure 8-13.

The Text is hard to read over the darker portions of the stamps

FIGURE 8-11

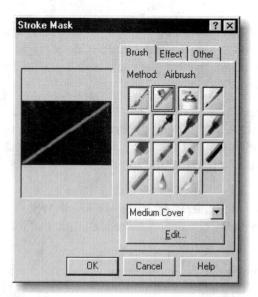

Stroke Mask dialog box for selecting brushes

FIGURE 8-12

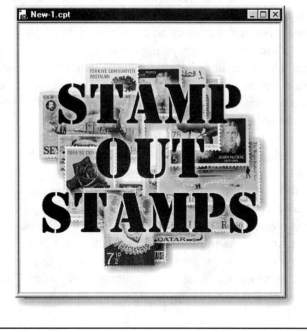

The
finished
exercise

FIGURE 8-13

11. Close the file and don't save any changes.

 TIP: *If you ever get an assignment from a group that wants to stamp out stamps, get paid in advance.*

There is one last subject under the heading Advanced Masks: Paths.

Paths

What are paths? *Paths* are line and curve segments connected by square endpoints called *nodes*. If you work with CorelDRAW, paths will be familiar to you. Masks and paths share some common characteristics. A mask is created from a bitmap image. A path, on the other hand, is a vector drawing that exists on a layer above the image and is independent of the image resolution. A path that completely encloses an area, as a mask would, is referred to as *closed*. A path with start and end nodes that are not connected, something that a mask cannot do, is called *open*.

Paths offer powerful and precise editing tools that allow you to modify isolated segments of the outline you create. The advantage of the path over the mask is in the word *precision*. You can only adjust a bitmap mask by adding or subtracting from it with a brush tool or something similar. With a path, you have full Bezier level control over the points and nodes, just as you have in CorelDRAW.

New paths can be created using the Path Node edit tool, or existing masks can be converted to paths. Double-clicking the Path Node edit tool opens the Node edit tool shown in Figure 8-14.

You can save the path if you wish to work on it later, use it in another image, or export its contents as a bitmap. You can save a path as a path or convert it to a mask. If you export a mask as a part of an encapsulated postscript (.EPS) image, the mask is converted to a path. You can stroke a path in the same manner that you learned to stroke a mask earlier.

Corel has produced a large volume of material on paths, how to manipulate them, and apply them. So, in the interest of saving space, I refer you to either the PHOTO-PAINT user's manual or the extensive online help. With the online help, I recommend opening the index and entering the word **Path**. You will find considerable material on the subject.

The Node
Edit Tool
Settings
roll-up
offers
a large
number of
controls to
create and
manipulate
paths

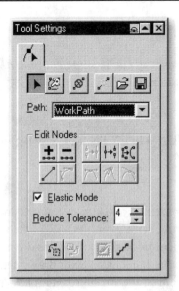

FIGURE 8-14

9

Correcting
Existing Images

Sometimes the most important operations we perform in PHOTO-PAINT are not found in the dazzling special effects we create or in the fantastic, surrealistic images produced using our vast array of filters. Some of the most important work done with PHOTO-PAINT is the correction and enhancement of existing images—in other words, making bad photographs look good.

In this chapter you will be introduced to some basic PHOTO-PAINT commands in the Image menu used to make an image look better either on a computer screen, when it is printed, or both. This is what photo-editing is about. It is not glamorous work, but more often than not it pays the bills. We will also mention other color-correction tools included with PHOTO-PAINT: PhotoLab, Intellihance, and the new Lens feature. We begin by covering some basic terms and concepts.

It's Not a Perfect World

The challenge facing anyone working with digital photo-editing that is destined to be printed is based on one fundamental fact. What you see on the screen is not, and will never be, what you get. The monitor that you stare at all day long has a greater range of color and shades than any output device can reproduce. Therefore, all of the tools that we will be looking at in this chapter essentially do one thing. They shuffle existing pixels around inside an image so that they will look their best on the media (inkjet, laser, or web offset) on which you will be doing your final output.

Understanding Image Correction and Targeting

The adjustment of lightness and darkness in an image is called *tonal manipulation*. We adjust the tones in an image for two reasons. The first is to correct flaws that are either inherent in the image or are introduced during the scanning process. This is called *image correction*. The second reason is to compensate for the limitations of the output device. This is called *targeting*. You can do both at once or one at a time; either way it is important to keep clear the distinction between image correction and targeting—at least for the remainder of the chapter. We will be concentrating on image correction in this chapter.

With few exceptions, if all you need to do is perform image correction on grayscale images, it can be accomplished using only two PHOTO-PAINT tools: Histogram and Level Equalization. The other tools related to image correction are either for color (and will be discussed later in this chapter), or their effects can be found in these tools. For example, Gamma is both a separate setting and part of Level Equalization.

Stop Before You Start

The most important step in image correction is to stop and examine the image you want to correct, for example, a photograph with debris (dust and hairs) that is painfully obvious. Does the photograph have detail in the shadows that you want to recover? Is it over-exposed? First decide what you want to do, and then plan a strategy to accomplish it. All of the stretching and squeezing of bits done by PHOTO-PAINT (or any photo-editing program) causes loss of image information. The loss is made worse by multiple applications of tonal corrections. It may not be obvious, but it is there. The damage may appear as posterization in areas of tonal shading, noise that begins to appear or general loss of detail. For this reason, your general rule should be to make only as many tonal corrections as are necessary.

Shades, Shadows, Highlights, and Histograms

Every digital image contains pixels that have a maximum range of 256 levels of brightness numbered 0-255. At this point, for simplicity's sake, we are going to restrict our discussion to grayscale images. These levels of brightness or shades range in value from black (0) to white (255). These values can be visually charted on a terribly complicated looking graph called a *histogram*. Figure 9-1 shows a portion of the histogram that is displayed by PHOTO-PAINT. It is divided into three regions: shadows, highlights, and midtones.

A histogram is a simple bar chart that plots the number of pixels at each brightness level in an image. It can tell you a good many things about an image before you begin to work on it. In Corel PHOTO-PAINT 7, you can see the histogram of an image by selecting Histogram in the Image menu.

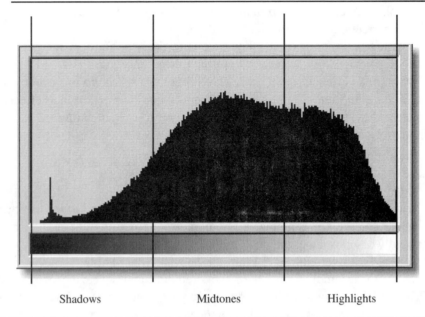

The three
major
regions of a
histogram

Shadows   Midtones   Highlights

FIGURE 9-1

How to Read a Histogram

The following examples will show the relationship between different types of photographs and their respective histograms. Only the actual histogram is displayed. The numerical information that is displayed with this histogram is not shown.

In the photograph shown in the following illustration, the histogram tells us things that are not apparent from looking at the image. Because the image is of a white subject taken against a dark background, most of the pixels are in the shadows area (far left). There are no midtones, and the highlights are the areas that contain the detail information. The purpose of the histogram is to provide a general overview of the image contents. From this one we learn there is no detail in the shadow area that can be recovered through image correction because it is all one shade of black and has no midtones. Even though the photograph is predominately dark, this is referred to as a *high-key* image because the details (the part we actually want to see) are in the highlights. This information in the highlights is very close to the high end of the spectrum (approaching paper white), so when adjusting the picture, it's necessary to move that range down in order to get all of the detail in the flower.

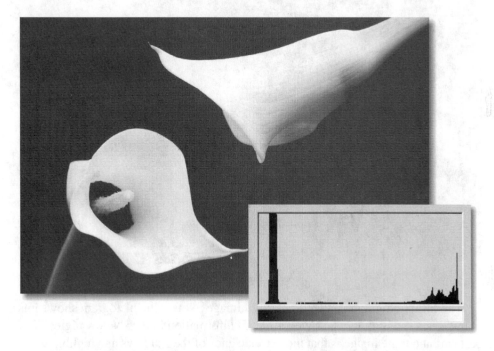

The next photograph and its histogram show that most of the information in the image is concentrated in the highlights. The reason the histogram doesn't show any midtones or shadows is because the display is adjusted so most of the image content is displayed. Since there is so much in the highlights, the midtones and shadows are there but in such small quantities they don't show up on this scale of graph. When planning a strategy for this type of image, you will have a problem. If you make the wall dark enough to pick up the detail in it, you will push everything in the shadows into solid black. Any image with extreme contrasts is a challenge.

The last photograph is a well-balanced image. Notice the histogram shows lots of midtones and highlights, as well as detail information in the shadow region. The best part about the image is that the extreme ends of the shadows and highlights are not clipped off. This is because they aren't concentrated at either end of the histogram.

9

Another thing histograms show is the quality of a scan. If the shadows or highlights are badly clipped, it was either a poor scan or a cheap scanner. We can also see if an image has already been manipulated. The histogram in the following illustration is the same one previously shown, after the output range was compressed using the Level Equalization tool. The spikes you see are normal after such a compression because when the image is compressed, the adjacent shades of pixels are pushed on top of one another. This increases the number of pixels in certain shades, which are represented by the spikes. The truth is, after you have applied tonal correction to an image, the histogram can begin to look downright ugly, which is fine. It's only a guide.

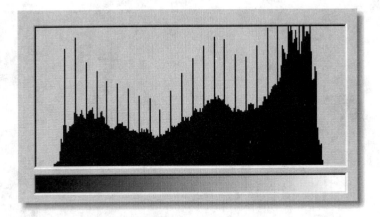

The Numerical Side of Histograms

Before we leave the subject of histograms, it is time to show you the entire display. I have not done this until now because I find most people are a little overwhelmed by the vast array of numbers that are associated with it. Figure 9-2 shows the entire display. Not many of the numbers will benefit you in the area of image correction, but there are a few you might find helpful or at least interesting.

Range

The Range section shows the Start and End points. These values are related to the *Percent* setting. You can click and drag your cursor over the histogram display to view the Percentage value (percentage of the histogram selected) and the tonal range of the selected area.

The Mean value is the average brightness of the image. The first photograph of the two flowers against the black background has a Mean value of 67 out of 255 (because it is a predominately dark photograph).

Std. Dev. is *standard deviation,* which represents numerically how widely the brightness values vary.

The Pixels value is the total number of pixels in the image. Aren't you glad you know that?

Individual

The Individual section reads the value of the cursor when it is positioned in the histogram and reflects the brightness value and the total number of pixels at that brightness value. For example, in Figure 9-2 the cursor was last at the shade value of 198, and there were a total of 1695 pixels of that brightness throughout the image.

Clipping

The Clipping section reminds me of judging at sports events where they throw out the high and low scores. Clipping removes a percentage of the extreme shadows and highlights.

Tools for Image Correction

PHOTO-PAINT provides two different types of image-correction tools: *linear* and *non-linear.* Don't go looking for them under those names because they're not listed as such.

Linear Correction Tools

The linear correction tools are probably familiar to you. They are Brightness-Contrast-Intensity, located in the Image menu under Adjust. They are called *linear*

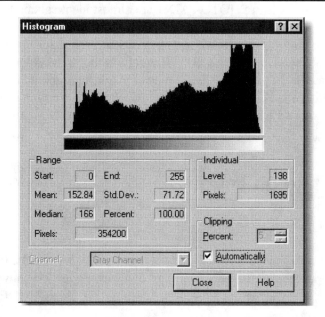

The entire Histogram dialog box with all of its amazing numbers

FIGURE 9-2

tools because they do exactly the same thing to every pixel in the image. This means that pixels are lost at one or both ends of the tonal range. For example, the Brightness control (-100 to 100) shifts all of the pixel values up or down the tonal range. If you were to increase the brightness by 10, PHOTO-PAINT adds 10 to the brightness value of every pixel. The pixels at 150 become 160, those at 200 become 210, those at 245 become 255, and those at 250 become 255 because you can't go above 255. This produces a clipping of the highlights. The Contrast control stretches the tonal range when you increase contrast, which effectively throws away image information. Does this mean these controls are bad? Not really, but I strongly recommend very moderate use of them. Once you learn how to use the non-linear tools—Level Equalize and Tone Curves—I doubt you will ever use Brightness-Contrast-Intensity again.

Non-Linear Correction Tools

These are the tools that you may have opened up, taken a good look at the dialog box, and immediately closed it again thinking that someday you would learn how to use them. We are going to learn how to use some of them in this book. It takes an entire book to learn all about what these and the other tools do. In fact, if you want to learn all of the things you can do with these tools, I highly recommend the book *Real World Photoshop 3* by David Blatner and Bruce Fraser. Even though it covers Photoshop, the tools in PHOTO-PAINT are almost identical and the principles are the same.

The two non-linear tools we use for grayscale and color image correction are Level Equalization and Tone Curve. Both are found in the Adjust category of the Image menu. Both change the distribution of pixels throughout the tonal range in an image. Rather than describe them in great detail, we are going to use them in a hands-on exercise to correct an image that Corel was kind enough to include on the CD.

Correcting an Image

In this hands-on exercise, we are going to take an overexposed, dirty photo and make it ready for publication.

1. Open the image \PHOTOS\PORTRAIT\570033.WI in the CD-ROM. Resample the image to a width of 6 inches. Figure 9-3 shows the starting photo. Using the Save As command, save the file as MODEL.CPT.

The original photo is in need of image correction

FIGURE 9-3

2. From the Image menu, select Histogram, opening the display shown in Figure 9-4. Looking at the histogram we see three areas of concentration. In the shadow region are the dark colors of the sweater vest. The upper end of the midtones contains most of the colors of the model, and the large number of pixels in the highlight area are the very bright background. Although we will eventually remove the background, we first need to shift the center of the curve that contains the details of the model more toward the middle. Since such a shift will shove all of the detail information in the sweater into black, we must first isolate it.

3. Select the Magic Wand mask tool from the Mask Tool flyout in the Toolbox. Ensure that the Tolerance setting is 10 on the Property bar and the Normal button is selected. Click the Additive button on the Property bar.

4. Place the cursor in the image and click inside on one side of the sweater vest. Click on the other side of the vest. Click the Grow button on the Property bar. The mask should cover the entire vest. Click the Invert Mask button. At this point the vest is protected.

9

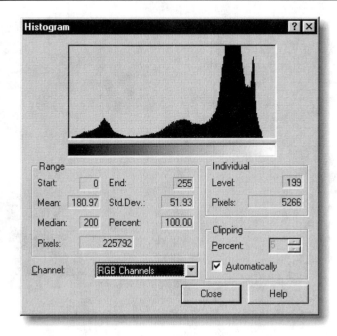

The
histogram
of the
original
photograph

FIGURE 9-4

5. From the Image menu, select Adjust and choose Level Equalize. A rather intimidating dialog box opens. Notice the histogram displayed in the dialog box is different from the one shown in Figure 9-4. This is because the sweater vest has been isolated from the image by the mask, and its pixels are no longer included in the histogram. Move the Gamma Adjustment slider to the left until it reads .72. The histogram displays an approximation of what the new histogram will look like after the Gamma adjustment is applied. The dialog box is shown in Figure 9-5. Click OK to apply.

6. The image now looks much less underexposed but the model has a bluish cast. From the Image menu, choose Adjust and select Color Tone. When the dialog box opens (Figure 9-6), move the position of the model in the preview window so you can see his face. Change the Step value to 6 and click Saturate one time. By increasing the saturation by a small percentage, we increase the overall color in his face. These changes are subtle but necessary. Click OK to apply. Next, we will apply a hue shift to one of the individual channels.

The Level Equalization dialog box after the Gamma adjustment is made

FIGURE 9-5

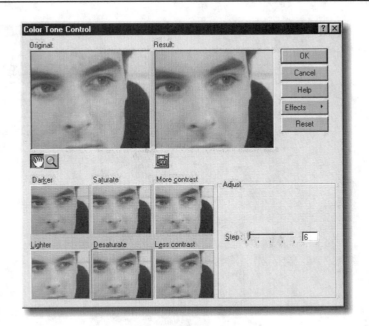

The Color Tone Control dialog box provides a highly visual method to adjust color in an image

FIGURE 9-6

9

7. From the Image menu, choose Adjust and select Color Hue. When the
dialog box opens (Figure 9-7), move the position of the model in the
preview window so you can see his face. Since most of his features are in
the midtones and highlights region, we will only apply the hue adjustment
to that region, so uncheck the Shadows box. Uncheck the Preserve
luminance box, too. Click the More yellow box one time and click
the OK button. The result is shown in Figure 9-8.

8. Save the file as MODEL1.CPT.

TIP: *Did you notice that Color Tone and Color Hue didn't have Undo
buttons? By clicking the opposite function, you can undo it. For example,
to undo a click of the Saturate, click the Desaturate.*

To Complete the Job...

There are some things that should be done to this photograph that are not tonal
correction. At this point our photograph no longer looks like an overexposed image

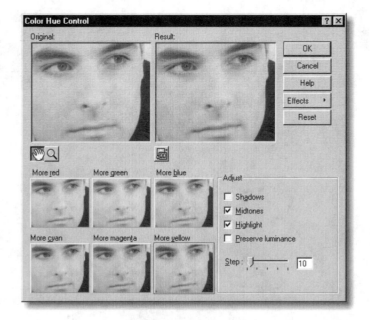

The
Color Hue
Control
dialog box
allows for
the fine
tuning of
each color
channel

FIGURE 9-7

Our
overexposed
photograph
now looks a
little more
normal

FIGURE 9-8

of a well-dressed cadaver. We have preserved the detail in the sweater vest. To finish the job, I recommend the following:

1. Use the Clone Tool to remove all of the debris on the photograph. The use of this tool is explored in Chapter 11.

2. Add to the existing mask to include the rest of the model (excluding the background). I recommend clicking the Magic Wand tool around his head, but when you get to his shirt, change the Tolerance to 5. There is a real tendency for the mask to break out into the background on the left side of the image.

3. After you have finished masking the model, apply Smooth at a Radius of 5, located in the Mask menu under Shape.

4. Invert the mask so only the background is selected. Select Fill from the Edit menu and from the Fountain fill, choose a fill like a Circular Green or Blue preset. Make sure it is a light color and apply it to the background.

5. Invert the mask again with only the model selected. From the Effects menu, select Sharpen and choose Directional Sharpen. Apply at 100%.

The Tone Curve Exercise

The Tone Curve command performs the same image correction that we accomplished with the previous exercise. The difference between the two is the degree of control that the Tone Curve offers. With the Tone Curve you can map individual tonal ranges that remap small portions of the tonal range. The following is a brief demonstration of the Tone Curve and an effect mentioned earlier.

1. Open the file MODEL.CPT (the one we saved earlier).

2. Select Adjust from the Image menu and choose the Tone Curve. This opens the Tone Curve dialog box, shown in Figure 9-9. Click the Load button. When the dialog box opens, select NEGGAMMA.MAP and click Open. Move the slider to the right until you get to the value of .72. Click the OK button.

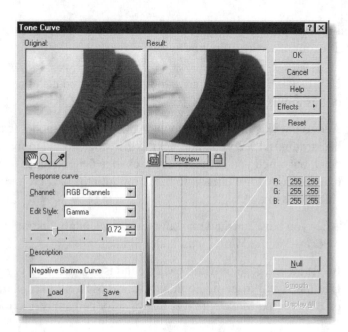

The Tone Curve dialog box

FIGURE 9-9

3. This applies the same gamma value as in the previous exercise. Look at the sweater. All of the detail has been lost, and the sweater has turned nearly solid black.

4. Undo the last command (CTRL+Z). Open the Tone Curve dialog box again (CTRL+T). This time, experiment by loading different settings. You can modify the curve by placing the cursor at a place on the curve, clicking, and dragging it. You will see the result immediately (well, almost) if the Auto preview button (looks like a lock next to the Preview button) is enabled. To reset the curve to a straight line, click the Null button. Class is over, click Cancel, close the file, and don't save any changes.

Other Tools

There are other tools available under Adjust, as follows.

Gamma   This allows you to quickly adjust only the Gamma without any other options.

Color Balance   This offers the same capability as Color Hue. Its only advantage is that you can apply all three effects without the delay of the automatic preview. Between the two, I like the interactive preview of the Color Hue. Likewise Hue-Saturation-Lightness does the same as Color Tone.

Auto Equalize   This is applied immediately and has no dialog box. It stretches the image's tonal information across the entire tonal range of 256 shades. The results are sometimes interesting. I recommend applying it at the beginning of work on an image, because you can never tell what the effect will be on any particular image. There have been several occasions when the application of Auto Equalize did the trick and no other correction was necessary.

Desaturate   This takes all of the colors in the pixels to a -100 percent setting. In this state the image looks like a grayscale. A popular way to emphasize an area or a subject in a photo is to leave the object you want to emphasize in color and apply Desaturate to the rest of the image.

Using the Desaturate Filter

Although this is a chapter about image correction, this hands-on exercise will allow you to quickly demonstrate a technique using the Desaturate file.

1. Open the file \PHOTOS\PEOPLE \677061.WI on the CD. Resample to a Width of 7 inches and click the OK button.

2. Select the Lasso Mask tool from the Mask Tools flyout in the Toolbox. Set the Tolerance on the Property bar to 20. Begin by clicking on the background and making a shape that includes the top portion of the bottle. Drag the horizontal bottom of the mask between the "S" and "h" of the word "Shampoo." The object is to use the Lasso Mask to create a tight mask around the top of the bottle.

3. Click the Additive mode button on the Property bar. Turn off the Mask marquee. If you want to see what is and is not included in the mask, use the Mask Overlay. The Mask marquee can be very distracting when working with masks like these.

4. Select the Freehand Mask tool from the Mask flyout in the Toolbox. Click on the edge of the bottle and begin to click at every point that encloses the bottle. Continue until you have enclosed the rest of the bottle with a mask.

5. Click the Mask Invert button.

6. From the Image menu, choose Adjust and select Desaturate. The result is shown in the color insert page.

PhotoLab

One of the new features in PHOTO-PAINT 7 was the addition of the PhotoLab filters created by CSI. PhotoLab consists of eight filters that are located in the Effects menu under PhotoLab. These filters are designed for use by professional photographers and prepress specialists. They are designed to bring out the maximum potential in your image by controlling and manipulating exposure, contrast, and color casts. Included are powerful controls for color negative reversal and special effects such as accurate sepia tones, infrared simulations and flexible noise generation.

Describing the operation of this software would take several chapters in itself. Fortunately, Corel has provided a copy of the CSI PhotoLab user's manual in the DOCUMENT\PLUGINS\PHOTOLAB folder of the PHOTO-PAINT CD-ROM. This is in Envoy format, so you will need to install the Envoy viewer that came with your Corel software to read it.

NOTE: *The PhotoLab Envoy file that shipped with the original release of CorelDRAW 7 has a minor corruption in it. Check with the CorelPHOTO-PAINT FTP site for an updated copy.*

Intellihance

Another plug-in filter provided by Corel, Intellihance improves the way digital images appear in print or on the screen by "intelligently analyzing each image's needs and then automatically applying filters to optimize contrast, brightness, saturation, sharpness and despeckle." That's straight from the horse's mouth…the user's manual. Located in the Effects menu under Intellihance, this set of filters is handy for providing quick fixes for images. The default settings for each type of image are effective much of the time.

Those who want to change the settings for these filters can refer to the user's manual, which, as with PhotoLab, is also in the DOCUMENT\PLUGINS\ INTELLIH folder of the PHOTO-PAINT CD-ROM. Again, this is in Envoy format, so you will need to install the Envoy viewer that came with your Corel software to read it.

TIP: *If you cannot find the PhotoLab or Intellihance filters in the Effects menu, you will need to install them. Refer to Chapter 14 for instructions.*

The Lenses

This is what puts the plus in PHOTO-PAINT Plus. Available only in the PHOTO-PAINT Plus release, a *lens* is an object that covers the entire image or a section of the image. You use a lens to try out various color or tonal corrections on your images.

There are 12 different lenses to choose from, each corresponding to an Image menu command found in either the Adjust or Transform flyout. In the previous hands-on exercise with the model, we applied the Level Equalize filter to the image. With a lens we can apply the Level Equalize setting to the lens and see the effect of the equalization through the lens.

The difference between applying a lens and using the Level Equalization command in the Image menu is that the lens does not modify the pixels in the image, whereas the Image menu command does. The lens is between you and the image pixels and shows you the result of the Equalization attributes you have selected. You can move the lens to see how the pixels in another area of your image look with the correction applied. Lenses that you use on an image are listed in the Objects roll-up just like any other object.

Using the Lens

The following hands-on exercise will show you how to create, modify, and apply a lens.

1. Open the file MODEL.CPT that was saved at the beginning of an earlier exercise at the beginning of this chapter.

2. Select the Circle Mask tool. Holding down the CTRL key, drag a circle mask over the image that covers the model's head.

3. From the Object menu, choose Create Lens from Mask. This opens the New Lens dialog box, shown in Figure 9-10. Select Level Equalization and click OK.

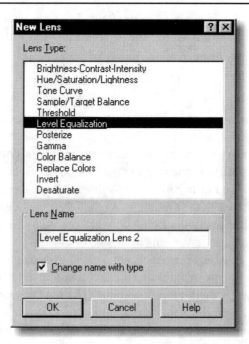

PHOTO-PAINT offers 12 different lenses to work with

■ FIGURE 9-10

4. When the dialog box opens, you will notice that the photograph is slightly different from the original we saw in the previous exercises. All of the controls are present except for the preview window because the image becomes the preview. Move the dialog box off of the image, if it is covering it, and move the Gamma Adjustment slider to .72. Watch the image change interactively as you move the slider. Click OK.

5. Use the Object Picker tool to move the lens around the image. As you do, the area viewed through the lens reflects the Gamma changes made by the filter.

6. Duplicate the Lens (CTRL+SHIFT+D). From the Objects roll-up, select the top lens. Ensure the bottom lens is deselected. From the Object menu, select Lens Properties.

7. When the Level Equalization dialog box opens, click the Lens button. This opens the New Lens dialog box. Choose Color Balance. In the Range portion of the dialog box, deselect the Shadows and Highlights. Enter 6 in the Magenta-Green channel. Click OK.

8. Now the two Lenses act together. From the Objects roll-up, select both lenses and click the Group button on the Property bar. The action of the resulting Lens is shown in Figure 9-11.

9. Close the file and don't save any changes.

Creating lenses

From the previous exercise, we learned we can create a lens from a mask. Actually, lenses can also be created from scratch using the New Lens command in the Object menu. This command creates a lens object that covers the entire image. However, you can edit the size and shape of the lens just as you would any other object.

The type of image you apply the lens to determines which lens types are available. For example, if you are working with a grayscale image, the Replace Color lens type is not available because the image consists only of different shades of gray.

The Create Lens from Mask command creates a lens that has the precise shape and size of the mask in the Image Window. When you create a new lens, you can assign a descriptive name to it in the New Lens dialog box.

You can create as many lenses as you need in an image. When you create a lens, it appears in the Objects roll-up at the top of the stacking order because it is on top of the image background. The name assigned to the lens in the roll-up is either the

Using the Lens feature allows selective preview and application of 12 different lens properties.

FIGURE 9-11

one you assigned to it in the New Lens dialog box, or the lens type. A number appears at the end of the lens' name in case you create more than one lens of the same type in a single image.

You can use the Objects roll-up to change the position of lenses in the stacking order, to hide or delete them, and to change their name. You can change the properties of a lens by selecting Lens Properties in the Objects roll-up.

When you are satisfied with result of the selected lens, you can apply it by selecting the lens and choosing Combine in the Objects roll-up. If the lens is not combined with the background, it will not have any effect on the output of the file. Only those lenses that are combined will cause changes in the printed output.

NOTE: *Lenses can be Grouped together but they cannot be Combined together as objects can.*

Lenses can be used for both previewing and applying different Transform and Adjust functions.

10

Exploring Corel
PHOTO-PAINT's
Brush Tools

By definition, PHOTO-PAINT's brush tools are classified as any effect applied with a brush. The Paint, Clone, Image Sprayer, Effect, Local Undo, Mask Brush, and Object Transparency tools are all brush tools in the Toolbox. In this chapter we will explore the Paint and Effect tools and their variations, some of which you have already seen in other chapters. While the purpose of each tool differs, all of them can be customized using the Property bars, Tool settings, and Nib roll-ups. Before discussing individual types of brushes, we will look first at the common features.

The Paint tool paints an area characteristic of the type of brush selected using the current Paint Color. Remember that the Paint tool's brushes replace (not cover) pixels with the currently selected Paint (foreground) color.

Selecting and Configuring Brush Tools

Once you've chosen one of these tools from the Toolbox, selection of a tool is accomplished by clicking its icon button from the Property bar or selecting it from the Tool Settings roll-up. You can vary the effect any tool has by changing the brush settings and using different paint modes. All of the brush tools are configured through the Tool Settings roll-up. Many, but not all, of the same Tool settings can be changed through the Property bar. Figure 10-1 shows the Tool Settings roll-up, the Property bar, and the associated menus and drop-down lists. The Tool Settings roll-up for most of the brush tools contain three tabs, each dealing with different qualities of the brush. The first tab offers a selection of preset brush types. You can customize any preset brush or create an entirely new brush that specifically suits your needs.

Parts of a Brush

Each brush type is a combination of different settings in the Tool Settings roll-up. The size and shape of the brush stroke is determined by the size and shape of the selected nib. A *nib* is the tip of the brush you use to apply effects with any of the brush tools. Brush nibs can be selected from several

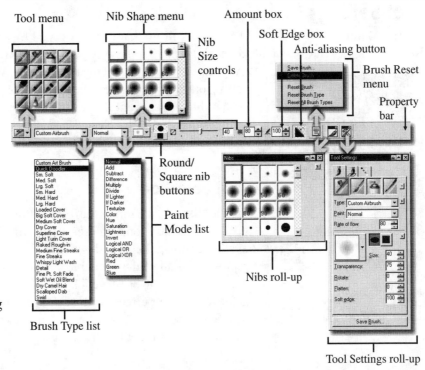

Tool menu **Nib Shape menu** **Amount box**

Soft Edge box

Nib Size controls

Anti-aliasing button

Brush Reset menu

Property bar

Round/ Square nib buttons

Paint Mode list

Nibs roll-up

Brush Type list

Customizing the Paint tools—plus much more

Tool Settings roll-up

■ **FIGURE 10-1**

different locations. The Nibs roll-up shown in Figure 10-1 actually contains a large number of presets (122) you can choose from to suit the style of brush you want. The size of the Nibs roll-up can be expanded by clicking and grabbing the edges until it reaches its maximum display area of 96 nibs. Clicking the Nib Shape button on the Property bar or the Tool Settings roll-up opens a smaller selection initially displaying 16 nibs. Its size is fixed. You can access all of the nibs by using the scroll bars. You can also customize any existing nib in the Tool Settings roll-up or create one from a mask for any of the brush tools. Any nib that has been created or customized can be saved. Once a nib has been saved, it appears at the bottom of the nib selection list.

10

Tool Settings Roll-Up

There are three tabs on the Tool Settings roll-up that can be opened by selecting Roll-Ups in the View menu and choosing Tool Settings, by pressing CTRL+F8, or

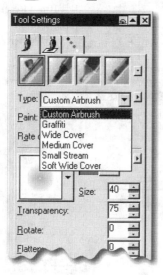

by double-clicking one of the tool buttons. With the roll-up open, you can select the brush preset and the type of brush you want. For example, here you see the Custom Airbrush selected and the six presets from the Type list.

Tool Selection

On the first tab, the top of the Tool Settings roll-up displays the last four brushes used. To view all available tools, click the down arrow to see icons representing all of the available choices, as shown here. To select a brush, click its icon. You can achieve different effects with each brush by using different types (available in the Type box), or by customizing different brush settings.

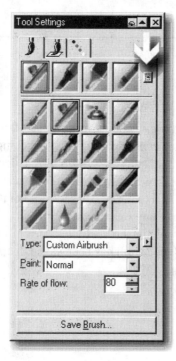

Type

This setting contains all of the saved brush styles for the selected tool. Many of these preset styles have names that indicate how they operate; you can see examples of them in the Tool Settings dialog box.

Brush Reset

In the Tool Settings box shown here, the arrow (pointing outward) to the right of the Type box opens a menu that allows you to reset the brushes to their default values. You can reset a single brush—i.e., a brush type—or all of the brush types. This is really handy when you have been making all kinds of changes to the tools and need to return them to their original values. You can open a similar menu by clicking the Brush Reset Option button on the Property bar, which is not available with all tools. The only extra item on this menu is the Save Brush command.

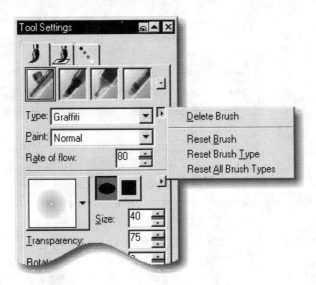

Paint

This setting determines the way the paint pixels are applied to the image. There are up to 20 different modes. The Paint Mode button on the Property bar offers the same selection of Paint modes (see Figure 10-1). Table 10-1 explains how these modes

Paint Mode	Method Used for Altering Color
Normal	Replaces the paint color with the base color. This is the default mode.
Add	Adds the values of the paint and base colors. Tends to make images brighter.
Subtract	Adds the values of the paint and base colors, then subtracts 255, generally creating a darker image.
Difference	Subtracts the paint color from the base color, then multiplies the result by 255. If the paint value is 0 (black), the result will always be 255 (white). It seems as if the result would always be white, but the result is usually a color shift.
Multiply	Multiplies the base color by the paint color, then divides the result by 255. Has a darkening effect unless you are painting on white. Multiplying black with any color results in black. Multiplying white with any color leaves the color unchanged. This mode can be very handy for pasting objects that have white areas (which often become invisible).
Divide	Divides the base color by the paint color, or vice versa, depending on which color has a higher value. Results are unpredictable and rarely useable.
If Lighter	Replaces any pixels in the base image that are a darker color than the paint color. Pixels in the base image that are lighter than the paint color are not affected.
If Darker	Replaces any pixels in the base image that are a lighter color than the paint color. Pixels in the base image that are darker than the paint color are not affected.
Texturize	Converts the paint color to grayscale, then multiplies the grayscale value by the base color.
Color	Combines the lightness of the base color with the hue and saturation of the paint color. This mode is the opposite of Lightness mode.

Paint Modes

TABLE 10-1

Paint Mode	Method Used for Altering Color
Hue	Combines the hue of the paint color with the saturation and lightnesss of the base color. If you are painting on a grayscale image, there will be no change, because the colors are desaturated.
Saturation	Combines the lightness and hue of the base color with the saturation of the paint color.
Lightness	Combines the hue and saturation of the base color with the lightness of the paint color. This mode is the opposite of Color mode.
Invert	Displays the paint color's complementary color, so the result appears as a negative of the original.
Logical AND*	Converts the paint and base colors to binary values, then applies the Boolean algebraic formula AND to those values.
Logical OR*	Converts the paint and base colors to binary values, then applies the Boolean algebraic formula OR to those values.
Logical XOR*	Converts the paint and base colors to binary values, then applies the Boolean algebraic formula XOR to those values.
Red*	Applies the paint color to the red channel of RGB images.
Green	Applies the paint color to the green channel of RGB images.
Blue*	Applies the paint color to the blue channel of RGB images.
Cyan*	Creates a result color by applying the paint color to the cyan channel of CMYK images.
Yellow*	Applies the paint color to the yellow channel of CMYK images.
Magenta*	Applies the paint color to the magenta channel of CMYK images.
Black*	Applies the paint color to the black channel of CMYK images.

Paint Modes
(*continued*)

TABLE 10-1

work. You'll find examples of some of them in the color insert at the center of the book. (Those paint modes with asterisks next to their names do not appear in the insert.)

Rate of Flow

This setting is only available on the Airbrush and Spray Can category of brush tools. Rate of Flow controls the rate at which the effect or paint is applied to the image, ranging from 1 to 100. A higher value results in a more pronounced effect or heavier application of paint. It controls the amount of the paint applied over time. If you have a low setting and place the tool over a spot and hold it there without moving the brush, the area will continue to have the effect applied at the rate set by this setting. This setting is called Amount on the Property bar; it replaces the Transparency setting on the Property bar when either the Airbrush or Spray Can tool is selected.

Shape Buttons

These determine the shape of the nib. The two basic shapes selectable by a button are Oval and Square. In addition to the two basic shapes, you can choose an existing nib from the Nib Shape box, which offers a large selection of different sizes and shapes. In addition to the size and shape of the selected nib, the custom preview area shows other characteristics of the nib. For example, if a nib has a high transparency setting or a soft edge, the preview area will reflect it in the nib that is displayed.

Size

This setting allows adjustment of Round or Square paintbrush sizes from 0 to 999 pixels. The size of nibs selected is shown by red text in the corner of the display for nibs whose size is greater than 30 pixels. The nib size can also be adjusted by moving the Nib Size slider or entering a value in the Nib Size box on the Property bar.

NOTE: *In earlier versions of PHOTO-PAINT, the size of the Custom brush was not adjustable. Now all of the brushes can have their size changed.*

Transparency

This setting (range 0-99) sets the level of transparency of the brush stroke. The higher the setting, the more transparent the brush stroke. At a high setting, the color acts like a tint. A setting of 0 has no transparency, whereas a setting of 99 makes the brush stroke almost invisible regardless of any other settings. The availability of the Transparency setting on the Property bar depends on the tool selected.

Rotate

This setting (range 0-360 degrees) rotates the nib by the amount entered. You can see the effect of the rotating in the preview window as the change is being applied. The Rotate setting is not available in the default configuration of the Property bar for all tools.

Flatten

The Flatten setting (range 0-99 percent) controls the height of the nibs. Flatten values are expressed as a percentage of nib height. You can see the effect of the flattening in the preview window as the change is being applied. Using combinations of the Rotate and Flatten settings allows you to create nibs for making calligraphic strokes, among other things.

Soft Edge

This determines the amount of transparency at the edges of the nib. Large settings produce soft edges, which make the brush stroke the least dense at the edges. Low settings produce hard edges that are dense up to the edge, with little to no softening, depending on the nib size and other brush settings. The preview box displays the softness of the nib selected.

Save Brush

This saves any customization made to a brush setting. Clicking the Save Brush button opens the Save Brush dialog box, shown here. Entering a name and clicking the OK button saves all of the current brush's settings in the Type list for the currently selected tool. The name will only appear in the Type box for the tool under which it was saved. This command is available as Save Brush in the Brush Reset Options button on the Property bar.

10

Controlling Texture, Watercolors and Brush Stroke Settings

The second tab, shown here, controls the Texture, Watercolors, and Brush Stroke settings. This tab has the greatest impact on any painterly effects produced by the brush strokes. Painterly effects are brush strokes that appear to be made by natural media tools like pastels, oils, etc. The controls on this tab are not available for the Image Sprayer, Mask Brush, Local Undo, and Object Transparency brush tools.

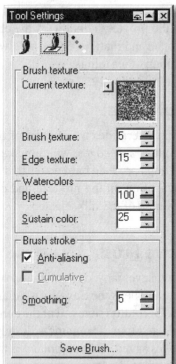

Brush Texture

Brush texture uses a bitmap texture to cause the paint color or effect to be applied in an uneven pattern so that it simulates the patterning exhibited by application of materials, like pastels or chalk over rough media. The setting has a range of 0-100. A setting of 0 produces no effect regardless of the texture pattern that is loaded. A setting of 100 produces a rough texture when the brush tool is applied. Figure 10-2 shows a sample of six different textures of the ten that are provided with Corel PHOTO-PAINT.

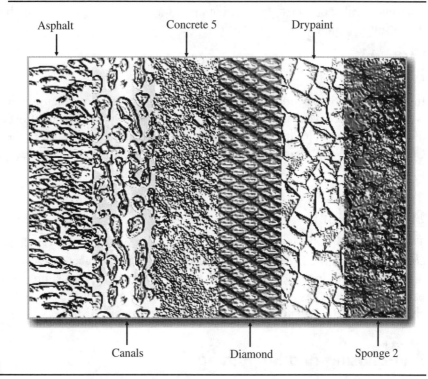

Asphalt   Concrete 5   Drypaint

Samples of
several
of the
available
brush
textures

Canals   Diamond   Sponge 2

FIGURE 10-2

To load a different texture, click the left-pointing arrow and select Load A Texture from the menu. By default, the COREL\DRAW70\PHOTOPNT\BRUSHTXR folder contains ten texture files. Select a drive and folder in the Look in list box, and double-click the texture filename to load it.

TIP: *The best images to use for brush textures possess high contrast. The dark areas apply paint and the light areas don't.*

Edge Texture

This works like Brush texture, except it controls the amount of "texture" (0-100) that is applied to the edge of the stroke. Edge texture displays the current edge texture setting, which controls the amount of texture applied to the edges of your brush stroke. Edge texture is only apparent if the nib has a soft edge. To adjust this setting,

10

type a new value or adjust the existing one using the scroll arrows. A higher value will result in a more pronounced effect.

Bleed

In the Watercolors section, the Bleed setting determines how many pixels in the image are affected when the brush is dragged across them. The Bleed setting controls the application of color throughout the brush stroke in conjunction with the Sustain Color control. With a range from 0-100, 100 produces the greatest effect, while 0 produces none.

Sustain Color

This setting controls the application of color throughout the brush stroke in conjunction with the Bleed control. A brush stroke with a bleed value will, during the course of an extended brush stroke, run out of paint and simply smear the background colors (as though you were painting with a wet brush). With Sustain color, traces of the Paint Color remain throughout the brush stroke.

Anti-aliasing and Smoothing

Enabling Anti-aliasing produces smooth-looking curved or diagonal edges when you use this tool and prevents jagged edges from appearing. In combination with the Anti-aliasing checkbox, the Smoothing setting determines the smoothness of the brush stroke. Both of these controls determine how faithfully the brush strokes follow the mouse/stylus movements. Without Anti-aliasing and Smoothing, the lines will appear to be very jagged. Apply too much smoothness and any sharp corners in the line become smoothed out, inaccurately representing the brush stroke that created them.

Cumulative

Only available when using the Clone tool and the Effect tools, this option, when enabled, makes the effects of brush strokes cumulative. It should be disabled if you want each brush stroke not to exceed the maximum effect. For example, if you are applying a tint to an area and wish it to appear uniform, you should disable the cumulative option.

Dab Variation and Color Variation

The third tab is divided into two parts, Dab variation and Color variation, as you can see here. This tab controls the number of dabs as well as the spacing, spread, and fade-out effects when any of the brush tools are applied.

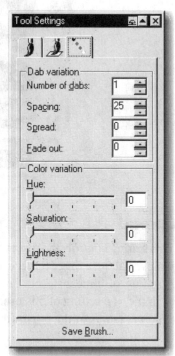

Number of Dabs

A brush stroke is composed of a number of dabs. The Number of dabs setting determines the number of dabs created during a brush stroke. This value, and the Spacing value, can have a significant effect on the speed at which your computer creates a brush stroke. It is recommended that you keep the number of dabs low and the spacing as high as practical to achieve the effect you require. The Spread and Spacing controls let you specify the layout of the dabs along the brush stroke.

Spacing

This sets the distance, in pixels, between applications of the brush. To create a brush stroke, the pointing device draws a line across the image. At a frequency determined by the Spacing setting, the brush is applied to the line. For example, if a brush stroke is made with a Spacing setting of 5 (pixels), Corel PHOTO-PAINT will produce the selected brush on the image area at a spacing of every 5 pixels. While it may seem that a setting of 1 would be desired, a lower setting slows down the generation of the brush stroke considerably. It can be really slow on some systems. This is especially true when using a large nib (greater than 70). When a large brush is being used, the Spacing setting can be larger (and this is recommended) because of the overlap caused by the larger brush. Here you can see the effect of a number of brush strokes at different Spacing settings.

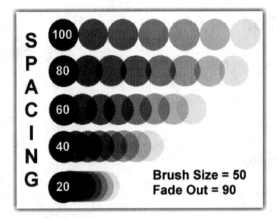

Spread

This setting controls the distance between dabs along the width of a brush stroke as
it moves along a line. Higher values make the distance between stroke lines greater.
A setting of 0 means each dab will be placed on the line of the brush stroke. For
example, if a setting of 5 is used, each dab of the brush stroke will be placed within
a 5 pixel radius of the brush stroke.

Fade Out

This setting determines the length of the
brush stroke before it fades entirely by
adjusting the rate at which the brush
stroke disappears. This is similar to
adjusting the pressure of the brush
against the canvas as the paint is
applied. The greater the Fade Out value,
the quicker the fade-out of the brush
stroke occurs, as shown here. As the
Fade Out value decreases, the amount
of fade-out applied to the brush stroke
diminishes; a value of 0 turns off the
Fade Out function completely.

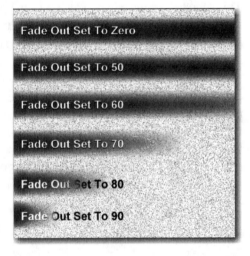

Fade Out works by counting the number of brush applications to determine when to begin applying the gradual fade-out function. This is important because spacing controls the distance between brush applications, and increasing spacing between brush applications increases the distance that the brush stroke will go before Fade Out begins.

With a steady hand it is theoretically possible to maintain a straight line with a brush tool but it is very difficult. Fortunately, Corel provides some features that allow you to create straight lines with any of the brush tools.

Constraining and Automating the Brush Tools

Use the CTRL key to constrain the tool to a vertical or horizontal direction. Pressing the SHIFT key changes the direction of constraint. You can automatically apply the Effect tool along a straight line between two points by clicking the brush at the beginning of a line and holding down the ALT key and clicking at the end of the line. The Effect tool will be applied between the two points automatically. Holding down the CTRL key while using automatic brush stroke application applies the line along either the horizontal or vertical.

The Paint Tools

The Paint tools are the virtual equivalent of a fully stocked artist's studio, but with the advantages of being able to work around things like the law of gravity. Choose from a wide selection of brush tools, such as watercolor, oil pastel, felt markers, chalk, crayons, several types of pens and pencils, spraypaint, and an artistic brush with a wide variety of settings. Each of the preset paint tools has a number of variations built in, and you can customize any aspect to suit your specific needs. Many of the tools are very similar in their appearance and purpose. For example, the Airbrush and the Spray Can are different brush tools but are very similar in the brush strokes they produce. In the following section is a brief description of the Paint tools and examples of the brush strokes they produce. For some of the Paint tools, I have included hands-on exercises.

NOTE: *The names of some of the brushes may seem, at times, inconsistent. For example, if you select the Pastel tool, it will say Oil Pastel. That is the first of several choices. I have named each tool according to its overall description rather than the name associated with the default brush type.*

Paintbrush Tool

The Paintbrush tool offers a wide selection of types. These types are also available with some of the other tools. I am not an artist, so I do very little original work with this tool. It is a great way to add texture to objects. The following hands-on exercise teaches how to create a wood texture using the Paintbrush tool.

Creating a Wood Texture

Even with the addition of a new program, Corel TEXTURE, this technique offers a quick way to make a texture that looks remarkably like real wood.

1. Create a new file that is 6 × 4 inches, 24-bit color at 72 dpi.

2. Click the color gold in the onscreen palette with the left mouse button, changing the Paint Color. Click the Text tool button in the Toolbox and click inside the image area. Change the font to Kabel Ult BT. Change the size to 96, centered, and inter-line spacing to 70.

3. Enter the text **CUSTOM WOOD WORKING**, as shown in Figure 10-3. Click the Object Picker tool. Move the text to the center of the image. Open the Objects roll-up (CTRL+F7) and click the Single button.

4. Click the Paintbrush tool button and in Type:, select Medium Fine Streaks. In Paint:, choose Logical AND. The Type: setting will change to Custom Art Brush. Click the color brown in the onscreen palette.

5. Click inside the image at the point to the upper-left of the word CUSTOM as indicated by the left arrow in Figure 10-3. Hold down the ALT key and click at the point indicated by the right arrow. Holding down the ALT key causes a straight line to be applied between the two points. Click again on the left side, moving the position of the cursor down approximately the width of the cursor, and repeat the procedure. Continue to do this until the brush strokes cover all of the text.

6. Click the Object Picker tool. In the Objects roll-up, click the Layer button.

7. From the Effects menu, select 3D Effects and choose Emboss. When the Emboss dialog box opens, click the Reset button and then change the Emboss color to Original color. Click the OK button. The resulting image should look like Figure 10-4.

Text for the woodwork example, showing start and ending points for the Paintbrush tool

FIGURE 10-3

It almost looks like wood after embossing

FIGURE 10-4

10

8. In the Objects roll-up, select the Single button. In the Object menu, choose Drop Shadow and change the Offset to bottom-left, Horizontal and Vertical to 0.05, Direction to Average, Feather to 10, and Opacity to 75. Click the OK button.

9. In the Objects roll-up, select the background by clicking between the Eye icon and the word background. This places a pencil icon. From the Edit menu, choose Fill. When the Edit Fill & Transparency dialog box opens, click the Bitmap Fill button and then click the Edit button. From the Bitmap Fill dialog box, click the Load button. On the Corel CD-ROM, locate and select the file \TILES\WOOD\LARGE\WOOD27L.CPT. Click the OK button three times to close all of the dialog boxes. The result is shown in Figure 10-5.

10. Close the file and do not save any changes when asked.

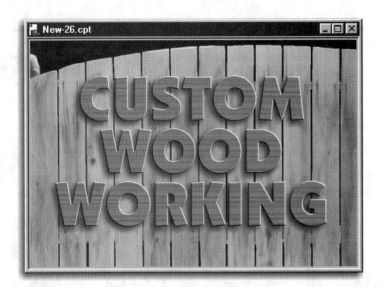

The finished project

FIGURE 10-5

The Airbrush Tool

The Airbrush tool is one of the most often used brush tools to create shadows and highlights on images. It produce a very soft diffuse edge. The following exercise depends on the Airbrush tool for the shadows.

Making a Flag

My editor for the first PHOTO-PAINT book is a race car buff. I was thinking about making something that would spruce up his Web page when I came up with this hands-on exercise. Your objective is to make a checkered flag, the kind that is associated with the finish of a race. During this exercise, you will be using some Effects filters that you will read about later in the book. Since there isn't a checker pattern in PHOTO-PAINT, you must first make one. That will be your first task.

1. Create a New image that is 2 × 2 inches, 24-bit color at 72 dpi. When the image is open, enable Snap To Grid (CTRL+Y) and from the View menu, select Grid. If your Paint Color is not black, click the color black in the onscreen palette with the left mouse button.

2. Select the Rectangle Mask tool from the Toolbox Mask flyout. Click at the top-left corner of the image and create a mask that covers the upper-left corner of the image. From the Edit menu, choose Fill. From the dialog box, select Paint Color and apply the fill. Repeat this procedure in the bottom-right corner. Remove the mask by clicking the Remove Mask button on the Property bar.

3. Save the file as CHECKER.CPT. Remember where you saved the file. Close the file and open a new file that is 6 × 5 inches, 24-bit color at 72 dpi.

4. Select the Rectangle tool (F6). Open the Tool Settings roll-up (CTRL+F8), click the Bitmap Fill icon, and click the Edit button. When the Bitmap Fill dialog box opens, click the Load button. Locate and select the file CHECKER.CPT. Click the Open button. In the Bitmap Fill dialog box, uncheck Use original size in the Tile section. Click OK.

5. In the Tools menu, ensure Snap To Grid is enabled. Enable the Rulers (CTRL+R). Ensure Render to object is enabled either by checking the option in the Tool Settings roll-up or by clicking the Render to Object button on the Property bar. Beginning about an inch from the top and left side, click and drag a rectangle that is 4 × 3 inches. Disable Snap To Grid and the Rulers. The result is shown in Figure 10-6.

10

6. Select the Object Picker tool. Click the Layer mode in the Objects roll-up. From the Effects menu, choose 2D Effects and select Ripple. Change the settings to those shown in Figure 10-7. Click the OK button. In the Objects Layer roll-up, click the Single button.

7. Select the Paint Tool button in the Toolbox. From the Tool Settings roll-up, select the Airbrush. If it is not one of the top four icons, click the button to the right of the icons and select it from the list, then close the list again. Change the Type: setting to Wide Cover.

8. Place the cursor at the point indicated as A in Figure 10-8. Click once and let go of the mouse button. Place (don't drag) the cursor at the point marked B. Hold down the ALT key and click the mouse button again. Now repeat that procedure at the other points beginning with the one marked C. Feel free to apply the Airbrush tool to an area more than once—I did.

9. Select the Object Picker tool and move the flag to the upper-right area of the image. Select the Rectangle tool and in the Tool Settings roll-up, click the Fountain Fill button and then the Edit button. From the Fountain Fill

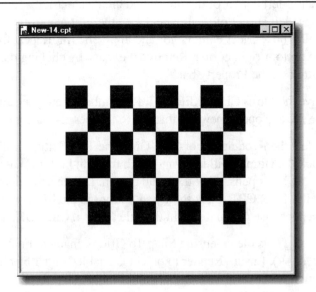

The
checkered
flag made
from the
bitmap
pattern you
created

FIGURE 10-6

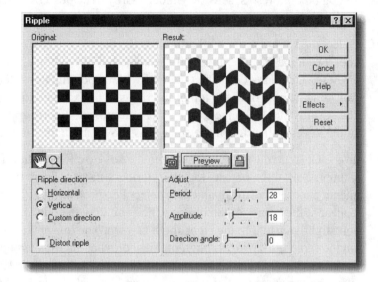

The Ripple filter dialog box

FIGURE 10-7

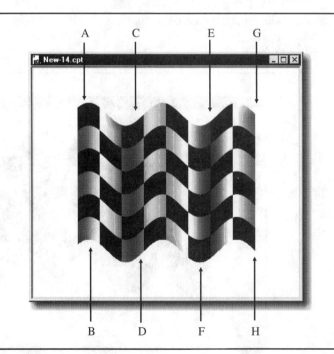

The addition of airbrush strokes at the points shown adds shadows

FIGURE 10-8

10

dialog box in Presets, select Cylinder - Grey 01. Click OK. Drag a rectangle that matches the one shown in Figure 10-9.

10. Select the Ellipse tool (F7). Ensure the Render to Object is enabled on this tool. From the Tool Settings roll-up, click the Edit button and change the Preset to Circular - Grey 01. Click OK. While holding down the CTRL key, drag a circle over the top of the flagpole you created in step 9. Select the Airbrush tool, change to a smaller soft nib, and lightly apply a shadow at the lower-right edge of the sphere, as shown in Figure 10-10.

11. In the Objects roll-up, select all three objects by clicking their icons. Combine all of the objects together (CTRL+SHIFT+L). From the Object menu, choose Transform and then select Perspective. Four handles will appear at the corner of the object. Click and drag the one at the bottom left slightly up and to the right about an inch. The image will be redrawn on the screen, showing a rough preview of what the finished object will look like. Move it until it looks like the one shown in Figure 10-11. To clear the temporary transformations at any time click the ESC key. Double-click the image to apply the Perspective transformation.

12. Close the file and don't save the changes.

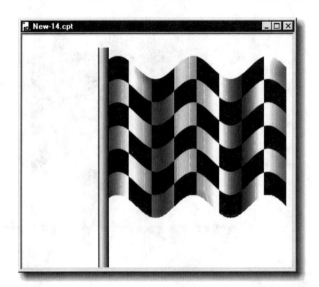

The Rectangle tool is used to create a flagpole

FIGURE 10-9

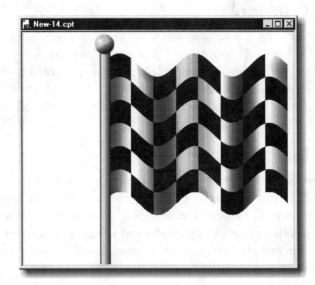

The Ellipse
tool is used
to create the
ball at the
top of
the pole

FIGURE 10-10

A flag fit
for the Indy
brickyard

FIGURE 10-11

Spray Can Tool

The Spray Can and the Airbrush tools share the same controls, but the brush strokes produced by each are noticeably different. Where the Airbrush produces soft diffused patterns of paint, the Spray Can creates a spattered brush stroke. This tool is used for creating a textured look to a surface. It is especially good when working with fonts that are associated with stencils—like the Stencil BT font.

Pencil Tool

This tool produces different types of brush strokes that appear to have been created by a pencil. If you are artistically gifted, you can actually create images that resemble pencil drawings using the pencil brush in conjunction with a stylus and digitizer pad. The recommendation for the stylus and pad is based on the well-known fact that most people on this planet cannot write, much less draw, with a mouse. If you are one of the few that can write and draw with a mouse, you are fortunate and you need to get out more.

Making Tracing Paper

As I said, the Pencil brush and the pen-related tools that follow require some artistic ability and a stylus to take advantage of their potential. However, there is a way to work around the lack of artistic gifting: use tracing paper. PHOTO-PAINT doesn't have any tracing paper commands, but the effect is easy to create. Using the Layer mode with help from the grid, it is possible to make excellent tracing paper, with the following steps.

1. Load the image you want to trace.

2. In the Objects roll-up (CTRL+F7), click the Layer Mode button and the New Object button that appears to the right of the Delete button with the Trashcan icon. You now have a transparent layer over the original and can trace to your heart's delight without affecting the original image.

3. You may find it helpful to display the grid by selecting the Grids and Ruler Setup on the Tools menu.

To dispel any illusions that you may have about my artistic abilities with pen and pencil, I have shown a hastily traced image of one of the flower photographs in

Figure 10-12. You can do better than this, but the point is, it does look a little like the original and it took less than four minutes.

 TIP: *If you are used to working with pencil and charcoal, you may find yourself looking for a smudge stick. Corel provided it. It is called Light Rub and is described later in this chapter.*

Ballpoint Brush

 This tool makes brush strokes that mimic a ballpoint pen. You may be wondering why you would use a computer costing several thousand dollars to make brush strokes that look like they were made with a .20 disposable pen. Actually, I was wondering the same thing.

Calligraphy Brush

 This tool can be used to add some real "non-computer-looking" touches to images created in PHOTO-PAINT. One of the benefits of PHOTO-PAINT over a vector

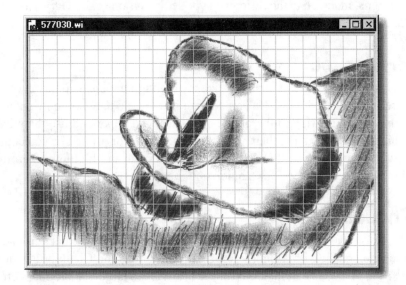

Tracing paper was used to make this sketch with the Pencil tool

FIGURE 10-12

program like DRAW is this ability to make things look "real." The Calligraphy brush, like the Pencil tool, is best used with a stylus and digitizer pad. The shape of the nibs with this brush tool makes possible many of the strokes associated with calligraphy. If you are using a pressure-sensitive stylus, you can achieve even more "realistic"-looking pen strokes.

Here you see a treble clef (left) that was created using the Calligraphy brush and one (right) that was created using the Calligraphy Old setting.

Fine Felt Pen Brush

This Paint tool operates like a real felt pen right down to the part where it makes darker spots when you keep it in one place too long. For drawing line art and cartoons in general, this one is my favorite. You really need a stylus to use this tool effectively.

Felt Marker Brush

This tool replicates the brush stroke of those felt markers we all use to write garage sale signs. Included in the different Type settings is one called Dry Tip, which drags out colors irregularly just like a felt marker that is running out of ink does.

Hi-Liter Tool

This is a fantastic tool. It acts just like the highlighter pens you buy at office supply stores. One of the things you can do with it is to scan the text you want to highlight with a scanner. Bring in the image of the scanned paper and use the highlight tool to highlight the text and then print it out on your color printer, or you could just use a real highlighter pen that costs less than a dollar and highlight the original. All kidding aside, it is good for a quick tint or shadow.

Chalk Brush

This brush tool requires two things to work correctly: that the background be a dark color, i.e., black with a light Paint Color chosen for the Chalk brush and that you use a small nib. The default nib for the brush is too large and produces effects more like those of the Pastel brush.

Wax Crayon Brush

This tool is similar to the Chalk and Pastel tools. It has a hard texture that makes the distinctive waxy look. For a more realistic appearance, you may want to apply it as a new object in Layer mode and then Emboss it.

Light Rub Brush

This is the tool you use with the Pencil and other pen-related tools to smear the pencil/pen strokes. It also contains the Custom Charcoal Type setting. Just as the Chalk brush needs to be on a dark background, the Charcoal brush needs to be on a light background with a dark Paint Color. The viewer's mind expects charcoal to be dark.

Pastel Brush

If you are working in grayscale, this will look a lot like the Charcoal. There are many choices for different pastel textures, which makes this a versatile Paint tool.

Watercolor Brush

This brush mixes all of the adjoining colors as it is dragged on the image. It can produce a brush stroke similar to watercolors and is good for making part of an image look like someone spilled water on it.

Pointillism Brush

The Pointillism brush offers the greatest variety of settings, not in number of settings but in the different types of effects. The effects include Impressionism, Cubist, Op Art and several others.

10

NOTE: *The names of some of the Effect tools may seem, at times, inconsistent. For example, if you select the Smear tool, it will say Pointy Smear. That is the default Type setting. I have named each tool according to its overall description rather than the name associated with the default type setting.*

The Effect Tools

The Effect tools discussed in this chapter are a category of brush tools in PHOTO-PAINT, hence the terms *tools* and *brushes* are used interchangeably throughout the chapters. The Effect tools are accessed by clicking the Effect tool button in the Toolbox. Selection and configuration of the tools is via the Tool Settings roll-up. Effect tools offer a rich assortment of effects, many of which can be found in the Effects and Image menus. Unlike their menu-based counterparts, the Effect tools can be applied selectively in small areas, sometimes without the necessity of creating a mask. Although the effects provided by many of the tools can also be achieved through various menu commands, others are unique to the Effect tools and not available elsewhere in Corel PHOTO-PAINT. In Corel PHOTO-PAINT 5, these tools are called the Freehand Editing tools, and they are all located on a flyout. No longer. In Corel PHOTO-PAINT 7, they can be accessed from the Property bar and the Tool Settings roll-up. There are 11 different tools that constitute the Effect tools. Like the Paint tools, the Effect tools offer multiple Types for each tool. We will begin our exploration of the Effect tools with the Smear tool.

Note for Corel PHOTO-PAINT 5 Users:

The Freehand Editing tools are no longer located on a flyout. They are now accessed through the Tool Settings roll-up or the Property bar.

The Smear Tool

The Smear tool smears colors. The same tool in Adobe Photoshop is called the Smudge tool (which can get confusing, because there is a Smudge tool in Corel PHOTO-PAINT). The Smear tool spreads colors in a picture, producing an effect similar to dragging your finger through wet oil paint. The size and shape of the Smear tool is set from either the Property bar or the Tool Settings roll-up.

Using the Smear Tool

The purpose of this tool is to smear colors. I know I said that before, but it's worth repeating, because many first-time users of Corel PHOTO-PAINT misuse the Smear tool. That is, they use it to soften color transitions. That is the purpose of the Blur tool. Think of it this way: The results of using the Smear tool are not that much different from finger painting (except you don't have to wash your hands after you're done). Blending an area causes the distinction between colors to become less pronounced. Choosing a blending amount of 0 percent in the Tool Settings roll-up causes no blending to occur although it stills smears existing pixels, while an amount of 100 percent will give you the maximum amount of blending possible. Adjacent pixels must be different colors for the effect to work correctly.

 TIP: *Make a practice of using the Checkpoint command (which makes a temporary copy of the image that can be quickly restored) before you begin application of the Smear tool or any other freehand editing tool.*

Have the Smear Tool Settings roll-up open when you work with this tool. For retouching, Soft Edge and Transparency should be adjusted to produce the greatest effect without being obvious. Remember that a higher Soft Edge setting causes the edges of the Smear tool to appear more feathered, which is desirable for most Smear tool applications. Fade Out and Spacing are not the critical settings. That said, you might want to play with the Fade Out settings for applications where you do not want the effect to end abruptly. The effect of the Smear tool is additive. Every time you apply it to the image, it will smear the pixels, no matter how many times you apply it.

For retouching, you may end up "scrubbing" the area with the tool to get the desired effect. When retouching a photo, you do not want a solid color after you are done—you need to have texture for the subject to look real.

 TIP: *If you start the Smear tool well off of the image, it pulls the pixels (Paper Color) onto the image. This can be used to give the brush-stroke effect on the edge.*

The last application of the tool can be removed with the Undo command (CTRL+Z), provided it was applied with one continuous stroke without letting go of the mouse button.

Creating Cloth Text

 The Smear tool is not limited to retouching photographs. The following hands-on exercise shows what you can do with the Smear tool if you only apply a little imagination.

1. Create a new file that is 3 × 3 inches at 96 dpi.

2. Click the Text tool and place an ampersand character in the middle of the image. Change the font to Century Schoolbook at a size of 300. Click the Bold button.

3. Open the Objects roll-up (CTRL+F7) and click the Layer button.

4. Select the Effect tools and from the Tool Settings roll-up (CTRL+F8), select the Smear tool. Click on the Nib tool preview window to the left of the shape buttons. When the nibs appear, as you see here, scroll down the list until you find the nib indicated by 49 in the following illustration. Remember, 49 is its size in pixels. After you have selected the nib, change the Transparency setting from 0 to 50.

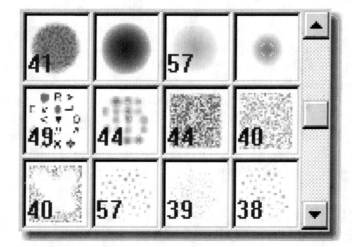

5. On the ampersand, click the inside of the character and drag outward. This creates a ragged edge. Continue to do this until it looks something like this:

6. Click the Single button in the Objects roll-up. From the Edit menu, select Fill. When the Edit Fill & Transparency dialog box opens, click the Texture Fill button (last one on the right) and click the Edit button. Choose the Samples 7 Texture library and the Aztec Cave Drawing from the Texture list. Click OK to close the dialog box. Click OK again to apply the fill.

7. From the Effects menu, choose 3D Effects and then Emboss. Change the Emboss color to Original color, Level to 60, Depth to 2, and Direction to 135. Click OK.

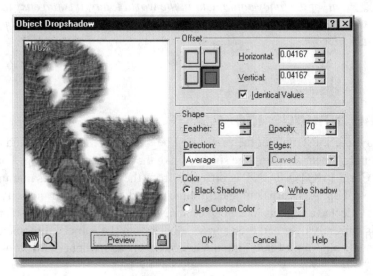

8. From the Object menu, choose Drop Shadow and change the settings of the dialog box to match those shown here. The finished project is shown next. The best part about this project is that it is an object, meaning you can apply a different background fill behind it.

 TIP: *If you are doing touch-up work with the Effect tools, never count on an image being small enough to cover the sins of sloppy touch-up. With all of the fancy equipment in the world today, it is too easy for people to get a photo blown up to poster size, and that is when they might get real ugly about your touch-up work.*

The Smudge Tool

 Maybe it's just me, but the first time I began exploring the freehand editing tools, I thought Smear and Smudge sounded like they did the same thing. The Smudge tool in Corel PHOTO-PAINT is different from the tool with the same name in Adobe Photoshop. As it turns out, the Smudge tool adds texture by randomly mixing pixels in a selected area. It is like a can of spraypaint that sucks up color from the area that it is currently over and then sprays it back onto the subject. Technically, it acts like a local color noise filter. I am not aware of any equivalent of this tool in Photoshop.

The Smudge Tool Settings Roll-Up

All of the controls here are identical to those shown for the Smear tool, with one exception. The Rate of Flow setting determines how fast the noise (texture) is placed on the image. A rate of flow of one causes the noise texture to flow very slowly; therefore, to create a noticeable change, the tool has to be held at the same location for a longer period.

Using the Smudge Tool

The Smudge tool adds texture. It is really color noise. The effect of the Smudge tool is additive. As long as you hold the button down, the effect is being applied, *even if the brush is not moving.*

Thoughts about Retouching Photographs

While the Smudge tool removes highlight very well, it must be used with caution. When the bright highlights are removed, the image appears to be "flatter" than before. This is a drawback as we seek perfection in a photograph. Too many highlights may distract, but they also add contrast to the photograph, which deceives the human eye into thinking the image looks sharper. Another consideration when you are touching up photographs is whether what you are removing or modifying is necessary for the overall effect the photograph is trying to convey. Ultimately, you must make the call, but consider what you are changing before you change it. The only photographs that are digitally manipulated to perfection without regard to the original subject generally are the type that fold out of magazines.

TIP: *Always remember when working with the Smudge tool that it acts like the Airbrush or Spray Can brush. That means that you do not need to drag it across the image unless you have a high Rate of Flow setting. Just put it over the area you want and hold down the mouse button until you get the desired effect.*

10

The Brightness Tool

Brightness is the degree of light reflected from an image or transmitted through it. The Brightness tool can be used to both lighten and darken areas of the image. It is similar to the Dodge-and-Burn tool in Photoshop. These tools are simulations of traditional darkroom techniques. Photographers can improve their work by using the dodge-and-burn technique to block out or add light from a negative in order to enhance an image. In photography, dodging is used to lighten shadow areas (the darkest portions of an image), and burning is used to darken the highlights (the brightest portions of an image). Both dodging and burning can increase the detail in a photograph. The Brightness/Darkness tools produce the same effect in a digital image.

Using the Brightness Tool

The Brightness brush brightens or darkens areas in an image. Choosing a brightness of 100 percent in the Tool Settings roll-up causes all the black to be removed from the affected area, resulting in a much lighter color. Conversely, choosing -100 percent turns the affected area black.

Special Effects with the Brightness Tool

This tool is great for giving a feeling of depth to images. In the following series of figures, I show how to use the Brightness tool to add shadows to an object to make it appear more real. This tool is an alternative to the Airbrush you used to create the shadows on the flag exercise earlier in the chapter.

Using the Brighten Tool

When using this tool, remember that you want the changes to be subtle, so make them in small increments using a Brighten tool with a round shape unless you are working near straight lines, as in a geometric figure. The effect of the tool is not additive. It will apply the effect at the level set in the Tool Setting dialog box each time it is applied.

To achieve any subtle effects in areas that have no naturally occurring visual boundaries, you must be prepared to apply the brush in several stages to reduce the sharp transition of the contrast effect.

The Contrast Tool

Contrast is the difference between the lightest and the darkest parts of an image. The Contrast tool intensifies the distinction between light and dark. It operates in the same manner as the Contrast filter, except that it can be applied to small areas without the need to create masks. The size, shape, and level of the Contrast tool are set from the Tool Settings roll-up on the View menu. The Contrast Tool Presets are Custom Contrast, Increase Contrast, and Decrease Contrast, plus small, medium, and large Soft and small, medium, and large Flat.

Using the Contrast Tool

Use the Contrast tool to bring out color in scanned photographs that appear dull or flat. Don't increase the contrast too much or the picture might appear overexposed. Some scanners have a tendency to darken the photographs when they are scanned, which causes them to lose contrast. Video images that are obtained through a frame grabber also tend to be dark. Both of these applications can benefit from the selective application of contrast.

Be careful not to overuse the Contrast tool, which can result in exaggerated white and dark areas. At the maximum Amount setting for Increase Contrast, highlights and shadows are blown out. That is, the areas that are lighter become white and almost all shades are lost. It is as if the image were converted to *bi-level,* which means the image is composed of only black and white pixels.

The effect of the Contrast tool is additive. It will apply the effect at the level set by the Tool Setting dialog box the first time it is applied. After the mouse button is released, progressive applications add to the effect already applied.

10

The Hue Tool

There are two hue tools, the Hue tool and the Hue Replacer tool, that at first seem to do the same thing. I found their names to be especially confusing. The Hue tool shifts the pixels of the image the number of degrees specified in the roll-up. The Hue Replacer is used to replace the hue of pixels in the image with the hue of the selected Paint (foreground) Color.

How the Hue Tool Works

The Hue tool actually changes the color of the pixels it touches by the amount of the setting. The number of degrees entered in the Amount setting relates to the HSB color wheel. The maximum setting is halfway around the color wheel (180 degrees), which represents the complementary color of the changed pixel.

 TIP: *The best way to get the most realistic color change is to experiment with the transparency settings for the Hue tool. I have found that the default setting has insufficient transparency.*

Limiting the Effect of the Hue Tool

The Hue tool is like using the tint control on your color TV. The difficulty with using this tool is that it will shift every pixel you paint with the tool. To prevent unwanted hue shifts, it is best to mask the area first. By using the Color Mask, you can create a mask that is limited to the colors that you want to change. The best part about this combination of Color Mask and Hue tools is that you need not concern yourself if the Color Mask exists in an unwanted portion of the image, since you will limit the application of the Hue shift by where you place the Hue tool.

 TIP: *Use the Hue brush to create interesting shifts in color within your image.*

The effect of the Hue brush tool is additive if the Cumulative option on the second Tab of the Tool Settings roll-up is selected. It will apply the effect at the level set by the Tool Settings dialog box the first time it is applied. Progressive applications after the mouse button is released will shift the hue of the pixels that much again.

The Hue Replacer Tool

 The Hue Replacer tool replaces the hue of pixels in the image with the hue of the selected Paint (foreground) Color. By changing the Hue, the color changes but the other two components (saturation and brightness) remain unchanged. The same considerations exist with the tool's masking and other settings, as mentioned with the Hue tool. The Hue Replacer brush changes the colors of pixels by the value set in the Amount number box. The color values relate to the degrees on the HSB Color Wheel.

Mixing Colors and Other Confusions

The amount of the original hue that remains is determined by the Amount setting in the Tool Settings roll-up or the Property bar. All of the traditional rules of color you learned, like yellow + blue = green, do not apply with digital color. To complicate matters further with regard to predicting the color outcome, the default color model of Corel PHOTO-PAINT is RGB. To accomplish the Hue mix, Corel PHOTO-PAINT must temporarily convert the model to HSB. This text is not here to discourage you, only to help you understand that predicting the color outcome is very difficult, and the best method I am aware of is experimentation.

 TIP: *Use this Hue Replacer effect tool to replace the color of an object without removing its shading and highlights. For instance, you can change the color of a red dress to yellow, while still retaining the shading that distinguishes the folds in the skirt.*

The Sponge (Saturation) Tool

 The Sponge tool acts in the same manner as the Saturation filter, discussed in Chapter 9. The Sponge tool is used to increase the saturation or intensity of a color. When saturation is added to a color, the gray level of a color diminishes; thus it becomes less neutral. The Sponge tool can also be used to desaturate or diminish the intensity of a color. When Saturation is reduced to -100 percent, the result is a grayscale image. The size, shape, and level of the Saturation tool is set from the Tool Settings roll-up on the View menu.

 TIP: *Also use the Sponge brush to make colors more vibrant. For the amount, select a low negative value (-5, for example) and brush over the desired area. Nonessential colors that cause dullness are stripped away, leaving pure, vivid colors.*

Using the Sponge Tool

The Sponge tool actually removes the color of the pixels it touches by the amount of the setting. The effect of the tool is not additive. It will apply the effect at the level set by the Tool Settings dialog box the first time it is applied. Progressive applications will not make any changes to the previously affected area unless the tool settings are changed.

The Tint Tool

 The Tint tool tints an area in the current paint color. This may seem the same as painting with a high-transparency paintbrush, but it is not. The paintbrush is additive. That is, when the same area continues to have the brush applied to it, the paint builds up until it reaches 100 percent. The Tint tool will apply the Paint Color as specified by the Tint setting, regardless of how many times it is applied. The amount of tint set in the Tool Settings roll-up is the maximum level of the Paint Color that can be applied to the pixels in the image.

Using the Tint Tool

The first thing to remember with the Tint tool is that 100 percent tint is a solid color without any transparency. The Tint tool provides a way to highlight a selected area with a color. The same effect can also be achieved over larger areas by using the Rectangle, Ellipse, or Polygon Draw tools and controlling the Transparency setting through the Tool Settings roll-up.

Another use of the Tint tool is for touching up an image. The technique is simple. When you have a discoloration to cover, pick an area of the image that is the desired color. Using the Eyedropper tool, select a large enough sample to get the average color that is needed to match the adjoining areas. Now apply the tint to the area with progressively larger percentage settings until the discolored areas disappear into the surrounding area. If the resulting tint application looks too smooth, use the Smudge Effect tool to add texture. You can also use the Blend tool to reduce spots where there are large differences in the shades.

The Blend Tool

 This is a better tool to use for some types of retouching than the Smear tool. The Blend tool enables you to blend colors in your picture. *Blending* is the mixing of different colors to cause less distinction among them. For example, if you have two areas of different colors and they overlap, it is possible to blend the two different colors so that the separation of the two areas is indistinct. You can use the Blend tool to soften hard edges in an image and to correct any pixelation caused by oversharpening.

 TIP: *You could use this effect to blend the edges of a pasted object with the background to make it appear more natural.*

Blending an area causes the distinction between colors to become less pronounced. Choosing a blending amount of 1 percent in the Tool Settings roll-up causes no blending to occur, while an amount of 100 percent will give you the maximum amount of blending possible. Adjacent pixels must be different colors for the effect to work.

Using the Blend Tool

The Blend tool acts like applying water to a watercolor. The effect of the tool is additive. It will apply the effect at the level set by the Tool Settings dialog box the first time it is applied.

The Sharpen Tool

 The Sharpen tool sharpens selected areas of the image by increasing the contrast between neighboring pixels. It operates in the same manner as the Sharpen filter except that it can be applied without the need to create masks. The size and shape of the Sharpen tool is set from the Tool Settings roll-up in the View menu.

Using the Sharpen Tool

Avoid overusing the Sharpen tool, which results in exaggerated white spots (pixelation) wherever the white component of the image approaches its maximum value. The effect of this tool is additive. It will apply the Sharpen effect to the Sharpen level set in the Tool Settings dialog box every time it is applied. Progressive applications intensify the changes. Any application of the tool can be removed with the Undo command (CTRL+Z) as long as it was applied with one continuous stroke without letting go of the mouse button. If you must be zoomed in at great magnification to do your work, keep a duplicate window open to a lower zoom value so you can see the effect in perspective.

Undither Tool

This brush is new with PHOTO-PAINT 7. The Undither tool allows you to create a smooth transition between adjacent pixels of different colors or brightness levels. It works by adding intermediate pixels whose values are between those of the adjacent pixels. Use this tool to remove dust and scratches and to smooth jagged edges. Its effect is similar to that of the Smear tool except it has a more pronounced effect.

Creating a Custom Nib from a Mask

You can create a custom nib for any of the tools discussed in this chapter using a mask. The following hands-on exercise uses some of the newer features in Corel PHOTO-PAINT 7 to create a custom nib.

1. Create a new image that is 6 × 4 inches at 96 dpi.

2. Open the Objects roll-up (CTRL+F7). Click the Layer button and then the New Layer in the lower-right portion of the roll-up.

3. Select the Image Sprayer tool and from the far left button on the Property bar, ensure it is set to BUTRFLY.CPT. If not, click the file folder to open the list and select it.

4. Click once on the image area and a single butterfly appears. If the one that appears doesn't match the one shown here, click Undo (CTRL+Z) and try again until you get the single butterfly. This may take a few moments since the Image Sprayer, by default, applies each of the 17 different butterflies randomly.

5. Click the Single button in the Objects roll-up. Ensure the Preserve Image button is not enabled and click the Create Mask button on the toolbar. The butterfly and its mask are now part of the background.

6. Select the Paint tool from the Toolbox and from the Tool Settings roll-up, click the small button to the right of the two shape buttons. This opens the Create from Mask function. Clicking it opens the Create from Mask dialog box. While we could change the size of the brush, leave it at 97 and click OK.

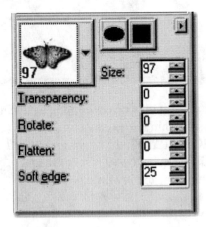

7. Congratulations, you have created a custom nib. Now, let's apply it.

8. From the Tools menu, choose Grid and Ruler Setup. Select Snap To Grid and Show Grid. Change the Spacing to .5 in both Horizontal and Vertical. Click OK.

9. Because your nib is large, you need to change the spacing of the dabs or all of the butterflies will overlap one another. Click the third tab in the Paint Tool Settings roll-up and change the Spacing setting to 90.

10. Click the color Red in the onscreen color palette to change the Paint Color. Click in the image window in the upper-left corner one time and then, while holding down the ALT key, click the upper-right end of the image. A single row of red butterflies is applied on the image. Continue to change the Paint Color and produce more rows. The following illustration has been cropped and is displayed without gridlines.

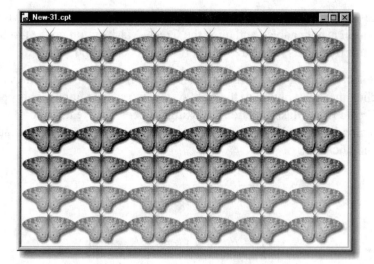

Just a few thoughts to leave you with concerning the creation of nibs from masks. The mask must contain something. You cannot make a nib from an empty mask. In previous versions of PHOTO-PAINT, the nibs were limited to 100 pixels. That is no longer true. You can make them up to 999 pixels. Of course, your system may throw a hairball, but hey, no one ever said it would be easy.

11

The Power Tools

This is called the Power Tool chapter because the two sets of tools in it, the Clone tool and the Image Sprayer, have lots of horsepower! The Clone tool has been around for some time. The Image Sprayer is new to PHOTO-PAINT 7. Let's begin our tour with the Clone tool.

The Clone Tool

This is the last set of tools in the Toolbox. The ability to clone images in Corel PHOTO-PAINT is one of the more valuable features in the program. Many people assume the primary use of the Clone tool is to duplicate people or things in an image. Actually, while the Clone tool is used to replicate images or portions of them for effect, it's more often used in photo-editing for repair and restoration. If you thought Clone tools were used to make the dinosaurs in *Jurassic Park* and *Lost World,* I hope you won't be too disappointed.

In the world of Corel PHOTO-PAINT, Clone tools are used to take part of an image and apply it to another part of the image. The cloned area can be on the same image or in a different image window. This is important when part of an image needs to be removed and something is required to replace it. The Clone Tool has a mode that lets it operate as the world's best Undo tool.

The Clone Tool Settings Roll-Up

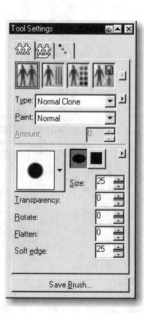

There are several ways to open the Clone Tools Settings roll-up, shown here. With the Clone Tool button selected, choose Roll-Ups and Tool Settings from the View menu, use the keyboard combination of CTRL+F8, or double-click the Clone tool button in the Toolbox. The Clone Tool Settings roll-up is identical to the Brush Tool Settings roll-up except for the Clone selections. The category headings are:

- Normal Clone

- Impressionism Clone

- Pointillism Clone

- Clone From Saved

Normal Clone

In this mode the Clone tool does not modify the pixels. The pixels from the source are painted precisely as they appear in the source. The process of cloning one object to another to create something that is missing is commonly used both in still photography and motion pictures. In the movie *Forrest Gump,* Gary Sinise, who played Lieutenant Dan, had special blue socks on when they shot the scenes that showed his legs. If you are one of the 50 people on the planet who missed the film, the character of Lieutenant Dan had lost both of his legs in the Vietnam war. By using a blue screen process, anywhere his blue socks appeared would not record on film. They used a clone tool similar to the one in Corel PHOTO-PAINT 7 to clone other parts of the background to replace the areas covered by his feet—one frame at a time. In Figure 11-1, I used the Normal Clone tool to remove the man from the image. Other parts of the image were cloned over the area occupied by him until he was gone.

How the Clone Tool Works

When the button is selected, the cursor icon becomes a circle with a blinking plus sign in it. The first time you click the mouse button, the blinking plus sign (the source point) remains at the point where you clicked it. The circle part of the cursor

Using the
Normal
Clone tool
to quickly
and easily
remove the
man from
the image

FIGURE 11-1

11

continues to follow your mouse or stylus movement until you click it again, at which time the Clone tool paints the pixels from the source point on the image. As you move the Clone tool, the source point moves. At this point they are operating in aligned mode. The source point and the tool can be on the same image or on different images. To reset the source point, hold down the SHIFT key and press the left mouse button at the same time. The Clone tool has been set to where your circle cursor was. The source point is now anchored at the new location. The plus and circle cursor momentarily line up and the process starts all over again.

Aligned and Non-Aligned Clone Modes

The clone has two modes in which it can operate: *aligned* and *non-aligned.* When it is in aligned mode, the source point moves in relation to the Clone tool. This mode is used to clone whole images. When it is in non-aligned mode, the Clone tool can move about, but the position of the source is restricted by the user. This mode is generally used to clone nondetailed areas like clouds or abstract backgrounds.

To use non-aligned mode, we place the cursor over a point in the background that contains the colors we want to clone. Next, while holding down the "S" key, drag the Clone tool and release the mouse button without releasing the "S" key. When the mouse button is released, the source crosshair jumps back to the original anchor point. This is what non-aligned mode is all about. It operates, like the mouse, in relative mode. As long as you hold down the "S" key, each time you release the mouse button, the source point will return to its previous (not the anchor) point. This allows us to "paint" an area using clones of the pixels under the source.

 TIP: *Give the Clone tool a soft edge with greater-than-normal transparency if you want to ensure the cloning will not be evident.*

How to Use the Clone Tools to Clone an Area

- Double-click the Clone tool in the Toolbox to open the Tool Settings roll-up.

- Select the type of Clone tool desired.

- Set a clone point on the area you want reproduced and then move the Clone tool to the new location. The cloned area can be on the same image or in a different image window.

- To re-anchor the clone point, place the cursor over the area you want to clone, hold down the SHIFT key, and click.

- To operate in non-align mode, hold down the "S" key.

- Holding down the CTRL key constrains the Clone tool to horizontal/vertical movements.

- To draw a straight line in any direction with the Clone tool, click to establish a starting point, hold down the ALT key, move to where you wish the line to end, and click again to create the line.

TIP: *You can use the Normal Clone tool to retouch photographs that contain scratches or other defects. Clone an area containing similar color and copy over the damaged section of the photograph.*

Removing Defects from a Photograph with the Clone Tool

Probably the most common use for the Clone tool is removing things from a photograph. In 1993, the film *My Fair Lady* was restored. Even though it is only 20 years old, it was in very poor condition. In the opening credits, several pieces of film had broken off, leaving black spots on the screen. Technicians used clone tools to clone part of another background to cover the spots. The result was that the black spots vanished without a trace.

Corel was considerate enough to provide an image on which to demonstrate this technique of using cloning to remove or repair damage.

Restoring a Photograph with the Clone Tool

In the following hands-on exercise, we are going to remove some dust and debris that was left on a negative when it was scanned.

1. Locate and open the file \PHOTOS\PEOPLE\651017.WI on the Corel CD-ROM. Resample the Width to 7 inches using the Resample command in the Image menu.

2. Look at the couch on the right side of the image. There is a large black spot there and some other debris. Hold down the "Z" key (the cursor becomes a magnifying glass) and enclose the area around that spot.

3. Double-click the Clone Tool to open the Tool Settings roll-up. Select the Normal Clone Tool button (it should be selected by default) and Normal Clone. The cursor should be a large circle (my image is zoomed at 600%) with a small plus in it. The size of the source point cursor never changes, but the Clone Brush cursor reflects the size of the Clone Tool brush.

4. From the Property Bar, change the brush size to 7. The cursor and source point should still be together. Click on a spot to the left of the debris. Move the Clone brush so it is over the ugly spot. The source point (plus sign) should remain where you clicked it. Click the left mouse button once. The debris should be gone.

5. Try this on the other debris on the shades in the background (a lot was left for you to practice on). Remember to reset the Clone brush when you move to a new area. The key to good clone repair is to locate source points that are the same general shade and texture as the area where you are cloning to prevent the cloning from being noticed. When you have finished here, hold down the "N" key. This opens the Pop-Up Navigator. In the small picture that just appeared on your screen, click and drag the rectangle over the smaller girl's nose and click the left mouse button.

6. The object in this area is to remove the dark spot at the tip of her nose. Change the Type to Small Soft Clone. Place the cursor just under and to the right of the spot. Hold down the SHIFT key and click the left mouse button. Now place the cursor over the dark spot and click the left mouse button. If it doesn't look right, click Undo (CTRL+Z).

7. Save the file as GIRLS.CPT.

Removing scratches, dust and other debris is initially a fun thing to do. After your hundredth one, it gets a little old, but I still never cease to be amazed at what can be done with the Clone tool.

Making an Oil Painting with the Clone Tool

As stated earlier, you can clone between two points on an image, which we did in the previous exercise, or clone from one image to another. In the following exercise, we will clone the image of the smaller child to another image, in a unique way.

1. Open the file GIRLS.CPT.

Replacing backgrounds is a simple task with the PHOTO-PAINT 7 masking tools. In Chapter 7, you will learn how to quickly mask the background for replacement.

Here is an easy hands-on exercise that will teach you how to use the Stroke Mask command and the new Image Sprayer.

Here is my favorite of all the exercises you will do in this book. What makes it interesting is that it involves only a few steps and that each image is different from the last, as demonstrated by the variation to the right. You will find this exercise in Chapter 8.

There is no need to sweep up the sawdust after you create this wooden sign and background in Chapter 10. The wood pattern that makes up the letters was created with one of PHOTO-PAINT's brush tools.

This second image of the project was created by converting the text into a mask, reducing the mask four pixels, and applying the Boss filter using the Wet Pastel type.

By changing the color of your paintbrush tool, you can create different types and shades of wood effects.

By using masks in combination with one another, we can produce photo-realistic effects like this one, which was made in the hands-on exercise in Chapter 8.

When you work through this exercise in Chapter 9, you will discover that removing color from certain elements in a photo can emphasize those where the color remains.

In Chapter 10, we explore the power of the Brush tools. These treble clef images were created with one of PHOTO-PAINT's Calligraphy Pens.

In Chapter 10 you will learn how to make realistic shadows and highlights when you create the flag you see here.

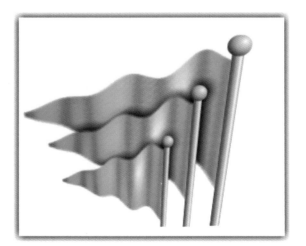

Using the same techniques, we are able to make duplicates and variations, as with these flags.

After removing the original blue sky from this photograph with the Color Mask tool in Chapter 8, you will replace it with the mountain photograph shown here.

In Chapter 11, you'll use the PHOTO-PAINT Clone Tools with custom nibs to create a new image, showing a painterly effect on the younger girl's picture.

Create images like the one shown here in less than two minutes using the new Drop Shadow and Layer modes in Corel PHOTO-PAINT 7.

By using the Smear Effect tool with the new Layer mode, you will learn to create cloth objects, like this one from Chapter 10.

By creating a custom paintbrush nib in Chapter 10, you will learn how to make repeating patterns like the one shown here.

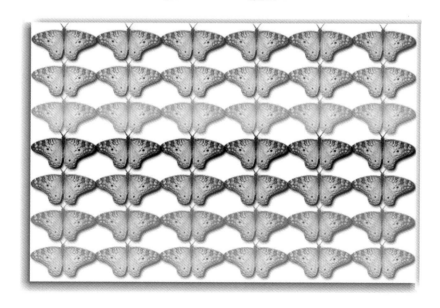

You will learn about using Merge modes in Chapter 13. Here are the results of applying different Merge modes to the Gears object: (A) Original; (B) Add; (C) Subtract; (D) Difference; (E) Multiply; (F) Divide; (G) If Lighter; (H) If Darker; (I) Texturize; (J) Color; (K) Hue; (L) Saturation; (M) Lightness; (N) Invert; (O) Green.

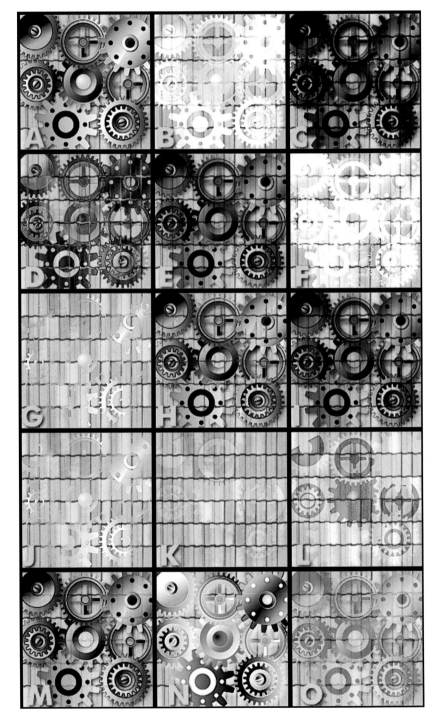

In Chapter 11 we learn how to use the new PHOTO-PAINT Image Sprayer tool in a step-by-step exercise, creating the company logo you see here.

In Chapter 13, you will discover how simple it is to use the new Lens feature to control effects on your text.

Learning to use Photo-Paint's new Perspective mode is the subject of the step-by-step cone exercise in Chapter 13.

Using objects and merge modes in Chapter 13, you will create the image shown here. Next, you will apply PHOTO-PAINT Lighting Effects filters and Object transformations to create the final version of the CD cover.

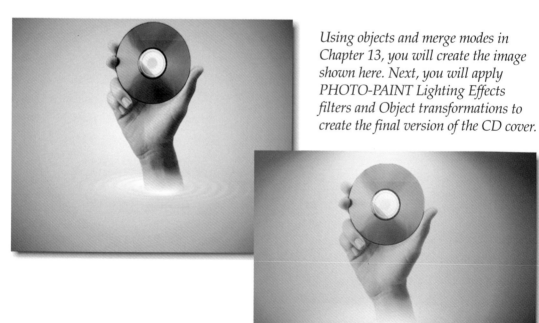

Chapter 21 includes a series of hands-on exercises in which you will learn how to use filters to create the cut-metal and rough-textured look of the letters you see here.

If the preceding Heavy Metal image is just too much, in Chapter 16 learn to create a milder version for a multimedia presentation.

Need some variety in your multimedia titles? Try some of the techniques described in Chapter 18 to create more lively and dynamic text like the titles shown here.

Using several of the 3D Filters, you will create the box of colors, and then make the text look like it belongs on the box. You'll find this exercise in Chapter 19.

In Chapter 15, we discover how to emphasize items in the foreground through the use of the PHOTO-PAINT Blur and Desaturate filters.

Sometimes we need to print black-and-white images. In Chapter 17, you will learn how to change this color photograph into the black-and-white pencil sketch shown below.

The
Gardener

In Chapter 18, you'll use one of the many PHOTO-PAINT filters to create this book cover from a single photograph of a shell.

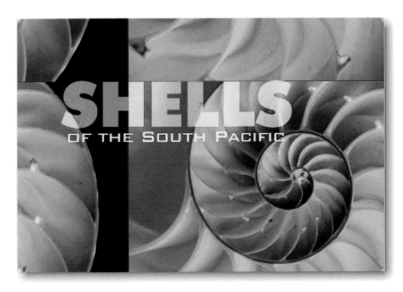

SHELLS
OF THE SOUTH PACIFIC

Blurring can convey a sense of action, as you will learn when you create this brochure cover in Chapter 15.

Using multiple filters together to create effects is another technique taught in Chapter 18, in which you will create this head for a magazine article.

In Chapter 22, you will go through the step-by-step process of changing this photograph into the European travel poster shown below.

During the course of three different exercises, you will use the powerful tools built into PHOTO-PAINT 7 to transform the image shown at the left into the one displayed below.

Learn to use the Boss filter to create 3D buttons like this one. You will find this exercise in Chapter 22.

One of the more interesting effects that can be achieved with PHOTO-PAINT is done by duplicating and rotating an object, then applying different transparency levels.

When you have PHOTO-PAINT and this book, you can make license plates without having to serve prison time (well, almost). Find this exercise in Chapter 22.

After scanning the Corel DRAW 7 CD-ROM, I scaled it and placed it in the hand coming out of the screen. Everything shown in this image is an object from Photo-Paint's library.

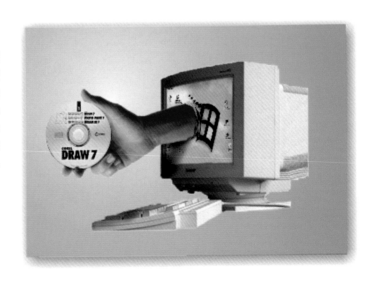

2. Create a new file that is 4 × 5 inches at 96 dpi.

3. Save the new file as HATGIRL.CPT.

4. Select the Clone tool and double-click the button to open the Tool Settings roll-up.

5. Click the title bar of GIRLS.CPT (to bring it forward). From the Tool Settings roll-up, select Fine Streaks as the Type. This changes the nib shape so the cloned area resembles the fine brush strokes of a paintbrush.

6. Place the cursor on the little girl's nose and click the left mouse button.

7. Click the title bar of HATGIRL.CPT or select HATGIRL.CPT from the Window menu. Place the Clone brush in about the middle of the image area, click the mouse button, and begin to drag the brush. The girl under the source is cloned in the new image looking a little like a painting, as shown in Figure 11-2.

8. To remove any portion of the material you have just cloned click the last button on the Tool Settings roll-up, choose either Custom From Saved, Eraser or Light Eraser and paint it away. This is the reason I had you save the blank image in step 3. The Clone From Saved mode requires a saved version to operate.

9. When you have finished, close the file and don't save any changes.

Impressionism Clone

In this mode the pixels from the source are modified using the Impressionist effect. The Impressionist effect applies brush strokes to the image, causing it to look like an Impressionist painting. Impressionist paintings are marked by the use of unmixed primary colors and small brush strokes to simulate reflected light. Notable Impressionist painters include Monet, Cezanne, and Degas.

This tool wins the big prize: I have been unable to find any practical use for this tool whatsoever. Think about it for a moment. A clone is an exact copy of the original, right? The Impressionist Clone tool makes randomly distorted copies of the original. Am I missing something here?

In using the tool, remember that by keeping your brush size and number of line settings small, your result will more closely approximate the original. At least the outcome will be recognizable. The results with this tool are unpredictable, so be sure to use the Checkpoint command before beginning your work.

11

Using the Clone tool to make a painterly copy of a girl in another image

FIGURE 11-2

Pointillism Clone

In this mode the pixels from the source are modified using the Pointillist effect. Pointillism adds a dotlike appearance to the image. The brush stroke made with the Clone tool incorporates a selected number of dots in colors that are similar (e.g., eight shades of red). The size, shape, and qualities of the Pointillist Clone tool are set from the Variation Tab in the Tool Settings roll-up. The effect can be subtle, retaining the overall appearance of the original image, or you can vary the dots and the colors to create very unusual special effects. The Pointillism Clone tool selects colors in an image and paints with those colors in a pointillist style. It does not reproduce areas in an image, as does the Normal Clone tool.

Experiment with this tool when you have lots of time on your hands and no deadlines. Use it to create special effects. Keeping the brush size very small (a setting between 2 and 5) enables the creation of a clone that looks vaguely similar to the original. As with the Impressionism filter, use objects that have definite shapes, making them easily recognizable, since the Clone tool distorts their appearance. The results with this tool can be unpredictable, so use the Checkpoint command before beginning your work.

Clone From Saved

This is the ultimate Undo tool, although it seems to have several names. It is called Clone from Saved and Custom from Saved, Eraser. Whatever the name, it uses the last saved version of the image file as a source, allowing you to selectively remove any changes that had been made since the last time the file was saved. It has three presets that are unique to it, each producing a different effect. The presets are:

■ Light Eraser

■ Eraser

■ Scrambler

The Eraser, Light Eraser, and Scrambler Presets

This is a wonderful feature for when you are cloning images. After you have cloned a portion of an image, you may end up with cloned material that you do not want. The Eraser and the Light Eraser allow you to restore the original pixels from the last saved version of the image. This restores areas to their saved states. The Light Eraser allows you to control how much of the changes you want to remove, requiring multiple passes to achieve the full restoration. The Eraser removes all of the cloned pixels. The Scrambler option is a pointillism version of the Clone from Saved, so it allows you to distort the current image from a saved version—what were they thinking?

TIP: *To restore background with the Clone From Saved feature, I recommend you use the Eraser setting with a soft edge setting of 60-80. This way the transition is gradual and you won't need to go over the area later with a Smear or Blend tool.*

All of the settings in the Tool Settings roll-up for the Clone Tool operate in the same fashion as the Brush tools described in Chapter 10. Now let's look at the Image Sprayer tool.

The Image Sprayer Tool

 The Image Sprayer allows you to load one or more images and then "spray" them across your image. We have already used this tool in several hands-on exercises in this book. The Image Sprayer tool makes it possible to paint with multiple images instead of simply a paint color. The images you paint with are contained within a special file called an *image list,* which you can create from selected objects, or you can use any of the image lists available in the ImgLists folder on the PHOTO-PAINT CD. You can adjust the size, transparency, and spraying sequence of the images by adjusting the brush settings on the Property bar or from the Tool Settings roll-up as shown in Figure 11-3.

Using the Image Sprayer Tool

 Here is a hands-on exercise to make a quick logo for a company.

1. Create a new file that is 6 × 3 inches at 96 dpi.

2. Click the Text tool in the Toolbox. Change the Font to Futura XBlt BT at a size of 96 and the inter-line spacing to 70. Ensure the Preserve Image button is enabled. Type GEARS Unlimited, Center (CTRL+A) text, choose Create Mask button, and delete the text, leaving only the mask.

3. Click the Image Sprayer tool in the Toolbox. By default it is set to Butterflys. Click the Load Image Sprayer List button on the far left of the Property bar. When the dialog box opens, select GEAR.CPT. Click the Open button.

4. The current size of the gears that would be painted are so large that they would lose their effect, so change the size of the image in the Property bar from 137 to 100.

5. Click in the image and paint the gears inside of the masked area. The result is shown in Figure 11-4, with the Mask marquee off. Because the gears are applied in a random fashion, yours will look different than the one shown.

6. Ensure the Preserve Image button is off and click the Create Object button in the Toolbar.

7. Select the Object Picker tool in the Toolbox. Open the Objects roll-up (CTRL+F7) and click the Layer button.

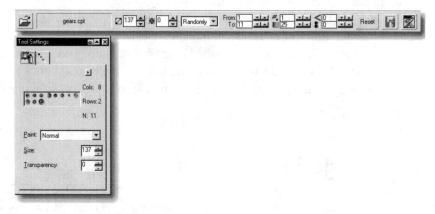

The Property bar and Tool Settings roll-up offer complete control over the Image Sprayer tool

FIGURE 11-3

8. From the Effects menu, choose 3D Effects and then Emboss. When the dialog box opens, click the Reset button. Change the Emboss color to Original and the Level to 150. Click the OK button. Click the Single button in the Objects roll-up.

9. From the Object menu, select Drop Shadow. From the Drop Shadow dialog box, choose the lower-left Offset button with an Offset value of .1 in both the Horizontal and the Vertical. Set the Feather to 12, the Opacity to 60, and the direction to Average. Click OK.

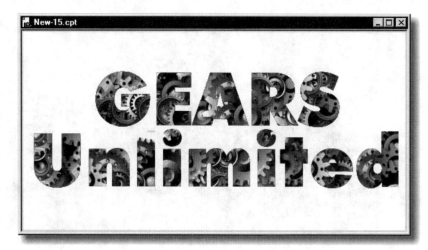

The Image Sprayer applied to the masked text creates a power visual

FIGURE 11-4

10. In the Objects roll-up, deselect the text by clicking on it. Click on the background so there is a pencil beside it. From the <u>E</u>dit menu, choose <u>F</u>ill. From the Edit Fill & Transparency dialog box, click the Fountain Fill button and choose <u>E</u>dit. From the Fountain Fill dialog box, change the preset value to Gold Plated. Click OK to close the box and click the OK button again to apply the fill. The finished logo is shown in Figure 11-5.

11. Close the file and don't save the changes.

More Image Sprayer Information

There are many more image lists that are included with PHOTO-PAINT 7 than the ones you saw when you opened the Image Sprayer List. Open the ImgLists folder on the PHOTO-PAINT CD to see a lot more of these jewels. To learn how to make your own image lists, click the F1 button in PHOTO-PAINT, select Index, and enter "Image Sprayer tool, using." Click the Display button and choose "Creating and editing image lists for the image Sprayer tool."

 TIP: *A good source for creating the Image Sprayer list is the Objects folder on the PHOTO-PAINT CD. Make sure you check out what has already been created, since many of the objects in the folder are already available as image lists.*

The finished company logo

12

Working with Fills and the Shape Tools

Until now you have looked at fill tools only as far as necessary. In this chapter you will learn everything there is to know about the subject of fills. All of the technical details are here, so if you are having trouble sleeping at night, start reading the definition of Pantone colors. That should put you out pretty quick. We will also look at the Shape tools. With the addition of the new Fill command in PHOTO-PAINT 7, the Shapes aren't used as much as they used to be, but they still remain an important part of the PHOTO-PAINT Toolbox.

What's New, Fill?

With the release of PHOTO-PAINT 7, several new fill features have been added and the way fills work has been slightly changed. Are you surprised? The newest addition to the fabulous world of fills is the new Fill command. Located in the Edit menu, the Fill command opens the Edit Fill & Transparency dialog box, shown in Figure 12-1. This command is a real time-saver because from this dialog box, you can access any of the individual roll-ups, like Fountain fill or Bitmap fill, and you can directly apply the fill to the image. In previous releases of PHOTO-PAINT, these required the use of the Fill tool or the Shape tools, which are both still available and necessary.

The Edit Fill & Transparency dialog box is like a jumping-off point for all of the fills in PHOTO-PAINT. The dialog box contains two tabs: Fill color and Transparency. The Fill color is used to set the color of the fill and the Transparency tab controls all of the different transparency options that are possible with the fill.

The Fill Roll-Up

In PHOTO-PAINT 6, the Fill roll-up was one of the most popular roll-ups. While it is still there, you may find yourself using it less and less. The Fill roll-up controls

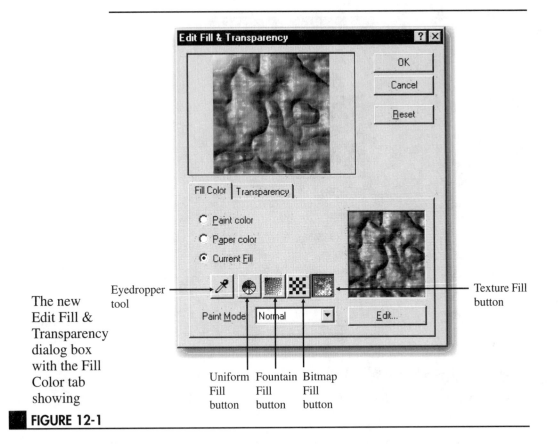

The new Edit Fill & Transparency dialog box with the Fill Color tab showing

FIGURE 12-1

what fill is applied when you use the Fill tool, or the Rectangle, Ellipse, and Polygon Shape tools. It provides access to a wide variety of preset and custom fills, ranging from simple spot colors to complex custom bitmap fills.

The Fill roll-up, shown here, can be accessed many ways, as follows.

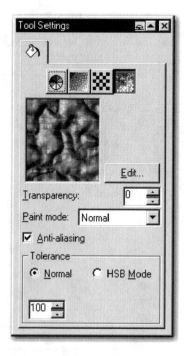

- Double-clicking the Fill tool in the Toolbox.

- Double-clicking the Rectangle, Ellipse, or Polygon Shape tool in the Toolbox.

- If any of these tools are selected, you can also access the Fill roll-up by using CTRL+F8 or selecting Roll-Ups and then Tool Settings from the View menu.

When you open the Fill roll-up, you will notice that there are four buttons near the top of the roll-up. Each of the buttons in the Fill roll-up is identical in appearance and operation to the ones shown in Figure 12-1. The icon on the buttons indicates the operational mode they activate.

NOTE: *If you open the Fill roll-up feature of the Tool Settings roll-up by double-clicking either the Rectangle, Ellipse, or Polygon tool, there will be five buttons at the top. The fifth is the No Fill button.*

The Mode Select Buttons

Before going into detailed descriptions, let's summarize the button functions.

The first button selects the Eyedropper tool (only on the Edit Fill & Transparency dialog box). Enabling this button activates the Eyedropper tool. In this mode, you place the cursor on the image and click the desired color and it becomes the Current Fill color.

The next button enables Uniform Color fill. From this mode, any solid (non-gradient) color can be selected either from the existing palette or from a custom palette.

The Fountain fill button enables the Fountain fill dialog box to produce Linear, Radial, Conical, Rectangular, and Square fills. This fill comes with a large selection of presets. All of the fountain fills can be customized.

The next button is the Bitmap fill, indicated by the Checkerboard icon on the button. Like its CorelDRAW counterpart, it can provide bitmap fills either from its existing library of fills or from custom fills that are created with Corel PHOTO-PAINT or other graphics programs. This is a powerful tiling engine. Any bitmap file can be used for Bitmap fill patterns (tiles).

The last button is the Texture fill, the most unique in the Fill roll-up. This mode does not use existing tiles or patterns. Instead, it creates them at the time of use through a powerful fractal generator. You can produce some unusual and exotic textures (or patterns) with this fill.

The Edit button is used to produce variations with any of the previous buttons.

NOTE: *The No Fill button that was available on previous releases has been removed. Use the Transparency control to prevent fills from being applied.*

Fill Status Line

You can see the currently selected fill color/pattern by viewing the Status bar. You will notice that there are three small rectangles located on the status line, as shown here. They are, from left to right, Paint color (foreground color), Paper Color (background color), and the Fill tool color/pattern. Because the area is small, it is sometimes difficult to accurately determine the selected type of fill.

12

Paint: Paper: Fill:

The Uniform Color Fill Mode

Uniform Color Fill is the simplest fill mode and is used to select and apply solid (uniform) colors to an image. When Uniform Color fill is selected, the Fill Color Swatch on the Status bar reflects the current Fill color that is selected.

Selecting a Uniform Color

The currently selected color is shown as a color swatch on the roll-up. There are several ways to change the color. The quickest is to click the desired color in the onscreen color palette with the left mouse button. If the color you want is not available in the onscreen palette, then from either the Edit Fill & Transparency or the Fill roll-up, select the Uniform Fill button and click the Edit button. This action opens the Uniform Fill dialog box, as shown in Figure 12-2. From this dialog box you can do just about anything you can think of in regard to color. In fact, there is

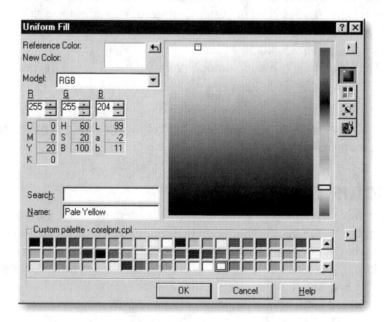

The
Uniform
Fill dialog
box

FIGURE 12-2

so much here it can be a little intimidating if you just opened it up to get a different color. You can select a color from the color palette in the lower portion of the dialog box. There are more colors in this palette that can be accessed by moving the scroll bars. Once you find the desired color, click the color in the palette. The name of the color appears in the Name box above the palette. Other actions occur and other information is displayed, but I will discuss these later in the chapter.

The Uniform Fill Dialog Box

The Uniform Fill dialog box is where you can literally pick any color in the universe. The operation of this dialog box can intimidate the faint of heart. The dialog box is an essential tool for defining and correcting colors for those doing prepress work. If you only want to make a simple modification to a color so it will look better in an image, you can do that as well.

Just so you know, the Uniform Fill dialog box is common throughout Corel PHOTO-PAINT as well as all of the CorelDRAW suite of applications. Changes made to the palette in this dialog box are global. That means that they apply to all of the CorelDRAW suite of applications. The Uniform Fill dialog box allows you to choose colors from various color models and custom palettes. You can also import and select individual colors from existing image files.

How to Approach the Uniform Fill Dialog Box

There are two general approaches to using the Uniform Fill dialog box. The simplest is to pick the color closest to the desired color from the palette, modify the color in the Uniform Fill dialog box, and then return to the Fill roll-up or to Edit Fill & Transparency. The advantage of this method is speed. The disadvantage is that you will be using an undefined color that may be difficult, if not impossible, for someone at a different location (like a service bureau) to duplicate.

The second approach is to create one or several colors, name them, and save them in a custom palette. This way you can use the colors in another image because the colors have been named and saved. Another site can duplicate your work since you can send the palette along with the image. The disadvantage is that it takes longer to do. That said, let's examine this cornucopia.

12

Setting the Mood—Models, Palettes, Blenders, or Mixers?

The operation of the dialog box is controlled by which of the four mode buttons on the right side of the dialog box is selected. These affect not only the operation but also the appearance of the dialog box. You have four choices, as follows.

- **Color Models**   This method of choosing a color allows you to select one of ten color models to establish the color you want. This is the mode shown in Figure 12-2. The reason for selecting a specific color model to use when choosing colors is based on the type of work you are doing. For example, if you are color-correcting a photograph that will be printed using the four-color printing process (CMYK), you should choose the CMYK or CMYK 255 color model.

- **Palette Mode**   Selecting this button changes the color selection to one based not on color models but on a series of predefined palettes as shown in Figure 12-3. Use Palettes to pick a system of predefined colors such as Pantone or Trumatch. These are the choices if you are using spot colors.

- **Color Blender Mode**   It slices, it dices, it's the Color Blender. This tool, shown in Figure 12-4, is very handy for selecting colors. You select four colors and it produces a range of colors for those selected using gradations between them across a square grid.

- **Mixing Area Mode**   The first two choices only offer about 30 million or so colors. There are always those who just cannot find that special color they want with only 30 million to choose from, so Corel provided mixers, shown in Figure 12-5, that provide two different ways to make their own colors.

Color Models

Color models are a method for representing the color of colored items, usually by their components as specified along at least three dimensions. The first button allows you to select one of ten color models. As you change color models, the numerical value system on the right and the 3D color model displayed below the model name change.

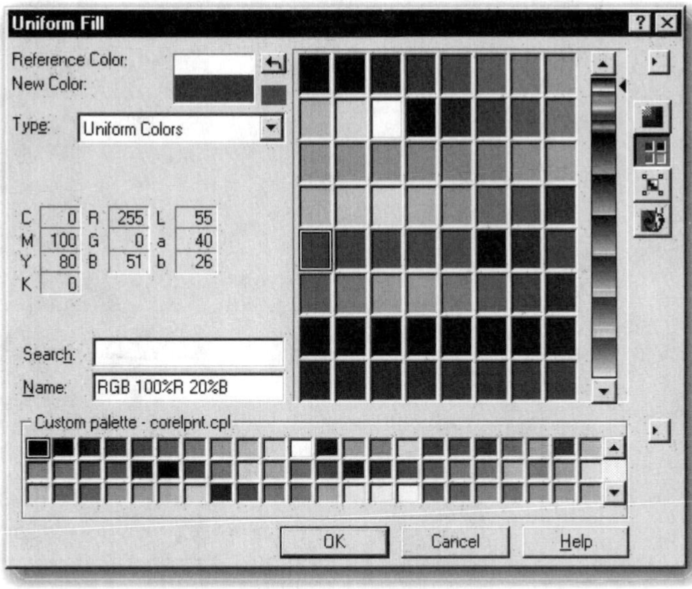

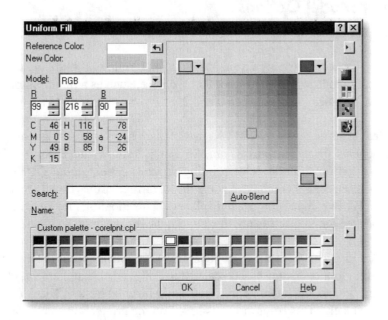

The
Uniform
Fill dialog
box in
Palette mode

FIGURE 12-3

The
Uniform
Fill dialog
box in
Color
Blender
mode

FIGURE 12-4

12

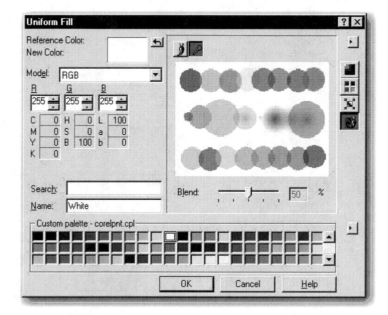

The Uniform Fill dialog box in Mixer mode

FIGURE 12-5

Color Model Options

The color model options available are described in the following sections.

CMY   This contains only Cyan, Magenta, and Yellow. You should only select it if the final output will be done on a CMY device, such as a three-ink printer. The C, M, and Y values range between 0 and 255.

CMYK   This shows the CMYK model and list value boxes for each of the components in percentages. Cyan, Magenta, Yellow, and Black (CMYK) is the model used for the four-color printing process. *A note about CMYK:* When this model is selected, there may be some display irregularities if you are using blended colors. When blended colors are displayed on the monitor, they show up as banding. The printed output itself is unaffected, but the display may be banded.

CMYK 255   This is like the previous CMYK model, except the values are listed according to a computer-based scale (0 to 255) rather than percentages. As in the previous model, the letters represent Cyan, Magenta, Yellow, Black ("K" is used to indicate black). This color model is based on the printer's primary colors.

RGB This is the standard of monitor color models. All computer displays are RGB (Red, Green, and Blue)—the same as your eyes. The RGB model is the default color model of Corel PHOTO-PAINT. This is the ground zero of all color models.

HSB The popularity of HSB (Hue, Saturation, and Brightness) isn't what it used to be, although components of this model are still used when working with the filters. HSB is an alternative to the RGB model.

HLS HLS (Hue, Lightness, Saturation) is a variation on HSB and another alternative to RGB. Hue determines color (yellow, orange, red, etc.), lightness determines perceived intensity (lighter or darker color), and saturation determines color depth (from dull to intense). The circular visual selector defines the H value (0 to 360) and the S value (0 to 100); the visual selector defines the L value (0 to 100).

L*a*b* This color model is becoming more and more popular. It was developed by Commission Internationale de l'Eclairage (CIE) based on three parameters: lightness (L*), green-to-red chromaticity (a*), and blue-to-yellow chromaticity (b*). The rectangular two-dimensional visual selector defines the a* and b* coordinates from -60 to 60; the vertical visual selector defines the L* value from 0 to 100. This model is device-independent, meaning that it does not need to have information about the devices it is working with to operate correctly. For the prepress industry, it encompasses the color gamuts of both the CMYK and the RGB color models.

YIQ The preferred model when working with video is YIQ, which is used in television broadcast systems (North American video standard: NTSC). Colors are split into a luminance value (Y) and two chromaticity values (I and Q). On a color monitor, all three components are visible; on a monochrome monitor, only the Y component is visible. The square two-dimensional visual selector defines the I and Q values, and the vertical visual selector defines the Y value. All values are scaled from 0 to 255. In Corel PHOTO-PAINT, the Y component of the splitting process produces a grayscale image that is often superior to results obtained with a grayscale conversion using the Convert To command from the Image menu.

12

GRAYSCALE This is your basic plain vanilla 256 shades of gray color model. No, that's not a typo—gray is a color. By using the arrows on the Gray Level list box, it is possible to select any of 255 levels of grayscale, with 255 being the lightest and 0 the darkest.

REGISTRATION COLOR The Registration color model consists of a single color in the CMYK color space, for which C, M, Y, and K are at 100 percent. You can use this color on any object that you want to appear on all separation plates. It is ideal for company logos, job numbers, or any other identifying marks that you may need for the job. This color cannot be added to the Custom palette.

TIP: *If the project you are working on is not going to an offset printer, select the RGB or Grayscale color model.*

How to Select or Create a Color Using Color Models Mode

The following is a general procedure to create a specific color in the Uniform Fill dialog box.

- The first step is to remember what color it was that you were working on to begin with. You'll find it in the upper-right corner, labeled Reference color. This was the color originally selected in the onscreen palette or on the palette in the Uniform Fill dialog box.

- Select a color model. This step is easy: use RGB unless you have good reason to use another model. If you are working with 32-bit color, use CMYK or CMYK 255.

- If the only change you want is to make the Reference color darker or lighter, click and drag the small square in the color model display, moving it to make the selected color darker or lighter. The color of the area under the square is shown in the New Color box under the Reference Color in the upper-right corner of the dialog box.

- If you want to create a completely different color, you can click on any point in the color model display area. To locate a different color area, click a color on the vertical spectrum on the right side of the color display area. The color value of the point will appear in the New Color swatch. You can then adjust the shade of the color in the color model display area. You can also enter values numerically. For example, with the RGB model, entering a value of 0,0,0 will produce black and 255,255,255 will produce white.

- When the New Color is the desired color, click the Update Reference Color button. Doing this makes the New Color the Reference Color. This is useful when you are matching colors and wish to update your reference point. To swap the Reference and New Colors, use the Color Options flyout, and choose Swap Color.

Using the Printable Color Swatch

As you adjust the square in the color model display area, a swatch of color will appear (and sometimes disappear) below the Update Reference Color button, as shown in the following illustration. This is an ingenious device that warns you of colors that cannot be printed using SWOP (Standard Web Offset Press). If you are not having your image printed on an offset press, don't be too concerned about this feature. The swatch continually displays an approximation of what the color will actually look like. To try it out find a vivid blue or green and you will see that the swatch will only display the closest color that can be reproduced.

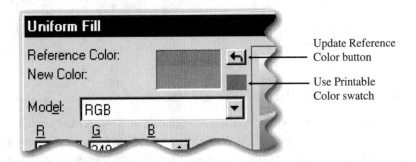

If you are new to color printing, you may not be aware that there are ranges of colors that cannot be reproduced by your printer. The Printable Color warns you when the color you are selecting is outside the capability of your printer. The swatch of color that appears displayed as Printable Color represents the closest approximation to the desired color that can be printed. To use the color that appears in Printable Color, click it. The color in the Printable Color will replace the New Color.

Once you are satisfied with the color displayed in the New Color swatch, click the OK button and you will return to the Edit Fill & Transparency dialog box or the Fill roll-up with the New Color selected.

Color Options Button

Clicking this button opens the Color Options menu, as shown in the following illustration. There are five choices on this menu.

- **Color Model** This allows you to choose from eight different ways to display the color model. Regardless of which color model you choose, the HSB - Hue Based display is the default. If the color model selected in the upper-left portion of the dialog box is either Grayscale or Registration color, this option is not available.

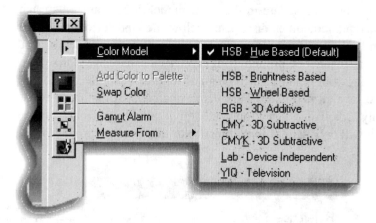

- **Add Color to Palette** This adds the New Color to the Custom palette.

- **Swap Color** When selected, this option will swap the New Color and the Reference color. This is different from the Update Reference Color button that changes the Reference Color to the current New Color. Getting a headache yet?

- **Gamut Alarm** This causes the Color Model Display area to display areas that contain colors that are outside of the color gamut for the printer selected in Corel Color Manager. The color of the Gamut Alarm is selected in the Color Manager.

- **Measure From** The last choice is for selection of color measuring devices. Choosing this opens a menu of several industry-standard measuring devices. If you have not used one of these before and think it might be a neat idea to hop down to your local computer superstore and check them out, think again. The least expensive ones I have seen cost over one thousand dollars.

Saving a New Color on a Palette

Now that you have created that special color you wanted, you need to save it. Colors are saved on palettes. Before I show you how to save a color to a palette, you need to understand a few things about palettes. *Palettes*, like the original artist's palette, are files that store colors. Palette files have a .CPL extension. The palette in the dialog box is the short palette that was originally shown in the Fill roll-up. The palette is displayed regardless of the color model selected. The only way to display another palette is to load a different one. This will be dealt with in more detail in the next section, which concerns Palette mode.

The Custom palette is the default Corel PHOTO-PAINT palette. The palettes discussed in this chapter store a large selection of colors. You can use a special palette to keep all of the colors used in a particular project or painting. Some people like to keep a palette that contains all of their favorite colors. The choice is yours. Here is how to save a color you have created.

1. After you are satisfied with the new color, enter a name for it in the Name value box. Naming colors is not necessary, but it is recommended.

2. Click the Color Options button below the color model, and a drop-down list appears. Choose Add Color to Palette and the new color will be added to the bottom of the current palette.

 TIP: *When creating new colors, especially for company logos, be sure to give the new color a specific name. This can be critical when the job needs to be modified and you are trying to guess which color you used out of a possible ten billion combinations.*

Removing a Color from the Palette

Fair is fair. If I am going to show you how to add a color to a palette, I should also show you how to get rid of it.

1. In the palette, click on the swatch of the color you want to delete.

2. Click the Palette Options button to the right of the palette and choose Delete Color from the drop-down list as shown here.

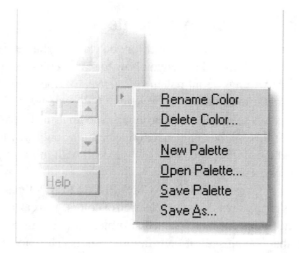

3. A confirmation box appears, giving you one last chance before deleting the color. Click the Yes button and the color is history.

Renaming a Color in the Palette

Sometimes you don't want to remove the color, just rename it. Renaming colors is simple as well.

1. Click on the color you want to rename.

2. Type the new name in the Name: box.

3. Click the Palette Options button below the palette and choose Rename Color from the drop-down list. To test it, click on a different color and then on the color you just renamed.

NOTE: *Don't rename existing industry-standard colors. For example, if you are using Pantone 1615V, don't call it Flaming Neon Ties. While you may find the nomenclature entertaining, it will not be understood by the service bureau or your printer. Another reason for sane color names is that human memory is frail, and if you give a color a cute name, there is a strong chance that when it comes time to look for it again, you may not be able to remember that specific shade of green that you created was called Aunt Fred's Toenail Clipping. Now that I've spoiled your fun, the good news is that Corel PHOTO-PAINT gives you 20 characters with which to name your new color creation. This is a vast improvement over the terse eight-character restriction of DOS naming conventions.*

Working with the Palettes

Now that you know how to get colors on and off the palettes as well as how to rename the colors, the only thing left is how to manage the palettes themselves.

The palette management options are listed on a drop-down list that appears when the Palette Options button is clicked. The drop-down list includes the following options.

NEW PALETTE   This palette option opens up an empty palette that you can fill with any combination of colors. If you attempt to create a new palette without saving the current one that you have modified, you will receive a warning message. To create a new palette, proceed as follows:

1. Select New Palette.

2. When the New Palette dialog box opens, enter the name for the new palette.

3. Click the Save button.

 TIP: *Sometimes when you are working on a project that requires a number of exact reference colors (e.g., Pantone), you may find it is easier to create a palette specifically for the project with the required colors.*

OPENING AN EXISTING PALETTE   The Open Palette option opens the Open Palette dialog box. The default palette is CORELPNT.CPL, an RGB color model palette. When opening an existing palette, you have the choice of three different types from the File of Type list:

- Custom palette (.CPL)

- Spot Palette (.IPL)

- Process palette (.PAL)

SAVING A PALETTE   Selecting this option opens the Save Palette dialog box, which saves the current palette under the same name. This is used to save any changes made to a palette. If you do not save a palette, any change made to it will be lost when Corel PHOTO-PAINT is closed or a new palette is selected.

12

SAVE PALETTE AS   Use this option when you have modified an existing palette but do not want to apply the change to the original palette. This is the best way to build a custom palette of favorite colors. The basic palette has 99 colors. By adding colors to the existing palette and saving it under a unique name, you have all of the basic colors plus your personal favorites or specific colors made for a project or client.

TIP: *Use the Save As command when you have made changes to the default palette. Many times, image files that you can get from various sources expect to find the default palette. If you have changed it, you may get unpredictable results.*

DELETING A PALETTE   To quote the caterpillar in *Alice Through the Looking Glass,* "You can't get there from here." Well, you actually can; it's just not obvious. OK, watch carefully. Click the Palette Options button and select the Open Palette option. When the dialog box opens, right-click the palette you want to delete. A pop-up menu appears and one of the choices is Delete. Like I said, not a direct route.

Palette Mode

Enabling the Palettes button of the Uniform Fill dialog box opens the Palette mode. This offers a collection of different color-matching system palettes available to the Corel PHOTO-PAINT user. The number of colors or shades available in each palette depends on the color mode of the image. The different palettes are provided for projects that work with Spot or color process systems like Pantone, TOYO and Trumatch. The palettes contain industry-standard colors that are essential for color-matching accuracy when the project is to be output to offset printing.

NOTE: *When using the Pantone color-matching system in Palette mode, be aware that the colors cannot be changed. Only the percentage of tint can be modified. This is because the ability of a system like Pantone to match the colors printed on the swatch (which you must buy from them) is based on the combination of inks that make up the color and do not change.*

Viewing Palette Selections by Name

Click the Color Options button and you will immediately notice some of the selections have changed. Selecting Show Color Names will cause the currently selected palette to change to an alphabetical listing of all of the color names for the color system selected, as shown here.

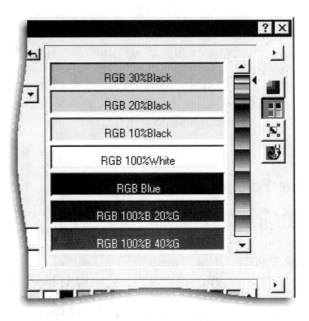

Each name is displayed on a color rectangle displaying a sample of the named color. Regarding the displayed colors, please remember that what you see is only a good approximation of what that actual color looks like, even when you are using a very expensive monitor and graphics card and even when you have done all of the calibration voodoo. When using color samples from a color-matching system, always trust the swatches provided by the manufacturer over the screen.

Searching for Colors by Name

The Search provides a quick way to locate a specific, named color in a color system. As each character is typed in, the computer begins its search. As subsequent characters are entered, the search field is narrowed. Here is a quick exercise to find the spot color blue.

1. In the Type: area, click the down arrow button and select Pantone®
   Matching System.

2. Type **BL** in the area labeled Search:. As the letters "BL" are entered under the Pantone spot system, the computer goes to the first BL in the system, which is "black."

3. Type **U**, and the search produces Pantone Blue 072 CV.

4. Since clients often will specify colors by number, enter 273 in the search area. As you type in each character, the list narrows the search until you have Pantone 273. The search system accepts both alphabetic and numeric characters, since many names of colors in color-matching systems have numeric designations.

Exploring the Palettes

When the Palette mode is enabled, the Type choices change as well. The 12 different palette choices available when you click the arrow in the Type box are as follows.

UNIFORM COLOR PALETTE   This is the default palette for Corel PHOTO-PAINT. The Uniform Color palette offers 255 standard RGB colors for quick selection. Colors are expressed as RGB values for all images and drawings. Use the scroll bar on the right to display other areas of the palette. Colors can be displayed by name through the Show Color Names option on the flyout menu (the color names correspond to the R, G, and B values). It is a sampling of the entire visible spectrum at 100 percent saturation.

FOCOLTONE PALETTE   This palette offers colors that are available through the FOCOLTONE color system. Because the colors are based on CMYK, there is no need to add additional color separation plates. When FOCOLTONE is selected, the dialog box shows the FOCOLTONE model and a Search For box. This box, located under the Color Options button, is used to search for specific FOCOLTONE color names. FOCOLTONE is a color-matching system. Like all color-matching systems, it provides a specimen swatch to printers and designers so there is a point of agreement as to what the color specified is supposed to look like.

PANTONE MATCHING SYSTEM PALETTE   This is one of three available Pantone palettes. This palette offers colors that are available through the Pantone Matching System (known as Pantone Spot Colors in previous releases of PHOTO-PAINT). In this system, you define tint through the Tint Number box, ranging from 0 (lightest) to 100 (darkest) to control saturation. This system also allows you to define

PostScript options. Since spot colors correspond to solid inks and are not CMYK-based, each unique color applied to an object results in an additional color separation plate. In Corel PHOTO-PAINT, you can use spot colors only in CMYK images to affect duotones. Colors can be displayed by name or swatch through the Color Options menu.

Selecting the Pantone Matching System opens the palette and the Search For box, which is used to search for specific Pantone Spot Color names. Spot colors are specific colors that are applied to an area and are not the result of multiple applications of inks. Pantone is one of the more popular color-matching systems. As with FOCOLTONE, when using Pantone, you pick out a specific color from a sample and then pick out the color name or number from the Pantone list. When it goes to the service bureau to be made into film, the computer then knows what particular Pantone color was specified.

PANTONE® HEXACHROME This displays the Pantone® Hexachrome colors, which are based on the CMYK color model, but it adds two additional inks for a total of six inks and a broader range of colors. While this system is gaining popularity, it still is more expensive than others to reproduce because it requires six printing stages instead of the traditional four-step process.

PANTONE PROCESS PALETTE This operates like the Pantone Matching System model except that it shows Process colors. Process colors are created by multiple applications of ink. Pantone specifies all the information that is necessary for the printer to be able to duplicate the color. When Pantone Process is selected, it shows the Process Color model and the Search For box. Tint is not an option with Pantone Process. The Search For box is used to search for specific Pantone Process Color names. The list offers a search capability for colors that are available through the Pantone Process Color system, which is based on the CMYK color model. The first 2000 colors are two-color combinations; the remainder are three- and four-color combinations. Colors are based on CMYK and therefore do not add additional color separation plates. Use the scroll bar on the right to display other areas of the palette. Colors can be displayed by name or swatch through the Color Options menu.

12

TRUMATCH PALETTE This is a competing color-matching system for Pantone. Like Pantone, the Trumatch palette allows specification of colors according to specific samples, but it offers colors that are available through the Trumatch color system. This system is based on the CMYK color model and therefore colors do not add additional color separation plates. Colors are organized by hue (red to violet), saturation (deep to pastel), and brightness (adding or removing black). Use the scroll bar on the right to display other areas of the palette. Colors can be displayed by name or swatch through the Color Options menu.

NETSCAPE NAVIGATOR   This displays the 8-bit palette of 256 colors used by the Web browser Netscape Navigator. By limiting your choices to the colors found on this palette, you ensure that your image colors will display clearly on systems using the Netscape Navigator browser.

MICROSOFT INTERNET EXPLORER   This is the same as the Netscape Navigator except the palette is for the Microsoft Internet Explorer.

SPECTRAMASTER PALETTE   This is a specialized color-matching system. The palette offers colors that are available through the DuPont Spectramaster solid color library. This library was developed to provide a paint color selection and matching tool for industrial coatings and colorants. Colors are based on L*a*b* and are converted to RGB for display and CMYK for printing. Colors can be displayed by name or swatch through the Color Options menu.

TOYO COLOR FINDER   If you have a printer that uses only TOYO inks, this is the palette that you will need to use. The TOYO palette offers colors that are available through the TOYO 88 Color Finder system. The range of colors offered here includes those created using TOYO process inks and those that are reproduced using TOYO standard inks. Colors can be displayed by name or swatch through the Color Options menu. These colors are defined using the L*a*b* color space and are converted to RGB for display and CMYK for printing. Colors can be displayed by name or swatch using the Show Color Names command found in the flyout menu.

DIC COLOR PALETTE   This palette offers colors that are available through the DIC Color Guide, DIC Color Guide Part II, and DIC Traditional Colors of Japan. Colors in these palettes are created by mixing DIC brand inks. Reproduction through Corel applications is achieved through the CMYK color space. Colors can be displayed by name or swatch through the Color Options menu. Swatches are identified by palette and color ID code.

USERINKS COLORS   This was called Custom Palette in the previous release. The palette to the right of the displayed color-matching system acts the same in this mode as it did in the previous Color Models mode.

NOTE: *The Custom palette in the Palette mode displays the contents of the currently selected custom palette and does not reflect the colors of the color-matching system in use.*

The Color Blender Mode

The Color Blender mode in the Uniform Fill dialog box allows creation of colors by mixing one or more colors together.

Color Blender

The Color Blender box provides a method of picking four colors, and the computer automatically generates all of the intermediate colors. It is from these intermediate colors that you can select the color you want. Use the Color Blender to create a four-way blend of color and choose from the range of color variations. Grids are square, ranging in size from 3 × 3 to 25 × 25 (smaller grids produce more distinct colors, while larger grids produce more subtle color variations). Colors are selected from the Custom palette and can be mapped to the CMYK, RGB, and HSB color models.

USING THE COLOR BLENDER MODE   The operation is simple enough. There are four colors at the four corners of a color square. Each of the four colors is selected by clicking the color square in the corner, which opens a palette. From the palette, select a color. If the Auto-Blend switch is enabled (depressed), every change in the corner changes all of the colors in the square appropriately. Clicking the Color Options button gives a great degree of control over the operation of Color Blender with the following options.

- **Grid Size**   This allows selection of one of ten different grid sizes ranging from 3 × 3 to 25 × 25.

- **Add All Grid Colors to Palette**   This option applies all of the colors in the Color Blender area to the Custom palette, which is very handy when you want to place a large range of colors in a palette.

The Mixing Area

The Mixing Area is a unique feature of Corel PHOTO-PAINT. The principle behind it is the equivalent of an artist's palette. Lucian Mustatea, who headed up the Corel

12

PHOTO-PAINT 5 team, came up with the idea of allowing the PAINT user to actually mix various colors together to make new custom colors. While I think the idea is neat, I personally do not have the necessary experience to use it effectively. That said, I can still show you how it works.

The Mixing Area contains two buttons: a brush and an eyedropper (color picker). The Color Options button opens additional choices, as follows.

USING THE MIXING AREA   By clicking the Brush button, you can select colors from the Custom palette. Once the color is selected, it can be applied to the Mixing Area. Additional colors can then be selected with the brush and mixed in the Mixing Area by painting over the previous colors. All colors applied in the Mixing Area are additive. Once you have achieved the desired color, select the color picker (eyedropper) and click the color. The newly created color will appear in the New Color swatch. The colors made in the Mixing Area can be saved.

The Color Options button displays the following commands:

- **Brush Size**   This allows selection of one of three sizes of brushes: Small, Medium, and Large.

- **Brush Type**   Hard, Medium, and Soft.

- **Load Bitmap...**   This command opens the Load Mixing Area File dialog box. You can load any .BMP file into the Mixing Area and use it for selecting individual colors from an existing image. The default Mixing Area file is PNTAREA.BMP, located in the COREL\CUSTOM folder.

   TIP: *This is an excellent way to get and keep colors from an existing image. For example, if you found a file that had a remarkable shade of ruby red, you could bring it into the paint area with the Load command and then select the color and save it to a palette. If the file you want is not a .BMP file, load it into PAINT and save it as a .BMP file.*

- **Save Bitmap...**   This opens the Save Mixing Area File As dialog box for saving mixing areas for later use.

- **Clear Bitmap...**   This clears the existing paint area.

Well, that does it for Uniform fills. The next section is less complicated and a lot more fun.

The Fountain Fill Tool

Next to the Effect filters, the Fountain Fill tools represent the greatest tools for creating stunning backgrounds and fills. A *fountain fill* is one that fades gradually from one color to another. This type of fill is also called a "gradient" or "graduated" fill. Corel PHOTO-PAINT lets you create linear, radial, conical, square, and rectangular fountains using the Fountain Fill icon in the Fill roll-up window. To open the Fountain Fill tool, click its button in the Edit Fill & Transparency dialog box or the Fill roll-up. To access the Fountain Fill dialog box, shown in Figure 12-6, click the Edit button in either the dialog box or the roll-up.

From this dialog box, it is easy to select and configure one of four types of fountain fills.

Advanced Features of the Fountain Fill Dialog Box

If you require greater control of the fills, there are more advanced control features in the Fountain Fill dialog box, which allows you to edit and create fountain fills.

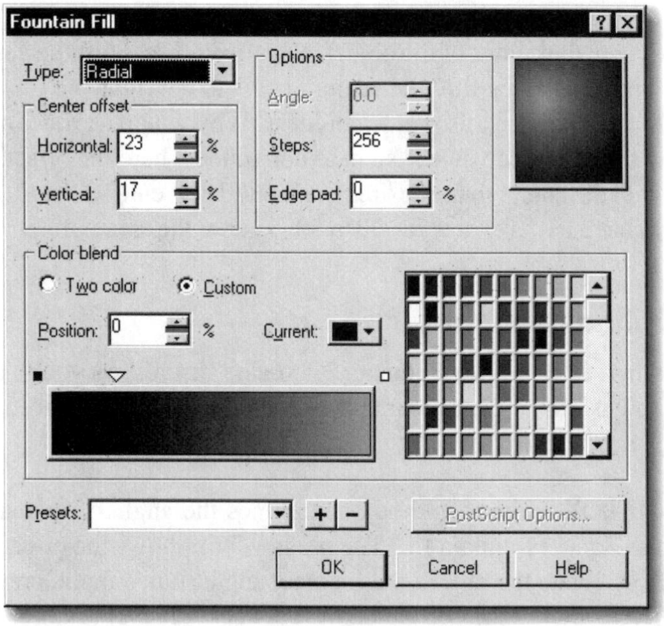

The Fountain Fill dialog box

FIGURE 12-6

It is laid out in four sections: Type, Options, Color Blender, and Presets. The Preview box shows you how the fountain fill will look with the colors you have chosen.

The Type Section

This section selects one of five types of fountain fills.

- **Linear**   This selects a fountain fill that changes color in one direction.

- **Radial**   This selects a fountain fill that changes color in concentric circles from the center of the object outwards.

- **Conical**   This selects a fountain fill that radiates from the center of the object like rays of light.

- **Square**   This selects a fountain fill that changes color in concentric squares from the center of the object outwards.

- **Rectangular**   This is the same as Square except that it uniformly radiates to all corners of the rectangle.

THE CENTER OFFSET SECTION OF THE FOUNTAIN FILL ROLL-UP   The Center Offset repositions the center of a Radial, Conical, or Square fountain fill so that it no longer coincides with the center of the object. Negative values shift the center down and to the left; positive values shift the center up and to the right.

At first appearance this seems pointless. Why would anyone in their right mind waste the time to use a value system to determine where the offset is when you can move it with the cursor to the desired position? The Center Offset is in fact necessary when you have to make several fills with exactly the same offset values.

The Options Section

The Options section of the Fountain Fill dialog box allows you to adjust any of the settings to customize the appearance of the fountain. The choices are described in the following paragraphs.

THE ANGLE BOX   The Angle box determines the angle of gradation in a Linear, Conical, or Square fountain fill. The preview box shows the effect of changing the angle. If you rotate the object, the fountain angle shown in the preview box adjusts automatically after a one-second delay. This delay prevents Corel PHOTO-PAINT from acting on a new setting before the entire value has been entered. You can also change the angle by dragging the line that appears when you click in the preview box. Use the right mouse button (or the left mouse button and SHIFT) to change the angle for Conical and Square fountains. Holding down the CTRL key while dragging constrains the angle to multiples of 15 degrees.

THE STEPS BOX   The Steps box displays the number of bands used to display and print the fountain. The preview display always shows 20 steps regardless of the Steps setting, so don't think that it is malfunctioning. The preview when you exit the Options section will correctly display the higher number of steps.

TIP: *When increasing the value of the Steps, be aware that a large number increases the smoothness of the transitions. The negative side of the increase is that the fountain fill becomes very complex and takes longer to display. In CorelDRAW, complex fountain fills take a long time to print. In Corel PHOTO-PAINT, they take no longer than anything else because it is all bitmaps.*

CAUTION: *Beware of producing too narrow a range of colors over a large area, which creates banding. For example, if a range of six shades of colors is spread over an 11 × 17 inch area, banding will result.*

THE EDGE PAD   The Edge Pad increases the amount of start and end color in the fountain fill. It is used primarily with circles and irregularly shaped objects in which the first and/or last few bands of color lie between the object and its highlighting box. The effect is to take away from the smooth transition between the starting and ending colors. The Edge Pad can be used when applying shading to an object such as text. Entering a large number into the Edge Pad box will cause a wide band to separate the top and bottom of a Linear fill. The Edge Pad option is not available for Conical fountain fills and therefore is grayed out.

The Color Blend Section

The Color Blend section of the Fountain Fill dialog box is where you select the colors you want to use in your fill. There are two modes of operation in the Color Blend area: Two Color (default) and Custom.

TWO COLOR BLEND   Two Color Blend is the system default. It takes the intermediate colors along a straight line beginning at the From color and continuing across the color wheel to the To color. This is best for appearances of shading and

12

highlights. The operation of the Two Color Blend is controlled by one of the three buttons to the right of the From and To colors. These buttons are:

- **Direct**   When selected, this determines the intermediate fill colors from a straight line beginning at the From color and continuing across the color wheel to the To color. This option produces a color series composed of blends of the From and To colors.

- **Clockwise Color Path**   This determines the fill's intermediate colors by traveling clockwise around the color wheel between the To and From colors.

- **Counter-Clockwise Color Path**   This determines the fill's intermediate colors by traveling counter-clockwise around the color wheel between the To and From colors.

- **Mid-Point Slider**   New to Corel PHOTO-PAINT 7, this is only available with Direct selected. It adjusts the midpoint between the From and To color. The Mid-point slider allows the user to control the distribution of color/shading of the fountain fills.

CUSTOM BLEND   The Custom Blend allows you to add more than two colors to a fill and in specific locations on the fill. In the Custom feature, even more incredible effects and backgrounds come to life. When the Custom button is clicked, the dialog box changes as shown here. The Custom option allows you to select up to 99 intermediate colors from the palette at the right of the dialog box. Specify where you want the color to appear by adding markers with a double-click above the preview box. The markers look a lot like the tab markers on my word-processing program.

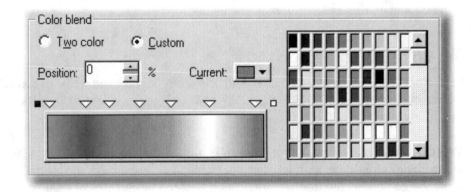

ADDING MARKERS   There are two ways to add markers, as follows. Double-click just above the preview box in the Color Blend area. The marker will appear, and the preview box in the Color Blend area and in the upper-right corner of the Fountain Fill dialog box will reflect the change after a one-second delay. (If you have a slower machine, it may take longer.)

Select the To or From color squares at either end of the preview ribbon and specify a new value in the Position box. (The first works best.)

 TIP: *Use the Position box to enter precise positions for the markers. An easy way to do this is by double-clicking where you want the marker and then putting the exact position for it in the Position box. For example, by double-clicking near the middle of the fill you can get an approximate center position. To be exact, enter 50 percent in the Position box. The halfway point between the middle and the end is 25 and 75 percent, and so on.*

After adding a marker, choose a color from the palette. To reposition a color, select its marker and drag it to the desired spot, or edit the value in the Position box. The preview box in the Color Blend area and in the upper-right corner of the Fountain Fill dialog box will reflect the change after a one-second delay. To delete a color, double-click the marker.

 NOTE: *More than one color marker can be selected at a time by holding down the SHIFT key when selecting or deselecting.*

The Presets Section

The Presets area lets you save the fountain settings you specified so that you can apply them to other objects at a later time. It also contains over 100 predesigned fills that were installed with Corel PHOTO-PAINT.

SELECTING A PRESET   To select a preset, click the down arrow to the right of the Preset text box and a list appears. Click on a preset name and the preset appears in the preview window. If you want to browse through the list, just click the first one you wish to view, and then each time you press the down or up arrow, the next preset will be selected and previewed. You might enjoy doing this if your cable TV is out and you are really bored.

12

SAVING A PRESET   To save a preset, type a name (up to 20 characters in length) in the Preset box, and then click the plus button. (Clicking the minus button removes the selected settings from the Preset list.)

Bitmap Fill

The Bitmap fill is enabled by selecting the Bitmap Fill button on either the Edit Fill & Transparency dialog box or the Fill roll-up. It is the one that looks like a checkerboard. The Bitmap fill allows you to fill a selected area with a bitmap image. There are a large number of images in the Corel library (located in the \TILES folder on your Corel PHOTO-PAINT CD-ROM). In addition to the bitmap images provided, you can import almost any bitmap that can be read by your PC.

NOTE: *Corel PHOTO-PAINT can import vector-based images for use as bitmap fills.*

Loading a Different Bitmap Image

When you invoke the Bitmap fill, you will see the currently selected image in the preview window. To change the image, you must click the Edit button. This will open the Bitmap Fill dialog box, as shown here.

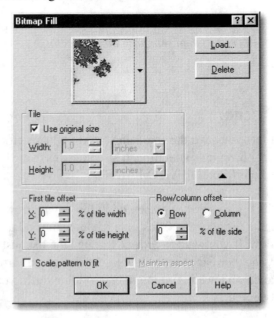

How the Bitmap Fill Operates

Here is a brief summary of how the Bitmap fill works. You have so much versatility when using bitmaps for fills that it is sometimes difficult to get a grip on all of it. Here are some pointers:

- Remember that if you use the Fill tool (the bucket), the fill will be calculated to the boundaries of the mask or the edges of the image. If the bitmap image is larger than the mask or the image, Corel PHOTO-PAINT will put as much as will fit, beginning with the lower-left corner of the original image.

- You can control what appears in a flood-filled area by using the many tile/offset controls in the Bitmap Fill dialog box.

- The Rectangle, Ellipse, and Polygon tools, on the other hand, will fill to the perimeter of the defined area. If there is a mask, the masked area that falls within the area will be filled.

 TIP: *When using Corel PHOTO-PAINT CD-ROMs as bitmap fills, make sure to crop them in the Import dialog box to get rid of any black film border. If you don't, the results can be really ugly.*

Controlling the Size and Position of the Bitmap Tiles

With the Bitmap Fill dialog box settings at their default, if the bitmap that you import is too small to fill the area, it is tiled. If the image is too large, the fill does not resize the bitmap but rather, beginning in the lower-left corner of the original bitmap, it takes all of the bitmap that can fit in the area that is being filled. As a result, if you have a large file you have used for a bitmap fill and a small area to fill, you might find that a large portion of the bitmap didn't make it into the fill area.

In Corel PHOTO-PAINT, you can control the size, offset, and several other parameters of the bitmap fill.

Tile

The controls in this section allow you to set the size of your pattern tiles. You can choose one of the preset sizes or enter custom dimensions. If you select Use original

12

size, the bitmap file will not be scaled to a new size. If it is not checked, the bitmap will be scaled to the size set in the Width and Height settings. These settings are grayed out if the Use original size option is enabled.

Scale Pattern to Fit

When enabled, it scales the tile pattern to fit entirely within the tile preview window. It also disables the entire dialog box when enabled.

Maintain Aspect

The Maintain Aspect feature, if selected, maintains identical tile width and height values. When enabled, any value entered in one number box will cause the other box to change automatically.

First Tile Offset

Controls in this section set the offset of the first tile (and therefore the rest of the pattern) relative to the top right-hand corner of the object. If you want the pattern to start flush with the corner, set the X and Y values to 0 percent.

Row/Column Offset

These controls shift either the rows or columns of tiles so that the pattern is staggered rather than continuous. The percentage of tile side setting shifts alternating rows or columns by the amount specified. This feature helps break up the repeating patterns, which would normally not allow many types of bitmap fills to be used.

Selecting Between Currently Loaded Bitmap Images

On the right side of the preview window in the Bitmap Pattern dialog box is a down arrow button. Clicking the button or anywhere in the preview window opens a color preview of the first nine bitmaps that have been imported into Corel PHOTO-PAINT. If there are more bitmaps than can be displayed, scroll bars appear on the right side of the preview window that allow the user to see the remainder of the bitmap fills in Corel PHOTO-PAINT.

Importing Bitmaps

Clicking the Load button opens the Import dialog box, where you can import a graphic to use as your bitmap pattern. The Import dialog box is the same one used to open a graphic file. The only exception is that none of the options like Crop and Resample are available. There is a large selection of bitmap fills available on the CD-ROM containing the \TILES folder.

Now on to the next section of the Fill roll-up: texture fills.

The Texture Fills

This is the feature that makes Corel PHOTO-PAINT unique. I do not know of another package that can do the things that can be done with texture fills. There are some tricks to using the fills effectively, but you will learn them here. The Texture Fill dialog box is used to select one of the 100-plus bitmap texture fills included in Corel PHOTO-PAINT. Each texture has a unique set of parameters that you can modify to create millions of variations. Although most of the textures look fine on color monitors, if you are using a monochrome monitor, you may not get a very good representation of the texture's appearance. If you are using a monochrome printer, you may get good results with some of the fills and poor results with others. This depends on your printer, your taste, and your willingness to experiment.

What's in a Name?

As with the filters, don't let the names of the fills confuse your thinking. As an example, using the Rain Drops, Hard Texture fill, I was able to obtain the effect of a cut metal edge.

I came across this cut metal effect when I was writing the Corel PHOTO-PAINT 5 Plus manual for Corel. I found that by filling each character individually, the size of the "raindrop" doesn't get too large. Too large? This leads to our first general rule regarding the texture fills. As in Boyle's law of expanding gases (gas expands to fit the volume of the container):

Rule of bitmap textures: A texture fill expands to fit the volume of the available area.

In the following example, I have created squares of various sizes and filled them with the same texture fill. As you can see, as the squares increase in area, the size

12

of the fill increases proportionally. While this can be used to create some unusual effects, it can also catch you by surprise, especially when working with a large image only to find that when it is applied, it looks nothing like the thumbnail preview.

 NOTE: *The fill size is calculated by creating a square that is determined by the greatest dimension of the mask. For example, if you made a mask that was 50 × 500 pixels, the resulting fill would be as if it was a 500 × 500 pixel square.*

Exploring the Bitmap Texture Fill Dialog Box

When the Texture Bitmap mode of the Fill roll-up is selected, the currently selected fill is displayed in the preview window. The Edit button opens the Texture Fill dialog box, which allows you to edit and create an unlimited number of new texture fills from existing fills. Unlike bitmap fills, you cannot import files for use as texture fills. The texture fills are actually fractals that are created as they are applied. This goes a long way toward explaining why some textures can take a long time to apply.

If you cannot find the exact file that you want in the 160+ preset textures that were shipped with Corel PHOTO-PAINT, you can edit the existing textures by clicking the Edit button. The Edit button below the preview of the fill opens the dialog box, shown here, that contains all of the controls for the fill.

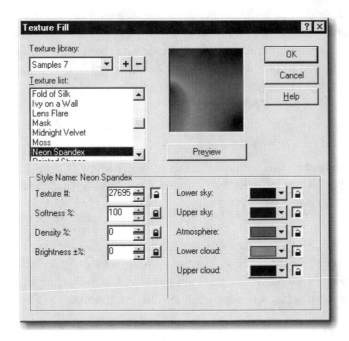

Texture Library

This list box displays the names of the texture libraries. Corel PHOTO-PAINT ships with four libraries described in the following paragraphs: Samples, Samples 5, Samples 6, Samples 7, and Styles.

SAMPLES   This is the original set of samples that were made with the Texture generator in the Styles library. For example, Clouds, Midday was created with Sky, 2 Colors. It is a quick way to get a texture without having to wade through all of the texture parameters to make it. The Samples library shipped with the original version of Corel 5.

SAMPLES 5/6/7   These libraries are like Samples except that there are more variations. Some of my personal favorites are in this library. I find that I use the Night Sky and Planets textures in the Samples 5 library more than almost any other texture. The Samples 5 library first shipped with the maintenance release of Corel PHOTO-PAINT 5. The Samples 6 shipped with Corel PHOTO-PAINT 6. Samples 7 is by far my favorite. Make sure you check it out.

12

STYLES   These are the building blocks of the bitmap texture fills. It is from the textures in this library that all of the other samples in the other three libraries are made. This is a read-only library. If you modify a texture and want to save it, you will not be allowed to save it here. You must either create a new library or save it in one of the Samples libraries.

Texture List

This lists the texture fills available in the currently selected library. Clicking on a texture in the Texture list will select it, and the default setting for the texture will display in the preview window.

 TIP: *Each time a library is selected, the texture list returns to the default texture for that library. For example, if you were in Samples 5 and had been working with Night Sky and then you switched over to look at something in Styles, when you went back to Samples 5, it would have returned to the default texture.*

Preview and Locked/Unlocked Parameters

Each time the Preview button is depressed, Corel PHOTO-PAINT varies the appearance of the selected texture by randomly changing all unlocked parameters. This button does more than is apparent at first. There are over 15,000 textures with several million possible combinations for each one. Rather than requiring you to wade through a sea of permutations, Corel PHOTO-PAINT textures have certain variables that are either locked or unlocked by default.

The unlocked parameters are the ones that the graphic engineers at Corel thought provided the best way to modify the textures. Every time the Preview button is depressed, the unlocked parameters change randomly. This is especially important for the texture pattern settings.

You can lock and unlock a parameter by clicking the Lock button next to it. You can also use the Preview button to update a texture after changing the parameters yourself.

 TIP: *Until you get used to using a texture, I recommend using the default settings for the locks. They generally provide the best, quickest results.*

Save As (Plus Button)

After changing the parameters of a texture in the library (or a new library you created), click the Plus button in the upper-right corner to overwrite the original. This opens a dialog box for naming (or renaming) a texture you have created. The texture name can be up to 32 characters (including spaces). The Library Name option allows you to create a new library in which to store the textures. You can type up to 32 characters (including spaces). The Library List displays libraries where you can store the modified texture. (*Note:* You must save any modified Style textures in a library other than the Styles library, because it is read-only.)

Delete (Minus Button)

This deletes the selected texture. You can only delete textures from libraries you created and added.

Style Name and Parameter Section

This part of the Texture Fill dialog box shows the name of the selected textures. Because each texture has different value assignments, methods, colors, and lights, it would take a separate book to list even a few of the combinations provided by the parameters. The value boxes in this area list parameters for the selected texture. Changing one or more of these parameters alters the appearance of the texture. The changes are displayed in the preview box whenever the Preview button is depressed. The Style Name fields list numeric parameters. All textures have a texture number, which ranges from 0 to 32,767. The names of the other parameters vary with the texture selected and have ranges from 0 to 100 or -100 to 100.

To change a numeric parameter, enter a value in the text box or use the cursor and click either the up or down arrow.

 TIP: *If you are going to ascend or descend very far on the numeric list, you can use a speedup feature of the up and down arrows. Place the cursor between the up and down arrows. It will change into a two-headed arrow cursor with a line between the two arrowheads. After the cursor changes, click and drag either up or down, and the selection list will move rapidly up or down the list (depending on which way you choose). To see the change entered, click the Preview button.*

12

The right side of the field lists up to six color parameters, depending on the texture selected. To change a color, click the color button and select a new color from the pop-up palette. If you desire a specific color or named color that is not on the color palette, click the Others button. This opens the same dialog box (here called Select Color) as the Uniform Fill dialog box. (See the Uniform Fill section for specific details regarding the use of this dialog box.) After you have made the desired changes, click the Preview button to see the effect the new color has on the selected texture.

The Transparency Tab

The Transparency tab of the Edit Fill & Transparency dialog box offers the ability to control the transparency of fills. With the Transparency tab, you apply fills with one of eight transparency fills by selecting it in the Type box.

Choosing None (default) means there is no transparency applied to the fill. This is the way fills are normally applied. Choosing Flat creates a transparency that is uniform throughout the fill. Because it is a uniform transparency, it only has a starting value. The default setting for the Start Transparency is zero. If this setting isn't changed, the Flat setting operates like the None setting. The photograph shown here had a bitmap fill applied to it at a Flat transparency setting of 60.

The Linear setting, shown in Figure 12-7, applies a fill beginning with the level of transparency specified in the <u>S</u>tart Transparency value and ending with the level defined by the <u>E</u>nd Transparency. The beginning and ending points of the fill are determined by the starting and ending points placed in the preview window. Using a value of 0 to 100, the Linear fill was applied to the picture of the mask in the image. In the next image, the cursor in the preview window (enlarged in the insert above the dialog box) indicates the starting and ending points of the transparency. The resulting image is displayed above and to the left of the dialog box.

The Elliptical setting (Figure 12-8) provides the greatest control in the creation of irregularly shaped fills. The original photograph has a solid black background. By applying a parchment fill through an elliptical transparency as shown in the dialog box, we are able to make the man appear to be part of the original paper. Believe me when I tell you it looked much better in color.

The Radial setting, like the Elliptical setting, offers the advantage of circular lines, which attracts the attention of the viewer by allowing another image to be

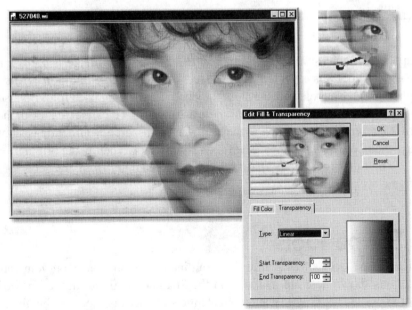

Applying
the Linear
setting
of the
Transparency
tab

FIGURE 12-7

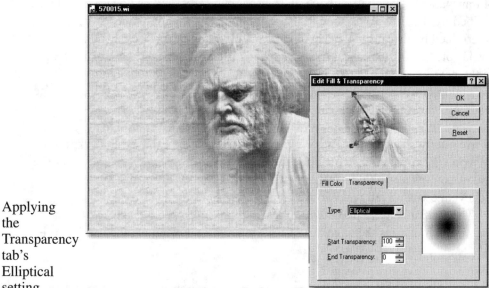

Applying
the
Transparency
tab's
Elliptical
setting

FIGURE 12-8

applied without straight lines. In Figure 12-9, the top image is the original. The Radial Type was selected and instead of one of the traditional fills, another photograph was selected. Because the photograph being used for a fill also had the subject in the center, it was necessary to use the First Tile offset feature of the Bitmap fill to move the photograph to the right. The transparency direction is shown in the expanded preview window. The final result is shown below the original.

The other two choices are Square and Rectangle. Both are good for creating frame-style effects.

The Shape Tools

The Shape tools allow you to draw outlined or filled shapes on your image. The buttons shown here are available in the Shape tools flyout in the Toolbox. If you

want to create the shape as an object, enable the Render to Object checkbox in the Tool Settings roll-up for the Shape tools or the Property bar. This allows you to reposition or edit your object before you merge it into your image. If you

Applying
the Radial
setting
of the
Transparency
tab

FIGURE 12-9

do not create the shape as an object, it will instantly merge into the background, so ensure you set the color, fill, and outline the way you want to in the Tool Settings roll-up before you begin. Another unique feature of the Shape tools is the No Fill tool. When enabled, the Shape tools create rectangles, circles, and polygon borders without applying a fill.

TIP: *The Render to Object option on the Property bar creates shapes as objects that can be moved and transformed without affecting the underlying image. This feature is not enabled for all of the Shape tools. If you enable it on the Rectangle tool, it is not automatically enabled on all of the other tools. This is true of all of the Shape tool properties.*

12

Width and Roundness of Borders

With the Tool Settings roll-up or the Property bar, you can control the size and shape of a border made by the Rectangle, Ellipse, or Polygon Shape tools.

Width

This determines the thickness of the border in points (remember, a point is 1/72 of an inch).

Transparency

The Transparency setting determines how transparent the fill will be when applied to the image. This setting can be of great benefit when you need to apply a fill for an effect. It can also be a real pain.

 TIP: *You must understand that when you change the transparency, it remains, and it is very easy to forget that you now have a transparency setting. What happens to me is that I will apply a color like red and notice that it looks washed out. I sit there puzzled, wondering if I have left some sort of mask on the image, and then after a few moments, I remember that I have a transparency setting. This setting only works for the Rectangle, Ellipse, or Polygon tool. It does not affect the transparency setting for the Fill tool.*

Roundness (Rectangle Tool Only)

The "roundness" of the corners is determined by the Roundness settings. A rough representation of the rounded curve is continuously updated as the value of roundness is increased or decreased.

Paint Mode

The Paint mode drop-down box lets you control the way paint colors and paper colors combine to create new colors and effects. With most paint tools, the Paint Color simply replaces the Paper Color (just as you would use a colored paint to paint a white wall). However, with the paint modes, it is the combination of paint colors and paper colors that produces the new color.

Anti-Aliasing

Anti-aliasing removes jagged edges from a mask, object, or image by adding duplicated pixels where the mask, object, or image edge contacts the background image.

Joints (Polygon Tool Only)

This setting gives you three choices for how Paint is to treat the joints of multiple line figures. Use the drop-down list to select the type of joint. Choices are Butt, Filled, Round, and Point.

- **Butt**   The Joints are the squared ends of the lines where they meet and overlap.

- **Filled**   The open areas caused by the overlap are filled.

- **Round**   The corners are rounded.

- **Point**   The corners end in points.

Using the Rectangle Tool

The Rectangle tool is used to draw hollow or filled rectangles and rounded rectangles. Without the tools in this flyout, we wouldn't be able to control the fill of masked areas as well as we do.

Here are the Rectangle drawing tool facts:

- If the CTRL key is held down while defining the shape, the rectangle is constrained to a square.

- Holding down the SHIFT key while creating a rectangle will cause the rectangle to shrink or grow (depending on the direction of the mouse movement) from the center.

- When the rectangle is produced, it is filled with the current fill setting in the Fill roll-up.

- If the No Fill setting is selected, a hollow rectangle is created. It doesn't consume system resources; it doesn't do anything. Sounds Zen. Very good, Grasshopper.

12

To Draw a Rectangle or Rounded Rectangle

Here are some hints about drawing rectangles or rounded rectangles.

- Select the Rectangle tool and choose the border color by left-clicking the desired color on the onscreen palette and the Fill color by right-clicking on the desired color. The paint (background) color determines border color.

- The rectangle is filled with the current Fill color when the left mouse button is released.

- The rectangle is hollow if No Fill is selected in the Fill roll-up.

- Specify the width and roundness of the border in the Tool Settings roll-up.

- Press the left mouse button to anchor the rectangle and drag until you have achieved the desired size.

- If the rectangle is not what you desire, it can be erased by pressing the ESC key *before* releasing the mouse button.

The Ellipse Tool

The Ellipse tool draws hollow or filled ellipses. If the CTRL key is held down while defining the shape, the ellipse is constrained to a circle. Holding down the SHIFT key will shrink or grow the ellipse/circle from the center.

To Draw an Ellipse

The following are some general guidelines for drawing circles and ellipses with the Ellipse tool.

- Click the Ellipse tool and choose the border color by clicking the desired color in the onscreen palette with the left mouse button.

- The paint (background) color determines border color. The ellipse is filled with the current Fill color unless No Fill is selected in the Fill roll-up.

- Specify the width of the border in the Tool Settings roll-up.

- Press the left mouse button to anchor the ellipse, and drag until you have achieved the desired size.

■ If the circle is not what you desire, it can be erased by pressing the ESC key *before* releasing the mouse button. Holding down the SHIFT key produces a circle.

The Polygon Tool

The Polygon tool produces closed multisided figures. By selecting different Joint settings in the Tools Settings roll-up, the Polygon tool can provide a wide variety of images.

To Draw a Polygon

The following are some procedural guides for using the Polygon tool:

■ Select the Polygon tool.

■ Choose Color, Width, type of joints, and Transparency of the border and fill.

■ Click where the polygon is to begin in order to anchor the starting point. Move the cursor where the first side of the polygon is to end. As the cursor is moved, the closed shape of the polygon is continually redrawn on the screen to assist the user in what the final shape will look like.

■ Click the left mouse button again to complete the first side. Continue moving the cursor to define the remaining sides.

■ Double-clicking the end of the last line completes the polygon.

■ Holding the CTRL key down while moving the cursor constrains the sides of the polygon vertically, horizontally, or at 45 degree angles.

The Line Tool

The last button on the Shape tools flyout is the Line tool. There are times when working with any photo-editing package that you just need to make a line. This tool draws single or joined straight line segments using the Paint Color. The Render to Object option on the Property bar creates new lines as objects that can be moved and transformed without affecting the underlying image. This is very handy because it allows you to correct mistakes that were impossible to fix before this feature was introduced.

12

13

Understanding Objects

U p to now we have been manipulating images with the help of various types of masks. In this chapter we will begin to work with one of the more powerful features of Corel PHOTO-PAINT: creating and controlling objects. The use of objects falls into a category I call fun stuff. There is a tabloid sold in the United States called *The Sun,* which may be one of the leading forums for unique photo-editing. If you live in the United States, you have probably seen *The Sun* while standing in grocery lines. Last night the headline was "Baby Born with Three Heads." The photograph showed a woman holding an infant who fit the headline's description. Someone on *The Sun* staff had masked the face of a small child, made it into an object, duplicated several copies, and placed them on the body of the baby. Like I said, fun stuff. If you are an avid reader of *The Sun,* do not take what I say as criticism of the tabloid. I love *The Sun*! I stand in a lot of grocery lines, and it provides entertainment during an otherwise boring wait.

In this chapter we will explore Objects, the Text tool, and all that can be done with them.

Pixels and Crazy Glue

When an image is placed in a bitmap program like Corel PHOTO-PAINT, it becomes part of the background of the image. Traditionally, with bitmap programs (like Microsoft PAINT), there is only one layer. With these one-layer programs, if we were to take a brush from the Toolbox and draw a wide brush stroke across an image, every pixel the brush touches would change to the color assigned to the brush. If we then removed the brush color, the original image would have vanished. This is because the brush color did not go on *top* of the original color, it replaced it. It is as if every pixel that is applied has super glue on it. When an action is applied to an image, it "sticks" to the image and cannot be moved. This is one of the reasons the Undo command can only "remember" what color(s) it replaced in the last action. Each Undo operation requires the entire image area to be replaced, a process that consumes large amounts of system resources. Anyone who has spent hours and hours trying to achieve an effect with these older, one-layer bitmap programs will testify that the process by which bitmaps merge into and become part of the base image is the major drawback to photo-editing programs.

Objects Defined

So what is an object? Here is the official Corel definition:

An object is an independent bitmap selection created with object tools and layered above the base image.

Let's expand that definition. In Corel PHOTO-PAINT, an object is a bitmap that "floats" above the background, which is also called the *base image.* Because it is not a part of the base image, but instead floats above the image, an object can be moved as many times as needed without limit. Objects can also be scaled, resized, rotated, and distorted. In PHOTO-PAINT 7, we have the ability to apply Perspective transform in addition to the other transformations already mentioned, as well as new Modes of operation that greatly increase the flexibility of many of the tools.

When the concept of objects was introduced in Corel PHOTO-PAINT 5, there were *simple* and *complex* objects. Now PHOTO-PAINT has only one kind of object. Here is the best part: objects are much easier to create in Corel PHOTO-PAINT 7 than they are with Corel PHOTO-PAINT 5. You are about to learn how to do some amazing things with objects. Most of the rules you learned in previous chapters regarding masks also apply to objects.

The Objects Roll-Up

The Objects roll-up is the control center for all object manipulations. The following is only a partial list of the functions that can be accomplished through the Property bar and the Objects roll-up:

- Render to Object
- Select object
- Lock or unlock objects
- Make objects visible or invisible
- Create objects from masks
- Create masks from objects

- Move objects between layers

- Control the transparency/opacity of objects

- Apply transformations to individual objects

- Select merge modes for individual objects

- Label different object layers

- Combine objects with the background

- Combine individual objects together

- Delete objects

Exploring the Objects Roll-Up and Property Bar

The Objects roll-up, shown in Figure 13-1, is a multifaceted roll-up. It can be opened by double-clicking on the Object Pointer in the Toolbox, pressing the keyboard combination CTRL+F7, or selecting objects from the Roll-Ups list in the View menu. The Property bar that is associated with objects offers many of the controls available on the Objects roll-up.

Grouping and Resizing the Objects Roll-Up

The top of the roll-up shows that there are two roll-ups grouped together. This is the default setting for the Objects roll-up. Holding the SHIFT key down and dragging the Channels roll-up from the roll-up is one of many ways to ungroup these two roll-ups. The only reason you may want to ungroup them is to use the new Object roll-up resize feature. When the roll-up isn't grouped, you can resize it by grabbing the bottom with a cursor and dragging it to the desired size, as shown next. This is very handy when working with many objects. For more information on the grouping of roll-ups, see the Corel PHOTO-PAINT user's manual or the Help file.

Object Editing Mode

New to PHOTO-PAINT 7 are the Object Editing Mode buttons. These modes are major improvements to the way objects are handled. The three mode buttons are:

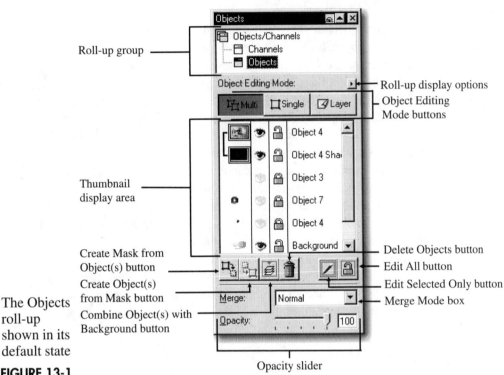

Roll-up group

Thumbnail display area

Create Mask from Object(s) button

Create Object(s) from Mask button

Combine Object(s) with Background button

Roll-up display options

Object Editing Mode buttons

Delete Objects button

Edit All button

Edit Selected Only button

Merge Mode box

Opacity slider

The Objects roll-up shown in its default state

FIGURE 13-1

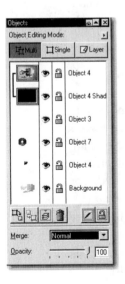

■ **Multi mode** In the default Object Editing mode, what you see is what you can edit using Corel PHOTO-PAINT's tools and commands. You use the Objects roll-up's Padlock icons to protect objects or the image background from editing changes.

■ **Single mode** This mode locks all objects except the one that is currently selected. A Pencil icon appears in the roll-up next to the name of the editable object. Only this object can be edited with Corel PHOTO-PAINT's tools; the rest of the image is protected.

■ **Layer mode** In this mode, the topmost object is placed on a transparent layer that covers the entire image. Only this object can be edited; changes are applied to the new layer and do not affect the underlying image. The Pencil icon in the roll-up identifies the object that is currently editable in this mode.

13

Thumbnail Display Area

The Thumbnail display is divided into four columns. The column on the far right shows the name of the object/layer. For purposes of clarification, the terms *object* and *layer* are used interchangeably. This is because each layer can contain only one object, and without an object there cannot be a layer. The bottom layer is named Background. It cannot be moved. Each time an object is created, Corel PHOTO-PAINT assigns a default name to it unless the user changes it. You can give an object a name by clicking on the default name and renaming it. There is a maximum length of 18 characters for Object names.

The column next to it contains a Padlock icon that shows if an object is locked or unlocked. When an object is locked, it cannot be selected, and it is protected from any effects being applied to it. Locking an object in Corel PHOTO-PAINT 7 is the equivalent of "hiding" the object in Corel PHOTO-PAINT 5. The advantage of being able to lock an object is that it remains visible, whereas in Corel PHOTO-PAINT 5 the "hidden" object disappears.

The Eye icon in the center column is either open or closed, indicating the object is either visible or invisible. When an object is invisible, it is automatically locked. The column on the left displays a thumbnail of the object in the layer.

Roll-Up Display Options

To the right and above the Object Edit Mode buttons is a small right-arrow button. Pushing it opens a drop-down list that determines the size of the thumbnails displayed. The choices are No Thumbnails; Small, Medium, and Large Thumbnails; and Update Thumbnails.

Other Available Functions

There are several buttons on the bottom of the roll-up. The availability of the buttons and the buttons that are displayed depend on the Object Editing mode. Create Mask from Object(s) and Create Object(s) from Mask perform the same as commands found in the Mask and Objects menus and the buttons in the standard toolbar.

The Combine button merges any selected object(s) with the background. The object is merged using the Merge mode setting displayed in the Merge Mode box at the bottom of the roll-up. The Delete Object button deletes the currently selected object(s) from the image.

The last two buttons are only available in Multi mode. The Edit Selected Only button locks all objects that are not selected. The Edit All button unlocks all objects in the current image. When you unlock the objects, the Padlock icons to the right of the objects are opened, indicating that each one can be accessed and manipulated independently.

The New Layer button is only available in Layer mode. It is the same as selecting New Object command in the Object menu. Clicking this button creates an empty transparent layer that covers the entire image: this layer is an object that is invisible. You can add elements to the layer to create visible elements in the new object. When you create an object using these instructions, the underlying image is not affected by any of the tools you use.

Merge Mode and Opacity

The Merge Mode box determines the way in which the colors of the object and the colors of the background image are combined when the object is merged with the background. You can preview the result of using each merge mode directly in the image window. The Opacity Slider determines the opacity of the selected object.

Object Picker Modes

There are seven different Object modes that provide all of the control you could ever dream about when it comes to manipulating and transforming objects. All of these modes are available either through the Property bar or by clicking on the object to cycle through the modes. Five of the modes can be selected and controlled through the Tool Settings roll-up, as shown here.

The Tool Settings roll-up for objects provides a very powerful and easy way to make precise manipulations to objects. There are five tabs that control the following:

- Object Position
- Object Rotation
- Object Scaling/Mirror
- Object Resizing
- Object Skewing

All of the tabs within the Tool Settings dialog box for objects have three common functions. They are:

13

- **Apply To Duplicate** This button, when selected, creates a copy of the selected object with the effects applied while leaving the original object unchanged. For example, the Object Rotation tab was selected and a value of 15 degrees was entered. Clicking the Apply to Duplicate button would create a copy of the object that was rotated 15 degrees while leaving the original unchanged.

- **Transform** Clicking this button displays a preview of the transformation of the selected object in the image window. This is a preview only. You can either press ESC or double-click outside the object or marquee in the image window to cancel the transformation and return to the original state.

- **Apply** After clicking the Transform button, click Apply in the Tool Settings roll-up, and press ENTER, or double-click inside the object to apply the transformation permanently. This control is available for both the Object Picker tool and the Mask Transform tool.

Object Position

Going from left to right, clicking on the first tab accesses the Object Position. These controls are used to reposition or move objects.

Using certain settings while attempting to move an object will result in the object being placed outside of the image area. The object is still there, just not in the viewing area. When these controls are used in conjunction with the rulers, you can position objects very precisely and quickly anywhere within the image.

Absolute/Relative Positioning

When the Relative Position option is unchecked, the Horizontal listing displays the leftmost position of the object and the Vertical listing displays the topmost position of the object in relation to the 0,0 point of the image (upper-left corner). Moving the object is accomplished by changing these values. Objects of equal size can be positioned on top of one another by entering the same values for each object in these settings.

When the Relative Position option is checked, the Horizontal and Vertical Settings start out at zero pixels in both the horizontal and vertical axis in reference to the object.

TIP: *You can quickly create a duplicate object that is precisely positioned over the original by pressing the Apply To Duplicate button without changing the Horizontal and Vertical settings.*

Object Rotate

The second tab provides access to the Object Rotation controls, as shown here. While rotation of objects can be accomplished from the Object menu or by dragging the Rotation handles, the Transform roll-up allows for precision rotation, which is very handy when you are applying it to multiple objects. Control of rotation is divided into two parts, angle and center of rotation.

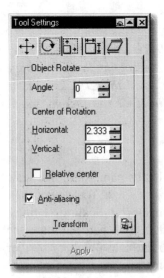

Angle of Rotation

The first control determines the Angle of Rotation. There is nothing mystical here; the value is in degrees. The range of rotation is +360 through -360 degrees. You can enter a number for the Angle of Rotation as low as one one-thousandth of a degree. If you rotate an object 15 degrees, close the Object Tool Settings roll-up, and then reopen it three hours later after having worked on several other files, the setting will still be 15 degrees for the Angle of Rotation. If you close and reopen Corel PHOTO-PAINT, the setting will default back to 0 degrees. Regardless of what rotation values are entered into this setting, the Center of Rotation setting remains centered on the object.

Center of Rotation

The next set of controls is a little more interesting. With the Center of Rotation controls, you can precisely position the center of rotation. With the Relative Center option turned off, the controls for Center of Rotation report where the center of rotation is located on the currently selected object. Whenever you need to reposition the center of rotation, simply use the rulers to locate the new position and enter those values into the Center of Rotation controls. For example, if your currently selected object has a center of rotation at the Horizontal and Vertical position of 1 inch each, you could easily change that to, say, 2 inches Horizontal and 3 inches Vertical by simply entering those values in the Center of Rotation controls.

Relative Center

When the Relative to Center option is turned on, the controls for Center of Rotation start off at 0. Units are controlled by the Preferences dialog box. Values entered in the Center of Rotation controls will move the center of rotation according to the values relative to its current position. For example, if you are working in inches and you enter a Center of Rotation value of 1 inch for both the Horizontal and Vertical settings, the center of rotation would be repositioned one inch down and to the right of the current center of rotation.

 TIP: *A quick way to rotate an object is to select it with the Object Picker and then click on the object a second time. The control handles will change to indicate it is in rotation mode. By holding down the CTRL key on the keyboard while dragging the handles, you get rotation in 15-degree increments.*

Object Scale/Flip

Object Scale, shown here, enables you to do exactly what its name suggests: scale objects. An object can be scaled by percentages of the object's size. You cannot enter

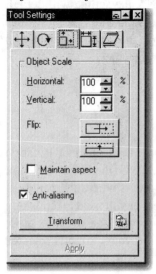

negative numbers for the Object Scaling settings. Rather, numbers larger than 100 percent scale the object larger than its current size; numbers smaller than 100 percent scale it smaller than its current size.

When Maintain Aspect is selected, the Horizontal and Vertical settings within the Object Scale remain the same. The Flip buttons flip the objects horizontally and vertically. The Object Scale settings and the Flip buttons can work in conjunction with one another. For example, if you have 50 percent Horizontal and Vertical settings for Object Scale with the Vertical Flip button on, the selected object will be flipped vertically at 50 percent of its original size when the Apply button is pressed.

TIP: *You can create a duplicate object exactly over another by hitting the Apply to Duplicate button with 100% Horizontal and Vertical Object Scale settings and the Mirror buttons not selected.*

Object Size

The Object Size settings, shown here, are a more accurate way to resize an object than Object Scale. The Object Size settings list the dimensions of the currently selected object. To change these dimensions, simply enter the new values, select Transform, and choose Apply or Apply to Duplicate. Units are determined by the default setting in the Options dialog box. Negative numbers should not be entered for the Object Size settings.

Maintain Aspect

When the Maintain Aspect option is checked, the aspect of the object will be maintained when you enter a new value in one of the Horizontal or Vertical settings. For example, if you have an object that is 1 inch horizontal and 2 inches vertical, and you enter 2 inches in the Horizontal setting with the Maintain Aspect option checked, the Vertical option will automatically maintain the aspect ratio of the object by changing to 4 inches.

13

Object Skew

Object Skew, shown here, allows you to numerically skew objects. Like all of the other settings in the Object Tool Settings roll-up, Object Skew simply provides a

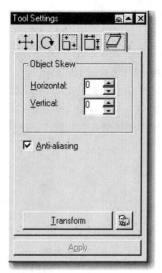

way to accurately enter values for alterations that could otherwise be performed manually. Negative degree values can be used. Once new values are entered into this setting, the Object Skew settings will remain the same until they are changed, even if the file you are working on is closed and another is opened.

Perspective Mode

This mode is new to the PHOTO-PAINT arsenal of object tools and is one of the most powerful. Although this mode is not selectable from the Tool Settings roll-up, it can be selected from the Property bar or by clicking on the object until the handles that look like small circles appear.

Perspective is the symmetrical distortion of an object that gives it a sense of depth, making it appear three-dimensional. The transformation is achieved by moving either of the two handles away from each other, making the side of the object moved longer and making it look closer to you than the other side. You can also move the handles closer to one another to make a side of the object appear further away.

Making 3D Objects Using Perspective

This is a hands-on exercise to create a 3D shape using the Perspective mode and then Duplicate and Scale—in other words, to make a much more complicated image.

1. Create a new image that is 4 × 5 inches at 96 dpi and 24-bit color.

2. From the Tools menu, select Grid and Ruler Setup. When the dialog box opens, select the Grid tab and check the Snap to Grid and the Show Grid boxes.

3. Choose the Rectangle shape tool from the Toolbox using the F6 key. From the Tool Settings roll-up, click the Fountain Fill button (second from the left) and click the Edit button. When the Fountain Fill dialog box opens, locate Cylinder - Green 04 on the Presets drop-down list. Click the OK button.

4. On the Property bar, ensure the Anti-aliasing and the Render to Object buttons are enabled. Beginning one square in from the top and left side, click the cursor and drag a square that is two by two squares in size.

5. Click the F7 key to open the Circle shape tool. Again ensure the Anti-aliasing and the Render To Object buttons are enabled on the Property bar, because each of the Shape tools maintains its own settings. Click at a point in the middle of the left side of the square and drag a circle that is two squares in diameter. The resulting image is shown in Figure 13-2

The new Render to Object command allows the instantaneous creation of the object shown

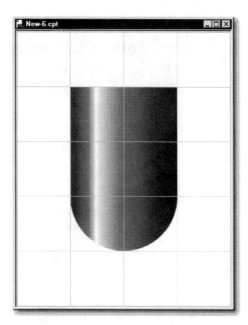

FIGURE 13-2

13

6. Open the Objects roll-up (CTRL+F7). Select the square object by clicking on its icon in the Objects roll-up. Both objects should be selected.

Combine the two objects together with the keyboard combination CTRL+SHIFT+L.

7. Select the Object Picker tool and choose the Perspective Mode button from the drop-down list on the left side of the Property bar. Four circle handles appear on the object.

8. Click and drag the upper-right handle to a point one square from the top and in the middle. Release the mouse button. The image changes into a "preview" of what the final transformation will look like. We could undo the temporary changes at this point by clicking the ESC key. Apply the transformation permanently by either clicking the Apply button on the Property bar or double-clicking the object. The resulting image is shown in Figure 13-3.

9. Save the File as CONE.CPT.

10. Duplicate the object (CTRL+SHIFT+D). Drag the one object to the left as shown and then drag the other. The resulting image is shown in Figure 13-4.

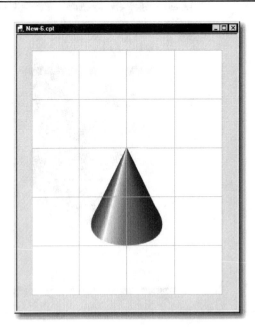

The object has a 3D appearance after applying a Perspective transform

FIGURE 13-3

11. Turn off Snap to Grid (CTRL+Y). SHIFT-select both objects and click the button labeled Group on the Property bar. Notice that the display in the Objects roll-up as shown in Figure 13-5 has changed to indicate the grouping status of the objects.

12. From the Object menu, choose Drop Shadow. When the dialog box opens, choose one of the lower offset buttons. Uncheck the Identical values box. Change the Horizontal value box to zero. Set the Vertical box to .07. Set the Feather value to 12 and the Opacity to 55. Click OK. The shadows appear directly below the cones. Notice that in the Objects roll-up (Figure 13-6) we now have four objects because each shadow is an object.

13. To minimize the number of objects we are working with for the next few steps, combine the objects together using CTRL+SHIFT+L. Duplicate the object (CTRL+SHIFT+D).

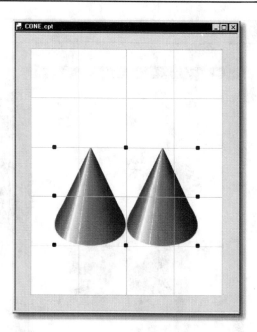

Duplicating
and moving
the object
creates two
cones

FIGURE 13-4

13

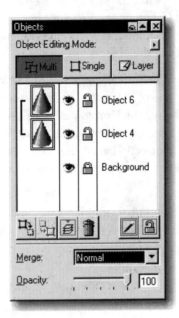

The
grouping
of objects,
indicated in
the Objects
roll-up

FIGURE 13-5

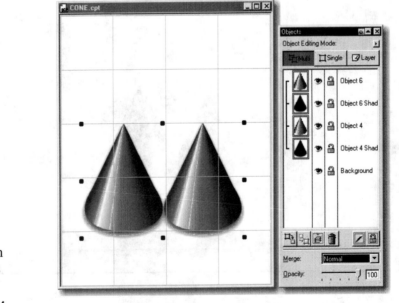

The
shadows
created by
the Drop
Shadow
command
are objects
as shown in
the Objects
roll-up

FIGURE 13-6

14. The new object appears at the top of the Objects roll-up. Deselect the new object and select the bottom object (closest to the background). Open the Tool Settings roll-up (CTRL+F8). Select Object Scale tab (middle tab). Ensure <u>M</u>aintain aspect is checked and enter a value of 75 percent in the <u>H</u>orizontal value box. Click the <u>T</u>ransform button. Notice how jagged the edges appear. Click the A<u>p</u>ply button. The transformed objects look smoother.

15. Click and drag the objects so that they look like those shown in Figure 13-7. Using the Objects roll-up, you may drag the name of one object above the other to alter the layering. Click the Single Mode button. Click between the Eye icon and the name of the bottom object. A Pencil icon will appear. Open the Hue/Saturation/Lightness dialog box (CTRL+SHIFT+U). When it opens, enter a value of 70 in the <u>H</u>ue value box. Click the OK button.

16. Duplicate the Object (CTRL+SHIFT+D). When the new object appears in the Objects roll-up click on its name and drag it down until it is just above

Using the Duplicate and Scaling capabilities to make another set of objects that appear further away from the viewer

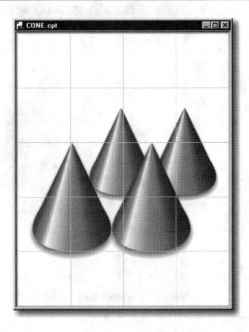

FIGURE 13-7

13

the background. Scale the object like we did in step 14. Repeat the Hue shift by clicking CTRL+F.

17. Position all of the objects so they appear to be evenly distributed in the image as shown in Figure 13-8. In the Objects roll-up, click in the column between the Eye icon and the word Background.

18. From the Edit menu, select Fill. Select the Texture Fill button (last one on the right) in the Edit Fill & Transparency dialog box and click the Edit button. When the dialog box opens, change the Texture library to Samples 7. From the Texture list, choose Neon Spandex (hey, I don't make up these names). Click OK to close the dialog box and OK again to apply the fill. You're done. From the View menu, click Grid to turn off the grid display. The final result should look like Figure 13-9 and is also shown in the color insert.

19. Save the file as MADONNA… (just kidding) CONES.CPT.

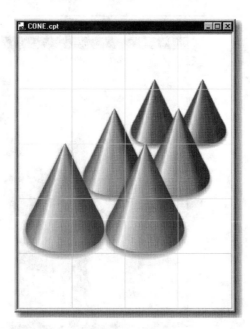

Now the cones are beginning to remind me of the brooms from *Fantasia*

FIGURE 13-8

The
finished
image—
a grand
exercise in
objects and
perspective

FIGURE 13-9

Additional Tips for Working with Objects

- Transform Options will be unavailable when anything other than the Object Picker tool is selected from the Toolbox.

- Objects do not have to be the same size as the image. You can paste or drag and drop an object into an image that is larger than the page size and not have the area outside the image boundaries clipped.

It is the ability to create, modify, and position objects that makes Corel PHOTO-PAINT 7 such a powerful photo-editing program. We have only covered the basics to this point.

13

How to Group Objects

To group objects, you must have two or more objects selected. There are several ways to select objects for grouping in an image.

- Using the Object Picker tool, you can drag a rectangle over the objects you want grouped together.

- From the Objects roll-up, you can select (by clicking on the thumbnail image) the objects you want.

- If you want to select all of the objects in the image, you can choose Select All… from the Object menu.

- You can select the first object, and then, holding down the SHIFT key, select more. Each time you select an object, it is added to the number of Objects selected. The action is a toggle, so if you select an object you do not want, click it again to deselect it. (Did you know "deselect" is not a real word? Isn't it amazing what we learn from our spelling checkers?)

After you have selected the objects, depress the keyboard combination CTRL+G. All of the selected objects will become grouped together. How will you know? Looking at the Object roll-up gives a visual clue to what objects are grouped. When objects are grouped, they are joined together with a black bar in the far left column of the Objects roll-up. To ungroup the objects, select the group and depress CTRL+U or choose Ungroup from the Object menu. You may also use the Group and Ungroup buttons on the Property bar.

Creating a CD Cover

In this hands-on exercise, we are going to use many of the commands and tools of PHOTO-PAINT 7 to create a CD cover for a fictional group called Excalibur. We want to convey visually the mystique associated with the sword Excalibur, King Arthur, et al., and yet convey the fact that this is a modern group. No problem.

Before beginning, please notice that when we load objects into an image, they all have white backgrounds that also appear as objects. Any object saved as a file will contain these backgrounds, which in most cases must be deleted.

1. Create a new image that is 5 × 4 inches at 96 dpi and 24-bit color.

2. Click the F6 function key to open the Rectangle shape tool. From the Tool Settings roll-up, click the Fountain Fill button and then the Edit button. When the dialog box opens, select the Circular - Green 02 Preset. Change the Horizontal setting to -12, the Vertical to 11 and the Steps to 999. Click OK.

3. Place the cursor in the image and click and drag a rectangle as shown in Figure 13-10.

4. Open the Objects roll-up (CTRL+F7) and click the Single button. From the Effects menu, choose 3D Effects and select Zigzag. When the dialog box opens, change the Type to Pond Ripples. Under Adjust, change Waves to 10 and Strength to 25. Click OK.

5. Select the Object Picker tool and on the far left of the Property bar, open the Mode Selector flyout and select the Perspective transform mode. Grab the upper-right handle of the rectangle and drag it down and to the left until it looks like the one shown in Figure 13-11.

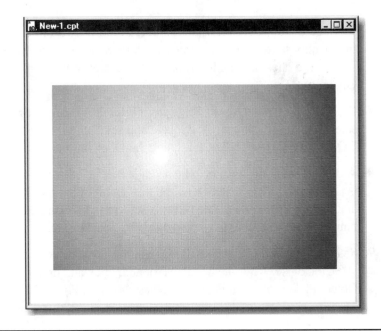

The
rectangle
object
created
with the
Rectangle
Shape tool

FIGURE 13-10

13

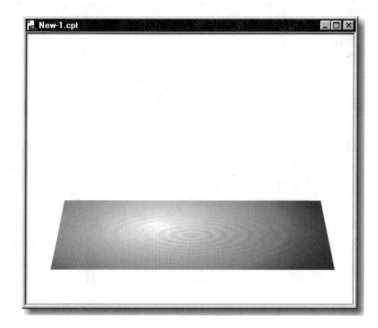

After
the Ripple
filter is
applied, the
Perspective
Object is
applied

FIGURE 13-11

6. Click on the object to return to the default handles. From the Effects menu, choose Render and then Lens Flare. Select the 105mm Prime setting and click at a point just above the center of the ripples. Click the OK button.

7. From the Edit menu, select Paste from File. From the dialog box, select the CD-ROM drive and locate and select the file \OBJECTS\ COMPUTER\HANDCD.CPT. Click the Open button.

8. Although the hand appears to be a single image, Objects roll-up shows it is actually two objects. Click on the thumbnail of the hand to deselect it and the object we just created (if it is selected). Click the Delete Object button (Trashcan icon) to remove the white background.

9. Select the hand object. From the Object menu, select Rotate and choose 90° Clockwise. After the hand has rotated, click and drag it with the Object Picker tool so it is positioned as shown in Figure 13-12.

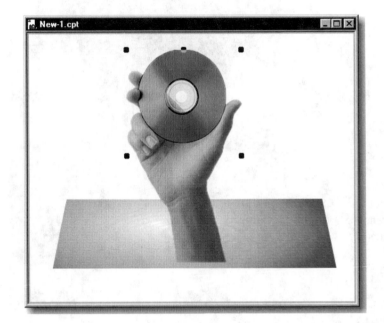

Position
the hand
as shown

FIGURE 13-12

10. Click the small black icon on the Object Picker tool to open the flyout. Select the Object Transparency tool (the one in the middle). Place the cursor on the hand, and click and drag a short line to the end of the hand object as shown in Figure 13-13. Click the Apply button on the Property bar.

11. In the Objects roll-up, deselect the hand object and click in the empty column between the word Background and the Eye icon. The Pencil icon appears. From the Edit menu, select Fill. When the Edit Fill & Transparency dialog box opens, click OK.

12. Ensure that only the original ripple object is selected in the Objects roll-up. Select If Lighter from the drop-down list in the Merge mode settings.

13. Click Multi mode. Select both objects. Click the Combine button (left of the trashcan) at the bottom of the Objects Roll-Up. The result is shown in Figure 13-14.

14. Save the file as EXCALIBUR.CPT.

13

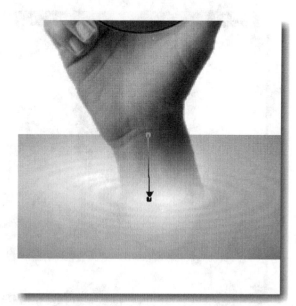

The Object
Transparency
tool creates
a smooth
transition
into the
ripples

FIGURE 13-13

We have
a basic
background
for our
CD label

FIGURE 13-14

15. Select the Text tool from the Toolbox. Click on a dark blue color in the onscreen palette. Change the Font on the Property bar to Century Schoolbook at a size of 48. Click the Bold button. Click the cursor on the image, type EXCALIBUR, and position it centered between the hand and the bottom of the image.

16. Select Perspective mode from the Property bar. Click and drag the upper-right handle until the text appears as shown in Figure 13-15.

17. Double-click on the text to apply the effect. From the Object menu, choose Drop Shado_w_. From the dialog box, uncheck the _I_dentical values box. Change _H_orizontal to 0 and _V_ertical to .03. Change the Feather to 6 and the Opacity to 100. Change the Color to White Shadow. Click OK. The result is shown in Figure 13-16.

18. I'm never willing to leave well enough alone. There is one final step. From the Objects roll-up, select Single mode and click the cursor between the word Background and the Eye icon. Click the Eye icon of the text to make it invisible.

Our finished CD label is almost ready, but the type needs something to make it stand out

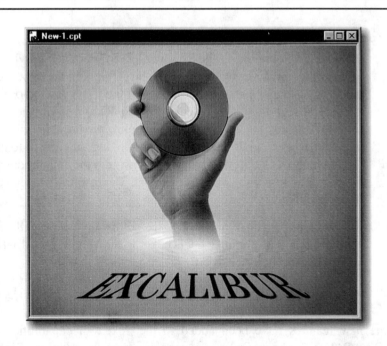

FIGURE 13-15

13

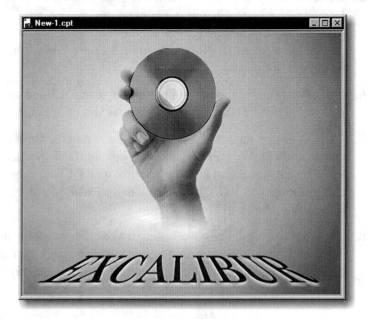

The final image is ready, now we only need to find a band called Excalibur

FIGURE 13-16

19. From the Effects menu, choose Render and then Lighting effects. When the dialog box opens, set the Style to Default. From the preview window, click the larger of the two dots on the bright light in the upper-left corner and drag it so it is directly over the top of the CD at the top of the image. Next, grab and drag the smaller connected dot to a point below the middle of the CD. Click the Add Light button below the preview window. When the light appears, grab the larger of the two dots and drag it to the bottom of the image in the preview window. Now grab the smaller dot and drag it to the beginning of the palm of the hand. The resulting image is shown in Figure 13-17.

20. In the Objects menu, click the Eye icon of the text and it will become visible again. The completed CD cover is shown in Figure 13-18 and is also shown in the color insert.

The Text Tool

Some new features have been added to the Text tool capabilities with Corel PHOTO-PAINT 7. The major improvement has been the addition of intercharacter

The icons
from the
Lighting
Effects
filter
preview
window
show the
direction
and height
of the
Lighting
Effects

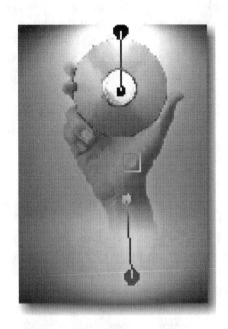

FIGURE 13-17

Now that
it really
is finished,
we really
should
locate a
band to
go with the
CD cover

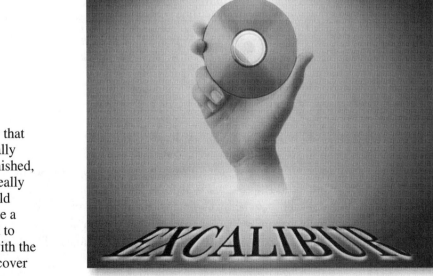

FIGURE 13-18

13

spacing (kerning) and interline spacing (leading). Another productivity enhancement has been the ability to render the text immediately to a mask.

Although introduced last year in PHOTO-PAINT 6, the most powerful feature of the Text tool remains the editable text capability. In Corel PHOTO-PAINT 5, the text becomes a bitmap image after it is entered and becomes an object. In Corel PHOTO-PAINT 7, we can return to text and change the fonts, size, or other attributes at any time. Only when the text is combined with the background does it cease to be editable. The Text tool, used in combination with the fill capabilities and layers/objects, can produce stunning effects quickly.

Before Adding Text in Corel PHOTO-PAINT

As great as Corel PHOTO-PAINT's text capabilities are, if you are planning to add paragraph-style text to a Corel PHOTO-PAINT image, it's best to use another program like CorelDRAW. The procedure is simple. First, finish whatever enhancements to the image are needed and save it as a .CPT file. Next, import the file into CorelDRAW or similar graphics program and add the text at that time. While I have mentioned this before, it bears repeating. When text is created in Corel PHOTO-PAINT, it is a bitmap image that is resolution-dependent. Text in a program like DRAW is resolution-independent. This means that text placed in Corel PHOTO-PAINT will be the resolution of the image. If it is 300 dpi (dots per inch), the text will be a bitmap image that is 300 dpi regardless if it is printed to a 300-dpi laser printer or a 2450-dpi imagesetter. If the same text is placed in DRAW, it remains text. If it is output to a 2450-dpi imagesetter, the resolution of the text will be 2450 dpi. The result is sharper text.

Basics of the Text Tool

 Use the Text tool to add text to an image. Text is by default an object that floats above the image background. Text properties—the font, style, size, kerning, leading, and other effects—are determined through the Property bar or the Tool Settings roll-up. You can manipulate, edit, format, and transform the text object while it is still an object. Once you've combined the text object with the background, you can no longer edit it as text. A new feature in PHOTO-PAINT 7 is Render Text to Mask. When selected, it automatically makes new text you type become a mask. This is a real time saver.

If you have worked with recent versions of word processors in Windows, everything on the Property bar, as well as the Tool Settings, should be familiar to you. The first box shows all of the available fonts that are installed in Windows 95. The second box displays the selected font sizes in points (72 points = 1 inch). While the font size drop-down list shows many available sizes, you can select any size you need by typing the desired font size (in points) in the Font Size box. Any change you make in the Text toolbar is instantly reflected in the text displayed in the image area. You can also move the rectangle containing the text by clicking on its edge and dragging it with the left mouse button.

 CAUTION: *Be careful when entering text in Layer mode. Any part of the text entered that is outside of the image window will be lost.*

There are no system default settings for the Text tool's font selection. The typeface is always the first element of the list of installed fonts. Since lists in Windows 95 are maintained alphabetically, the typeface whose name is first alphabetically (i.e., AARDVARK) will always appear as the default. The last settings of the Text toolbar remains until changed again or Corel PHOTO-PAINT is shut down.

Here are the facts about the Corel PHOTO-PAINT Text tool:

- The color of the text is determined by the setting of the Paint (foreground) color. It is very easy to change the color of the text in Corel PHOTO-PAINT 7. With the text selected with the Text tool, click any color in the palette with the left mouse button. The color of the text will change to match the color you just clicked.

- When you select existing text with the Text tool, all transformations that have been applied to that text will be lost.

- To correct a text entry, use the BACKSPACE or DELETE key.

- To check the spelling of text, use a dictionary. Sorry, no spell checker.

- The selected alignment of text (left, center, or right) does not occur until the ENTER key is pressed.

- There is no automatic line wrap (soft carriage returns) of text. This is because Corel PHOTO-PAINT has no idea where to wrap the line.

13

- Text always looks ragged until it becomes an object.

NOTE: *When you go into Text Edit mode, the text will look pretty ugly (lots of jaggies). Don't worry! It will look fine once you exit Text Edit mode by selecting a different tool.*

Note For Corel PHOTO-PAINT 5 Users

In Corel PHOTO-PAINT 5, the text is a bitmap after it becomes an object. In Corel PHOTO-PAINT 7, the text remains editable as text after it becomes an object until it is combined with the background or another object.

Highlighted Text

Two of the new features of PHOTO-PAINT 7 make this hands-on exercise very simple. They are Render to Mask and Lenses. When you have a dark background, it is sometimes difficult to create text that doesn't stand out too much but is still readable. In previous versions of PHOTO-PAINT, this process took as many as 15 steps.

1. Locate and open the file PHOTOS\SUNSETS\345092.WI. After it is loaded, Resample to a width of 6 inches.

2. Select the Text tool in the Toolbox and change the Font to Futura XBlk BT at a size of 72, Centered, and Line Spacing of 70. Enable the Render to Mask button on the Property bar. Click on the image and type **SUNSET CRUISES**.

3. Select the Object Picker from the Toolbox. The text has become a mask. From the Object menu, select Create Lens from Mask. When the New Lens dialog box opens, choose Gamma. When the Gamma dialog box opens, change the slider to 2.2 and click OK. You are done. You can see the result in Figure 13-19 and is also shown in the color insert.

You can
almost feel
the sea
breeze

FIGURE 13-19

The beauty of using the lens is twofold. You can move the lens anywhere in the image that you want. Second, you can change the Gamma settings by selecting Lens Properties in the Object menu. The only limitation, if you can call it that, is that any lens must be combined with the image if the effect is to appear when it prints.

There are many other hands-on exercises involving text throughout this book. Check the table of contents or the index for their location.

14

Third-Party Filters

Given the capabilities of filters, support for the plug-in standard provides even more power to PHOTO-PAINT's already strong feature set. In this chapter I'll discuss how to enable the filters that are included in PHOTO-PAINT, how to install filters from other vendors, and I'll include some tips about the use of filters in general.

Understanding Plug-in Filters

The concept is simple. A company (like Corel) provides an access that can be used by programmers to control parts of the PHOTO-PAINT program. This access comes in the form of *plug-in filters,* which can be called from within an application (like PHOTO-PAINT) to provide a wide variety of functions and effects. The plug-in concept first appeared in photo-editing programs several years ago and is now being used in other applications, including page layout and vector drawing programs. In this chapter and the ones that follow, we are going to explore the filters that are provided with PHOTO-PAINT 7.

Different Jobs, Different Filters

Just as there are many different tasks in photo-editing, there are also many different types of plug-in filters. For purposes of discussion, filters can be loosely classified as either utility or artistic. An example of a *utility* filter would be one that converts images to a format not normally supported by the application. Those that provide artistic, or painterly, effects represent an *artistic* type of filter. Examples of artistic type filters can be found in Kai's Power Tools 3.0, which is included in PHOTO-PAINT 7. Some of the filters fall into both categories. Regardless of the type, they must first be installed.

Installation of Filters

The first time you launch PHOTO-PAINT after installation, you will notice that not all of the filters are available when you open the Effects menu, shown at the left of Figure 14-1. After you have installed all of the filter sets that came with PHOTO-PAINT, your drop-down list will look more like the middle menu in Figure

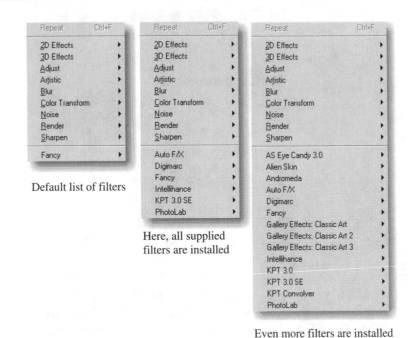

Default list of filters

Here, all supplied
filters are installed

The more
filters you
install, the
longer your
Effects list
will be

Even more filters are installed

FIGURE 14-1

14-1. Any filter that can be installed by the user appears in the list (alphabetically) under the dividing line below the Sharpen category. The menu on the right shows the list that appears when some additional third-party filters are installed. This brings us to the subject of actually installing the filters.

Installing Plug-in Filters

Installing plug-in filters in Corel PHOTO-PAINT means you are making the filters available so that they appear on the Effects drop-down list. The procedure for doing this is a breeze. Simply select Options from the Tools menu (or CTRL+J) and click the Plug-In Filters tab, shown next.

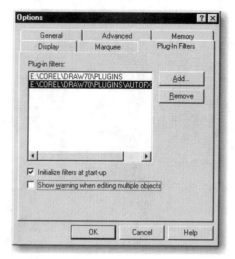

Click the <u>A</u>dd... button to open the Select A Plug-In Folder dialog box, and locate the directory where the plug-in filters have been installed. PHOTO-PAINT keeps all of its plug-ins in separate folders in COREL\DRAW70\PLUGINS. For example, to install the PhotoLab filters, select the Photolab folder in the Plug-ins folder.

There are two options in the Plug-In Filter tab. With the Initialize filters at <u>s</u>tart-up checkbox enabled, all of the Plug-In filters are initialized at the time Corel PHOTO-PAINT is launched. When disabled, Plug-In filters are not initialized until the first time you click the Effe<u>c</u>ts menu. This process may take a few minutes. I recommend you leave it enabled. The other option, Show <u>w</u>arning when editing multiple objects, displays a message advising you that the preview area in the Filters dialog box may not be completely accurate when working with an image that contains objects. You may want to leave this option on until you get used to how the filters work and then disable it to stop the message from displaying.

When you install the filters, you may wonder if they must be in their own subdirectory (that was created by their installation program) or if you can just copy them into the \COREL\DRAW7\PLUGINS folder. While you can copy all of the filter files into the same PLUGINS directory, be aware that by installing them all in the same folder you cannot selectively turn sets of filters on and off. This is because you cannot select individual filters within a folder. All of the filters in a folder are made available when the folder is selected. Corel PHOTO-PAINT can use filters installed in folders just about anywhere in the system, so while it may be more tidy to have all of the sets of filters in folders under PLUGINS, it is by no means necessary.

TIP: *You may find that some of the filters give you a choice of automatically installing the filters for Corel PHOTO-PAINT. If this choice is offered, make sure where the program will install them, since the location of the filters is different in PHOTO-PAINT 5, 6, and 7, and it may load them in an unexpected area.*

While it is a matter of personal preference, it can be useful to only load those filters that you need during your PHOTO-PAINT session. Some filters take up system resources when they are loaded into PHOTO-PAINT. Making available a set of filters that won't be used during a PHOTO-PAINT session is a waste of system resources. Since the program can load and unload filter sets on the fly, you can load and unload filter sets as you need them. When you have a lot of filter sets loaded, it also takes a little longer to load each set initially.

Removing filters from PHOTO-PAINT is like installation in reverse: select the folder where the filters are located and hit the Delete button. Once you exit the dialog box by clicking the OK button, PHOTO-PAINT automatically removes any deleted filters and loads any filters that are selected. It takes a moment for PHOTO-PAINT to find the plug-in filters and rebuild the Effects menu. You will have access to your filters without having to restart PHOTO-PAINT.

Some Technical Information about Plug-in Filters

Filter files for plug-ins are easily identified by an .8BF file extension. All of the noninstallable filter files provided with PHOTO-PAINT are contained in dynamic link libraries that have a .DLL extension. The reason they do not have a *.8BF extension is twofold. First, DLLs provide a faster way for PAINT to access the filters. Second, this way you can only use the filters with Corel PHOTO-PAINT. The second point is worth mentioning in case you're wondering how to load Alchemy or one of the other Corel filters into another photo-editing program, such as Photoshop or Picture Publisher. It won't work.

Not All Filters Are Created Equal

All of the filters that appear on the market today are designed to work in a 32-bit environment like PHOTO-PAINT 7. These 32-bit versions offer the advantage of greater processing speed and functional capabilities. Many of the older filters in the marketplace are 16-bit. Corel PHOTO-PAINT 7 allows the use of these filters in most cases, but I strongly recommend the 32-bit versions. At the time of this writing, all of the vendors for third-party plug-ins are offering 32-bit versions. Some of the newest ones are available only in 32-bit versions.

Will plug-in filters designed for Adobe Photoshop work in PHOTO-PAINT 7? I get this question a lot. The answer is a definite maybe. Whether a filter works or not depends on whether the program was written as a general plug-in filter (it will probably work) or to control specific and unique Photoshop commands (it won't). The best way to find out is to call the vendor who wrote the program and ask.

Where Can I Get Additional Plug-Ins?

This isn't always easy since most of the plug-ins are not sold in the normal reseller channel. This is because with few exceptions, the companies that make these filters are very small. So where do you find out about them? Look in the magazines and catalogs that specialize in DTP. *Corel* magazine, *Adobe* magazine, and *Publish* all contain both articles and advertisements about plug-in filters.

A Note on Downloading Free Filters

If you are an avid user of the Internet or other online services, you will find a lot of plug-in filters available as freeware or shareware. Before you begin downloading all of these wonderful filters, carefully read the description. Many of the filters I have found in online services are only for use on a Mac. However, some of the descriptions that accompany the filters do not specify they are Mac filters. The filter designers are not being deceptive. In most cases they don't know or can't imagine that anyone from the Windows world uses plug-in filters. There are several telltale signs that the filter is for a Mac. First, there won't be any mention of Windows in the description. I have found if a filter is available for Windows, the filter designers tend to shout it from the rooftops. Second, look at the extension of the file to be downloaded. If it has an .SEA or any other extension that is not a standard IBM PC type compression extension like .ZIP, .ARC, etc., then it is for a Mac.

As long as I am discussing downloading filters, I should point out that PHOTO-PAINT 7 now works with nearly all of the Filter Factory filters that are available on the Internet. The Filter Factory is a user-definable type of filter that many people have used to create unique effects. By downloading the filter files and reading a lot of text files, you can use the filters they have made or roll your own.

Introducing the Filter Dialog Box

The filter dialog box has changed somewhat since PHOTO-PAINT 6. We are going to take a quick look at how the dialog box works and what options are available. Figure 14-2 shows the dialog box for the Zigzag filter. While the lower portion of each dialog box changes to accommodate the different filter controls, the upper portion remains generally the same.

The Hand and Zoom buttons on the left control the positioning and zoom level of the preview window. Both of the tools are applied in the Original window, and the Result window changes accordingly. With the Hand tool selected, you can drag

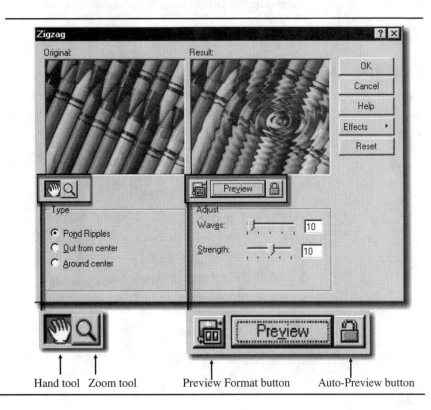

The Zigzag filter dialog box has many of the controls common to all filter dialog boxes

FIGURE 14-2

Hand tool   Zoom tool   Preview Format button   Auto-Preview button the image anywhere you want to get the best possible view of an effect. The Zoom tool zooms in with left mouse clicks and zooms out with right mouse clicks. The same zoom in/zoom out associated with the left and right mouse buttons also exists for the Hand tool.

On the right, below the Result window, are the Preview Format, Preview, and Auto-Preview enable buttons. The Preview Format button toggles between viewing the Original and Result windows side by side and viewing a single, larger Result window. The Preview button updates the Result window anytime it is clicked. The Auto-Preview button automatically updates the Result window to reflect any changes you make to settings in the dialog box.

 NOTE: *In Single Result window mode, the Preview button has an icon on it that looks like an eye.*

The Reset button returns the filter to its default settings. The Effects button allows access to any of the other installed filters without the need to close and reenter the Effects menu.

Into the Undiscovered Country

The fun of filters is that there seems to be something new every day. While writing this chapter, I received prerelease copies of two new plug-in filters that will be available by the time you read this. As you can see, it never stops. Our filter odyssey continues in the next chapter with a look at the Blur filters.

15

The Blur Filters

This is a fun chapter for me. There are so many things that you can do with the Blur filters, it's almost scary.

The Blur category in the Effects menu contains a collection of eight filters that produce a variety of blur effects. The type of blur filter you select is chiefly determined by the type of image you are working with and by the effect you want to obtain. Along with the blur filters that were in previous releases, Corel PHOTO-PAINT 7 introduced a new one, Radial Blur, that adds dramatic effects to images. The filters in this chapter are not listed in order of their appearance in the menu, but in order of their day-to-day usefulness, which leads us to the Gaussian Blur filter.

The Gaussian Blur Filter

This filter, although deceptively simple, is used every day to make shadows, produce glows, diffuse backgrounds, and create many of the special effects available with Corel PHOTO-PAINT. It produces a hazy effect that gives the image a slightly out-of-focus look. It can also be used to improve the quality of images containing jaggies, although with some loss of detail.

All Things Gaussian

In digital photo-editing, you often hear the term *Gaussian*. I am sometimes asked why Gaussian is capitalized and who is this person with a Blur filter named after him. The term *Gaussian* comes from Dr. Carl Friedrich Gauss, a German mathematician who was born in 1777. Dr. Gauss did not invent the Gaussian Blur, but he did discover the mathematical principles that the programmers use to create it.

Dr. Gauss demonstrated the mathematical principle of normal distribution, which is the distribution of values described by what is called a *normal curve*. The few of you who actually stayed awake in Statistics 101 recognize normal distribution as one of the first things you were shown just before you dozed off. Because the shape resembles that of a bell, the curve is also known as a *bell-shaped* or *bell curve*.

When I was going to school (way back when) and everyone in the class was doing poorly, the teacher often graded "on the curve," meaning that all of the grades would be distributed uniformly above and below the average of all the test scores. The result would have been a few "A"s, more "B"s, mostly "C"s, some "D"s, and a few "F"s. That is because the score necessary to get a grade of "C" would be the center of the curve (the average of all the scores), rather than an absolute, like 70 percent. This principle of Gaussian distribution is the basis for the Gaussian Blur filter and many other tools in Corel PHOTO-PAINT.

In photo-editing, the Gaussian Blur filter distributes the blur effect based on a bell-shaped curve. This curve is generated by mapping the color values of the pixels in the selected area and then distributing the blurring around the center value. So what's so hot about Gaussian blurring? Good question. It provides a true blurring, not a smearing, of the pixels, resulting in the blurred area appearing to be out of focus. End of history and math lessons.

The Gaussian Blur Filter Dialog Box

Selecting Blur in the Effects Menu and selecting Gaussian Blur... opens the dialog box, shown next. For information on the operation of the common filter dialog box controls, see Chapter 14. The following discussion describes the Gaussian Blur controls in detail.

The Radius Slider

The Radius slider controls the amount of filter action. Adobe Photoshop users are accustomed to seeing three separate controls for Gaussian Blur. Corel PHOTO-PAINT has combined the functionality of three controls so that a single percentage setting will allow you to determine the filter's effect. While it can be argued that three separate control settings gives the user a greater degree of control, I have found the single slider to be more than sufficient to produce the necessary blur.

To operate, set the Radius slider in the dialog box to a value between 1 and 50 percent to specify the degree to which you want to blur the selected image or masked area. For the more technically minded, the percentage would be more accurately described as *pixel radius*. With a setting of 5, the blur will be averaged over a radius of five pixels around each pixel in the image. The greater the Percentage slider setting, the greater the amount of blurring of the image. High percentage values (more than 30) can turn almost any image into fog. Use the preview window to see the effects of different slider settings before applying the filter. Click the OK button to apply it.

Subtle Emphasis by Creating a Depth of Field

15

Creating a pseudo depth of field by slightly blurring an area of the image is a good way to subtly emphasize a subject without making a big show of it. The hands-on exercise in Chapter 7 showed us how to use the Freehand <u>m</u>ask tool to create a slightly blurred background with some buildings. That was easy since the buildings had nicely defined edges. In day-to-day photo-editing, you have edges that are more difficult to define. In this hands-on exercise, you will learn some unique ways to create that blurred background with such subjects.

1. Open the image \PHOTOS\COUPLES\598053.WI on the CD-ROM. When the image appears, select Resamp<u>le</u>… from the <u>I</u>mage menu. When the dialog box opens, the width will be highlighted. Type in the number 5 (for 5 inches) and click the OK button.

2. Use either the Freehand Mask tool or the Scissors Mask tool and create a rough mask around the woman's face as shown in Figure 15-1. Don't spend a lot of time on the mask. It doesn't need to follow her face accurately. When you are done, invert the mask by clicking the Invert Mask button on the toolbar.

3. Select <u>B</u>lur in the Effe<u>c</u>ts Menu and choose <u>G</u>aussian Blur…, opening the filter dialog box. Ensure it is at the default setting of 5 and click the OK button. The result is shown in Figure 15-2.

4. Close the file when you have finished.

The man in Figure 15-2 now appears to be some distance away from the woman. This exercise was easy because the area between the two of them consisted of naturally blurred or dark areas. These areas prevented the rough edges of our crude mask from making the transition areas between the blurred and non-blurred areas apparent to the viewer. In our next exercise, creating the mask won't be as easy.

The mask
roughly
outlines the
woman's
face

FIGURE 15-1

The man
now
appears
more distant

FIGURE 15-2

Subtle Emphasis by Creating a Depth of Field II (the Sequel)

In the food shot you see here, we want to make the background slightly blurred—but the kind of mask we made in the previous exercise will not work. We require the blurring to occur gradually beginning near the front (bottom) of the image and moving back (up). In this exercise we want to emphasize that beautiful tomato in the center for an ad for a new restaurant, The Red Tomato. To accomplish this, we must isolate the tomato from the gradual blur we are going to apply to the background.

1. Open the file PHOTOS\FOOD\577054.WI. When the image appears, select Resample... from the Image menu. When the dialog box opens, the width will be highlighted. Type in the number 5 (for 5 inches) and click the OK button.

2. Select Paint on Mask in the Mask menu (CTRL+K). Next, choose Fill... in the Edit menu. When the Edit Fill & Transparency dialog box opens, select the Fountain fill button and click the Edit button. Change the values in the Fountain Fill dialog box to match those shown here. The From color is black and the To color is white. Click the OK button to close the dialog box, and click OK again to apply the fill.

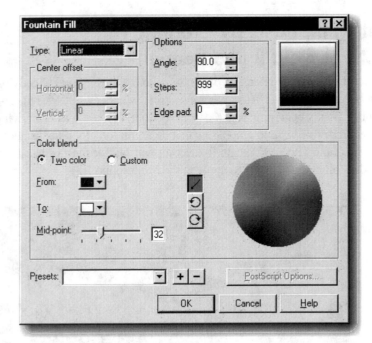

3. Switch off <u>P</u>aint on Mask mode (CTRL+K). We now have a mask that allows any effect we use to be applied gradually from top (maximum) to bottom (minimum).

4. To isolate the tomato, click the Circle Mask tool in the Toolbox. Change the Mask mode to Subtractive. Beginning above and to the left of the tomato, click and drag a circle that covers the tomato. This doesn't need to be exact. It is better if it is slightly inside of the tomato. If it doesn't work the first time, select Undo (CTRL+Z) and try, try again. It took me three attempts to get a mask that covered most of the tomato.

5. Switch on <u>P</u>aint on Mask mode (CTRL+K). The mask should look something like the one shown at the upper-left of Figure 15-3. The edges of the circle we just made are too hard to use. Select the Gaussian Blur filter and change the Radius setting to 10. Click OK. The result is shown at the lower right of Figure 15-3.

6. Switch off <u>P</u>aint on Mask mode (CTRL+K). Select the Gaussian Blur filter and change the Radius setting to 7. Click OK. The result is shown in Figure 15-4.

The mask shown at the upper left exhibits hard edges. An application of Gaussian Blur in Paint On Mask mode does wonders.

FIGURE 15-3

The finished work, ready to be made into an ad

FIGURE 15-4

7. Before closing the file, select <u>A</u>djust from the <u>I</u>mage menu and select <u>D</u>esaturate. This command removes the color content of the image, resulting in what looks like the background for an expensive ad in some gourmet-cooking magazine as shown in the color insert. Notice there is a slight glow appearing around the tomato where the mask went out too far into the background. Close the file without saving it.

When applying blurring to a background, you must remember how the human eye sees things. Objects near the viewer are usually slightly out of focus, while those further away are more out of focus. If you create effects that go against what the mind expects to see, it looks fake or artificial—even though the viewer in most cases cannot tell you why it looks fake.

The Shadow Knows...

One of the more frequently used features of the Gaussian Blur is its ability to make very realistic-looking shadows. Corel included a Drop Shadow command in PHOTO-PAINT 7 to do the routine drop shadows, which takes away much of the need for using the Gaussian Blur in this way. While for the most part the drop shadows created by the Drop Shadow command are satisfactory (all of the ones in this book were made with that command), there will be times when you need a more diffused edge to the shadow.

Here is a simple procedure to improve the blur on a shadow created by the Drop Shadow command.

1. After creating the shadow, click <u>U</u>ngroup on the <u>O</u>bject menu (CTRL+G) to ungroup the original object and the shadow object.

2. In the Objects roll-up, click the Layer button and select the shadow object.

3. Apply a Gaussian Blur to the shadow until you are satisfied with the appearance.

4. Click the Multi mode button in the Objects roll-up, and select both the shadow and the original object.

5. Click the Group button on the Property bar.

You're done. The Gaussian Blur filter produces a more diffuse shadow than the one created by the Drop Shadow command.

Removal of Banding Using the Gaussian Blur Filter

The Gaussian Blur filter can also be used to diminish the effect of banding in a fountain fill. The text at the top of Figure 15-5 contains a six-step fountain fill to make the banding apparent. The same image is shown below the original, after it has had a Gaussian Blur filter applied to it. Now it shows no evidence of the original banding. Be careful of setting amount of Gaussian Blur too high. At very high settings you will turn the entire image into fog.

The Motion Blur Filter

The Motion Blur filter was designed to create the impression of movement in an image. It is supposed to achieve this effect by determining the edges of the image for the direction selected and smearing them into the adjacent pixels. When choosing a subject for use with the Motion Blur filter, you should consider people, events,

The text on top has serious banding problems; the Gaussian Blur filter removes the banding

FIGURE 15-5

and things associated with speed. It looks wrong to see a photograph of two chess players in Central park with the speed blurs coming off of them.

The proper application of the Motion Blur filter can be a little tricky. Figure 15-6 shows an image of a snowmobile that was obviously photographed while it was moving. High speed films can freeze the action so the subject in the photograph looks like it is standing still. In fact, the only indication of movement in this photo is the snow flying up behind the snowmobile. When using a photograph like this in an ad or brochure, you want to convey a sense of action to the viewer. While no one viewing the image would say the snowmobile is parked, it still doesn't "look" like it is moving. We can achieve this apparent motion with the Motion Blur filter.

There are two ways to approach the application of motion—blur the subject or blur the background. The popular technique used in the car advertisements these days is to blur the background. This is most effective since blurring the background conveys the sense of speed and keeps the product (car) in focus.

The best way to apply the filter is to do so selectively. If you apply the Motion Blur filter to the entire image, it will just look like an out-of-focus picture, as shown in Figure 15-7. By creating a mask around the snowmobile and the driver and then

The original
photograph
of a
snowmobile

FIGURE 15-6

Blurring the entire image just makes it appear out of focus

FIGURE 15-7

inverting the mask, you can limit the effect to just the background. If you create a normal mask with hard borders, you will end up with hard borders, causing the blur to begin and end abruptly, which looks very strange. To eliminate this, you need to feather the mask with a wide soft feather. This is what was done in Figure 15-8. Notice the front (leading edge) of the snowmobile that is in the lower-left corner of the photograph. I deliberately included this part of the snowmobile in the masked area so that it would be lightly blurred. This again helps convey the sense of motion to the viewer. This is more a result of perceptions we humans have regarding things in motion than a function of laws of physics.

The Jaggy Despeckle Filter

The Jaggy Despeckle filter scatters colors in an image to create a soft, blurred effect with very little distortion. It also smoothes out jagged edges (jaggies) on images. It is most effective in removing jaggies on high-contrast images. If the image has them, the Jaggy Despeckle filter will probably work well for you.

Blurring only the background gives the impression of speed

FIGURE 15-8

Using the Jaggy Despeckle filter

This filter will not work with line art, images composed of only black-and-white pixels. The image must be either grayscale or color. When applied to a photograph, it has a tendency to blur the image slightly, depending on your setting. Jaggy Despeckle operates by performing edge detection on the image. After the filter thinks it knows where all the hard edges are, it applies anti-aliasing to the edges to give them a smoother appearance. Figure 15-9 shows a portion of a script letter magnified to 500 percent. This is a worst case for a bitmap graphic. Diagonal lines, zoomed in at 500 percent, and little to no gray areas. A perfect candidate for Jaggy Despeckle?

The Jaggy Despeckle was applied at the default settings, resulting in the improvement you see in Figure 15-10. After the application of the Jaggy Despeckle filter, the "jaggies" have been visibly reduced. Don't forget, you are looking at 500 percent zoom level. So is it only used to smooth out text? One of its most popular uses is to apply the filter to an individual color channel that has a lot of noise or areas that are exhibiting jaggies. Applying filters to separate color channels is explored in Chapter 24.

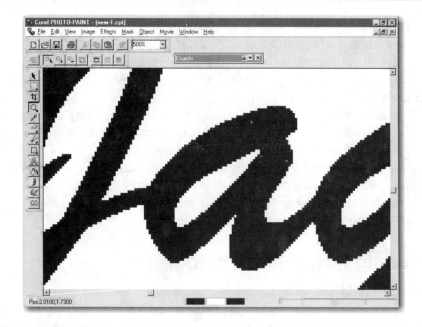

This is a
close-up of
some text at
500% zoom

FIGURE 15-9

The Jaggy
Despeckle
filter helps
smooth the
edges

FIGURE 15-10

The Radial Blur Filter

A new addition to PHOTO-PAINT 7, the Radial Blur filter allows you to create a blurring effect that radiates outward from a central point. You can reposition the center point, set the intensity of the effect, and choose between two blur modes. Spin rotates the blur around the point. Zoom blurs outwards from the point. The Cross-hairs button to the right of the Zoom button (Magnifying Glass icon) is used to set the center point of this effect. Click this button and then click in the Original preview window to place the center point of the effect.

The key to using this filter most efficiently is controlling affected areas with masks. Without masks, the Radial Blur effect causes sufficient distortion to make the original subject unrecognizable. The following hands-on exercise demonstrates the use of the filter.

Adding Power to a Photograph with Radial Blur

When creating an insert for a dirt bike racing brochure, you may run across a perfectly vivid photograph of the subject matter like the one shown in Figure 15-11.

This photograph looks like it is frozen in time

FIGURE 15-11

The problem is it is too perfect. The rider, the bike, and the background are all in focus and appear frozen. Our mission is to make this appealing to people who like the smell of gas, the feel of mud, and enough noise to start a major geological shift. We need the look of POWER! The Motion Blur filter wouldn't be a good candidate, since it can only create the appearance of speed. For the look of power, we need a different type of distortion. In the following hands-on exercise, we will create a power photo that will get the viewer's motor running.

1. Open the photograph \PHOTOS\SPORTS\511091.WI. Select Resample in the Image menu and choose a Width of 7 inches. Click OK.

2. Click the Paint on Mask button. From the Edit menu, choose Fill…. From the Edit Fill & Transparency box, click the Fountain Fill button and then the Edit button. Change the settings in the dialog box to match those shown here.

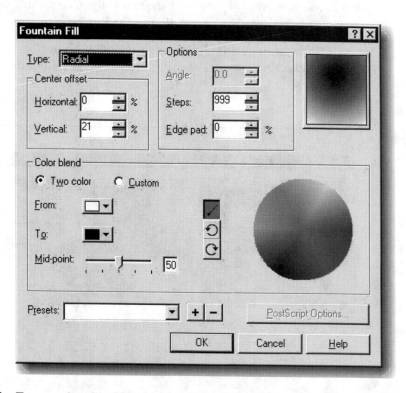

The From: color should be black and the To: color, white. This setting will produce a mask that allows very little effect to be applied to the rider and most of the effect to be applied to the background. Click OK to close the dialog box, and click OK again to apply the fill. Click the Paint on Mask button to return to the photograph.

3. Select Effects, Blur, and Radial Blur... and change the settings to those you see in Figure 15-12.

   Center the effect using the Effect Center tool at the point indicated by the arrow in the Original preview window. Click the OK button. It will take a few moments to apply. The effect will be very subtle at this point, so we need to apply it again (CTRL+F). The photograph should now look like Figure 15-13.

4. Click the Text tool in the Toolbox. Select Kabel Ult BT at a size of 72. Click the left mouse button on the color yellow in the onscreen palette to set the Paint color. Click the Object Picker tool in the Toolbox. Open the Objects roll-up (CTRL+F7) and, with the text still selected, click the Single button. Click the Remove mask button on the Property bar.

5. In the Effects menu, choose Noise, and from the list, select Add Noise.... Click the Reset button to restore the filter to its default values. Click the OK button.

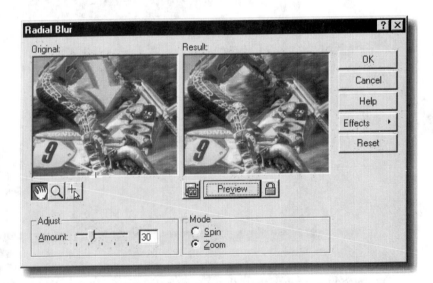

The Radial Blur dialog box settings

FIGURE 15-12

The photograph is now ready, except for the text

■ FIGURE 15-13

6. Select Effe<u>c</u>ts, <u>B</u>lur, and <u>M</u>otion Blur…. Click the Reset button to restore the filter to its default values, and then change the <u>D</u>irection to 90 degrees. Click the OK button.

7. With the Object Picker tool, click on the text until the handles on the corners are small circles. Grab the handle in the upper-right corner of the text and drag it in and up until the text looks like Figure 15-14. Then double-click the text to apply the changes.

8. Use the Drop Shadow command in the Object menu to create a shadow that is directly under the text using a Vertical setting of 0.1 and a Horizontal of 0. The Feather was set to 15, Direction to Average, and the Opacity to 70.

9. To help the top of the text blend into the photograph, select the Object Transparency tool from the Toolbox and, beginning at the bottom-center of the text, click and drag the tool until you reach the top of the text. Select the Object Picker tool to complete the action. You are done. You can see the resulting image in the color insert.

10. Close the file and don't save any of the changes.

Now there
is a photo
with
POWER!

FIGURE 15-14

The Directional Smooth Filter

The Directional Smooth filter analyzes values of pixels of similar color shades to determine in which direction to apply the greatest amount of smoothing. Sounds great, right? As great as the description sounds, it is still a Blur filter. It and the following two filters (Smooth and Soften filters) are nearly identical in operation, although the results obtained are slightly different.

The Smooth Filter

The Smooth filter tones down differences in adjacent pixels, resulting in only a slight loss of detail while smoothing the image or the selected area. The differences between the effect of the Smooth and Soften filters are subtle and may only be apparent on a high-resolution display and sometimes not even then.

The Soften Filter

The Soften filter smoothes and tones down harshness without losing detail. The differences between the effects of the Smooth and Soften filters are subtle and may only be apparent on a high-resolution display or in the mind of the person who programmed this filter.

Getting It All Together—The Blur Control

The Blur option is found in the Effects menu by selecting Adjust. Enabling this opens a very large dialog box called Blur Control, shown in Figure 15-15, which displays thumbnails side by side, showing the results of applying each of the five Blur filters—Gaussian Blur, Motion Blur, Smooth, Directional Smooth, and Soften—to the current image. Blur control should not be confused with government information agencies.

The Blur Control Dialog Box

This provides a quick way to compare the results of different filters side by side. By default, the operation is centered on the Before/After format, which appears in Original and Result windows at the top of the dialog box. Clicking the thumbnail of the desired filter applies that filter to the image in the Result window. To Undo the

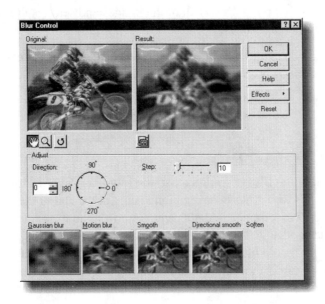

The Blur Control dialog box shows the comparative effects of all the blur filters

FIGURE 15-15

last filter application, you can click the Undo button to the right of the Zoom button. Repeatedly clicking this button lets you step back through a group of effects applied. Different filters can be applied multiple times using the Blur Control dialog box.

- The Original (before) window never changes and always reflects the current image or the portion of the image that is masked.

- The Result (after) window shows the effects of the applied filter.

- The Step slider controls the number of steps for all of the filters simultaneously. For example, a setting at 10 means this setting would be applied each time the Motion Blur thumbnail, or any of the other filters, is clicked. This is important since a setting of 10 would be very small and therefore impossible to see with either the Smooth, Soften, or Directional Smooth filters.

- The Help button opens our ever-sensitive, context-sensitive Help screen. You can also display information about a specific button by right-clicking the button or control. When the What's This? message appears, click on it with the left mouse button. A description of the tool/function is displayed.

- Click the Undo button to undo the last action taken. Repeatedly clicking this button lets you step back through a group of effects applied.

- The Reset button resets all of the images and settings in Blur Control to their default values.

- The Filters button allows you to open up additional filters without closing this dialog box.

- If you are wondering what Cancel does, I am seriously worried about you.

The Low Pass Filter

Also found in the Blur drop-down list, the Low Pass filter is not a traditional Blur filter, which is why it has been mentioned only at the end of the chapter. The effect of this filter is to remove highlights and color from an image, leaving shadows and low-frequency detail. The dialog box contains two Slider bars, one for Percentage and the other for Radius. The Percentage value controls the intensity of the effect, and Radius controls the range of pixels that are affected. At higher settings, the Low Pass filter creates a blurring effect, which is why it is in the Blur filter section. This action erases much of the image's detail. If you need only to de-emphasize (smooth) highlights, use a lower percentage setting.

Congratulations! You have made it through yet another chapter of filters. The next chapter introduces you to the exciting world of noise. Noise, not the kind that comes from a boom box, is a fact of life in digital imagery and these filters help create, remove, and control it.

16

Noise Filters

The Noise filters are very important to photo-editing. Noise, which is composed of random pixels, can be used to add an apparent sharpness to a soft image. It can be used to add "grit" to an otherwise smooth surface. Naturally occurring noise in an image can result from poorly scanned images or from the film grain of certain film types. Whether noise needs to be removed or added, Corel PHOTO-PAINT provides the necessary filters to accomplish it. The Noise subgroup in the Effects menu has the following seven filters: Add Noise, Diffuse, Dust & Scratch, Maximum, Median, Minimum, and Remove Noise.

Noise in digital images is normally a "bad" thing, akin to visual static. Like an uninvited guest at a party, noise seems to show up in the worst possible places in an image. For example, when scanning an image, it is difficult for the scanner elements to pick out detail in the darker (shadow) regions of a photograph. As a result, these areas will contain more than their fair share of noise. All of those ugly little specks on the faxes you receive are caused by noise. Because of the physical composition of noise, it tends to stand out and make itself known in a photograph, especially when you sharpen an image, as you will learn in the following chapter. Noise is everywhere and you cannot avoid it. You can control it, get rid of it, and even add it to your images. In fact, in this chapter you will learn that noise can be pretty useful to have around.

The Add Noise Filter

Why would you want to add noise? Actually, adding noise has more uses than you would first imagine. Noise (random pixels) can give the effect of grit and texture to a picture. It can add a dusting of pixels to an image in a way that emulates film grain. When the grain color is not quite compatible with the image, adding noise can be helpful in softening the look of stark image areas. When you are retouching photographs that have existing film-grain texture, it can be helpful to add noise so the blending is less apparent. If you are an old hand with Photoshop, you probably know much of this already.

The Add Noise filter creates a granular effect that adds texture to a flat or overly blended image. There are several neat tricks that can be done with this filter. Let's begin with a description of how it operates.

The Add Noise Filter Dialog Box

The default setting of the dialog box, as shown here, consists of two viewing windows arranged in a Before and After format. The Original window, on the left, shows a thumbnail of the original image. The Result window, on the right, displays the results of the filter action based on the current settings.

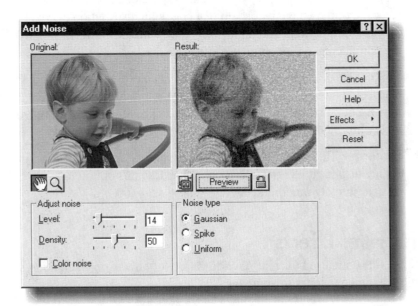

Understanding What the Controls Do

The Level slider controls the intensity of the noise pixels. The slider operates on a percentage scale of 0-100. A lower setting makes the noise barely visible; a higher setting produces higher-visibility noise pixels. The default setting for this slider is way too high for most applications. A Level setting of 10 is recommended as a starting point.

The Density slider controls the number of noise pixels added to the image. The slider also operates on a percentage scale of 0-100. A lower setting adds very few noise pixels; a higher setting produces a higher density of noise pixels. When Color Noise is checked, the Noise filter create noises that contain color values. When left unchecked, the noise that is introduced is grayscale.

TYPES OF NOISE Three types of noise are available: Gaussian, Spike, and Uniform. The difference between the Gaussian and Uniform noise is slight. The Spike noise appears as tiny speckles on the image.

- **Gaussian** This filter prioritizes shades or colors, if color noise is selected, of the image pixels along a Gaussian distribution curve. The results are more light and dark pixels than with the Uniform Noise option, thus producing a more dramatic effect.

- **Spike** This filter uses shades or colors, if color noise is selected, that are distributed around a narrow curve (spike). It produces a thinner, lighter-colored grain. In fact, it is almost impossible to see unless you use a very high setting.

- **Uniform** This filter provides an overall grainy appearance that is not evenly dispersed like the Gaussian Noise. Use this option to apply colors in an absolutely random fashion.

Noise Filter Effects

The Noise filters are used to create a wide variety of effects, from creating textures to adding dramatic touches to an image.

Removing Banding from a Radial Fill

Many times, if a radial fill (or any gradient fill, for that matter) is applied to a large area, some banding occurs. *Banding* is the phenomenon wherein the changes of color or shades appear as bands in the image. This effect is more pronounced in low-resolution than in higher-resolution output. It is also more apparent in grayscale or 256-color fills than in 24-bit color. In Chapter 15 we learned that a blur could reduce or remove banding. The limitation of using the Gaussian Blur is that it blurs the subject matter. You can remove the effect of banding with noise. Figure 16-1 shows an 8-step fountain fill applied to some text (top). We next applied a Gaussian Noise with a Level setting of 29 and a Density setting of 100 (bottom).

Noise can make banding less apparent in an image

FIGURE 16-1

Making Metallic Effects

The Noise filter can not only remove banding from fountain fills, but also create unusual textures as well. In the following hands-on exercise we will apply several different filters to some applied noise to create gold metallic characters.

1. Create a new image that is 24-bit color, 6 × 4 inches at a resolution of 72 dpi.

2. Click the Text tool in the Toolbox. The font used is Futura XBlk BT at a size of 120. The line spacing was set to 80 so the two lines aren't too far apart. Locate the gold color in the On-screen palette and click on it with the left mouse button. Click the Object Picker button in the Toolbox and type the text **HEAVY METAL**.

3. Open the Objects roll-up (CTRL+F7) and, with the text selected, click the Single button.

4. From the Effects menu, select Noise. Choose Add Noise… from the list to open the dialog box. Change the Level slider to 25, Density to 100, and choose Gaussian as the Noise type. Click OK. The result is shown in Figure 16-2.

5. From the Effects menu, select Blur and choose Motion Blur… from the list. In the filter dialog box, change the settings to Speed: 10; Direction: 225; Off-image sampling: Ignore pixels outside image. Click the OK button. The pixels are blurred up and to the right as shown in Figure 16-3.

Text with
Gaussian
Noise
applied

FIGURE 16-2

6. In the Effects menu, choose 3D Effects and select Emboss…. Change the settings in the Emboss filter dialog box as follows: Emboss color: Original color; Depth: 7; Level: 25; Direction: 45. Click OK. The text now has a three-dimensional quality as shown in Figure 16-4.

7. The texture of the text now looks smooth so to roughen it up, we will use the Sharpen filter. From the Effects menu, choose Sharpen and then choose Sharpen…. Change the dialog box settings to Edge level (percent): 27, Threshold: 53. Click the OK button.

8. Select the Drop Shadow command in the Object menu to add a drop shadow as shown in Figure 16-5. Nearly any setting works with the Drop Shadow command.

9. To put the finishing touch on the exercise, in the Objects roll-up, click the Single button and select the Background. In the Edit menu, choose Fill…. In the Edit Fill & Transparency dialog box, select the Fountain Fill button and click the Edit button. Choose Preset: Circular - Green 02. Click OK and the OK button again to apply the fill.

10. Repeat step 4.

Motion Blur makes the noise into a texture

FIGURE 16-3

The Emboss filter gives the letters some depth

FIGURE 16-4

Sharpening the image gives it a sharp edge and the Drop Shadow lifts it off of the page

FIGURE 16-5

11. From the Effects menu, select <u>B</u>lur, choose <u>R</u>adial Blur..., set the <u>A</u>mount to 30, and ensure <u>Z</u>oom is selected. Click the OK button. The complete image is shown in Figure 16-6 and in the color insert.

Noise and Embossing

Noise serves as the foundation for many textures and effects. Using a combination of noise and embossing to make a stucco-like texture is a favorite technique of mine. Try this little hands-on exercise.

1. Create a new image that is 24-bit color, 6 × 2 inches at a resolution of 72 dpi.

2. Click the Text tool in the Toolbox. The font used is Futura XBlk BT at a size of 120. Pick a light color in the On-screen palette with the left mouse button. Click the Object Picker roll-up in the Toolbox and type the text **NOISE**.

3. In the Objects roll-up (CTRL+F7), click the Single button.

4. Apply a Gaussian Noise at a Level of 50 percent and a Density of 100 percent.

The final image

FIGURE 16-6

5. Next, apply the Emboss filter under 3D Effects in the Effects menu. Click the Reset button, click OK, and add a Drop Shadow. The resulting image is shown here.

Noise and Focus

Noise can also make the focus of an image appear sharper than it actually is. This is because the human eye believes images are in sharper focus when it sees areas of higher contrast. So the viewer can be tricked into seeing an image as being in sharper focus by introducing a very small amount of Uniform noise onto a soft image. This process is often referred to as "dusting" the image. When you see the results, you may think, at first, that nothing was accomplished. In fact, to the operator, the image appears noisier. That's because (1) it does have more noise, and (2) you know what the original looked like before you added the noise. To a first-time viewer of the photograph, it will appear sharper.

The Diffuse Filter

Before the Gaussian Blur filter was added to Corel PHOTO-PAINT 5, the Diffuse filter was all that was available to blur an image. Corel's PAINT team received so many requests for Gaussian Blur that it was added to Corel PHOTO-PAINT 5 in the first Maintenance release. So where does that leave the Diffuse filter? It still has uses. First, it scatters colors in an image or a selected area, creating a smooth appearance. Unlike the Gaussian Blur, the Diffuse filter scatters the pixels in a way that produces a harsher or grittier blur. So why is it in the Noise section of Effects? Because its operation is based on noise.

The Diffuse Filter Dialog Box

The Level slider in the Diffuse Filter dialog box controls the amount of diffusion in the image. Set the level slider in the dialog box to a value between 1 and 255. The number specifies the number of shades that adjoining pixels are shifted, which controls the amount of diffusion of the selected image. Higher values produce more pronounced effects. Use the preview window to see the effects of different slider settings.

When enabled, the Shuffle Edge Pixels option causes the pixels that make up edges (areas of high contrast) to be affected. When it is not selected, the edges are maintained. In Figure 16-7, Shuffle Edge Pixels was not selected. As a result, the edges of the sailboat masts and numbers on the sails have been preserved. In Figure 16-8, Shuffle edge pixels was selected and the entire image has been diffused.

Notes on Using the Diffuse Filter

When selecting a level setting, watch the preview window for the appearance of an edge. When some objects are diffused at too high a setting, they develop an outline, which may be undesirable. To overcome this, do multiple applications of the diffuse filter at a lower setting.

The Diffuse filter applied without Shuffle edge pixels selected, preserving the edges in the photo

 FIGURE 16-7

The Diffuse filter applied with Shuffle edge pixels selected, causing the entire photograph to be diffused

 FIGURE 16-8

The Dust & Scratch Filter

The Dust & Scratch filter reduces image noise. Use this effect to eliminate dust and scratch faults in an image. Located in the Effects menu under Noise, the Dust & Scratch filter is not a magic cure-all. The best way to use this filter is to first apply a mask around the damaged areas of the image before selecting the effect. This will let you eliminate the problem areas without affecting the rest of the image. The filter will give a softer appearance to the area to which it is applied. To prevent the areas affected from being visible when you create a mask, you should feather it before applying the filter.

Using the Dust & Scratch Filter Controls

Adjust the Threshold slider (0-255) to reduce image noise. The lower the setting, the greater the amount of noise removed. By setting it low, you are telling the filter that all levels of contrast above the Threshold setting are considered noise. Adjust the Radius slider (1-20) to set the range of the effect. The Radius setting determines the number of pixels surrounding the noise that will be included in the removal process. Be advised that increasing the Radius setting increases the processing time for the filter's operation.

The Maximum Filter

The Maximum filter is not a traditional noise filter. Actually, it is a bit of a mystery why it's under Noise in the Effects menu. The Maximum filter lightens an image by adjusting the pixel values of the image, decreasing the number of colors. By using the Percentage slider (1-100 percent), you can control the percentage of filtering that is applied. This filter provides a method of lightening an image without washing it out (as would happen with brightness or intensity adjustments). With the Radius slider (1-20), move the slider to the right to increase the number of pixels that are successively selected and evaluated when you apply the effect. If you are an experienced Photoshop user, the Maximum filter that you are already used to does something different.

Fundamentally, Maximum as used in Photoshop creates a spread trap. In layman's terms, the Maximum filter spreads the white areas and chokes the black areas. Spreading and choking are used to compensate for minute misalignments in the printing process. While the Maximum filter in Corel PHOTO-PAINT can be used as a traditional Maximum (Choke) filter, it doesn't do it as well as other programs. The effect is applied along a radius rather than on the pixel edge. (If you didn't understand the last sentence, don't bother rereading it. It will not become any clearer the second time around. If you live and breathe digital imaging and prepress, you understood it.)

Notes on Using the Maximum Filter

The Maximum filter does reduce the number of colors in an image area to achieve the lightening effect. In addition to color-depth reduction, it also causes a mild blurring of the image if applied in large percentages or multiple times. This blurring should be taken into consideration when using the Maximum filter.

The Median Filter

This filter reads the brightness of the pixels within a selection and averages them. Median simplifies an image by reducing noise (produced when pixels of different brightness levels adjoin one another) and by averaging the differences out of the selection.

The Median filter is used to smooth the rough areas in scanned images that have a grainy appearance. This filter uses a slider to set the percentage of Noise removal that is applied. The filter looks for pixels that are isolated and, based on the percentage setting in the dialog box, removes them.

Notes on Using the Median Filter

There is nothing magic about the Median filter. Its ability to remove noise is dependent on the type of noise (sharp and high-contrast or blurred and low-contrast) that is in the image. The Median filter tends to blur the image if it is set too high. Use the Result window to experiment with various settings. If a particular area of the image has noise, mask it off and apply the filter to the noisy areas rather than to the entire image.

The Minimum Filter

The Minimum filter, like the Maximum filter, is not a traditional noise filter. This filter darkens an image by adjusting the pixel values of the image, decreasing the number of colors. By using the slider, the percentage of filtering applied can be controlled. This filter provides a method of lightening an image without washing it out (as would occur using brightness or intensity). Converse to the Maximum filter, this filter spreads out black or dark areas into the white or light areas of an image.

Notes on Using the Minimum Filter

The Minimum filter reduces the number of colors in an image area to achieve the darkening effect. In addition to color-depth reduction, it also causes a mild blurring of the image if applied in large percentages or multiple times. This should be taken into consideration when using the Minimum filter.

What's Really Going On with the Maximum, Median, and Minimum Filters?

These filters are each taking a look at an image's brightness values, pixel by pixel, and replacing adjacent pixels with the maximum or minimum brightness value of the neighboring pixel. Thus the names Maximum and Minimum. (The Median filter is obviously named after that thing in the middle of the highway.)

The Remove Noise Filter

This filter acts like a combination Jaggy Despeckle and Median filter. The Remove Noise filter softens edges and reduces the speckled effect created by the scanning process or from line noise in faxes. Each pixel is compared to surrounding pixels and an average value is computed. The pixels that then exceed the threshold set with the slider control in the dialog box are removed. This operates in the same manner as the Jaggy Despeckle does on objects (it reduces jaggies by softening edges), but, unlike Jaggy Despeckle, it also removes random pixels (noise) in the image.

Controlling the Remove Noise Filter

The operation of a majority of the controls on the dialog box is identical to that of the Add Noise filter described at the beginning of the chapter. The most important setting on this dialog box is the Auto checkbox. Use it! The Auto checkbox, when enabled, automatically analyzes the image and determines the best Threshold setting for it. The Threshold setting is not available when Auto is set. The Threshold slider controls the amount of threshold the program uses to differentiate between noise and non-noise. Set the level slider in the dialog box to a value between 1 and 255. Use the preview window to see the effects of different slider settings. While this slider can be set manually, I don't recommend it.

This filter is good for cleaning up faxes and poor scans. Like the other Noise filters, it cannot take a real garbage scan and make it look pristine. It can, however, improve a poor scan or a scan of a fax.

Figure 16-9 shows a before and after type sample. The top image had Spike noise applied to it. This most closely resembles the noise one can expect in real life. Using

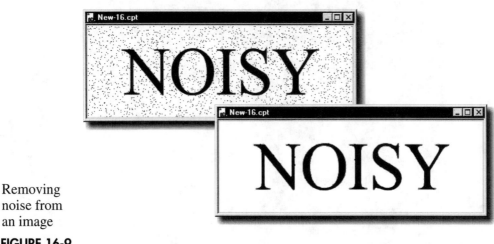

Removing
noise from
an image

FIGURE 16-9

the Auto setting, the Remove Noise filter lived up to its name and did an excellent job cleaning up the noise as shown in the lower image.

 TIP: *You can improve the performance of this filter on really trashy scans by masking the worst areas and applying the Remove Noise filter to them first. This speeds up the operation (because the area is smaller) and also keeps the filter from modifying areas that do not need to have any noise removed.*

17

The Sharpen Filters

No matter how crisp your original photograph and how great your scanner is, you will always lose some sharpness when any image is digitized. An image also loses sharpness when it is sent to an output device. As a result, most images will appear "soft" when printed without some degree of sharpening being applied. To compensate for this unavoidable reduction in sharpness, you must sharpen the images. Corel PHOTO-PAINT contains several sharpening filters that can help make your images as sharp as possible. The Sharpen subgroup of the Effects menu contains six filters that provide a wide range of sharpening effects both for improving image quality and creating special effects.

When to Apply Sharpening

Some people argue that the best time to apply sharpening is when an image is scanned. I have seen several comparisons between images that were sharpened during scanning and those done with sharpen filters after the scan, and the sharpening on the scanned images was visibly sharper. In fairness, the scanner was a $500,000 drum scanner and the operator was an experienced professional. If your image is from a Photo-CD or other source, the decision of whether to apply sharpening during the scanning process has already been made for you. If you need to sharpen it, you will need to use one of the filters included with Corel PHOTO-PAINT.

Sharpening is one of the last effects you should apply. Apply it after tonal and color correction, as it will affect the results of both.

The Sharpen Filters

The Sharpen subgroup of the Effects menu has the following filters:

- Adaptive Unsharp
- Directional Sharpen
- Find Edges
- High Pass

- Sharpen

- Unsharp Mask

Three of these filters, Adaptive Unsharp, Unsharp Mask, and Directional Sharpen, act in roughly the same way, by introducing small amounts of distortion to the image to reduce noise enhancement. The Sharpen filter sharpens both the image and its noise equally. The High Pass filter removes low-frequency detail and shading and emphasizes highlights and luminous areas of an image. The Find Edges filter, which is not a traditional sharpening filter, is in the Sharpen group because internally it uses the same sharpening techniques as the traditional sharpen filters to determine the edges in an image. Before we learn more about the individual filters, let's look at what happens when we sharpen an image.

What Is Sharpening?

Edges are what sharpening is all about. The human eye is influenced by the presence of edges in an image. Without these edges, an image appears dull. By increasing the contrast between neighboring pixels, PHOTO-PAINT can enhance the edges, thus making the image appear to be sharper to the viewer, whether it is or not. Sharpening filters enable you to compensate for images or image elements that were photographed or scanned slightly out of focus. Sharpening cannot bring a blurred photograph into sharp focus. Figure 17-1 shows a photograph before sharpening was applied, and Figure 17-2 shows the result of selective application using one of the filters in the Sharpen group. In this example, the background was protected by a mask and the sharpening was applied to the architecture.

Before discussing the various sharpen filters, it would be beneficial to understand a little more about how sharpening affects different parts of an image. As a point of clarification, there are a group of filters called the sharpen filters and in that group there is a filter called the Sharpen filter. When I talk about the Sharpen filter, I am referring to the specific filter and not to a general type of filter. If you find that confusing, wait until you learn that the best sharpening filter is called the Unsharp filter!

How Sharpening Affects Noise

In Chapter 16 we learned that all computer images include noise. Noise is unwanted pixels that may appear as a grainy pattern or as the odd dark or light spot. Images

The shapes
on this
ancient
monument
lack detail

FIGURE 17-1

from photographs will always have noise. The noise associated with camera film is called *grain*. Actually, any image, including those captured with digital cameras, will have noise of some sort. The most pristine photo in your stock photo collection that was scanned on a ten-zillion-dollar drum scanner will exhibit some noise. The only exception to this concept of universal noise is the Uniform color fill, which has no noise—or detail. Are you beginning to wonder if this chapter was supposed to be in another part of the book, on noise? Not to worry. This really is the sharpen chapter, and there is a reason for this noisy introduction.

So why do we care about noise in the sharpen chapter? Because when we sharpen an image, we "sharpen" the noise as well. In fact, the noise generally sharpens up much better and faster than the rest of the image, which is undesirable. Why does noise sharpen up so well? Because noise pixels (like the tiny white specks in a black background) appear in sharper contrast to their background than the non-noise pixels in the image. These unwanted high-contrast visitors are usually so small as not to be noticed. But, since they are high contrast, they contain the one component that sharpening filters look for—differences between adjoining pixels. The act of

Using
one of the
sharpen
filters
brings out
the detail

FIGURE 17-2

sharpening seeks out the differences (edges) and increases the contrast at those edges. The existing edges of the noise are enhanced and enlarged more than the rest of the pixels in the image. That is why they show up against the adjacent pixels so well, and that's what makes noise so noticeable after a sharpen filter is applied.

A Noisy Demonstration

To illustrate how noise rears its ugly head, I have scanned a photograph of Sandy, a good friend of mine who has always wanted to have her picture in a nationally published book (not the kind with foldout pages). In Figure 17-3, the upper image shows a normal scan with no sharpening applied. It is one of those "glamour shots"—always (intentionally) a little out of focus—so popular these days at the shopping malls.

Next, I masked only the dark areas of the photograph (background and gloves) and applied an excessive amount of the Sharpen filter to the masked area. The result, shown in the lower-right part of Figure 17-3, looks like she had dandruff and it got on the black curtain. The white specks in the background are the enhanced noise.

The upper image shows Sandy before sharpening is applied; after sharpening, the picture looks like a dandruff commercial

FIGURE 17-3

The noise in the background was always there; the application of the Sharpen filter made it visible.

Specular Highlights and Dark Areas

As the Sharpen filter increases the difference between adjoining pixels, eventually the limits of the tonal spectrum are reached. The white can only have a maximum value of 256, and the black can't be any lower than zero. Shades that were nearly white are all pushed to the maximum, resulting in the white specks we see in the background and in Sandy's hair. These areas where light shades have all been pushed to the same value are known by several different names. They are called blowouts, specular highlights, or tiny white blotches. The effect is the same whether it is caused by noise, dust specks on the original negative, or small bright reflections—the kind you get from glass or highly polished metal. When the same effect happens on the dark side of the tonal spectrum (you thought I was going to say Force didn't you?), the result is loss of detail in the shadow region as the darker shades all become the same shade of black. This is often referred to as plugging up the shadows.

The Sharpen filter can easily create these unwanted bright and dark areas. It is not the preferred filter for sharpening an image. Does this mean you can't use the Sharpen filter? Not at all. It is useful for creating effects, just not for general sharpening. So if the Sharpen filter is not recommended for sharpening an image, what filter is? The Unsharp Mask filter.

The Unsharp Mask Filter

Using the Unsharp Mask filter, we can minimize the effect of the noise by distorting the image. Don't panic—when I say distortion, I mean distortion in the technical sense, not the kind that produces a distorted image. The distortion I am referring to has the effect of toning down the sharp borders of noise while providing general sharpening of the other pixels in the image. The result is an overall sharpening of the image without enhancing the noise. This is how the unsharp filters in Corel PHOTO-PAINT work. These filters have a strange name. In the trade they are generically referred to as Unsharp Masking (USM) filters. The term *unsharping* is confusing to first-time users of photo-editing programs. Unsharping is named after a traditional film compositing technique that highlights the edges in an image by combining a blurred film negative with the original film positive, which results in a sharper image without enhancing the noise.

The Unsharp Mask filter, like the Sharpen filter, compares each pixel in the image to its neighboring pixels. The filter then looks for amounts of contrast between adjacent pixels. PHOTO-PAINT assumes that a certain amount of contrast between adjoining pixels represents an edge. After it has found pixels that appear to be an edge, it creates a light corona around those pixels. USM can also produce an undesired effect by creating halos around detected edges if it is applied in excessive amounts. The best use of this filter (or any other filter in the Sharpen group) is to learn to apply the filter selectively.

Using the Unsharp Mask (USM) Filter

The filter dialog box offers two control sliders, Percentage and Radius. Radius is the first control you should consider adjusting. It controls the width of the halo that is produced around each pixel. Start with an exaggerated amount and reduce it until you get the desired sharpening. The Percentage slider controls the amount of the halo created. Increasing the Percentage value creates big tonal shifts that push the shades that make up the edge closer to black and white. If you are familiar with Photoshop's USM filter, the Percentage slider relates to the Amount.

Enhancing a Selected Part of an Image

This is a simple exercise that enhances the company name on the jet used in a brochure. It is a funny thing about corporations, but they seem to want their names not only to be legible but to stand out in an image as well. The photograph we will be using is the FEDEX.CPT file we created in Chapter 4. The name on the jet, while legible, doesn't stand out enough to suit the people that pay the check, so we are going to enhance it.

1. Open the file FEDEX.CPT and click the Remove Mask button if a mask is present.

2. Select the Freehand Mask tool from the Toolbox and create a mask around the name, as shown in Figure 17-4. Make sure the mask stays on the plane and you don't get too close to the letters.

The company name is first masked

FIGURE 17-4

17

3. Select Feather from the Mask menu and change the settings to a Width of 10 and a Direction setting of Average. Click the OK button. This will smooth the transition between the sharpened area and the rest of the photograph. Your mask marquee may look like it is going to include part of the sky. This has to do with where the mask marquee is displayed in relation to a feathered mask boundary. To see a more accurate representation of the mask boundary, click the Mask Overlay button, and then click it again to turn it off.

4. Choose Sharpen from the Effects menu and select Unsharp mask. When the dialog box opens, change the settings to 40 for Percentage and 10 for Radius. Click the OK button. The result, in comparison, is shown in Figure 17-5.

5. Save the file.

The upper photo is the original; in the lower image, the name has been sharpened

FIGURE 17-5

The changes in the company name on the jet are subtle yet necessary if we are to produce an image using PHOTO-PAINT that is vivid and sharp.

The Adaptive Unsharp and Directional Sharpen Filters

Two other filters, Adaptive Unsharp and Directional Sharpen, produce effects similar to the Unsharp Mask filter. Because the radius setting of these filters is fixed, the effects produced by these two filters is more subtle than those created by the Unsharp Mask filter. It is not uncommon to make several applications of these filters, even at a setting of 100 percent. Beware of applying too much of any of the unsharp filters, however. At some point, the image edges will begin to exhibit halos when too much unsharp masking is applied.

Because it can be difficult to evaluate the effect of these filters in the Original/Result windows of the filter dialog box, the recommended approach for applying these filters is to use the Checkpoint command to save a copy of the image before you begin. After applying the filter at an exaggerated level, reduce the filter settings in 50 percent increments and evaluate how your image looks after each application.

Technical Notes About the Adaptive Unsharp Filter

The Adaptive Unsharp filter uses a sharpening process with local control around each pixel, rather than a global sharpening amount. It uses statistical differences (Adaptive) between adjacent pixels to determine the sharpening amount for each pixel. The effect of the Adaptive Unsharp filter is very similar to the other two unsharp filters. The Adaptive Unsharp filter seems to produce slightly less contrast than either the Unsharp Mask or Directional Sharpen filter.

Technical Notes About the Directional Sharpen Filter

In the Directional Sharpen filter, the sharpening amount for each pixel is computed for several compass directions, and the greatest amount will be used as the final sharpening amount for that pixel. In other words, the Directional Sharpen filter analyzes values of pixels of similar color shades to determine the direction in which to apply the greatest amount of sharpening. I have found that the Directional Sharpen filter usually increases the contrast of the image more than the Unsharp Mask filter does. The Directional Sharpen filter also produces good sharpening, but with higher contrast than either the Unsharp Mask or Adaptive Unsharp filter.

The Sharpen Filter

The most important thing to remember about sharpening an image is that the Sharpen filter is rarely the best filter to use. Use one of the three filters discussed in the previous sections to achieve general sharpening of an image. Why? Because the Sharpen filter doesn't ignore noise, it just sharpens everything in the photograph. It is a powerful filter that will blow the socks off your image, if you are not careful. The Sharpen filter sharpens the appearance of the image or a masked area by intensifying the contrast of neighboring pixels. There are times when this filter may be preferred over any of the previously described filters, but they are rare.

Using the Sharpen Filter

The Sharpen Filter dialog box contains only two controls. The Edge Level (%) slider controls the amount of sharpening applied to the photograph. Use this slider at higher settings with some degree of caution. Higher values usually produce blowouts. The Threshold slider determines the level of contrast between adjoining pixels that is necessary for the filter action to occur. For example, if the Threshold value is set low, it means more pixels meet the minimum requirement and the sharpen effect will be applied to more of the image. If the Threshold is set high, only the elements of the image that are high contrast will be affected.

NOTE: *Unlike the previously discussed filters, the Sharpen filter has a much greater effect at 5 percent than the USM filters do at the 100 percent level.*

The Find Edges Filter

The Find Edges filter is unlike any other filter in this chapter. Even though it is not a general image enhancement tool like the sharpen filters, it allows you to obtain some effects that would not otherwise be possible.

Find Edges Dialog Box

Behind-the-scenes operation of the Find Edges dialog box is like the Adaptive Unsharp filter dialog box. The Level slider controls the threshold that triggers the Find Edges filter. As the value increases, the threshold decreases, allowing the filter to include more of the edge. As the slider value decreases, less of the edge component is included, making the edges thinner and therefore lighter. Adjust the Level slider to define a sensitivity value. The higher the number, the more edges are enhanced. The Edge Type setting determines the type of outline produced. For dark bold lines, choose Solid. For lighter, more diffused outlines, choose Soft.

What Can You Do with Find Edges?

The Find Edges filter can create an outline effect. I've placed some text over a photograph of leaves in Figure 17-6. The Find Edges filter determines the edges on everything in the image and removes everything that is not an edge. For the image shown in Figure 17-7, the Level setting was 80, which produced dark lines, and the Edge Type was Soft.

The original image, showing text over a photograph

FIGURE 17-6

The same
image after
application
of the Find
Edges filter

FIGURE 17-7

Making Pencil Sketches with Find Edges

One of the unique things you can do with Find Edges is make fake pencil sketches. In this hands-on exercise we will make a banner for a local garden column that will be reproduced on a photocopy machine. Our primary task will be to convert the photograph of a beautiful flower shot against a black background into something that is reproducible. Because Find Edges looks only for edges, the black background will go away immediately when the filter is applied.

1. Open the image \PHOTOS\FLOWERS\514081.WI on the Corel CD. Use the Resample command in the Image menu, change the Width to 6 inches, and click OK.

2. Select Convert To from the Image menu and choose Grayscale (8-bit).

3. Select the Effects menu and choose Sharpen; then select Find Edges. From the dialog box change the Level slider in the Adjust section to 80 and the Edge type to Soft. Click OK. The result is shown in the following illustration.

4. To clean up the background, select the Magic Wand Mask tool from the Toolbox and ensure the Tolerance level in the Property bar is 10. Click anywhere on the background outside of the flower.

5. From the <u>E</u>dit menu select Cle<u>a</u>r. Invert the mask. Ensure the Preserve Image button is not enabled and click the Create Object button.

6. The flower object should now be selected, as indicated by the handles appearing on the corners. Click and drag one of the corner handles and reduce the size of the flower until it is approximately one third of its original size.

7. When you are satisfied with the size, double-click the flower to apply the transformation, or click the Apply button. You may see a slight edge from the original flower left behind. To remove it, you must lock the flower object from the Objects roll-up (CTRL+F7) by clicking the padlock icon and selecting Cle<u>a</u>r from the <u>E</u>dit menu. Click the object thumbnail in the Objects roll-up to unlock and select it.

8. From the <u>O</u>bject menu choose Drop Shado<u>w</u>. The shadow I created on the lower left had an Average setting, with a Feather setting of 15 and an Opacity of 55. It is all a matter of personal taste. Click OK.

9. The text is Times New Roman at 96 points. I applied the same drop shadow to it that I applied to the flower. The final result is shown in Figure 17-8 and in the color insert.

The
completed
banner for a
gardening
column

FIGURE 17-8

Another way to use the Find Edges filter with flowers is shown in Figure 17-9. The flower was imported into DRAW and then duplicated, aligned, and distributed to make the border. The text with the drop shadow and the scalloped lower border were created in PHOTO-PAINT.

The High Pass Filter

I placed the High Pass filter last because it is unique. Officially, this filter removes low-frequency detail and shading, and emphasizes highlights and luminous areas of an image. This filter enables you to isolate high-contrast image areas from their low-contrast counterparts. The action of the filter makes a high-contrast image into a murky gray one. You may rightly ask why you would ever want a filter to do something like that. The answer is that this filter is best used as preparation for other filter actions.

High Pass Filter Controls

The Percentage slider controls the intensity of the High Pass filter's effect. The default setting is 100 percent, which is far too high for many applications. Low

Using a single photograph of a flower and the Fine Edges filter, we produce an attractive banner for a menu

FIGURE 17-9

Percentage values distinguish areas of high and low contrast only slightly. Large values change all high-contrast areas to dark gray and low-contrast areas to a slightly lighter shade of gray. At higher settings, the High Pass effect removes most of the image detail, leaving only the edge details clearly visible. If you only want to emphasize highlights, use lower percentage settings. The Radius slider determines how many pixels near the edge (areas of high contrast) are included in the effect. The result is, the higher the setting, the more contrast is preserved.

What Can You Do with the High Pass Filter?

The High Pass filter is especially useful as a precursor to the application of the Threshold filter (Chapter 23). By first applying different levels of High Pass to an image, you can produce a wider variety of effects with the Threshold filter. You can also use the High Pass filter to help differentiate objects in an image when creating a mask. This is because the High Pass filter sees an image in terms of contrast levels, which is one of the ways your eyes perceive images in real life. Using the High Pass filter as the first step helps prepare the image so you can mask an element that is visually unique but proves difficult to isolate with a mask. By applying the High Pass filter set to a Percentage level of 50 and a Radius of 20, you can often create an outline around the object you want to isolate. After the mask is created, save it and use the Revert command to restore the image to its last saved state. Then reload the mask.

The Sharpness Control Dialog Box

Now that you know what all of the sharpen filters do, you can see them all (except High Pass) at once with the Sharpness Control dialog box, shown here. You access the dialog box by choosing Adjust in the Effects menu and selecting Sharpness.

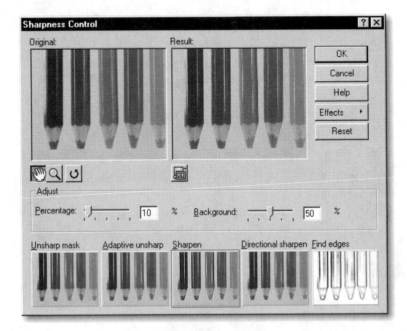

This dialog box provides a quick way to compare the results of different filters side by side. The operation is centered on the before-and-after format. The windows, called Original and Result, are at the top of the dialog box. Clicking the thumbnail of the desired filter applies the filter to the image in the Result window. To undo the last filter application, you can click the Undo button that is to the right of the Zoom button. Repeatedly clicking this button lets you step back through a group of effects applied. Different filters can be applied multiple times using the Sharpness Control dialog box.

Final Thoughts

Now you know a lot more about the sharpen filters. A few more ways to sharpen an image by sharpening individual channels are explored in Chapter 24. The next chapter deals with the wild and woolly world of the 2D Effect filters.

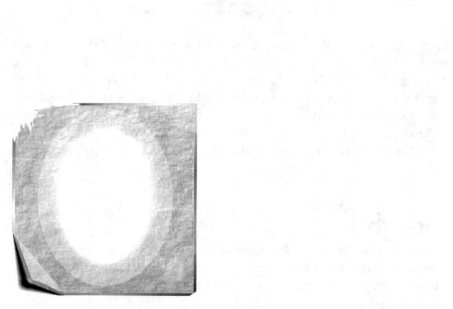

18

The 2D Effect Filters

This group of filters comprises some of the most unusual and complex in Corel PHOTO-PAINT 7. Many of the 2D filters are not needed for day-to-day photo-editing but can be genuine lifesavers in some situations. Many of these filters first appeared in Corel PHOTO-PAINT 6. The filters in this chapter are discussed in the order of their appearance in the drop-down list.

The Band Pass Filter

Leading off the lineup in the 2D Effect category of the Effects menu is the Band Pass filter. While the operation of this filter is a little difficult to comprehend, it does have its uses. The Band Pass filter lets you adjust the balance of high contrast and smooth areas in an image. The Frequency plot, in the lower right-hand part of the screen, displays a graph that shows the occurrence of sharp (high contrast) and smooth (low contrast) areas in the image. Smooth areas are located toward the center of the graph, while sharp areas are distributed toward the outer edges. By adjusting the radius and weightings of the bands, you can screen out unwanted tonal characteristics in an image. A low weighting for the center of the plot emphasizes image detail; a low weighting for the outside of the plot reduces image detail.

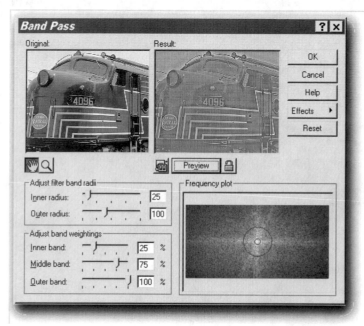

Reading the Frequency plot can be a little tricky. The area outside of the larger red circle is the Outer band; the area outside of the smaller red circle, but inside the larger one, is the Middle band. Everything inside of the smaller red circle is the Inner band. Use the Inner/Outer radius slider to determine which areas of the image (by frequency content) are in the Inner, Outer, and Middle bands. Then adjust the Inner, Outer, and Middle band sliders to set the intensity of each band. To eliminate either the sharp or smooth areas within a band, set the weighting to 0. To emphasize them, set the slider to the maximum of 100 percent.

Experiment with different weightings to see which provide the best results. For example, you can use the bands to eliminate unwanted noise by isolating the frequency of the noise within the middle band and reducing its weighting to 0. The only challenge you may experience with this experimentation method of using the filter is that its internal operation is very complex and therefore very, very slow. I thought it was slow and I am using a Pentium at 200MHz!

Using the Band Pass Filter

One of the four uses I have found for the Band Pass filter is balancing the contrast by applying it to an image before applying the Threshold. Figure 18-1 is the photograph of a train after it has had the Threshold filter (set to bi-level) applied to it. Figure 18-2 is the result of applying the Band Pass filter before the Threshold filter. Notice the difference between the two resulting images. The application of the Band Pass filter brings a balance between the high and low contrast areas. This means that the Threshold effect will be able to produce more detail. Note that in Figure 18-2 you can read the "New York Central" on the nose plate of the train. You can also see much more detail in the wheel carriage assembly. I confess that setting up the Band Pass filter was done by experimentation, but the results are worth it if you must reduce an image to bi-level and need to preserve as much image information as possible.

The Displace Filter

The Displace filter enables you to distort or add texture to an image by moving individual pixels. The direction and distance that the pixels move are determined by an image in the dialog box called a *displacement map*. The brightness values of the pixels in the displacement map tell Corel PHOTO-PAINT which pixels to move and how far to move them. It is important to remember that we are talking about Brightness values, so the following three values apply to grayscale and color images.

Here the
Threshold
filter
has been
applied
to the
photograph

FIGURE 18-1

Here the
Band Pass
filter has
been
applied,
followed
by the
Threshold
filter

FIGURE 18-2

- **Black** Areas in the displacement map that contain black will move the corresponding pixels in an image to the right and/or down by the maximum amount defined by the Scale settings in the Displace dialog box. Values between black and 50 percent gray move pixels a shorter distance.

- **White** Areas in the displacement map that contain white will move the corresponding pixels in an image to the left and/or up by the maximum amount defined by the Scale settings in the Displace dialog box. Values between white and 50 percent gray move pixels a shorter distance.

- **Middle gray** Areas in the displacement map that are composed of gray with a brightness of 50 percent cause the pixels to remain unmoved.

Creating a Watercolor Effect

In this hands-on exercise we are going to make a displacement map and apply it to an existing image to change its overall appearance to resemble a watercolor painting. I encourage you to do this exercise because the resulting image looks much better in color than the grayscale printed in this book.

Our first step is to make a displacement map. We have a choice of making the map either the same size as the image or small so that it can be tiled. To achieve the effect we desire, we will make a small one.

1. Select File, New. From the Create A New Image dialog box, choose 24-bit color mode; Width/Height: 150×150 pixels; Resolution: 144 dpi.

2. To make the displacement map, we will use the Texture Fill feature of PHOTO-PAINT. Select Fill from the Edit menu to open the Edit Fill & Transparency dialog box. On the Fill Color tab, select the Texture Fill button (on the far right) and click the Edit button. This action opens the Texture Fill dialog box, as shown on the next page.

3. Select Styles in the Texture Library and from the Texture list, choose Surface-Rainbow. We will use the pattern without modification. Click OK to return to Edit Fill & Transparency and click OK to apply the fill. Save the image using File, Save to the \COREL\ DRAW70\PHOTOPNT\

DISPLACE folder. Select the "PaintBrush (*.PCX)" setting for the Save as type and name the file WATERCOLOR.PCX. Close the file after it has been saved.

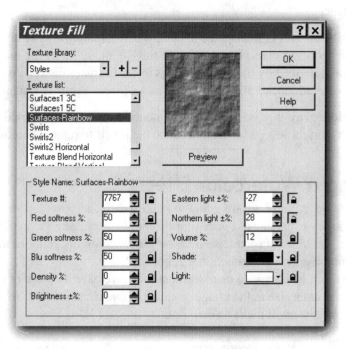

4. Using the File Open command in the File menu, find the image 514075.WI located in the \PHOTOS\SEASONS folder of either CorelDRAW 7 CD-ROM Disk #2 or the Corel PHOTO-PAINT 7 CD-ROM. Because this is a large file, use the Resample option. When the Resample dialog box opens, change the Width to 500 pixels and click the OK button. The image opens, as shown in Figure 18-3.

5. Under 2D Effects in the Effects menu, select Displace…. This opens the filter's dialog box, shown next. Locate and click the Load button on the right side of the dialog box. This opens the Load Displacement Map dialog box. It should be at COREL\DRAW70\PHOTOPNT\DISPLACE, which is the default location for the displacement maps provided with Corel PHOTO-PAINT.

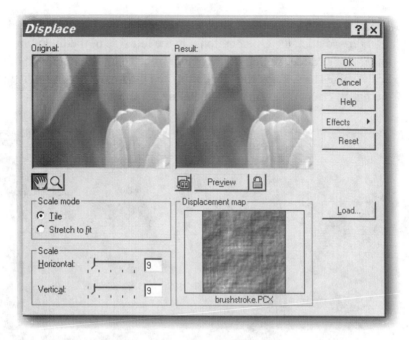

Use the
Resample
option to
open this
large file

FIGURE 18-3

6. Locate the file WATERCOLOR.PCX and either double-click on it or select it and click the Open button. On the left side of the dialog box under Scale Mode, keep the Tile option selected and change both of the Scale Values to 8. Click the OK button and the image becomes displaced, giving the effect of a watercolor painting, as shown here.

Suggestions for Creating Displacement Maps

This filter sounds very complicated, and I speak from experience when I tell you that it is possible to waste many hours playing with it. Here are some practical suggestions for creating displacement maps to work with the Displace filter.

Remember that 50 percent gray is the neutral color that keeps the pixels from moving; therefore, it is a good background color when creating a displacement map. Next, when making displacement maps, keep the image area small. Some of the most effective displacement maps that Corel provides are smaller than 20 × 20 pixels. Keep the Horizontal and Vertical displacement settings small for the best effects. Also, you will find that the some of the more effective maps are those that contain smooth transitions between the bright and dark components. Resolution and file formats are not critical factors. PHOTO-PAINT is not restricted to PCX format.

Some other Texture fills that make interesting displacement maps follow, using the format of LIBRARY/Texture name: STYLES/Surface1 2C; SAMPLES 5/Bacteria; SAMPLES 5/Beads; SAMPLES 5/Block Rainbow.

The Edge Detect Filter

Often it is necessary to create images that will be reproduced on a photocopier rather than a printing press. Because a photocopier doesn't faithfully reproduce grayscale images, you can use the Edge Detect filter to convert images into lines on a single-colored background. Best results are obtained with a high-contrast image. This filter is similar to the Find Edges filter in the Sharpen group of the Effects menu, as described in Chapter 17.

The operation of this filter is extremely simple. The Edge Detect Filter dialog box has only two areas in which to make a choice. The first involves choosing the Background Color. This color will replace every part of the image that doesn't have a line in it. The other is setting the Sensitivity slider (1-10), which determines the intensity of edge detection.

Using the Edge Detect Filter

Move the slider to the right to increase the effect, which means that more of the original area surrounding the edges is included. A high sensitivity value can create the appearance of noise in the finished image. When this happens, and it will, use the eraser tool to remove the noise from the image. Figure 18-4 shows a photograph of a nautilus shell that is great for use in offset printing but suffers considerably when reproduced on a photocopy machine. Applying the Edge Detect filter makes the photograph into something that can be used to advertise an upcoming shell exhibit. In Figure 18-5 the process of using the Edge Detect filter created a lot of noise around the shell that was removed with the Eraser tool.

The Edge Detect filter can work with both color and grayscale images. When used on a color image, it will generally produce lightly multicolored lines. To make all of the lines black, convert the image to grayscale. Be aware that some images, especially low-contrast photographs, look really ugly when applying this filter. If that happens, try using the Band Pass filter and then applying the Threshold filter, as discussed earlier in the chapter.

This
photograph
will not
reproduce
well on a
photocopy
machine

FIGURE 18-4

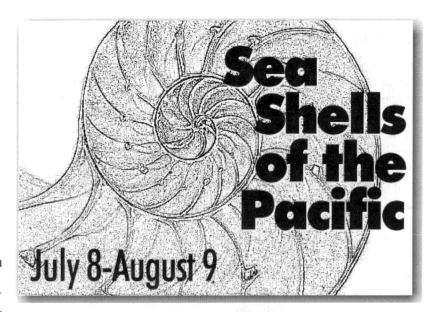

An outline
of the shell
created with
the Edge
Detect filter

FIGURE 18-5

TIP: *An application of contrast or equalization before applying the Edge Detect filter improves the resulting effect in most photographs.*

The Offset Filter

The Offset filter moves an image according to a specified number of pixels or a percentage of image size. We are not talking about moving an object; this filter actually moves pixels in an image. It is a favorite of those Photoshop users who were heavily involved in channel operations (called CHOPS). This filter remains critical to many techniques described in numerous Photoshop books. Most of these techniques involving the Offset filter were developed before the advent of objects and layers. It allowed you to create an image, save it to a channel, and offset the duplicate to create highlights and shadows. Today it is easier to do that by creating and positioning objects. Still, the Offset filter can be used for effects that no other filter can create, as shown in the hands-on project that follows.

Creating a Book Cover with the Offset Filter

This is a hands-on exercise using the Offset Filter to create a book cover. It seems our little shell exhibit has done so well we need to design a cover for it.

1. Find the file \PHOTOS\PATTERNS\594011.WI, select the Resample option from the Open An Image dialog box, and click the Open button. When the Resample Image dialog box opens, ensure that Units is set to inches and change Width to a value of 5 inches. Click the OK button and the original image appears, as shown in Figure 18-6.

2. Select the Offset... from the 2D Effects in the Effects menu, opening the 2D Effects dialog box. Click the button to enable Wrap around in the Fill empty area with: section. In the Shift section, set the Horizontal to 30 and the Vertical to 25. Ensure the Shift value as a percent of dimensions option is checked. The result of the offset is shown next.

3. For the Book title, select the Text tool in the Toolbox and click somewhere in the image. In the Property bar, change the font to Futura XBlk BT at a size of 72 and click the Render Text to Mask button to enable it. You may want to ensure the Mask Marquee button is enabled so you can see the mask we are going to make. Click somewhere in the image and type the word **SHELLS** in all caps. Then grab the edge of the text and move it to the location shown here.

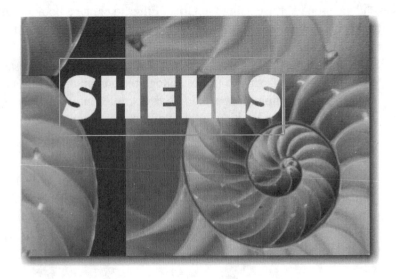

4. Click the Object Picker tool in the Toolbox and the text will become a mask. Select Adjust in the Image menu and choose Gamma. Set the Gamma to a value of 5.0 and click the OK button. If you used Gamma in previous releases of PAINT, the value of 5.0 corresponds to a value of 500 in those versions.

5. Select the Text tool again and change the Font to Bank Gothic Md BT and the size to 20. Disable the Render Text to Mask button, change the Character Line Spacing to a value of –2, and click on white in the onscreen palette, if your Paint color is not white. Type in the words **OF THE SOUTH PACIFIC**. Click the Object Picker tool and move the text, as shown in Figure 18-6. The completed cover is shown in the color insert.

Controlling the Offset Filter

The Offset Filter dialog box controls are divided into two areas: the Shift controls and the Fill empty area options. Horizontal and Vertical Shift sliders determine the

The finished book cover

FIGURE 18-6

amount of shift in the Horizontal and Vertical. The values in the boxes to the right of the sliders represent either the number of pixels shifted or the percentage, depending on whether the Shift Value box is checked. When the Shift Value as Percentage of Dimensions checkbox is enabled, it causes the coordinates of the horizontal and vertical shift values to be calculated as a percentage of the size of the object. When this checkbox is enabled and a vertical shift value of 50 and a horizontal value of 0 are selected, the image will shift along the vertical plane a distance corresponding to exactly one-half the size of the image.

Fill Empty Area Options

The key to the operation of this filter is determined by the following options:

- **Wrap around** This wraps another part of the image around the edges of the window when shifted.

- **Repeat edges** This fills the space vacated by the shifted image with the color(s) currently appearing along the edge of the image.

- **Paint color** This fills the space vacated by the shifted image with the current paint color.

Using the Offset Filter

There are a few things to consider when using this filter. First, the filter will shift either the entire image or an area enclosed by a mask. None of the pixels in the image being shifted will shift outside of the mask. Therefore, depending on the Fill Empty space option chosen, all of the effects will happen inside the mask. If the object being masked is a solid color and Wrap around is chosen as the option, it will appear as though nothing had happened.

The Pixelate Filter

The Pixelate filter gives a blocklike appearance to the selected area of an image. You have seen the effect many times on newscasts where the process disguises a person's features from the viewer. Because the pixelation was done on a frame-by-frame basis, the boundaries of the pixelation varied from frame to frame, which produced an apparent movement around the edges.

You can control the Pixelate effect by selecting either Rectangular or Circular mode and changing the size and opacity of the blocks. This filter can be used to create backgrounds that have the appearance of mosaic tiles.

Width and Height values (1-100 pixels) for the size of the pixel blocks can be entered independently. The effects of pixel block size are dependent on the image size. A value of 10 in a small image will create large pixel blocks. A value of 10 in a very large image will produce small pixel blocks. Use the Opacity slider (range is 1-100 percent) to control the transparency of the pixel blocks. Lower values are more transparent. The shape of the blocks of pixels is controlled with the Pixelate mode buttons. Square mode arranges the pixel blocks on horizontal lines. Circular mode bends the blocks of pixels and arranges them on concentric circles beginning at the center of the image or the masked area.

Using the Pixelate Filter

Since Corel PHOTO-PAINT 7 can import and work on video files (if you have a video capture board), the most obvious use for the Pixelate filter is to pixelate the faces of key witnesses to gangland murders for the local news station. If that opportunity is not readily available, Pixelate is very handy for creating unusual backdrops or converting backgrounds into something akin to mosaic tile. When working with backgrounds, remember that the best effects occur when there are contrasts in the image that is being pixelated. For example, if you pixelate a solid blue sky, you will hardly see any effect on the image.

Adding Action to a Scene

At times you may want to convey action in a photograph, and the Pixelate filter can be used to provide that effect. In the original photograph, shown next, the Land Rover appears to be parked, although it was shot at an angle and is clearly driving off the road. The absence of a driver is another visual indicator that the vehicle is parked. All of these problems can be solved.

If we want to convey action in this vehicle, we must make it appear to jump out of the page. The Motion Blur filter (Chapter 15) gives the effect of speed but does not give us what we want. In Figure 18-7 the portion of the Land Rover that will remain unchanged is first isolated with a mask. The area that will be affected is indicated by the lightened section. The mask is feathered so there are no abrupt transitions.

The Opacity percent slider is an import control feature of this filter. Many times, applying a 100 percent Pixelate filter overwhelms the image, whereas applying it with 20-60 percent Opacity produces a more subtle effect. In Figure 18-8, the area around the vehicle has been masked and the Pixelate filter applied at 100 percent opacity in Circular mode. In Figure 18-9, the same filter has been applied at 50 percent opacity, creating a feeling of action without being distracting.

A small remaining detail is the absence of a driver. It is hard for the viewer to imagine a vehicle racing through the page without one. This is not a difficult problem to resolve. From another photo I mask and drag in (as an object) a photograph of a man, as shown in Figure 18-10. Applying perspective, rotation, and scaling changes the size and angle of the man to make him appear to be driving the vehicle. Selecting Layer mode allows you to use the Eraser tool to remove all of the parts of his body that would be hidden if he were actually driving. To complete the illusion, a tint of 30 percent gray is painted over him so it will look like he is behind the glass. The

Mask the
area to be
pixelated

FIGURE 18-7

completed driver is shown in Figure 18-11. The final touch is to apply the Radial Blur filter to the pixelated background. The completed image is shown in Figure 18-12.

The Puzzle Filter

The Puzzle filter lets you break down the image into "puzzle-like pieces, or blocks, resembling a jigsaw puzzle." The preceding quotation is from the definition in the Help file. Now, maybe the puzzles look different in Canada, but I have worked with puzzles most of my life, and the results of this filter look like several things, but a puzzle is not one of them. It does change images or the selected portions of them into nice blocks that can give the effect of mosaic tile.

Using the Puzzle Filter

Just a few notes about the operation of the Puzzle filter. Adjust Block Width and Height sliders control the width and height of the blocks created by the filter. The range is 1-100 pixels, meaning it will create blocks of a size determined by these

Here the Pixelate filter has been applied at an opacity setting of 100 percent

FIGURE 18-8

Here the Pixelate filter has been applied at 50 percent opacity

FIGURE 18-9

A photograph of a man is added

FIGURE 18-10

The man is made to fit behind the wheel

FIGURE 18-11

The Radial
Blur filter
adds the
finishing
touch

FIGURE 18-12

settings. If the Square Blocks checkbox is enabled, the controls are locked together. The Max Offset (Percentage) slider controls the offsetting, or shifting, of puzzle blocks. It is important to note that the Offset is a percentage of the Block size. For example, if the Block size is set to a width of 50 pixels and the Max offset slider is set to 10 (percent), the Offset will have a maximum shift of 5 pixels (10 percent of 50 = 5). Therefore, increasing or decreasing block size changes the effect the Maximum amount of Offset has, even though the numbers don't change. To make the effect look more like blocks, the actual amount of offset for each block is random. This setting only determines the maximum amount of offset that can be applied. Fill Empty Space With is the remaining option. When the blocks are offset, something must take their place unless PHOTO-PAINT is in Layer mode. Choose from one of the following five options from the Fill empty areas with settings to fill the empty spaces.

- **Black** Applies a black background.

- **White** Applies a white background.

- **Paint Color** Applies the current Paint color.

- **Original image** Uses the colors from the original image as a background.

- **Inverse image** Inverts the image adjacent to the shifted blocks and applies it as the background.

Hands-on Practice with Puzzle and Pixelate Filters

Now that we have learned about these two filters, let's put them to use. In the previous release of PHOTO-PAINT, the Puzzle filter was pretty limited. With the addition of the Layer mode, it can now be used for some pretty spectacular effects. In the following hands-on exercise, we are going to create a masthead for an article about stress in today's workplace. To save time in doing the exercise, we are going to use an image that is smaller than we would use in a magazine, thus producing a smaller file.

1. Create a new file using File, New. When the Create A New Image dialog box opens, change the settings to 24-bit color; Paper color: white; Width: 3 inches; Height: 1 inch; Resolution: 300 dpi.

2. Select the Text tool. In the Property bar, set the Font to SWISS921 BT at a size of 72 points. Click in the image area and enter the text **STRESS**. The text will be filled with the current Paint color. Color is not important here; we will apply a specific fill in the final steps. If you don't have SWISS 921 BT, you can install it from the Corel CD-ROM.

3. Select the Object picker in the Toolbox to make the text into an object and make sure the text is not outside the image boundary. Open the Objects roll-up (CTRL+F7) and click the Layer button, as shown here.

4. Choose 2D Effects from the Effects menu and select Puzzle.... When the Puzzle Filter dialog box opens, click the Reset button and then change the Height and Width values to

15 (pixels). Because we are in Layer mode, the normal choices of Replace with colors are not available. Click the OK button. The text becomes fragmented, as you can see here.

5. Next, we will create a suitable background. Both the context and the shape of the word demand something other than a pastoral background. To fill the background, click the Single button on the Objects roll-up and make sure the Background layer has the Pencil icon next to it. From the Edit menu, choose Fill…. This opens the Edit Fill & Transparency dialog box. On the Fill Color tab, click the Texture Fill button and then the Edit button. Select Styles in the Texture Library and from the Texture list, choose Threads. Click the OK button. The image background becomes really stressful, but it makes the text hard to read.

6. Now we apply the Pixelate Filter to the new background by selecting 2D Effects from the Effects menu and choosing Pixelate. When the dialog box opens, click the Reset button and then change the Pixelate mode to Circular. Click the OK button. The resulting background is still too distracting.

7. Choose Blur in the Effects menu and select Gaussian Blur. When the dialog box opens click the Reset button and click the OK button. This completes the basic portion. Completing the artwork involves adding the remainder of the text and then applying a black glow behind it to help it to stand out. (This technique is described in Chapter 13.) The completed masthead is shown in Figure 18-13.

In the color insert, this image had the fractured text filled with a Fountain Fill (Sunset preset) and a light dusting of Gaussian Noise (Chapter 15) applied to the text.

The Ripple Filter

Ripple is one of the "fun" filters. There is just so much you can do with it. While it is of little use in the day-to-day work of photo-editing, when it comes to photo-composition, it is a very powerful tool. The Ripple filter creates vertical and/or horizontal rippled wavelengths through the image. This filter first appeared in Corel PHOTO-PAINT 5 and has been improved since.

Controlling the Ripple Filter

The Ripple dialog box provides control over the amount and direction of the Ripple effect. The direction controls are obvious but a few other controls are not. The Period Slider controls the distance between each cycle of waves. A value of 100 creates the greatest distance between each wave, resulting in the fewest number of waves. New

The completed masthead

FIGURE 18-13

with PHOTO-PAINT 7, the Period setting works on a percentage basis of image size—the larger the image, the larger the number of waves created. The Amplitude slider determines how big the ripples (amount of distortion) are. Enabling the Distort Ripple option causes the ripple produced by the filter to be distorted by placing a ripple on the ripple.

Doing Something with the Ripple

I don't know, maybe it's because I was raised in California, maybe it was the '60s, but just thinking about Ripple gives me a headache. Back to work. So what can you do with this filter? Like I told you before, have fun.

Note for Corel PHOTO-PAINT 5 Users

You probably noticed that one of the options for the Ripple filter, the one that applied both the Horizontal and Vertical ripple effects simultaneously, did not make it into the current Corel PHOTO-PAINT release. I am sure the three people who used it are really disappointed.

A Simple Ripple Border Exercise

Here is a quick hands-on exercise to create a ripple-shaped border, which has become very popular with Web sites these days.

1. Create a new file (CTRL+N) with the settings of 24-bit, 4 × 6 inches, and a resolution of 72 dpi.

2. Select the Rectangle tool in the Toolbox (F6). Enable the Render to Object button in the Property bar. Click and drag a vertical rectangle that is the height of the image covering the left third of the width.

3. Click the Object Picker tool in the Toolbox. Open the Objects roll-up (CTRL+F7) and click the Layer button. You might get a warning: "Objects that are off the paper will get clipped to the paper size if activated. Do you wish to continue?" Click yes.

4. From the Effects menu, choose 2D Effects, and from the drop-down list, select Ripple.... Set the filter to the settings shown here. Change the Amplitude to 9 and click the OK button. The object has the ripple effect applied to both sides.

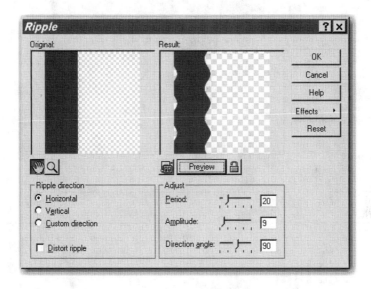

5. To trim off one side of the object, click and drag it so the rippled portion on the left side is off the paper (outside of the image area). Because we are in Layer mode, any part of the image that extends beyond the edge is removed.

6. Click the Single button in the Objects roll-up. Choose Fill from the Edit menu and choose a fill you like. I selected the Fountain Fill and used the preset Cylinder - Blue 03. Click the OK button.

7. To finish the border, select Drop Shadow... from the Object menu and use the preview area of the dialog box to make the drop shadow look like you want. Click OK and you have a border that looks like the one shown in Figure 18-14.

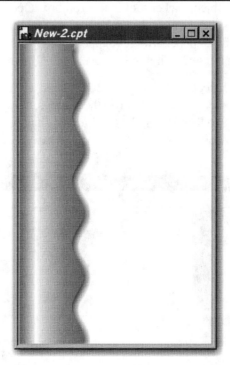

A
professional-
looking
edge border

■ FIGURE 18-14

The Shear Filter

Here is another distortion filter that is lots of fun—a real time waster. The Shear filter distorts an image, or the masked portion of it, along a path known as a Shear map.

Using the Shear Filter

Figure 18-15 shows a good action photograph. By using the Shear filter with the Tilt preset, we add more energy to the image as well as create space to add a short banner under the motorcycle if desired. The results are shown in Figure 18-16.

As I said, this is a fun filter. Applying the Wave preset to a rectangle of ducks, I was able to quickly create a flag for the land of Duck (where Howard sought asylum after his movie bombed). The flagpole is an object I created from a photograph of a flag and placed in the image, shown in Figure 18-17.

18

The original
photo of a
racer

FIGURE 18-15

The Shear
filter adds
a little
lift to the
photograph

FIGURE 18-16

The official flag of "Rubber Ducky Land," courtesy of the Shear filter

FIGURE 18-17

The Swirl Filter

The Swirl filter rotates the center of the image or masked area while leaving the sides fixed. The direction of the movement is determined by Clockwise or Counter-Clockwise options. The angle is set with the Whole Rotations slider (0-10) and the Additional Degrees slider (0-359°). Multiple applications produce a more pronounced effect.

Using the Swirl Filter

In the following example I have made a simple conical fill and applied it to a 200×200 pixels square. Next, I applied the Swirl filter set to 360°. Using the CTRL+F keyboard shortcut, I applied the Swirl filter twice more. The last image shows the application a total of six times. By using the Swirl filter, you can make excellent ornaments and effects for your desktop publishing projects, as shown in Figure 18-18.

The Tile Filter

This is a very simple and therefore quite useful filter. The Tile filter creates blocks of a selected image in a grid. You can adjust the width and height of the blocks (tiles) using the Horizontal and Vertical sliders in the dialog box. The values entered represent the number of images duplicated on each axis. The Horizontal slider determines how many columns of the tile will be present in the image. The Vertical slider determines the number of rows of tiles that will be produced.

The Tile effect can be used in combination with flood fills to create backgrounds as well as making wallpaper for Windows. The best effects are achieved when the number of tiles in relation to the original image is small. If you have a large number, the original subject becomes so small as to be unrecognizable.

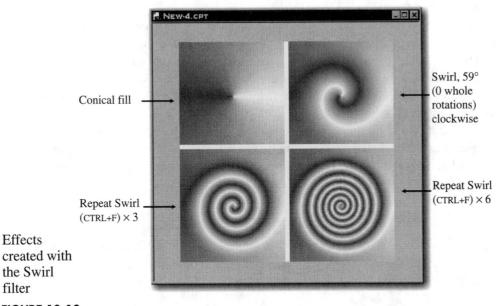

Conical fill

Swirl, 59° (0 whole rotations) clockwise

Repeat Swirl (CTRL+F) × 3

Repeat Swirl (CTRL+F) × 6

Effects created with the Swirl filter

FIGURE 18-18

The Trace Contour Filter

The Trace Contour filter effect lets you outline the edges of an image. This is one of those filters that is difficult to find uses for. It is similar in operation to the Edge Detect except it detects edges by their brightness values instead of their contrast component. Use the Level slider in the dialog box to set the edge threshold level. The Level slider in the dialog box ranges from 1 to 255. A lower setting leaves more of the image; a higher setting reduces the amount of the original image remaining after the effect is applied. Choose an edge type from the Edge Type settings. The Lower setting will trace the inside edges of an image, and Upper will trace the outside edges. The best effects are achieved when the subject matter is easily recognizable.

The User Defined Filter

The User Defined effect lets you "roll your own." Yes, you can make your own filters. The User Defined filter enables you to design your own *convolution kernel,* which is a type of filter in which adjacent pixels get mixed together. The filter that you make can be a variation on sharpening, embossing, blurring, or almost any other effect you can name.

The User Defined dialog box, shown in Figure 18-19, displays a matrix that represents a single pixel of the image shown at the center and 24 of its adjacent pixels. The values you enter into the matrix determine the type of effect you create. You can enter positive or negative values. The range of the effect is determined by the number of the values you enter into the matrix. The more boxes you give values to, the more pixels are affected.

This filter is not for the faint of heart. To understand its operation would take a chapter in itself. To show you what the filter does, Corel has provided several sample user-defined effects. Use the Load button for this. These effects have been provided to help you determine what values to enter into the matrix.

NOTE: *For more information about user defined filters, depress the F1 function key and select the Index tab. Type in* **User** *and select User Defined Filters, Using. Click the Display button.*

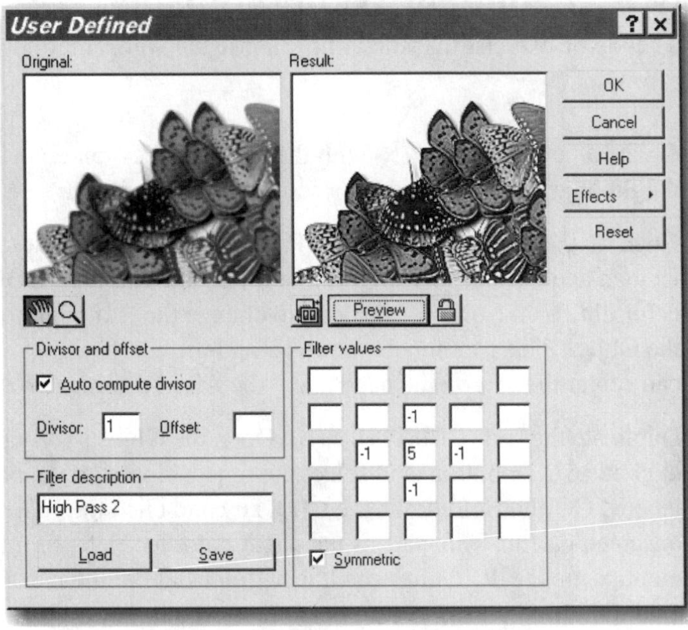

The User
Defined
dialog box,
which
represents a
single pixel
of the image

■ FIGURE 18-19

The Wet Paint Filter

After applying the Wet Paint filter, the image has the appearance of ... wet paint. This filter can quickly create some neat effects. You can set the percentage and the degree of wetness. Percentage refers to the depth to which the wet paint look is applied. For example, if you set low percentages, the amount of wetness appears to affect only the surface of the image.

Technically, Percent controls the amount (how far down) the drip travels. The Wetness values determine which colors drip. Negative (–) wetness values cause the dark colors to drip. Positive (+) wetness values cause light colors to drip. The magnitude of the Wetness values determines how large a range of colors drip. Maximum values are +/–50 percent.

With the addition of the Layer mode in PHOTO-PAINT 7, the Wet Paint filter can now be used to provide many different effects. Several combinations of positive and negative wetness can be applied to the same object to produce drop shadows, giving a 3D appearance to rounded text.

Frosty Text with the Wet Paint Filter

Here is a hands-on exercise that shows how to use the Wet Paint filter to make icicles hanging from text.

1. Create a new file (CTRL+N) with the settings of 24-bit color; Paper Color: a light blue; 6 × 4 inches; and a resolution of 72 dpi.

2. Click on the Text tool and on the Property bar, set the font to Times New Roman and the size to 150. Click in the image and type **COLD**. Click the color blue on the onscreen palette to change the text color to blue. Click the Object Picker tool in the Toolbox and the text becomes an object. You can center the text on the page using the Align command (CTRL+SHIFT+A).

3. Duplicate the text (CTRL+SHIFT+D). Open the Objects roll-up (CTRL+F7), click the Single button, and select the object closest to the background labeled COLD. Hold down the CTRL key and click the color white on the onscreen palette. This returns the paper color to white. From the Edit menu, choose Fill..., click the Paper Color button in the dialog box, and click OK. This makes the duplicate text, which may be hidden behind the original text, white.

4. Click the Layer mode in the Objects roll-up. Select Effects, 2D Effects, Wet Paint... and, using the default settings, click OK. Hide the Object marquee. Here is the result.

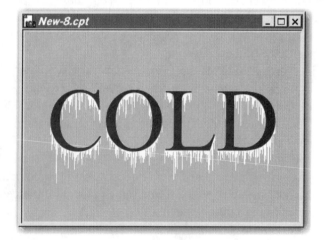

5. For the finishing touches, select Effe<u>c</u>ts, <u>3</u>D Effects, <u>E</u>mboss.... From the Emboss filter dialog box, use the default settings, with one exception: change <u>E</u>mboss to the original color. Click the OK button. In the Objects roll-up, click the Single mode button, select the top object and, from the <u>O</u>bject menu, choose <u>F</u>eather... (CTRL+SHIFT+F). Enter a <u>W</u>idth value of **5** and select Curved <u>E</u>dges. Click OK and we are finished, as shown in Figure 18-20.

The Wind Filter

18

The Wind filter is described as creating the effect of wind blowing on the objects in the image. This filter is normally ignored by most PHOTO-PAINT users because they rarely have a desire to put wind into their image. The problem is not with the filter or the description of it. It is important to learn what the filters do and how they do it. Then you can use them effectively. The Wind filter can be used to create some artistic effects with objects and masks.

The Wind filter smears pixels as a function of their brightness. The brighter the pixel, the more it gets smeared. Click and drag the Opacity slider (1-100) to

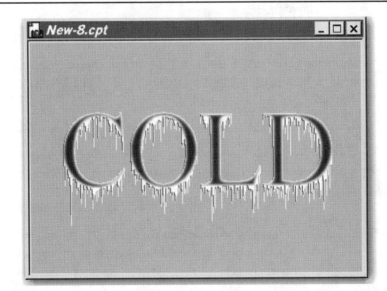

Our finished icicles

FIGURE 18-20

determine the visibility of the wind effect. Higher values make the effect more visible, and lower values make the effect more subtle. The amount of the wind effect (distortion) applied is controlled by the Strength slider. The direction of the smearing can be entered numerically or by clicking on the direction compass in the dialog box.

There are a few things to know about the operation of this filter when working with objects. It needs to have a source for the pixels it is "blowing" across the image. This means if you apply the Wind filter to an object, it will not work unless the background is unlocked or there is some unlocked object behind it. This also means it cannot be used in Layer mode.

Fuzzy Masks with the Wind Filter

One of the best things you can do with the Wind filter is to make masks with ragged edges, which I call *fuzzy masks*. Because this effect involves multiple applications of the Wind filter, I strongly recommend that you make a custom toolbar with the Wind filter button in it. The creation of custom toolbars is discussed in Chapter 3.

1. Create a new file: 24-bit color, 6 × 4 inches at 72 dpi.

2. Select the Rectangle Mask tool and create about a 5 × 3-inch rectangle in the middle of the image.

3. Choose Paint on Mask (CTRL+K) to make the mask into an image.

4. Select the 2D effects in the Effects menu and choose Wind…. Change the settings to an Opacity of 90, a Strength of 50, and a Direction of 90 degrees. Click the OK button.

TIP: *Using the Command Recorder (described in Chapter 24), you can quickly make a script that will automatically apply the Wind filter in multiple directions.*

5. Repeat step 4 three more times, but change the Direction setting to 180, 270, and 0. The result is a feathered fuzzy edge, as shown next.

6. Click the Paint on Mask button to return to normal mask mode.

7. The feathering needs to be removed for this exercise. From the Mask menu, select Shape and choose Threshold…. Enter a value of **90** and click OK. This will convert any part of the mask image with a brightness value of 90 or less to white, resulting in a firmer looking edge. Clicking the Paint on Mask button shows the resulting mask, which you can also see here.

8. Click the button again to return.

9. Select <u>F</u>ill… in the <u>E</u>dit menu. Choose the Texture Fill and, from the Samples 7 Texture Library, select Aztec Cave Drawing. Click the OK button in the Fill & Transparency dialog box.

10. To make the fill look like a furry mat, select <u>2</u>D effects in the Effe<u>c</u>ts menu and choose W<u>h</u>irlpool…. Select the Crystallize setting from the Style drop-down list and click the OK button.

11. To give it some depth, ensure Preserve Image is not selected and convert the mask to an object (CTRL+UP ARROW). Create a suitable shadow with the Drop Shado<u>w</u> command in the <u>O</u>bject menu. (Use an opacity setting to make it look like the figure.) The result is shown in Figure 18-21.

12. Save the file as RUG.CPT.

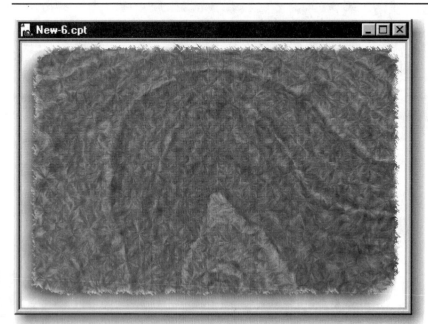

A background for the next exercise

FIGURE 18-21

The Whirlpool Filter

I used to refer to the Whirlpool filter as a poor man's Terrazzo. (I have also called it the "Smear tool on Steroids," which may be a more accurate description.) Since Terrazzo is now part of Corel PHOTO-PAINT, one would assume that there is no need for this filter. This is not true. Instead of making tiles, the Whirlpool filter does a blender operation on the selected area and creates some nice textures for use as backgrounds. Jeff Butterworth of Alien Skin Software, the original creator of the filter, states, "We just couldn't resist throwing in something fun. Swirl uses state-of-the-art scientific visualization techniques for examining complex fluid simulations. This technique smears the image along artificial fluid streamlines." This also may be one of the most CPU-intensive filters in the bunch. Be prepared for it to take a little time to complete its action. By clicking on Whirlpool, you open the Whirlpool Filter dialog box. This filter does not require a mask to operate.

Note for Corel PHOTO-PAINT 5 Users

The Whirlpool filter is called Swirl in Corel PHOTO-PAINT 5.

The Whirlpool Filter Dialog Box

The Whirlpool filter has several options that are unique to this type of filter. These controls are described in the next section.

SPACING SLIDER   All you really need to understand about spacing (of Whirlpools) is that the Whirlpool Filter randomly places whirlpools in the selection and then smears the selected area with them. The Spacing slider controls approximately how far apart these whirlpools are from one another. A large spacing setting creates more of a "painterly" effect. Smaller settings make the whirlpools close together and create effects that are reminiscent of 1960s design.

SMEAR LENGTH SLIDER   Smear Length controls how much the underlying image is blurred. Low values create noisy results, while large settings create smoother results. This is the one setting that has the greatest effect on how long the filter will take to process the image. A longer (higher) Smear Length setting results in longer processing time.

TWIST SLIDER   The Twist slider controls whether the fluid flows *around* or *out* of the whirlpools. Twist angles near 0 degrees make the whirlpools act more like fountains, because the fluid flows outward in a starlike pattern. Twist angles approaching 90° flow around in rings.

STREAK DETAIL SLIDER   Whirlpool is a form of blurring, so it can remove detail from your image or make your image altogether unrecognizable. To recover some of the image detail, increase the setting of Streak Detail.

WARP   When the Warp checkbox is checked, the simulated fluid stretches the image "downstream" along the streamlines. Warping makes the Whirlpool effect more striking, but it may not be desirable if you want the original image to remain recognizable. Turning the Warp off causes smearing without moving the underlying image.

STYLE   The Style drop-down list box lists several Whirlpool effect presets. When you choose a preset, dialog box values change to reflect its settings.

Making Distorted Text

While this filter is always useful for making blended backgrounds, the addition of the Layers command greatly expands the use of this filter, as the following hands-on exercise shows.

1. Create a new file: 24-bit color, 6 × 4 inches at 72 dpi.

2. Click the Text tool button in the Toolbox and after clicking on the image, type the word **TACOS**. Change the font to Kabel Ult BT at a size of 150 (points). Select the Object Picker tool. You may want to turn off the Object marquee.

18

3. Open the Objects roll-up (CTRL+F7), select the Single mode button, and select the Text object in the Objects roll-up. Select Fill... in the Edit menu and click the OK button in the dialog box.

4. Select the Rectangle Tool (F6) and enable the Render to Object button in the Property bar. Drag a rectangle below the word TACOS, as shown here. Select the Object Picker in the Toolbox and select both objects in the Objects roll-up.

5. Combine both objects (CTRL+SHIFT+L). Select Fill... in the Edit menu. From the Edit Fill & Transparency dialog box, click the Fountain fill button. Click the Edit button and from the Fountain fill dialog box, apply the Sunset setting from the Presets.

6. Click the Layer button in the Objects roll-up.

7. Select 3D Effects in the Effects menu and choose Emboss. Change the Depth and Direction settings as shown next, and click the OK button.

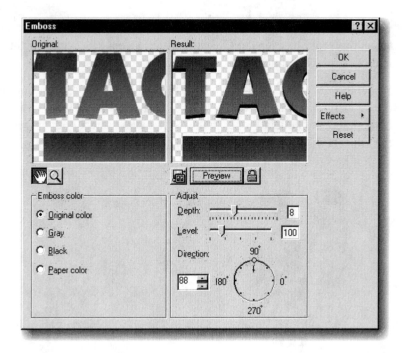

8. Select the 2D effects in the Effects menu and choose Whirlpool.... Select the Rings setting from the Style drop-down menu and click the OK button. The text is distorted, but we now need to trim the text.

9. With the Preserve Image button enabled, select the Create Mask command. We now have a mask that roughly corresponds to the shape of the letters and the underlying bar. From the Mask menu, select Shape and choose Threshold.... Enter a value of **170** and click OK. Now select Clip Object to Mask from the Object menu. Remove the mask (CTRL+D).

10. Create a suitable shadow with the Drop Shadow command in the Object menu. The result is shown next.

18

11. As a finishing touch, open the file RUG.CPT and drag the text /shadow object into it. You can see the result in Figure 18-22.

I hope this chapter stirs your imagination a little. Always remember not to let the name given a filter dictate what you use that filter for. I know the original designer of the Wind filter didn't think, "Boy, this would be great for making textures and other stuff." Now that we understand the 2D side of the filters world, let's move on to 3D filters, which should be called pseudo-3D. Why, you ask? Read on and find out.

The
completed
project

FIGURE 18-22

19

3D Effect Filters

Corel PHOTO-PAINT has a rich collection of filters that can be loosely grouped under the 3D category. This can be confusing since there is a 3D program in the Corel 7 Suite. Some of the filters in this group give effects that appear to be 3D, but none are true 3D filters. Please note that all of them are available with grayscale, Duotone®, 24-bit, and 32-bit color images. You can use 3D Rotate, Emboss, Map to Object, Perspective, Pinch/Punch, and Zigzag filters with Paletted (256 color) images.

3D Rotate Filter

The 3D Rotate filter rotates the image according to the horizontal and vertical limits set in the 3D Rotate dialog box. The rotation is applied as if the image were one side of a 3D box.

The 3D Rotate Filter Dialog Box

The dialog box is shown in Figure 19-1. The preview window shows the perspective of the image with the current slider settings. The plane of the box in the preview window that is shaded represents the image. By moving the vertical and horizontal sliders, the preview box can be oriented into the correct position. The preview window shows an approximation of the resulting application of the 3D Rotate filter.

If the Best fit checkbox is checked, the 3D image will not exceed the image window borders.

Using the 3D Rotate Filter

Applying the 3D Rotate filter to objects in any mode other than Layer mode is not recommended, as the results may be unpredictable. The basic problem is that while the rotation of the image occurs within the object, the object retains the same shape.

There are some real limitations to this filter. Although you can apply rotation to both the horizontal and vertical axes simultaneously, it is not recommended. The resulting image loses varying degrees of perspective. Also note that the preview doesn't always display the 3D perspective correctly.

Now that I have told you the bad news, let's make a box of crayons with this filter—and a few others.

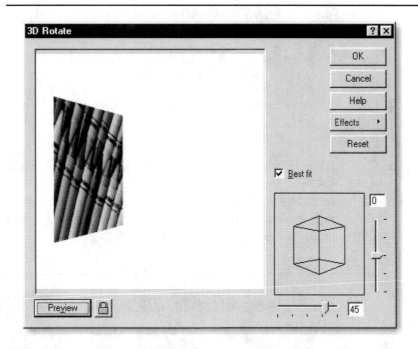

The 3D
Rotate filter
dialog box

FIGURE 19-1

Making a Big Box of Crayons

In this hands-on exercise you are going to create a box of crayons. In this super-turbo, extra-large world, it is only a matter of time before someone comes up with the idea for a box of crayons the size of a car, so why not design it now and beat the rush? It will require a little preliminary work to make the crayon art you will use for the box.

1. Open the file \PHOTOS\COLOR\593029.WI using the Resample option. Click the OK button. When the Resample dialog box opens, change Units to Inches. Change the Width to 6 inches. Click OK.

2. From the Image menu, select Paper Size and disable the Maintain aspect ratio checkbox. Change the Width to 4 inches. Click the OK button. Save the file as CRAYON.CPT. Close the file.

3. Create a new file that is 6 × 6 inches at 72 dpi. From the Edit menu, select Paste from File. When the dialog box opens, select CRAYON.CPT.

Change the option from Resample to Full Image. Click the Open button. Your image should look like Figure 19-2.

4. Select the Object Picker tool in the Toolbox. Open the Objects roll-up (CTRL+F7) and click the Layer button.

5. From the Effects menu, choose 3D Effects and 3D Rotate. When the dialog box opens, enter a value of **45** next to the Horizontal slider. Check the Best Fit box. Click OK.

6. Click the Single button in the Objects roll-up. Duplicate the object (CTRL+SHIFT+D). From the Object menu, select Flip and choose Horizontally. Use the Object Picker tool to move the objects so they look like the ones shown Figure 19-3. Use the arrow keys to make minor adjustments to the position of either object.

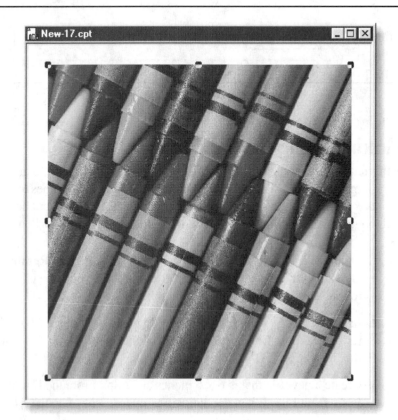

The crayons are ready to be made into a box

FIGURE 19-2

New-17.cpt

The 3D
Rotate
command
and the Flip
command
made the
box parts

FIGURE 19-3

7. With the Object Picker, select the right object. Open the Brightness-
   Contrast-Intensity control (CTRL+B) and change the Brightness setting
   to -20. Click the OK button.

8. SHIFT+select the other object (both should now be selected). Combine the
   objects (CTRL+SHIFT+L).

9. Duplicate the remaining object (CTRL+SHIFT+D). With your Paint color set
   to black, from the Edit menu, select Fill. Click Paint color and click OK.

10. Click the black object until the handles turn into circles (indicating it is
    in Perspective mode). Click and drag the upper-right handle and drag it
    down and to the left until the shape approximates what is shown in Figure
    19-4. The crayons in the figure have been made partially transparent to

make seeing the shadow object easier. Double-click the shadow object to apply the transform. If you make a mistake, click the ESC key to remove all temporary transforms.

11. With the shadow selected and the crayon object not, click SHIFT+PAGE DOWN. Click the Layers button in the Objects roll-up. From the Effects menu, choose <u>B</u>lur and then <u>G</u>aussian Blur. Change the <u>R</u>adius setting to 10 and click OK. Click CTRL+F to apply it again.

12. From the Objects roll-up, change the <u>O</u>pacity slider to 70. Move the shadow so it is where it looks good to you. The final image is shown in Figure 19-5.

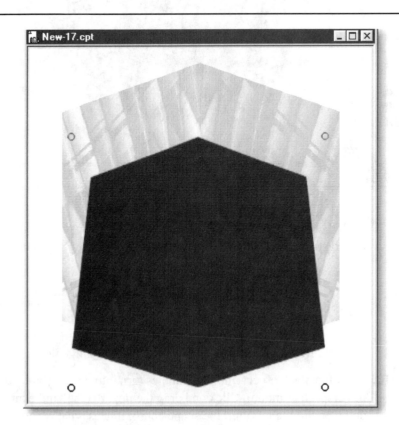

The shape of the shadow object doesn't need to be exact

FIGURE 19-4

Now, that's
a box of
crayons

FIGURE 19-5

13. Save the file as BIGBOX.CPT.

14. Click the Single button in the Objects roll-up. Set the Paint color to white. Select the Text tool from the Toolbox. Change the Font to Kabel Ult BT at a size of 60. Change the Interline spacing to 80. Click inside the image and type **BIG BOX OF COLOR,** as shown in Figure 19-6.

15. Click the Object Picker tool and position the text as you see in the figure. Click the object until the handles turn into circles (indicating it is in Perspective mode). Click and drag the lower-right handle and drag it down and to the left until the bottom line of the text is approximately parallel with the edge of the box. When you are satisfied with it, double-click the text to apply the transform. Use the Object Picker to position the text in the box.

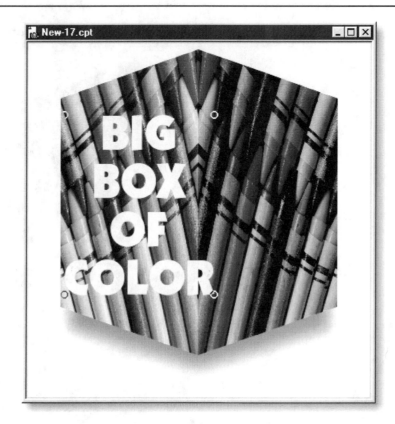

Adding the
text to your
image

FIGURE 19-6

16. So viewers will know how BIG this box of crayons is, from the Edit menu, select Paste from File. Locate the file \OBJECTS\PEOPLE\BOY.CPT and click Open. From the Objects roll-up, deselect the boy and leave the white background object selected. Click the Trashcan icon button at the bottom of the roll-up. Now we need to remove the white fringe that is apparent on the child when he is placed in front of a dark background.

17. Click on the boy to select him and, from the Object menu, choose Mating and Defringe. The default value of 10 is way too high; change it to 2. Click the OK button.

18. Click and drag one of the corner handles (they should be solid squares) to scale him down a little. Double-click on the child to apply the transformation. Move him as shown in Figure 19-7.

Now that's
a really BIG
box of
crayons

FIGURE 19-7

19. Select Drop Shadow and set it for a 0.1 Offset (lower-left) with a Feather
of 11 and Opacity of 50. You are done for now. Save the file.

The Emboss Filter

Corel PHOTO-PAINT has two emboss filters. One is called Emboss; the other one,
originally created by Alien Skin Software, is called The Boss and is found in the
Fancy category of the Effects menu.

Embossing creates a 3D relief effect. Directional arrows point to the location of
the light source and determine the angle of the highlights and shadows. The Emboss
filter has its most dramatic effect on medium- to high-contrast images. Several filters
can be used in combination with the Emboss filter to produce photo-realistic effects.

The Emboss Filter Dialog Box

The Emboss Filter dialog box, shown here, provides all of the controls necessary to produce a wide variety of embossing effects.

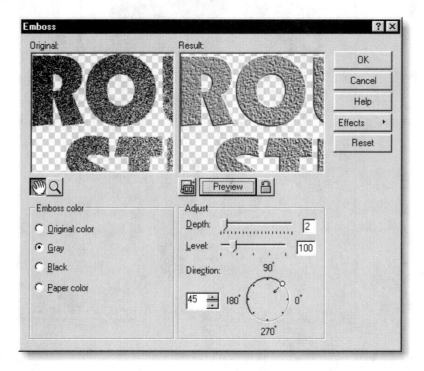

The Emboss Color option determines the color of the embossed image. When Original color is selected, the Emboss filter uses the colors of the image to simulate the relief effect. When Black or Gray is selected, the entire image becomes filled with that color. To select another solid color, other than black or gray, you must change the Paper Color (background color) to the desired color and select the Paper color button. The Depth slider sets the intensity of the embossing effect. Care should be taken not to use an excessive value since it can cause minor image displacement that will make you think you need to schedule an eye appointment. The Level slider controls the radius of the effect. You can use a larger amount of Depth without distorting the image. Direction specifies the location of the light source. Light direction is very important. It can make the image look like it has either a raised or sunken surface.

TIP: *To reduce the "jaggies" when applying the Emboss filter to high-contrast images (like text), apply a Gaussian Blur filter at a setting of 1 before applying the Emboss filter.*

Using the Emboss Filter

The Emboss filter is used in many of the hands-on exercises throughout this book. There are very few tricks to using it effectively. One of the standard techniques that the Emboss filter is used for is to produce textures. You can try this one yourself. Mask an area and apply the default setting of Add noise in the Effects menu. Apply the default setting of the Emboss filter. Instant sandpaper.

The Map to Object Filter

19

The Map to Object filter creates the impression that the image has been wrapped around a sphere, a vertical cylinder, or a horizontal cylinder. The sphere is easy to work with. The vertical and horizontal cylinders require the addition of highlights and shadows to make them look like cylinders.

The Map To Object Dialog Box

The Map To Object dialog box, shown here, has controls that are common to many other dialog boxes. In addition, there are two unique areas: Mapping mode and Adjust.

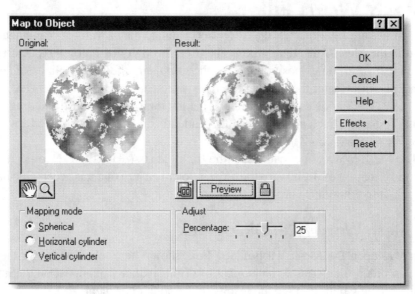

Clicking Spherical, Horizontal cylinder, or Vertical cylinder allows selection of the model used for wrapping. In the Adjust section, the Percentage slider is used to choose the amount of wrapping. Negative values wrap the image toward the back, and positive values wrap it toward the front. The default setting for the dialog box is a good one for Spherical. The amount of Percentage needed to achieve a noticeable effect with the Vertical or Horizontal cylinder is generally the maximum.

Note for Corel PHOTO-PAINT 5 Users

The Map to Object filter is called Map to Sphere in Corel PHOTO-PAINT 5.

While the filter can be applied to the entire image, some of the most dramatic effects are achieved by applying it to a smaller area of the image that has been defined by a mask. The effect is more pronounced and effective if the object has horizontal and vertical lines. Almost all uses of the Map to Object filter will require the application of highlights and shadows with an airbrush to enhance their appearance.

The Mesh Warp Filter

The Mesh Warp filter distorts the image according to the movement of the nodes on a grid in the Mesh Warp dialog box. The user, through the dialog box, determines the number of gridlines positioned over the grid using the No. gridlines slider bar. (Generally, the greater the number of nodes selected, the smoother the Mesh Warp distortion.) Each node can be moved by clicking on it with a mouse and dragging it to a new position. Each node moves independently and can be positioned anywhere in the Preview window.

The Mesh Warp effect can be a little tricky at first. Use the Preview button to view the effects of a Mesh Warp transformation to ensure that it is acceptable before applying it to your entire image.

The Mesh Warp Filter Dialog Box

When you open the Mesh Warp dialog box, shown here, click and drag the No. gridlines slider to determine the number of gridlines that will appear on the image. Use the Preview button to see the results of the node placement.

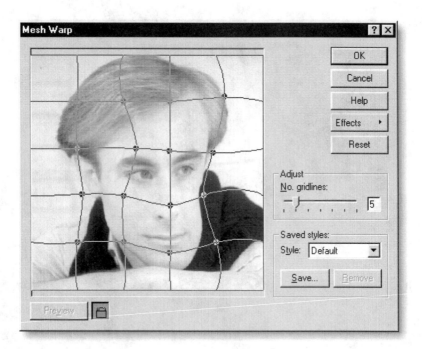

The No. gridlines slider controls the number of gridlines on the grid. The first horizontal gridline lies along the top and the first vertical gridline is on the left. Be aware that they can be hard to see, depending on your display. At each point where a horizontal and a vertical gridline intersect, a node is positioned. It is the manipulation of the nodes along the grid that creates the effect. Each node moves independently of one another. Generally, the more nodes you use in the Mesh Warp operation, the smoother the effect will be.

So…What Do You Do with It?

From a practical day-to-day standpoint, not very much. You can use the selective distortion capability to distort people and places. While this can be cute, it isn't very useful. It does allow you to distort or "morph" images or photos with some interesting results. The upper image in Figure 19-8 is the original photograph of an owl, looking curious. After the application of the Warp Mesh filter (lower image), he looks mad enough to start a fight.

People and owls aren't the only things to which you can apply the Mesh Warp filter. In Figure 19-9 we've improved the shape of a beer glass. Finally, the wrench and nut in Figure 19-10 has definitely gained an attitude.

With a
little help
from Mesh
Warp, a
curious-
looking owl
becomes
an owl with
attitude

FIGURE 19-8

Mesh Warp
can really
improve a
glass of beer

FIGURE 19-9

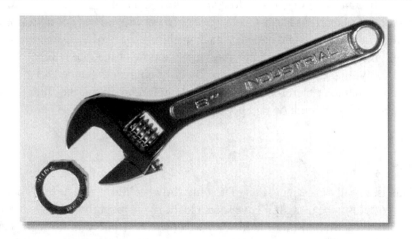

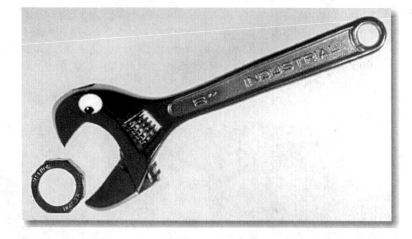

The wrench is less than interesting until we apply the Mesh Warp and make it hungry for a nut

FIGURE 19-10

Notes about Using the Mesh Warp Filter

As I said before, the greater the number of nodes, the smoother the transitions on the image. Because each node is independent, each must be individually moved. There is a trade-off between the smoothness of the transition and the time required to move all of the nodes. Since there are no constrain keys to keep the gridlines on the horizontal or vertical planes, use the gridlines themselves as your guide. As long as the line in the preview window appears straight, the line is still in line with its respective plane. The Mesh Grid value represents the number of nodes on each line of the grid. (The two end nodes on each gridline are out of view and not adjustable.) There is no zoom function in the preview window of the dialog box.

Applying the Mesh Warp filter to objects is not recommended, as the results may be unpredictable; therefore, merge objects before applying the filter. Hide or lock objects the filter is not being applied to.

Page Curl

This is a really excellent filter. The only drawback to it is that everybody and his uncle seems to be using it. I have seen a lot of flyers recently that have used the Page Curl filter. I wouldn't let that deter you, however; I just want to warn you in case your client seems less than enthusiastic when you show them something with the Page Curl filter. Page Curl simulates the effect of a page being peeled back, with a highlight running along the center of the curl and a shadow being thrown from beneath the image (if your image is light enough to contrast with a shadow). The area behind the image, revealed by the page curl, is filled with the current paper color. An example is shown here.

The Page Curl Dialog Box

The Page Curl dialog box, shown here with a curled edge that I added, has been improved again with the release of Corel PHOTO-PAINT 7. The curl effect begins in one corner of your selection and follows a diagonal line to the opposite corner.

You also may notice a slight transparency to the curl if there is any pattern or texture in the selected portion of your image.

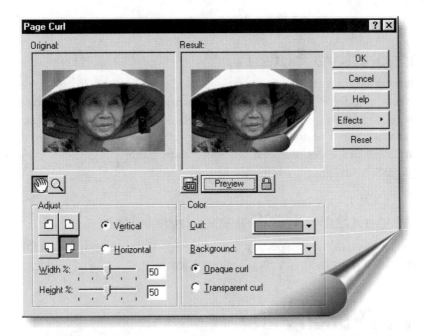

The origination point of the curl is controlled by using one of the four keys in the Page Curl dialog box. The Vertical button creates a vertically oriented page curl, which curls the page across the image (from left to right or right to left). Experiment with this setting to achieve the page curl you want. The buttons are mutually exclusive; that is, selecting one deselects the other. The Horizontal button creates a horizontally oriented page curl, which curls the page upward or downward through the image (from top to bottom or bottom to top).

Opaque curl or Transparent curl determines if the underside of the curled page is opaque or transparent. Choose the Opaque option if you want the curl to be filled with a blend of gray and white to simulate a highlight. Choose the Transparent option if you want the underlying image to be displayed through the curled paper.

The Width % slider controls the vertical component of the page curl regardless of whether it is a vertical or horizontal page curl. The curl Height slider controls the horizontal component of the page curl regardless of whether it is a vertical or horizontal page curl.

TIP: *To apply the effect to a portion of the image, select an area using a mask before you choose the effect. The page will only curl inside the masked area.*

The Perspective Filter

The Perspective filter creates the impression of 3D perspective in an image. There are two modes in the Perspective filter: *Perspective* and *Shear*. Perspective applies the look of 3D perspective to the image according to the movement of the four nodes in the preview box. The nodes are moved by clicking on them with the mouse and dragging them to the desired location. Shear also applies perspective, but it holds the original size and shape, similar to skewing.

Notes on Using the Perspective Filter

Since the addition of the Perspective Transform mode for objects, the usefulness of the Perspective filter has been greatly diminished.

The Pinch/Punch Filter

The Pinch/Punch filter either squeezes the image so that the center appears to come forward (pinch) or depresses the image so that the center appears to be sunken (punch). The result makes the image look as if it has been either pulled out or pushed in from the center.

The Pinch/Punch Dialog Box

This filter reminds me of the house of mirrors in the amusement park near where I grew up. They had all of these mirrors that distorted your features. This filter does the same thing. The Pinch/Punch dialog box lets you set the effect attribute. In the dialog box, moving the slider in a positive (+) direction applies a Pinch effect, and moving it in a negative direction (-) produces a Punch effect. While the filter can be applied to the entire image, some of the most dramatic effects are achieved by applying it to a smaller area of the image that has been defined by a mask. The effect is more pronounced if the object has horizontal and vertical lines.

The image in Figure 19-11 demonstrates one of the sillier things you can do to a photograph.

The Pinch/Punch filter can radically change the appearance of people, places, and things

FIGURE 19-11

Using the Pinch/Punch Filter

Besides distorting people's faces and bodies beyond recognition, there are actually some productive things you can do with this filter. The best way to use it is to limit the effects to small, manageable areas. Next, make applications in small amounts. For instance, in Figure 19-12, I have made a very loose-fitting mask around the head of the Statue of Liberty. Then I applied a small amount of Punch to it, which gives it a different perspective without the obvious distortion that attracts attention. In the "punched" photograph, shown in Figure 19-13, the only indication that the photo has been manipulated is one of the rays protruding from the crown. Even this telltale sign could have been eliminated if I had invested the time.

The Zigzag Filter

The Zigzag filter is a distortion filter. In short, you will get an effect but will, most likely, not be able to recognize the original image when you have finished. Zigzag distorts an image by bending the image lines that run from the center to the edge of the masked area or the circumference. This produces a wavelike action that changes

The original
photograph

FIGURE 19-12

A different
look after
the
Pinch/Punch
filter is
applied

FIGURE 19-13

curves to straight lines and creates angles that seem to twist the image from its center outwards. The Zigzag filter is great for simulating ripples and reflections in water. While the effect is slick, its uses are limited.

The Zigzag Filter Dialog Box

The dialog box for the Zigzag filter, shown here, has three options that allow you a wide range of control.

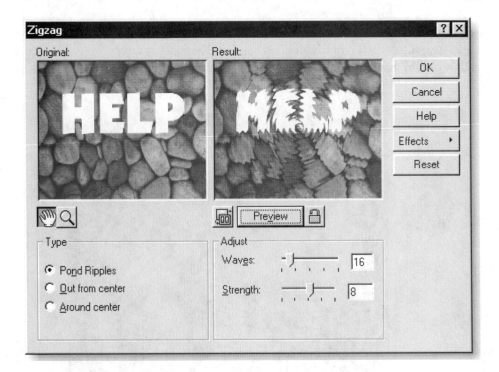

 NOTE: *The preview window for the Zigzag filter doesn't give a very accurate portrayal of the final result, so be prepared to experiment a little.*

The three options are as follows:

■ **Type** The Type settings control the direction and overall effect of the distortion.

- **Waves slider**   The Waves slider controls the distance between each cycle in the wave. Using larger values creates greater distances between each wave, resulting in a minimal number of waves. Smaller values create so many waves that it almost looks like a Fresnel lens.

- **Strength slider**   The Strength slider is used to control the intensity of the zigzag distortion. Keeping this value low helps the most when trying to imitate the effect of ripples in the water. With the Around center Type option selected, an additional Adjust option, Damping, becomes available.

To create Figure 19-14, I applied the stone bitmap fill to an empty image. Next the Zigzag filter with Pond Ripples was applied. The clock is an object (which Corel calls a watch) that was placed in the center using the Paste from File command.

Ripples in Time was easy to create with the Zigzag filter

FIGURE 19-14

20

The Render Filters

Render filters are used to produce special effects and backgrounds, and to make novelty images. Two of the filters, Lens Flare and Lighting Effects, were introduced in Corel PHOTO-PAINT 6. The Lighting Effects filter has been enhanced with this release of PHOTO-PAINT. In case you were looking here for the Julia Set Explorer 2.0, it has been moved to the Fancy category. The Render filters are

- 3D Stereo Noise

- Lens Flare

- Lighting Effects

3D Stereo Noise Filter

The 3D Stereo Noise filter (originally from the Kai Power Tools 2.0 collection) is my least favorite because it has become such a fad. This filter takes a perfectly good image and converts it to something akin to a printer failure all over your paper. By staring at the paper, you can see the original image with depth effect. (It is rumored that if you can stare at it for over an hour, just before the onset of a migraine, you can see Elvis.) The 3D Stereo Noise filter, or a program just like it, is what is used to produce those stereogram posters that have gained such popularity at suburban shopping malls in recent seasons. If you stare at them, you can actually see an embedded image with your depth perception.

3D Stereo Noise was discovered a long time ago at Bell Laboratories. The researchers observed that when certain points on an image where shifted, it gave the appearance of depth. As used here, the term *stereo* should not be confused with music. Human beings were designed with stereoscopic sight—two eyes that render a single image from two slightly different angles, thus producing depth perception.

The images that produce the best results with the 3D Stereo Noise effect use gray levels, are slightly blurred, and do not have extreme contrast. Don't waste precious system resources by using 24-bit color. The result will be grayscale. The 3D Stereo Noise filter generates a pixelated noise pattern that has horizontal frequencies corresponding to the gray levels of the initial image. This means that white will map to the highest frequency and appear closest to the viewer; black will map to the lowest frequency and appear farthest away.

Making an Image

First, create a grayscale image that uses text and simple objects. Although the filter will apply in all modes, the best images initially use gray levels. The smaller and more detailed the image you choose, the harder it will be to focus the stereo image. Apply a standard Gaussian Blur filter to the objects. This will soften the edges of the image for easier viewing. Make sure there are no masks and open the Effects menu. Then, under the Render subgroup, click on the 3D Stereo Noise filter. This opens the Preview dialog box. There are only two options with this dialog box: Depth control, with a relative depth range of 1-9; and a Show Dots check box, which enables the creation of two dots in a box near the bottom of the image to help the user focus on the 3D image. The two dots that appear in the Result window are used to guide you in focusing correctly on the image. Adjust your focus so that the dots fuse into one, and a three-dimensional effect is achieved.

Apply the filter to the entire image. The results will appear to be a random array of black-and-white noise.

Viewing 3D Stereo Noise Pictures

After you have created a stereo noise picture, it is time to focus your eyes and energies to see the image. I was never able to view the depth onscreen. Maybe you can do better here than I did. Don't feel bad if you don't see the image right away; it may take a few tries. In fact, there are some people who just cannot see it at all. I have included a sample image below. Can you figure out what it says?

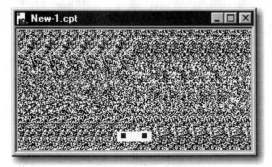

There are several ways to view the image in-depth. Try enabling the Show Dots check box to produce black dots about a half inch apart at the bottom of the image. Don't focus your eyes, but gaze through the image as if you were looking into the distance. The dots you placed at the bottom will separate into four. If you focus so that the middle two dots fuse, depth should pop in or out. Another way to view the image is to try crossing your eyes to fuse the four dots into three. You may also try holding the edge of a thin object such as a floppy disk or your hand between your eyes in order to separate each eye's vision. Were you able to see the word? I thought about putting the answer upside down but the production crew at Osborne had other thoughts about that. The answer is (drum roll please…) COREL. How original.

Controlling Depth in Stereo Images

When you see a 3D object up close, the object seems to be in a slightly different place depending on which eye looks at it. For instance, hold your finger about five inches from your computer monitor and look at it with one eye, then the other. Observe how it seems to move left and right with respect to objects on the screen. This discrepancy gives your brain information on how far away the object is. Against the background of your screen, your finger that is five inches away is displaced about one inch, depending on which eye views it.

Lens Flare Filter

The Lens Flare effect produces a spot of light that resembles a reflection within an optical system. In photography, lenses of different focal lengths produce different lens flare effects. Photographers work very hard to make sure the effects added by this filter do not occur. With this filter, you can add what they try to get out of a photograph.

When you first open the dialog box, shown in Figure 20-1, it will immediately render and provide a preview of the selected image. Choose from three lens types to produce the type of lens flare you want. You can also adjust the brightness (1-200 percent) of the lens flare with the slider bar. To change the position of the "flare," click the preview window at the point where you want the flare to be. You cannot "drag" the existing point in the preview window to the new location. Be aware that the preview function is automatic. This means that changing the lens type will start a preview cycle.

The Lens
Flare dialog
box
provides a
selection of
different
lenses and
levels of
brightness

FIGURE 20-1

Applying the Lens Flare to an Existing Image

In this hands-on exercise we are going to use the Lens Flare filter to add a final touch
to our Federal Express jet.

1. Open the file FEDEX.CPT.

2. Remove any existing masks by clicking the Remove Mask button in the
standard toolbar.

3. From the Effects menu select Render and choose Lens Flare.

4. Change the Lens type to <u>3</u>5mm prime and click the point at the end of the jet indicated by the plus sign in Figure 20-1. Click the OK button.

5. Save the file as FINAL FEDEX.CPT.

The Lens Flare filter gives the photograph a dynamic quality. The image is now ready for insertion in a brochure. In Figure 20-2 I have overlaid our starting photograph with the final photograph.

 TIP: *The Lens Flare filter only works with 24-bit color images. To apply this effect to a grayscale, convert the grayscale to a 24-bit color image, apply the Lens Flare filter, and then convert it back to grayscale.*

The original photograph compared with the final image

■ FIGURE 20-2

Lighting Effects Filter

The Lighting Effects filter lets you add one or more light sources to your image. Choose from a list of preset lights or create your own customized lights using the controls in the dialog box shown in Figure 20-3. You can add multiple lights and individually control the attributes of each light. The rather intimidating dialog box for the lighting effects is a little less than intuitive. After opening the filter, the preview window displays what the lighting effect will look like with the default or the last used setting.

Setting Up the Lighting Effects Filter

The first step in using the Lighting Effects filter is to choose a Light type from the Style list box. The list box contains a drop-down box with several preset light types available—for example, Spotlight, Directional. You can also add and remove your own styles. Each light source has been assigned appropriate settings to achieve a

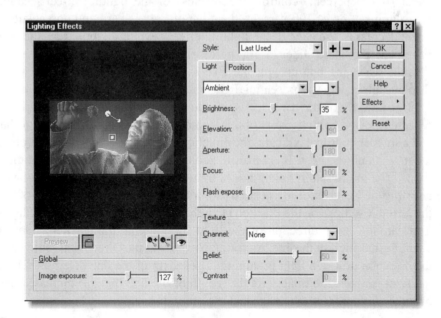

The
Lighting
Effects
dialog box

FIGURE 20-3

unique effect. For the purposes of discussing the various controls, we will use the Spotlight setting. After selecting Spotlight, the next step is to choose a color for the light; white is now the default setting, which provides a good starting point. Remember that colors add a color cast to an image. For example, I recently changed the background of a brightly lighted photograph to that of a sunset. I used the Lighting Effects filter with an orange light to add the color cast that was necessary to make the foreground look like it belonged in the same picture as the background.

Next, adjust the Brightness slider (used for spotlights) to set the brightness of the light (range of −200-400 percent), but be careful not to set it too high, as this can quickly wash out colors. The Elevation slider (0-90°) controls the angle of the light in relation to the surface of the image. For example, at a setting of 90° it would be as if a spotlight positioned above the image was pointed straight down. The Elevation slider confused me at first. Here is another example: think of the light as a flashlight. At an elevation of 90°, the flashlight is perpendicular to the image; that is, the actual light is pointing directly at the image. At 0°, the flashlight would be parallel to the image and only a small portion of the light would be striking the image.

The Aperture slider (1-180°) is used to set the range (width) of the light. The greater the aperture percentage, the greater the area affected by the light. The Focus slider (0-100 percent) controls the softness of the lighting effect's edge. At a maximum setting of 100 percent, the edge of light is hard and unrealistic. As the value decreases, the edge of the lighting effect develops a more realistic feathered edge. The Exposure slider (1-100 percent) controls the intensity of the light. By default, when the button with the Eye icon is depressed, the preview window displays all the icons representing light sources currently active in the image.

Initially, there are two icons in the preview window. The barbell icon, representing the light, consists of a large node that indicates the focus of the light, and a smaller node that indicates the direction and height of the light. The other icon, a dot, is Ambient light. It controls the color, and other settings control the "room light." The initial settings are a bright light with a dark color. Click the large node and drag the light source to a desired position. As you adjust the position of the light, the X and Y settings on the Position tab indicate the horizontal and vertical position. You can adjust the direction of the light by dragging the smaller node, thereby changing the angle of the line. As you adjust the line, the Directional setting indicates the direction in which light is shining. The length of the line determines how high the light is above the image. As the length of the line (height) increases, the light becomes farther from the image and therefore dimmer.

The Lighting Effects filter allows you to add up to 18 additional lights. Of course, with 19 lights, your rendering time will drastically increase. Clicking the Plus button below the preview window adds a light. Clicking the Minus button under the preview window removes the currently selected light.

I have included a sample before-and-after image in Figure 20-4 that demonstrates the application of the Lighting Effects filter to an image. Notice that you can use the Lighting Effects to change the entire mood of a photograph. Remember, when working with images like this one, to compensate for the type of lighting used. Can you see what is missing in the image? This type of light should be creating deep shadows under the old mariner. The absence of these shadows makes the photograph look fake.

Creating a Background for a Web Page

Until now, we haven't discussed the newest addition to the Lighting Effects filter, textures. This is not to be confused with CorelTEXTURE, which is something entirely different. The texture part of the lighting control creates pseudoshadows on surfaces, which greatly enhances the effect of the filter. To demonstrate some of the

The Lighting Effects filter can make day into night with the press of a button.

FIGURE 20-4

things we can do with the texture controls, the following hands-on exercise shows you how to create a splash screen for a new Internet Web news service using many of the filters we have already looked at in this and previous chapters.

1. Create a new file that is 6 × 5 inches, 24-bit color, and 72 dpi resolution.

2. Select the Circle Mask tool from the Toolbox. Holding down the CTRL key, click and drag a circle that is 4 inches in diameter (2-inch radius).

3. Center the mask on the image using the following method: ensure Preserve Image is disabled. Select the Mask Transform tool, click the Create Object button, open the Align dialog box (CTRL+SHIFT+A) and enable Align to Center of Page, and click OK. Click the Create Mask button.

4. From the Edit menu select Fill. Click the Texture Fill button and click the Edit button. From the Texture Fill dialog box select the Texture library: Styles. From the Texture list choose Satellite Photography. Click the OK button to close both dialog boxes. The result is shown in Figure 20-5 with the mask marquee turned off.

5. To make the world look round, choose 3D Effects from the Effects menu and select Map to Object. Click the Reset button to ensure it is at the default settings and click the OK button. Figure 20-6 shows the result.

6. From the Effects menu select Render and choose Lighting Effects. Change dialog box settings to match those shown in Figure 20-7.

7. Click the Invert Mask button. Repeat step 4 and change the Texture library to Samples 5 and the Texture list to Night Sky. Click the OK button to close both dialog boxes.

8. From the Effects menu select Render and choose Lens Flare. Change the Lens type to 35mm prime and click the point at the bright area of the planet. Click the OK button. The finished background is shown in Figure 20-8.

Satellite Photography fill applied to a circle mask

FIGURE 20-5

The Map to Object filter makes the world look round

FIGURE 20-6

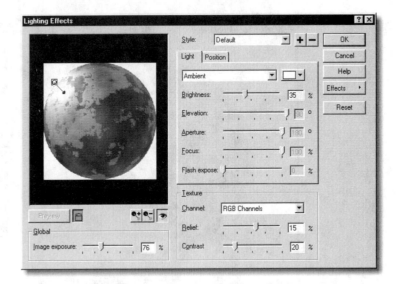

Settings for
lighting
effects

FIGURE 20-7

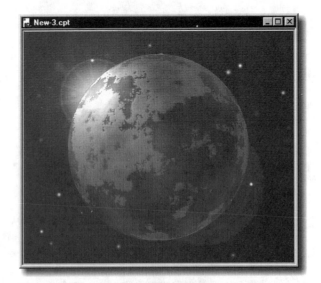

The
finished
planet
backdrop

FIGURE 20-8

9. Click the Text tool in the Toolbox and type **WEB NEWS**. Use Futura XBlk BT, Size: 96, Line Spacing: 80. Click the Center Text button on the Property bar. Click the Object Picker tool. Open the Objects roll-up (CTRL+F7), click the Single button, and select the text object.

10. Click the Remove Mask button. Repeat step 4, changing the Texture library to Styles and the Texture list to Flames. Click the OK button to close both dialog boxes.

11. From the Effects menu select Render and choose Lighting Effects. Change the Style to Texturize and click OK.

12. From the Object menu select Drop Shadow and change the settings as they are shown in Figure 20-9. Click OK. The resulting image is shown in Figure 20-10.

This is only a sampling of some of the many things that you can do with the Lighting Effects filter. In Chapter 13 it is used in a hands-on exercise for producing

Settings of the drop shadow for the text

FIGURE 20-9

The
finished
project

FIGURE 20-10

some final touches on a CD cover. As you work with the different features, you will discover more and more things that can be done with it. Now it's on to the strange world of the Artistic filters.

21

The Artistic Filters

The Artistic filters contain five filters—Canvas, Glass Block, Impressionist, Smoked Glass, and Vignette—that are best described as unique. These filters are for the creation of special effects.

Canvas Filter

In Corel PHOTO-PAINT 5, the Canvas filter is a roll-up. Changing it to a filter was a good move on Corel's part. The Canvas filter does not need to be kept available as other roll-ups do. Actually, Canvas was always a filter that thought it was a roll-up. The Canvas filter lets you apply any tile pattern or bitmap for use as an image background. If you set the transparency level to a higher percentage, the canvas can also be used to overlay an existing image.

Using the Canvas Filter

The Canvas filter is a simple filter that allows you to add unusual-looking effects with little experience or effort. A Corel PHOTO-PAINT Canvas can be made from any color (monotone or grayscale images have to be converted to color first) bitmap image. The Canvas filter applies the selected bitmap pattern to an image to give it the texture of the applied pattern. As mentioned earlier, the canvas can also be used with a high transparency setting to overlay an existing picture. The canvas shows through the image and any future application of paint. The Canvas effect is used to load a bitmap pattern over an existing image (creating a screening effect) or to serve as a background image (or canvas).

The Canvas Filter Dialog Box

The Canvas filter is accessed by selecting Artistic in the Effects menu and choosing Canvas. The dialog box consists of two viewing windows arranged in an Original and Result format. The window on the left shows a thumbnail of the existing image (before). The window on the right is a preview window that displays the results of the filter action based on the current settings (after). The canvas map, located below the preview window, displays the selected canvas. By default the canvas bitmap file MARBLE2C.PCX is loaded.

Transparency sets the level of transparency, expressed in percentage. High levels make the canvas more transparent and the underlying image more visible. Lower levels make the canvas opaque, and less of the image is visible. Emboss gives the canvas a raised relief effect. X and Y offset values allow you to control the size and placement of the bitmap tiles through scaling.

The Rows and Columns settings in the Tile Offset section provide control over the placement of the bitmap tiles in relation to one another. For example, changing the Row Offset value to 50 percent means that each successive row of bitmap tiles will overlap by 50 percent. Row and Column settings are mutually exclusive, meaning that if a value is entered in one, the other is zeroed out. The Stretch to fit setting simply takes the tile and stretches it to fit the image. If the image is large and the tile is small, the results can get either very artistic or very ugly. After all, beauty is in the eye of the beholder.

Clicking the Load button displays the Load A Canvas From Disk dialog box. Select a canvas from the PHOTOPNT\CANVAS directory, or choose another image.

Corel PHOTO-PAINT installs ten .PCX files for canvases in the \PHOTOPNT\ Canvas folder. Each .PCX file is 128 × 128 pixels at 300 dpi in 256-color mode.

Finding Custom Bitmaps to Use for Canvas

You can use any color bitmap file that can be imported by Corel PHOTO-PAINT to create a new canvas by loading it into the Canvas dialog box through the Load Canvas Map Files dialog box. The files that can be used for canvases include Photo-CDs and the files that you create with Corel PHOTO-PAINT 7. If you have a vector-based file that you want to use, simply load it into Corel PHOTO-PAINT and save it as a color bitmap file.

If the Canvas Bitmap Is the Wrong Size

If the bitmap image that is selected for use as a canvas is too small to fit the image area where it is being applied, the image will be tiled by Corel PHOTO-PAINT to fit the image area. If the image used for a canvas is too large to fit into the image area, it will be cropped (not resized) to fit the image area.

 TIP: *If the image is going to be tiled, you may want to consider cropping the bitmap with the Cropping tool, feathering the edge of the object with a small value, and dragging the image into the Corel PHOTO-PAINT workspace to create a new cropped image. The feathering will reduce the lines and, therefore, the "kitchen tile" look.*

Applying a Canvas Background

I may be going out on a limb here, but it seems appropriate to make a background that looks like canvas with the Canvas filter. In this hands-on exercise we are going to make a photograph look like a painting.

1. Load the file PHOTO\COASTS\557039.WI. Select <u>R</u>esample from the Image menu and change the <u>W</u>idth to 7 inches. Click the OK button. The original photograph is shown in Figure 21-1.

2. From the Effe<u>c</u>ts menu select Auto F/X and choose Photo/Graphic Edges 3.0. Click the Select Outset Effect button. You will be asked for the CD-ROM that contains the Photo/Graphic edges (Phot_edg folder) if it is not in your CD-ROM drive. Click on the file named AF109.AFX and click the Open button. It will take a few moments for PHOTO-PAINT to generate a preview. Click the Apply button. The resulting image is shown in Figure 21-2. When you have completed this step, skip to step 4. If you haven't installed the filters yet, please be aware that this step isn't

Original
image

■ **FIGURE 21-1**

The Photo/Graphic edge makes the image look more painterly

FIGURE 21-2

necessary to apply the Canvas filter. If you want to install the Auto F/X filter, follow the instructions in step 3.

3. Select <u>O</u>ptions in the <u>T</u>ools menu. Click the <u>A</u>dd button on the Plug-In Filters page. Locate the folder \PLUGINS\AUTOFX and click OK, and then click OK again to close the Options dialog box.

4. Open the file \TILES\PAPER\LARGE\PAPER01L.CPT located on the same CD-ROM that contains the photos. This image contains the right pattern but it lacks the contrast necessary to work with the Canvas filter.

5. Select <u>A</u>djust from the <u>I</u>mage menu and choose <u>A</u>uto-Equalize. Use the Save <u>A</u>s command in the <u>F</u>ile menu and save the file in \PHOTOPNT\CANVAS AS PAPER01L.PCX. Close the file.

6. Open the Canvas filter by selecting Ar<u>t</u>istic in the Effe<u>c</u>ts menu and choosing <u>C</u>anvas. When the dialog box opens, click the <u>L</u>oad button and select the PAPER01L.PCX file. Change the <u>T</u>ransparency setting to 92 percent and the <u>E</u>mboss setting to 20 percent. Click the OK button.

7. For the finishing touch, select <u>3</u>D Effects from the Effe<u>c</u>ts menu and choose <u>E</u>mboss. Click the Reset button, and then change the Emboss color to <u>O</u>riginal color. Change the <u>L</u>evel to 135. Click the OK button. The result is shown in Figure 21-3.

8. Close the file. It is not necessary to save this image.

Considerations About Using the Canvas Filter

If you are going to apply the canvas to an image, be aware that it will make the image more opaque to some extent. The best canvases are those with little color, lots of white area, and contrast. Cement is a good example of a canvas to place on top. It is a high-contrast canvas and therefore the effect of the embossing really stands out.

There is good news and bad news about using the Canvas filter. The bad news? One of the effects of applying the Canvas filter can be that the resulting image looks washed out. The good news? There is a cure. After you have applied the canvas,

The
finished
image looks
as if it were
painted

■ FIGURE 21-3

apply the Auto Equalize filter in the Image menu under Adjust. Applying this filter generally restores most of the tonal depth that is lost when the canvas is applied.

Although it has been mentioned before, remember that the preview for this filter does not always faithfully reflect what the final output will look like.

Canvases can be placed on top of and behind images, and they can be applied to objects. In fact, the canvas provides a way to add texture only to specific objects. Figure 21-4 shows the application of a canvas (default settings of Stucco) to the text with the background locked. Only the objects that are unlocked have the canvas applied to them.

Glass Block Filter

This filter, which is only available with Duotone, Paletted (8-bit), 24-bit, 32-bit color, and grayscale images, creates the effect of viewing the image through thick transparent blocks of glass. The dialog box is very simple. The two settings, Width and Height of the glass blocks in pixels, can be set independently of each other. The setting range is 1 through 100. The lowest setting (1 Width, 1 Height) produces glass blocks that are 1×1 pixels in the image area.

21

Application of the Canvas filter to the text gives the image a photorealistic texture

FIGURE 21-4

Using the Glass Block Filter to Make a Multimedia Background

The Glass Block filter is good for distorting an image for use in backgrounds. Here is a quick hands-on exercise to make a background that would be a nice addition to a multimedia presentation.

1. Open a new file that is 6 × 6 inches, 72 dpi, and 24-bit color.

2. From the Edit menu select Fill. Click the Fountain Fill button and then the Edit button. Change Presets to 11 for Cylinder, Angle: 45.0, and Steps: 999. Click the OK button and OK again to close the Edit Fill & Transparency dialog box.

3. From the Effects menu choose Artistic and select Glass Block. Change the Block width and Block height to 30. Click the OK button.

4. Close the file and do not save the changes.

That's all there is to it. The glass blocks made by this filter also make good borders for masks by clicking the blocks with a Magic Wand mask tool. The blocks cause the masks to align with the grid formed by the blocks. Make the mask into an object, then use the Drop Shadow command. The result is shown in Figure 21-5.

Impressionist Filter

Like the Glass Block filter, the Impressionist filter is only available with Duotone, Paletted (8-bit), 24-bit, 32-bit, and grayscale images. This filter gives an image the appearance of an impressionist brush (not really, but that's the official description). The amount of Impressionist effect can be applied independently as Horizontal or Vertical values. The range is 1-100 and is measured in the amount of scatter (displacement) in pixels. For example, a setting of 10 for Vertical will diffuse the image over a ten-pixel region in the vertical direction. Using a setting larger than the default (or 10) will scatter the pixels in the original image to the point where it becomes unrecognizable. In the previous edition of this book, I referred to this filter as "one of those 'what-were-they-thinking-about?'-type filters that ends up in every photo-editing package." I have since changed my mind. With the addition of the Layer mode, this filter has taken on a new life.

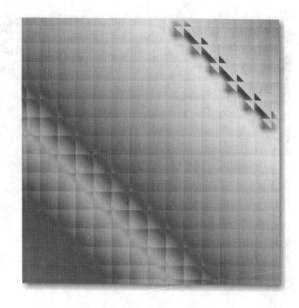

The Glass
Block filter
can produce
excellent
backgrounds
for Web
pages

■ FIGURE 21-5

The key to using this filter is to be aware that when it scatters pixels on an object it replaces the scattered pixels with the current Paper color. This would seem to restrict the filter's usefulness. It doesn't if you remember another part of PHOTO-PAINT that thinks in such a binary format. I am referring to the mask! Here is a hands-on exercise that I think you will like.

Making Cut Metal Objects

This hands-on exercise may seem complicated, but the results are worth it. In it we are going to make a title screen for a multimedia presentation that introduces one of the rock-and-roll categories. Using several filters, we are going to make letters that look like they were cut out of metal flooring.

1. Locate and open the file 537099.WI in the \PHOTOS\BORDERS folder. Select Resample in the Image menu and change the Width to 6 inches. Click the OK button.

2. Select the Text tool from the Toolbox and type **HEAVY METAL** on two lines with a line spacing of 80. The font is Kabel Ult BT at a size of 96

Note—Heavy
Metal is not
a reference
to the tuba
section

FIGURE 21-6

and centered. The result is shown in Figure 21-6. The figure has white
type so it will stand out in the book. The color of the type is not important.

3. Open the Object roll-up (CTRL+F7) and click the Single button. The text
   should be selected.

4. In the Edit menu select Fill and click the Bitmap Fill button; then click the
   Edit button. In the Bitmap Fill dialog box click the Load button. From the
   Import dialog box locate \TILES\METAL\MEDIUM\METAL01M.CPT
   on the Corel CD-ROM. Click the OK buttons to close all of the dialog
   boxes. The text will fill with the metal texture.

5. Click the Preserve Image button. Click the Create Mask button. Click the
   Paint On Mask option in the Mask menu (CTRL+K) or the Paint On Mask
   button on the standard toolbar. From the Effects menu select Artistic and
   choose Impressionist. Change both of the Scatter settings to 6. Click the
   OK button. The result is shown in Figure 21-7.

6. The edge of the mask needs to be smoothed out a bit. From the Effects
   menu select Blur and choose Gaussian Blur. Change the Radius setting
   to 1. Click the OK button.

The Impressionist filter scatters the edge of the mask

FIGURE 21-7

7. Click the Paint On Mask button again to return to the image. In the Objects roll-up click the Layer button. In the Object menu select Clip Object To Mask. There won't seem to be any difference at this point.

8. From the Effects menu select 3D Effects and choose Emboss. Change the Emboss color to Original color, Depth: 5, Level: 120, Direction: 128, and click the OK button.

9. From the Effects menu select Sharpen and choose Sharpen. Change the Edge level (percent) to 45 and the Threshold to 100. Remove the mask.

10. Select the Text object and choose Drop Shadow in the Object menu. For settings use a Horizontal and Vertical setting of 0.1, a Feather of 10, and an Opacity of 100. Offset direction is bottom right. The result is shown in Figure 21-8.

11. Close the file. You do not need to save this file.

You can use this technique on just about any object to get a rough cut effect. The Sharpen filter was applied to add specular highlights to the edges of the metal. You

We are now
ready to
rock and roll

FIGURE 21-8

can also use this same technique (without the sharpening and the embossing) to make text that looks like a stencil.

Smoked Glass Filter

The Smoked Glass filter applies a transparent mask over the image to give the appearance of smoked glass. You can determine the color of the tint (before opening the filter), the percentage of transparency, and the degree of blurring.

The color of the tint is determined by the Paint (foreground) color, which is controlled in the Tool Settings roll-up before opening the filter dialog box, or from the color controls within the dialog box. The Tint slider controls the opacity of the tint being applied. Larger values mean greater amounts of color tint applied to the image. A value of 100 fills the area with a solid color. The Percentage slider controls the amount of blurring applied to the image to give the appearance of the distortion caused by glass. A value of 100 percent produces the greatest amount of blurring, while 0 percent produces no blurring of the image. There are two ways to determine the color of the Tint. You can use the existing Paint color or choose another color from the Color section.

The Smoked Glass filter is used in a hands-on exercise in Chapter 19 for darkening one side of a giant box of crayons to give the box a 3D appearance.

Vignette Filter

The Vignette filter applies a mask over the image through the creation of a transparent shape in the center. The remainder of the mask is opaque. It is designed to appear as an old-style photograph when the image is placed in an oval or other shape.

A Vignette filter can be applied to the entire image or just a masked area. By clicking and dragging the Offset slider, you can control how large the selected shape is around the center of the image. The larger the percentage, the smaller the transparent oval. The Fade slider controls the fade (feathering) at the edge of the oval. Using the Vignette dialog box, you can determine the color of the mask by selecting black, white, or Paint color. The Paint color must be selected before opening the Vignette filter dialog box.

The only restriction on using this filter is the inability to select the area that is to be the image center. This is logical when you consider that the Vignette is supposed to be equal on all sides, therefore it always uses the very center of the image as its center. The problem occurs when your subject is not in the center. The only way to correct an off-center subject is to crop the image so the subject is centered, and then, if the resulting image is too small, use the Paper Size command to restore part or all of the image size after applying the filter.

That wraps up the Artistic filters. While these are not the most powerful filters on the planet, I think we have seen that they can be used to create some unusual effects, even if they are not what the original filter programmer had in mind.

21

22

The Fancy Filters

The filters in this category of the Effects menu offer unique special effects that cannot be obtained through any other means.

The Fancy Filters

As diverse as the Fancy Filters are, they all have one thing in common—they are all popular third-party plug-in filters in their own right. Two of them, Paint Alchemy and Terrazzo, are only available as plug-in filters on the Macintosh platform. The Boss and Glass filters are from Alien Skin Software, and Julia Set Explorer 2.0 is from Kai's Power Tools. Together they represent an awesome array of special effects capability.

Paint Alchemy

Paint Alchemy and its counterpart Terrazzo are both incredible filters that offer many levels of customization. Since there is very little documentation for these filters and they are, without a doubt, the most complex ones, they are presented in greater detail than the other filters in this chapter. To ensure the most accurate documentation, I have been assisted greatly by Xaos Tools' documentation for the Macintosh and their tech-support people, who have been a world of help. Acknowledgments and kudos given, let's play with Paint Alchemy.

Paint Alchemy applies brush strokes to selected areas of your image in a precisely controlled manner. As with all filters, you can use masks to apply Paint Alchemy to part of an image or the entire image. You can use one of the many brushes provided with the filter or create your own brushes. It is not hard to create effects with Paint Alchemy; the key to using and enjoying it is experimentation.

 TIP: *As you learn how to make changes to the Paint Alchemy filter styles, I recommend limiting your changes to one at a time so that you can keep track of the effects.*

Starting Paint Alchemy

The Paint Alchemy filter is located under Fancy in the Effects menu. Clicking Alchemy in the drop-down list opens the Paint Alchemy dialog box as shown in Figure 22-1.

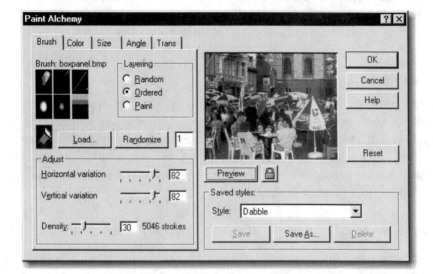

The Paint
Alchemy
dialog box

FIGURE 22-1

 NOTE: *Paint Alchemy is only available when 24-bit color images are selected. If a grayscale, back-and-white, 16-color, 256-color, or 32-bit image is open, the Alchemy filter is unavailable (grayed out).*

The Paint Alchemy Dialog Box

The dialog box is divided into three sections: control tabs, style controls, and preview controls.

The Control Tabs

These are the controls that let you customize Paint Alchemy. They are arranged on five control tabs. Only one tab can be visible at a time, but the controls on all five tabs are always active. To switch between tabs, click the tab labels at the top.

The Style Controls

The style controls let you select one of the 75 preset styles included with Paint Alchemy, modify an existing style so that it may be saved as a new style, or remove an old style. Before you begin modifying the preset styles, I encourage you to work with and learn the preset styles to get a feel for what they do. If you do change a style and like the results, you can save these settings as a style.

The Preview Controls

The preview controls allow you to zoom in or out of the preview image. They also allow you to move the image inside of the preview window. Clicking the left mouse button in the preview area zooms the preview image in; right-clicking zooms it out. Clicking the left mouse button and dragging produces a hand for moving the image around in the preview window. Two seconds after any change is made in the preview window, filter preview is automatically invoked.

Using Styles

You can use Paint Alchemy to create an enormous variety of effects. With 30 parameters to change and the ability to use custom brushes in addition to the ones provided, the number of possibilities is virtually infinite. To allow you to keep track of your favorite settings, Paint Alchemy offers the ability to save all of the filter settings as styles.

Each style is a complete record of the settings of all the controls. By loading a style, you can reproduce exactly that incredible filter effect that so wowed your client.

Loading a style is very simple. You only need to click the down arrow to the right of the Style box, and a drop-down list of 75 predefined styles appears. You can use the styles that Corel provides with Paint Alchemy, or you can create your own. Any of the predefined styles can be customized.

 TIP: *Altering existing styles and saving the new settings under a new name is often the best way to begin creating your own styles.*

Creating a Custom Style

Paint Alchemy, like many paint-oriented filters, can take a long time to apply to an image. When you begin experimentation in search of the custom look that is going to win the Corel Design contest for you, consider selecting a small area of the total image by using a mask. Smaller image areas can be processed much faster. When you find the style you want, you can then apply it to a larger image to make sure all of the settings work before you save it as a style.

The following is a recommended procedure for creating new styles. There is nothing about it that is set in stone; it is only a guideline.

- Find an existing style that is closest to the one you want to create. Use the settings from that style as your starting point.

- Reduce the number of brush strokes (the Density) on the Brush tab until you can see what the individual brushes are doing. Using the Zoom feature of the preview window, zoom in on individual brush strokes and make necessary adjustments to appropriate parameters (i.e., size, transparency, etc.).

- Change the attributes on the Color control tab until you can see how the controls change each brush stroke. Once you are comfortable with the color controls, adjust your colors.

- Increase the density (number of brush strokes) until the angle of application becomes clear. Now you can adjust the brush stroke angle.

- To save a new custom style, click the Save As button. You are asked to enter a name for the new file (it can seemingly be a name of endless length, but you can only see the first 40 characters in the Style box). The current settings are saved with the name you provide, and the new style is added to the Style drop-down list in alphabetical order.

Changing a Custom Style

To change a custom style, do the following:

1. Select the style to be changed.

2. Make the changes desired.

3. Click the Save As button. (You cannot change and save a preset style. With preset styles, only the Save As button is available.)

Saving a custom style will substitute the current style settings for those of the Paint Alchemy style with the same name.

TIP: *A quick way to return to the default setting for any style is to click on the style name. Use either the up or down arrow key to move to an adjacent style, and then, using the opposite arrow key, return to the original setting.*

Removing a Custom Style

To delete a custom style, you need only select the style you want to delete and click the Delete button. A warning box (I like to call them "second chance" boxes) asks if you are sure that want to delete the style. If you click OK, it's all over.

The Brush Tab

The Brush tab is the one you see when Paint Alchemy is first opened. This tab is the heart of Paint Alchemy. The description that is in the Xaos Tools' Paint Alchemy manual can't be beat: "The simplest description of what Paint Alchemy does it this: It applies a whole bunch of brush strokes to your image. As a result, the shape of the brush has a profound effect on the look that is produced."

The Brush tab displays seven of the standard brushes. When I first began working with this program, I thought that they displayed the best brush for the application and then showed brushes that were also likely candidates for the effects. Wow, was I ever wrong! The seven standard brushes that are displayed never change, regardless of the current brush that is loaded. The currently selected brush has a highlighted border around it. (On my system, it is red.)

Loading a Custom Brush

There are 30 custom brushes included with Paint Alchemy. They are located in the COREL\DRAW70\PHOTOPNT\PLGBRUSH directory. Click the Load button and the Load Brush dialog box opens as shown here.

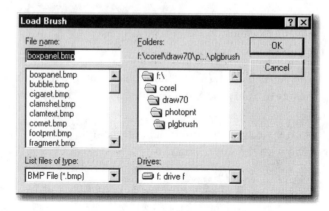

It allows you to select any .BMP file as a custom brush. Here are the general rules regarding brushes.

You can load any .BMP file as a brush as long as it meets the following parameters: 128 × 128 pixels, grayscale (8-bit), and 300 dpi. If any of these parameters are different, the custom brush won't work. The exception is that the resolution can be 100 dpi. The Brush icon will appear, but the resulting brush may be distorted.

Using the default settings, brushes are completely opaque where white and transparent where black. Gray areas are semitransparent; the darker they are, the more transparent they are. Black portions of your brush will not change your image, while the white portions define the area in which your selected effect is applied.

 TIP: *When making brushes in Corel PHOTO-PAINT, it is not necessary to paint white-on-black. Do all of your work in black-on-white, and then use the Invert filter.*

Styles that are built around custom brushes depend on the brushes remaining in the PLGBRUSH folder. If the brush that a selected style needs is not available when the style is selected, a default brush is loaded in its place.

22

Density

The Density slider controls the number of brush strokes that will be applied to the selected area. The density is a factor that is used to calculate how many brush strokes should be used for a given image size. The absolute number of strokes that will be used with the current image size is displayed above the slider. All of the calculations are based on the image size, not the mask size. Unlike the Texture Bitmap fills, the size of the brush effects does not increase or decrease as a result of the image size or the mask size.

 TIP: *The time required to apply the effect depends directly on the number of brush strokes: the more strokes, the longer the effect will take. The other factor is the size of the image or the size of the mask. If the image is large and the mask is small, the processing will still occur more quickly because the effect is only calculated for and applied to the masked area.*

Positioning

These sliders are far less than self-explanatory. They add randomness to the position of the brush strokes. When the Horizontal and Vertical Variation sliders are both set at 0, the strokes are placed on a regular grid. The Horizontal Variation slider controls side-to-side brush stroke deviation. The Vertical Variation slider controls the up-and-down motion of the brush stroke deviation. With most of the styles applying brush strokes one on top of another multiple times, there are many styles that seem to be changed very little by the positioning controls.

Layering Methods

There are three choices for layering methods in the Brush tab: Random, Ordered, and Paint Layering.

RANDOM LAYERING   The brush strokes are applied so that they randomly overlap each other.

ORDERED LAYERING   The brush strokes are applied so that strokes that are above and to the left always overlap those that are below and to the right. With a square brush, this can look like roofing shingles. With a round brush, it can look like fish scales.

PAINT LAYERING   With Paint layering, the brightest portions of each brush stroke take priority in the layering. The effect it produces is highly dependent on the shape and coloring of the brush. You will need to experiment with Paint layering to find out what it can do. Paint layering can also cause brush shape to be lost when brushes overlap too much. The overlapping brush problem is resolved by lowering the density setting or reducing the brush size (on the Size tab) to reveal more of the brush.

 CAUTION: *The Paint method of layering can cause aliasing (the dreaded "jaggies") when a brush that has hard black-and-white (or bright) edges is used.*

Randomize

Before you read this, click the Randomize button and see if you can figure out what it does. For those of you who understand techno-babble, it is a *random-seed generator.* For those that do not speak the language, it is the Randomize setting, which lets you set the initial value used in the random-number generation, a value that is called the *seed number.*

Clicking the Randomize button will randomly change the seed. You can also type a number directly into the box that is adjacent to the button. As a rule, forget the button. The fine folks at Xaos Tools, however, give two examples where you might actually want to use this function, as follows.

CHANGING THE SEED TO SUBTLY CHANGE THE EFFECT   You may want to change the seed if you like the general effect that Paint Alchemy is producing but not the way some brushes work. Changing the seed puts the brush strokes in slightly different random positions, and this may produce that final correction you were looking for.

MAINTAINING THE SEED TO ENSURE REPEATABILITY   Using the same seed number guarantees that the exact same series of random numbers will be used for Paint Alchemy's internal calculations and thus all of the effects will be identical. This application, however, sounds a little fishy to me. How can it be a true random-number generator if identical results occur every time you use it?

BONUS: PICKING THE NUMBERS FOR YOUR STATE LOTTERY   This is my idea. The numbers that you get each time you click the Random button are indeed random, so you can use this function to pick lottery numbers in much the same way that they are picked by the state, untainted by the sentimental and unscientific "favorite numbers" technique. The only hitch is that most big-money lotteries are based on two-digit numbers. No problem. Just use the last two digits of the random number for the lottery. By the way, if you win using this method, it is only fair for you to split the winnings with myself and the editors who let this piece of nonsense get into print.

Creating Your Own Brushes

Creating brushes is one on the slicker things you can do with Paint Alchemy. It is easy to make a brush, but it is a little more difficult to make one that looks great when it is used in Paint Alchemy. Here is a summary of brush-making tips from Xaos Tools and from my own experience working with Corel PHOTO-PAINT and Paint Alchemy.

You can open the existing brush files in Corel PHOTO-PAINT. (The brushes are .BMP files located in the PLGBRUSH folder.) You can then use Corel

PHOTO-PAINT to alter the appearance of the brushes. If you change one of the original brushes that came with the program, make sure you only save it under a new name. All of the styles in Paint Alchemy were designed to use one of these brushes. If you change the brush, you will need to reinstall PAINT to restore the original brushes. If you want to save changes you made, use Save As.

When you create a new brush from scratch, use an image size of 128×128 pixels with a resolution of 300 dpi. Also, remember to make the image a grayscale. If the brush you create is too large, it will not load into Paint Alchemy.

For more texture in the effect, create brush designs with a lot of gradation between black and white. Xaos Tools offers a collection called Floppy Full of Brushes. This collection is available at this time only for the Macintosh. The brushes on the Mac side are PICT files (.PCT in DOS lingo). To use them, I took the Mac disk to a copy center, where we copied the Xaos Tools original diskette to a high-density disk (it comes from Xaos on a low-density disk that cannot be read on a PC) and had the PICT files saved in a format that my IBM could read. Finally, I loaded each one into Corel PHOTO-PAINT as Mac .PCT files (did you remember that we could read Mac files?) and saved them as .BMP files. I know that may seem like a lot of work, but it's worth it. The best part is they all have long descriptive filenames, which I was able to keep under Windows 95's file-naming convention.

TIP: *To change the brush that is used by a style, select the style before you select the brush. This is because every style has a brush associated with it. If you load the brush and then the style, the style will load its own brush, forcing you to reload your brush.*

The Color Tab

You can use the Color tab, shown in Figure 22-2, to create effects such as pastel-like colors or even create improved black-and-white styles.

TIP: *To create pastel-like colors using the Color tab, set the Brush Color to From Image and the Background to Solid Color (white). Then set your brush strokes to be partially transparent.*

Brush Color

Each brush stroke is a single, solid color. To determine the color of your brush strokes, use the Color tab. You can set the colors of your brush strokes by using the

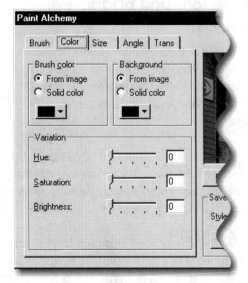

The Color
tab portion
of the Paint
Alchemy
dialog box

FIGURE 22-2

colors of the image you are working on or by selecting a specific color using the Brush Color controls.

FROM IMAGE   The color of each brush stroke is based on the color of the image at the center of each brush stroke.

SOLID COLOR   The color of all the brush strokes is based on the color that you select. To select the color, click on the color preview window to the right of the Solid Color button to open up the standard color-selection palette.

Background

You can choose to apply Paint Alchemy brush strokes with a Paper (background) of solid color using the Background controls.

FROM IMAGE   The brush strokes are applied to your image based on the color of each brush stroke.

SOLID COLOR   The brush strokes are applied to a Paper (background) of a solid color. To select the color, click on the color preview window to the right of the Solid Color button to open up the standard color-selection palette.

The Hue, Saturation, and Brightness Variation Controls

These controls operate in a similar manner to the Impressionism or Pointillism brush tools. They allow you to vary from the initial Brush Color settings. The amount of variation can be controlled independently for the hue, saturation, and brightness of the brush color. These controls affect the brush stroke of both the From Image and the Solid Color settings.

HUE VARIATION Hue Variation controls how much the color varies from the starting color. A small setting causes the colors in the brush to vary just a few shades to either side of the original color. A large setting produces a rainbow of colors, producing a confetti-like effect.

SATURATION VARIATION Saturation Variation has the least noticeable effect of the three. It controls the amount of gray level in the image. It isn't a simple relationship; for example, 100 percent gives lots of gray. It has a greater effect in images whose color scheme contains large quantities of gray. Play with this control, but expect subtle rather than great changes in the image.

BRIGHTNESS VARIATION Brightness Variation has the effect of controlling contrast. Officially, it controls the amount of variance in brightness between the starting color and the additional colors that are created by Paint Alchemy.

Image Enhancement

As with many of the other filters, you can increase the effectiveness of the Color tab by using the other controls and filters in Corel PHOTO-PAINT to modify the image before working on it with the Paint Alchemy filter. If you have a low-contrast image, you should consider applying the Equalization filter to stretch the dynamic range of the image or increase the contrast of the image to produce more dramatic results.

The Size Tab

The Size tab, shown in Figure 22-3, does just what it says: It enables you to vary the size of the brush strokes that are applied. There are several controls on this tab that

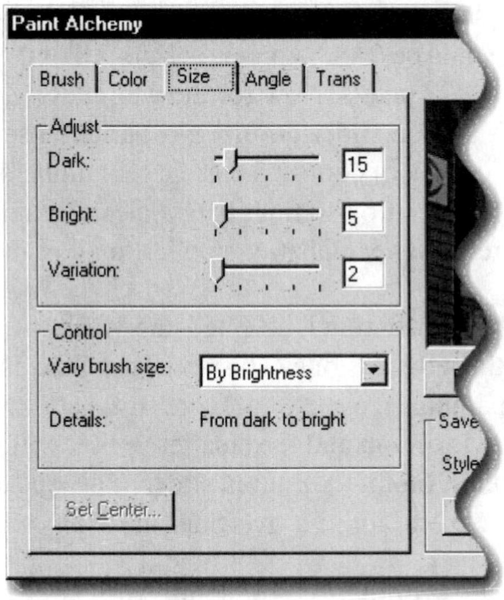

The Size
tab portion
of the Paint
Alchemy
dialog box

FIGURE 22-3

are evident when you open it. They are Vary Brush Size, Adjust Size, and Variation. The setting for Vary Brush Size determines what controls are available in the rest of the Size tab. When I first opened the Vary Brush Size drop-down list, I was greeted by a lengthy list of, shall we say, interesting names. However, once you understand the thinking behind the designers at Xaos, these might make a little more sense.

The Vary Brush Size Control

Clicking the arrow button to the right of the name box produces a list of eight sets of brush variations. The names of the presets are the same on the Size, Angle, and Transparency tabs. What follows is a description of the action of each of these variation sets.

NO VARIATION   Here's the only set that is self-explanatory. Well, sort of. When this option is selected, all of the brush strokes will be the same size. The size of the brush is set using the Size slider. The size is scaled from the actual size of the brush image selected. In practice, it is a percentage of the size of the original. For example, since the .BMP file that makes up the brush is 128×128 pixels, a size value of 128 would produce brush strokes of the same size. If the value was set for 50 (50 percent), the brush strokes would be 64×64 pixels in size. All of the brushes included in Paint Alchemy are 128×128 pixels. Now for the weirdness.

What does a Variation slider do in a No Variation setting? It overrides the No Variations In Size option, of course. Thus, larger numbers cause larger variations in brush size in the No Variation setting. Is that clear? I think I'm getting a headache. By the way, the preceding explanation applies to all of the Variation sliders.

RANDOMLY   When this option is selected, the brush strokes vary in size randomly. I love the two settings for this one: This and That. You use This and That to set the minimum and maximum size allowed. It doesn't matter which is which. The larger setting will be the Maximum and the smaller setting will be the Minimum. Look at the bottom of the tab. Another Variation slider! This one does the same thing as the Variation slider in No Variation: It overrides the This and That slider settings.

BY RADIAL DISTANCE   With this option, the brush strokes will change smoothly in size, in a circular manner. The brush strokes start out one size in the center and gradually change to another size at the edge of the circle.

- **Center slider** This determines the size of the brush at the center of the circle. Because the size of the brush varies as a function of its distance, this slider and the Edge slider control how the brush stroke will appear.

- **Edge slider** This sets the size of the brush at the edge of the circle.

Variation Slider: Center and Edge Sliders

To set the location of the center point, click the Set Center button. This brings up a dialog box that contains a thumbnail of the image or of the area selected by the mask. If more than one area is masked, an area of the image that is determined by the boundaries of the various masks makes up the preview image. By clicking at the place that you want to be the center of the circle, a small crosshair is placed on the image at the point where you clicked.

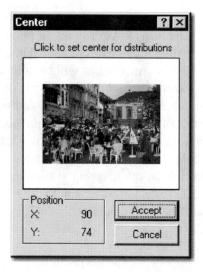

Below the thumbnail is exact X/Y-position information (in pixels) for the point where the circle is centered. Actually, I haven't got a clue why this information is provided. It wasn't in the Mac version, and when I asked some members of the Paint development team, they didn't know either, except that it had been requested from higher up in the command chain.

 NOTE: *The Set Center point determines the center of the circle used by the Size, Angle, and Transparency tabs. The Set Center point is available on the Size, Angle, and Transparency tabs when By Radial Distance is selected on each.*

BY VERTICAL POSITION   With this option, the brush strokes change smoothly in size from the top to the bottom of the image. You set the sizes using the Top and Bottom sliders.

BY HORIZONTAL POSITION   With this option, the brush strokes change smoothly in size from the left to the right of the image. The sizes of the brushes are set using the Left and Right sliders.

BY HUE With this option, each brush stroke is scaled according to the hue of the image at the location of each brush stroke. You set the minimum and maximum sizes using the Warm and Cool sliders. For example, the default setting for the Spatula style is Warm 5, Cool 30. The warmer colors will be limited to variations of up to 5 percent of the brush size, while the cool colors will be allowed to become up to 30 percent of brush size. So what do we mean by cool and warm? On a color wheel, the dividing line between cool and warm runs through red. Therefore, by using the By Hue option for determining brush size, brush strokes that are applied to areas of the image that contain colors on the yellow side of red are given the Warm size values. Those colors that fall on the magenta side of red are given the Cool size values. (This detailed explanation is so that you know how it works. I have yet to sit down with a color wheel that can calculate this stuff. Experiment on small images or the preview window.)

BY SATURATION With this selection, each brush stroke is scaled according to the saturation of the image color at the location of the brush stroke. You set the minimum and maximum sizes using the Unsaturated and Saturated sliders. If you are very health conscious, you can use these settings to make images that are high in unsaturates (just kidding). Setting the values for Saturated to be larger than the values for Unsaturated results in brush strokes over richly colored areas that will be larger than the brush strokes over black, white, or gray areas.

 TIP: *While working with this larger/smaller brush stroke thing, remember that smaller brush strokes retain more detail of the original image and may be more desirable than larger ones.*

BY BRIGHTNESS With this option, each brush stroke is scaled according to the brightness of the image color at the location of the brush stroke. You set the minimum and maximum sizes using the Bright and Dark sliders. Setting the values for Bright to be larger than the values for Dark results in brush strokes over bright areas of the image that will be larger than brush strokes over dark areas.

The Angle Tab

You use the Angle tab, shown in Figure 22-4, to set the angle of your brush stroke and to change brush angle based on its position in your image. Depending on the

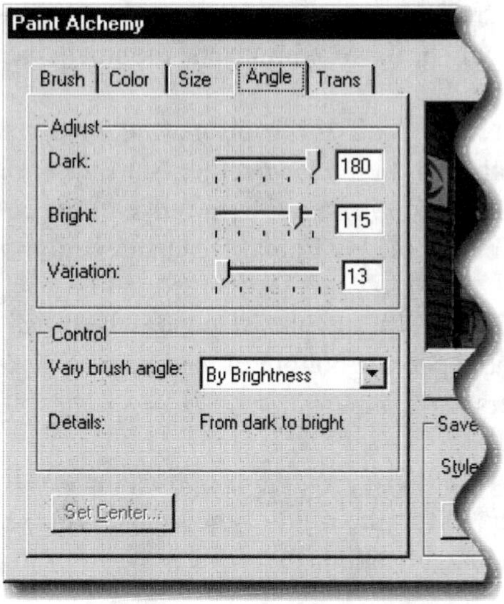

The Angle
tab portion
of the Paint
Alchemy
dialog box

FIGURE 22-4

Control option chosen, the Adjust options vary. You can also control brush angle based on the color content of your image, or you can change brush angle randomly. This tab is similar in operation to the Size tab.

Vary Brush Angle

The Vary Brush Angle drop-down list lets you specify what should control the orientation (the amount of rotation) of your brush strokes. You can apply all of the brush strokes at the same angle, or you can have them vary randomly, according to information in the image, or by their position. The following is what each option does.

NO VARIATION   When this option is selected, all of the brush strokes will be rotated by the same angular amount. The amount of rotation (-180 to +180) is set using the Angle slider. If the Angle is set to 0, the brush strokes will not be rotated at all; they will have the same orientation as the picture of the brush that is displayed on the Brush tab. If the angle is set to 180 degrees, the brushes will be upside-down.

RANDOMLY   With this option, the brush stroke angle varies randomly. You use This and That to set the minimum and maximum angles. It doesn't matter which is which. The larger setting will be the Maximum and the smaller setting will be the Minimum.

BY RADIAL DISTANCE   With this option, the brush strokes will change their orientation smoothly in a circular manner, starting at one angle in the center and gradually changing to another angle at the edge of the circle. The operation of these controls is described in the By Radial Distance section on the Size tab.

BY VERTICAL POSITION   Using this selection, the brush strokes change their angle smoothly from the top to the bottom of the image. You set the angles using the Top and Bottom sliders.

BY HORIZONTAL POSITION   With this option, the brush strokes change their angle smoothly from the left to the right of the image. You set the angles of the brushes using the Left and Right sliders.

BY HUE   With By Hue selected, each brush stroke is rotated according to the hue of the image at the location of each brush stroke. You set the minimum and maximum angles using the Warm and Cool sliders. Therefore, when using By Hue for determining brush stroke angles, areas of the image that contain colors on the yellow side of red are given the Warm size values. Those colors that fall on the magenta side of the red are given the Cool size values. If you set the angle for Cool to be larger than the angle for Warm, brush strokes over the blue areas of the image will be rotated more than brush strokes over yellow areas. (You should feel free to experiment on small images or the preview window.)

BY SATURATION   With this option, each brush stroke is rotated according to the saturation of the image color at the location of the brush stroke. You set the minimum and maximum angles using the Saturated and Unsaturated sliders. Setting the values for Saturated to be larger than the values for Unsaturated results in brush strokes over richly colored areas that will be rotated more than brush strokes over black, white, or gray areas.

BY BRIGHTNESS   With this option, each brush stroke is rotated according to the brightness of the image color at the location of the brush stroke. You set the minimum and maximum angles using the Bright and Dark sliders. Setting the values for Bright to be larger than the values for Dark results in brush strokes over bright areas of the image that will be larger than brush strokes over dark areas.

Angle Variation

The Variation slider lets you add randomness to the stroke angles. The higher this value, the more your strokes will vary from their set angles.

The variation is calculated as degrees of offset from the brush angle. Thus, if you set Vary Brush Angle to No Variation, the Angle to 90, and the Variation to 10, you will get brush strokes that range in angle from 80 to 100 degrees.

The Transparency Tab

The Transparency tab, shown in Figure 22-5, is used to control brush stroke transparency and to change the transparency based on brush position in your image. Depending on the Control option chosen, the Adjust options vary. You can also control transparency based on the color content of your image, or you can control it randomly. This tab is similar in operation to the Size tab.

The Vary Brush Transparency Controls

See the Size tab for information on using these controls.

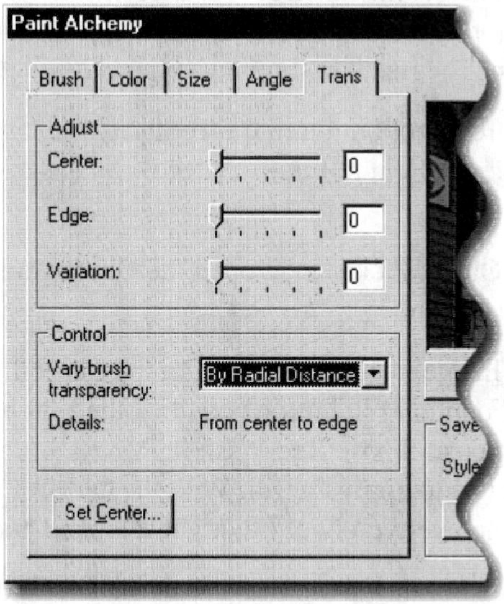

22

The
Transparency
tab portion
of the Paint
Alchemy
dialog box

FIGURE 22-5

The Power of Paint Alchemy

I have given you many pages of reference material about the Paint Alchemy filter. While perhaps not the most exciting reading, this material will be very useful when you begin experimenting with creating your own brushes and styles. What follows is a hands-on exercise to give you a taste of what Paint Alchemy can do.

Making a Travel Poster

The purpose of most travel posters is not to provide information but to convey a thought or feeling. We are going to create one for Europe that has an artistic theme.

1. Open the file \PHOTOS\EUROPE\673069.WI. Select Resample from the Image menu and change the Width setting to 7 inches. Click the OK button.

2. From the Effects menu, select Fancy and choose Alchemy. When the dialog box opens, ensure the Style is set to Default. Click OK. The result is shown in Figure 22-6.

3. From the Effects menu, select Auto F/X and then Photo/Graphic Edges 3.0. Click the Select Outset Effect button. Select AF073.AFX and click the Open button. Click the Apply button.

4. From the Effects menu, select 3D Effects and choose Emboss. Click the Reset button and change the Emboss Color to Original color. Click the OK button. The result is shown in Figure 22-7.

5. Click the Text tool button in the Toolbox. Click the cursor in the image and change the Font to Futura XBlk BT at a size of 72. Type the word **EUROPE**.

6. Click the Object Picker tool, open the Objects roll-up (CTRL+F7) and click the Single button.

7. From the Image menu, select Fill. In the Edit Fill & Transparency roll-up, click the Fountain Fill button and click the Edit button. From the Fountain Fill dialog box, choose Red Wash in Presets. Click OK to close the box and OK again to apply the fill. With the Object Picker tool, you can place the text wherever you like. I thought it looked good in the upper-left edge.

8. Select Drop Shadow from the Object menu. We do not want to make a drop shadow but a back glow to make the letters stand out. Set the

The result
of applying
the Default
Paint
Alchemy
filter

FIGURE 22-6

22

After the
Auto F/X
and Emboss
filters, it
looks more
like a
painting

FIGURE 22-7

Horizontal and Vertical values to .02. Click the White shadow color, Opacity of 50, and a Feather of 12. Click OK. Figure 22-8 shows the finished picture.

 TIP: *A problem with many of the Alchemy filter effects is that they tend to make an image nearly unrecognizable. A way to reduce the effect is to make a duplicate of the original as an object. Apply the effect to the object in Single mode and then reduce the Opacity of the object, letting more of the original show through.*

The Glass Filter

The Glass filter creates the effect of a layer of glass on top of the image. Keep in mind that the sheet of glass is the 3D part, while the image remains flat. By adjusting the combination of light filtering, refraction, and highlights, you can achieve some striking effects with this filter.

Ready for printing and hanging on the travel office wall

FIGURE 22-8

The Glass filter requires a mask to do its job. The shape of the glass sheet is controlled by the shape of the mask. The top edge of the glass bevel occurs along the mask. Feathering the mask has no effect on this filter's operation.

The Glass Filter Dialog Box

The Glass filter dialog box, shown here, is opened by selecting Glass in the Fancy category of the Effects menu.

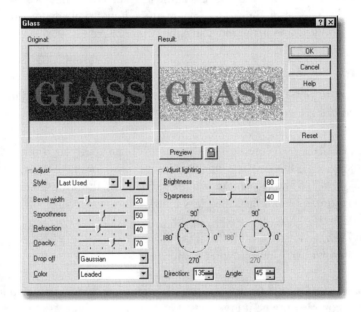

STYLE This contains a drop-down list of presets that are provided with the Glass filter. Choosing any of the presets changes the controls in the dialog box for the selected presets. Custom settings are also saved in the Style area by changing the controls to the desired settings and clicking the plus button to the right of the Style name. Another dialog box opens that allows you to name the new style. The minus button is used to remove a saved style.

THE BEVEL WIDTH SLIDER The Bevel Width slider is used to set the width of the bevel. The bevel is the area around a masked object that is slanted to produce that glassy 3D look.

THE SMOOTHNESS SLIDER   The Smoothness slider is used to set the sharpness of the edges of the bevel. A low-level smoothness produces sharper edges but may also display the steps used to create the embossed look. A higher smoothness level removes the jagged edges and makes for rounded edges.

THE REFRACTION SLIDER   The most striking 3D effect of the Glass filter is *refraction,* which occurs when the direction of light rays is changed (bent) as a result of passing through a material such as glass or water. Since we are looking directly at the glass sheet, refraction only occurs at the beveled edges. The Refraction slider sets the angle at which the light is to be bent at the bevel. This distorts the image at the bevel location, which is the most striking effect of the Glass filter.

 TIP: *To make the refraction effect more noticeable, try using a wider bevel. This will increase the area of glass that does not directly face the viewer.*

THE OPACITY SLIDER   Colored glass affects light, and it affects it more where the material (the glass) is thicker. The Opacity slider is used to set the transparency level of the glass sheet. The more opaque you make the glass, the stronger the underlying image will be tinted to look like the glass color.

DROP-OFF TYPE   The drop-off is the area adjacent to the bevel effect and is selected from a drop-down list. The following choices are available.

- **Gaussian** Use the Gaussian drop-off when you want a very subtle effect. On a complex image it gives a wet appearance to the masked area edge. The Gaussian drop-off has an "S" shape; it starts and ends with a round and gradual slope that becomes steep in between. It results in a smooth and less noticeable transition between the bevel and the rest of the image.

- **Flat** Because the Flat drop-off produces a sharp drop-off bevel, the areas around the edges are very sharp. The effect on text with dark colors may not even be noticeable. This effect works best with objects that have smooth, rounded edges. The Flat drop-off is a straight diagonal line starting at the bevel area and ending on the image. The transition is not as smooth as a rounded bevel, but the slope of the bevel is less steep.

- **Mesa** This drop-off style probably gives the best overall glass effect of the three. The Mesa drop-off is a curve that begins abruptly (almost a 90-degree angle) and ends with a rounded gradual slope.

COLOR   The glass can be the Paint (foreground) color, the Paper (background) color, or leaded. *Leaded* is really the same as dark gray, but it makes it somehow seem a little more "real" to call it leaded. Dark glass colors the underlying image more strongly than light glass does, so if you are experiencing difficulty in getting a noticeable glass effect, try darkening the glass color. There is a drop-down list from which you choose a color for the glass, but Paper and Paint colors need to be chosen before you open the filters.

THE BRIGHTNESS SLIDER   The Brightness slider in the Adjust Lighting section controls the intensity of the highlights in the glass. A higher setting produces more highlights on the glass.

THE SHARPNESS SLIDER   The Sharpness slider controls the sharpness of the light striking the edges of the bevel. So what is "sharpness of light"? This setting actually controls the amount of sharpness that occurs as a function of light striking the affected area.

DIRECTION AND ANGLE CONTROLS   You can control the direction that the sun or light source comes from by using the Direction and Angle controls. High light angle values illuminate the selection from directly above the surface, which tends to cause lighting that is bright and even. Low light angle values tend to make shadows stronger, thus accentuating the 3D effect. The angles are referenced to the horizon. High angle (90°) is similar to the sun being directly overhead, whereas low angle (0°) is like the sun sitting on the horizon.

- **Direction Dial and Value Box** The Direction dial controls the direction of the light striking the bevel. The bevel is the area around a masked object that is slanted to produce the 3D look. You can drag the dial to point toward the light source, or you can enter a value directly in the value box.

- **Angle Dial and Value Box** The Angle dial controls the angle at which the light is to be bent at the bevel. This distorts the image at the bevel location, which is the most striking effect of the Glass filter. The bevel is the area around a masked object that is slanted to produce the 3D look.

TIP: *You get better effects with Glass if you have a textured or high-contrast background to accentuate the glass effect.*

Glass Raised Text Using the Glass Filter

 The Glass filter is an excellent tool, but it takes some practice to get the hang of how and what to apply it to. The hands-on exercise in this section will give you some experience using the glass filter and will present some tricks that will help make it work better for you. We are going to create some text that looks like it is composed of raised glass.

1. Create a new image that is 7 × 3 inches, 72-dpi, 24-bit color. For the Paper color, select a light blue pastel. I used the blue that was to the right of the brown swatch on the drop-down palette. Click the OK button.

2. The glass effect looks better when there is a high-contrast content in the background. From the Effects menu, select Noise and choose Add Noise. Select Gaussian Noise at a Level of 30 and a Density of 50. Click OK.

3. Click the Text button in the Toolbox. Click the color red in the onscreen palette with the left mouse button. Click inside the image and type the word **GLASS**. Change the Font to Century Schoolbook at a size of 150 and select Bold. If you do not have Century Schoolbook, use Times New Roman.

4. Click the Object Picker tool. Open the Align dialog box (CTRL+SHIFT+A) and select Align to center of Page. Open the Objects roll-up (CTRL+F7).

5. Duplicate the text object (CTRL+SHIFT+D). Click Single mode in the Objects roll-up. Select the bottom object and unselect the top object. Ensure the Preserve Image button is not enabled. Click the Create Mask button on the toolbar.

6. From the Effects menu, select Fancy and choose Glass. When the Glass dialog box opens, select the Wet Style setting. Change the Refraction setting to 40. Click the OK button.

7. For the final touch, use the Object Picker and select the remaining object. Change the Merge mode at the bottom of the Objects roll-up to Color. This lets the highlights created on the background text by the Glass filter

appear through the text object. Click the Combine button on the Objects roll-up to merge the object to the background. The result is shown in Figure 22-9.

The important thing to remember is that this filter tends to make the image darker. We worked around that in the previous exercise by placing a copy of the original object on top of the background and working in Single mode, which protected the image from that effect.

Julia Set Explorer 2.0

The operation of this filter is explained in the Kai's Power Tools 3.0 Explorer Guide that is included on the CD-ROM. It is in Envoy format so you will need to ensure that the Envoy reader included with Corel PHOTO-PAINT is installed. If not, you can run Install again and ensure it is there.

The Terrazzo Filter

The next plug-in filter we will discuss from Corel PHOTO-PAINT's Fancy filters group is called Terrazzo. (The name comes from the Italian word for "terrace" and originally referred to a kind of mosaic floor covering.) I again acknowledge my

22

The Glass
Filter
makes the
text look
like it is on
embossed
glass

FIGURE 22-9

gratitude to the fine folks at Xaos, who have let me borrow heavily from their manual so that the material in this chapter would be accurate.

Terrazzo enables you to create beautiful, regular patterns taken from elements in existing source images. With Terrazzo, the patterns are very easy to create and infinitely repeatable. The best part is that Terrazzo is simple to use. Xaos Tools ships a wonderful manual with their product that covers Terrazzo in incredible detail. Since detailed information about this filter is not otherwise available, I have done my best to give you a condensed version of the major features and functions of Terrazzo.

An Overview of Terrazzo

The regular patterns you can create with Terrazzo are based on 17 symmetry groups, which are known in the math and design worlds by several names, including *planar, ornamental,* or *wallpaper* symmetry groups. You choose the symmetry you want to use from a Symmetry selection box in the Terrazzo dialog box.

The 17 symmetries in the Terrazzo filter are named after common American patchwork quilt patterns. Each of these symmetries also has a mathematical name. Because these mathematical names (such as p-4m) aren't very exciting or as easy to remember as the quilt names (such as Sunflower), Xaos has only used the quilt names in the interface.

Tiles, Motifs, and Patterns

Each Terrazzo-generated pattern is made from a *motif,* which is the shape that builds a *tile* when a *symmetry* is applied to it. The tile, in turn, repeats to build a regular pattern. These three terms will be used throughout this discussion.

The motif in Terrazzo is very similar to the masks in Corel PHOTO-PAINT. The area that is enclosed by the motif is the foundation of the tile. There are eight different motif shapes. Different symmetries use different motifs.

Although each of the 17 symmetries produces different results, all of them perform one or more of the following operations:

- **Translations** These move the motif up, down, right, left, or diagonally without changing the orientation.

- **Rotations** These turn the motif one or more times around a center at a specific angle.

- **Mirror Reflections** These create one or more mirror images of the motif.

- **Glide Reflections** These create one or more mirror images of a motif and move the motif up, down, right, left, or diagonally.

The Terrazzo Filter Dialog Box

Terrazzo is located in the Effects menu under Fancy. Clicking on the name produces an hourglass for a moment. (Of all of the filters that were available at the time this book was written, Terrazzo takes the longest to initialize. Still, on my system we are only talking about ten seconds. After it is initialized, Terrazzo operates very fast.)

Terrazzo works on grayscale, duotone, 24-bit, and 32-bit color images, but not on black-and-white (1-bit) images. As with Paint Alchemy and all of the other filters, you must have an image open before you can access the filter.

When you first open Terrazzo, you will see the opening screen as shown in Figure 22-10. Let's take a closer look at it.

The Original preview on the left side of the Terrazzo dialog box displays the masked area of the image, or the entire source image if you haven't selected any areas with a mask. (Color masks don't count.)

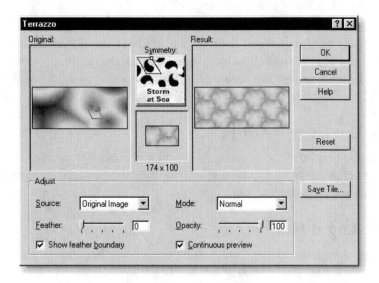

The Terrazzo filter dialog box

FIGURE 22-10

The large image on the right of the dialog box displays the source image with the current symmetry applied to it, which is referred to as the Result image.

NOTE: *The Result image is the one to which you are applying a pattern. Although you can open a new source image from within Terrazzo, you cannot open a new Result image without closing Terrazzo and returning to Corel PHOTO-PAINT's main screen.*

The Continuous Preview Option

When the Continuous Preview checkbox is checked, the destination image is continuously updated as you change any of the settings in the Terrazzo dialog box. This allows you to see the effects of your adjustments in real time as you are making them.

TIP: *Leaving the Continuous Preview options selected may slow down some older systems. This is especially true if you are using a large motif, one of the triangular motifs such as Sunflower, or a kite-shaped motif such as Whirlpool. If you experience system slow-down, you may want to consider switching off the Continuous Preview option. That said, I find that having it on really helps in finding some nice patterns quickly.*

By default, Continuous Preview is turned off in the Terrazzo dialog box. When the Continuous Preview checkbox is not selected, the destination image is updated only when you release the mouse button after making an adjustment to one of the controls in the Terrazzo dialog box.

The Terrazzo Motifs

When you first open the Terrazzo dialog box, the motif is positioned in the center of the source image; if you have already opened the Terrazzo dialog box, the motif is in the position where you last placed it.

Adjusting a Motif

You can change the tile you are creating by moving the motif to a new position on the source image, thus selecting a different part of the image to make into a tile.

In addition to moving the motif, you can also adjust the size and, in the case of the Gold Brick symmetry, the shape of the motif. Each motif has a handle on it that enables you to resize it.

To Adjust the Motif's Position

Place the cursor anywhere inside the motif and hold down the left mouse button. The cursor becomes a hand, and while you hold down the mouse button, you can drag the motif anywhere inside the source image.

If the Continuous Preview option is on, the Result image on the right side is constantly updated to show the results of repositioning the motif on the source image.

To Adjust the Motif's Size

Place the cursor over the motif control handle and drag it to increase or decrease the size. The only exception to this is the Gold Brick, which has two handles. The handle in the upper-right corner of the motif resizes the width, and the handle in the lower left lets you resize the height of the motif and skew its shape.

 TIP: *To constrain the Gold Brick motif to a rectangular shape, or to return to a rectangular motif after you have skewed the motif, hold down the SHIFT key as you drag the lower-left handle. The motif automatically becomes rectangular as long as you hold down the SHIFT key.*

22

Selecting a Symmetry

The first time you open Terrazzo, the active symmetry is Pinwheel. This symmetry is displayed between the Original and the Result images in the Terrazzo dialog box. Each symmetry swatch displays a simple representation of the selected symmetry.

To select a different symmetry, click the currently displayed symmetry swatch and the Symmetry selection box opens as shown here. Clicking the desired symmetry causes it to be highlighted with a blue border. Click the OK button when you are satisfied with your selection, and the selected symmetry appears between the Original and Result image.

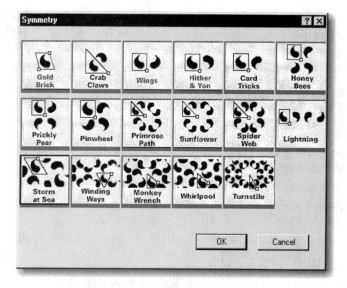

Creating Seamless Patterns

With most of the Terrazzo symmetries, you may notice a visible edge or seam between the tiles. The feather option in the Terrazzo dialog box allows you to feather the edge of a motif so that the seams between tiles fade away.

Feathering in Terrazzo is produced in an area outside the motif (called the *feather boundary*), and the pixels inside the feather boundary are dispersed, thus creating a gradual transition between motifs.

CAUTION: *Sometimes there is such a thing as too much of a good thing. With certain patterns, using too large a feathering value causes faint black seams to develop on certain patterns.*

Using the Feather Option

The Feather option in the Terrazzo dialog box sets the width of the feather edge around the motif. This option is dimmed (not available) if you have selected the Sunflower, Prickly Pear, Turnstile, or Winding Ways symmetry. It is not available because these four symmetries are kaleidoscopic and therefore always seamless.

To adjust a motif's feather edge, drag the slider to increase or decrease the feather edge around the motif, or enter a value directly into the data box to the right of the slider. The value is a percentage based on the size of the image. For example, setting the Feather value to 25 creates a feather with a width of 25 percent of the distance from the edge of the motif to its center.

When you set the Feather value above 0, you will notice that a second border appears around the motif in the source image. This border represents the area included in the feather edge of the motif.

TIP: *You cannot move the motif by clicking and dragging inside the feather border. You must be inside the motif itself to move a feathered motif. (This little jewel drove me crazy till I figured it out.)*

If you don't want to see the feather boundary around the motif, you can turn it off by clearing the Show Feather Boundary checkbox in the Terrazzo dialog box. This only turns off the visible border; if you have feathering selected, the feathering is still applied.

You may notice that setting a Feather value slows down your system a wee bit. The folks at Corel have done a wonderful job of speeding up these filters in comparison to the Mac versions. However, if you noticed that the feathering is slowing your system down, keep it off until you are ready to fine-tune your image.

TIP: *Some symmetries create mirror lines as they reflect a motif to create a pattern. Feather does not occur on mirror lines, because these are "seamless" lines; feathering only appears on edges with visible seams.*

Feather Boundary Constraints

If the Show Feather boundary is off and you have some value of feathering entered, you will discover that you cannot position the motif any closer to the edge of the source image than the feather boundary.

If the motif is already positioned near the edge of the source image and you attempt to enter a value for Feather, that would create a boundary that goes beyond the image edge. You would then receive a warning and the maximum allowable value would automatically be entered in the Feather value box. The slider or values will not exceed that value unless the motif is moved.

One last feathering note: If you have a very small motif, you may not be able to see the feather boundary, even if you have the Show Feather Boundary option turned on. Although you can't see it, the feather will still appear when you apply the pattern.

The Mode Settings

The Mode drop-down list in the Terrazzo dialog box lets you control the way a pattern is applied to a selection.

The Opacity Slider

The Opacity slider in the Terrazzo dialog box lets you adjust the opacity of the pattern when you apply it to a selection. You may want the effect of an almost invisible pattern (low opacity), or you may want a bold application of a pattern, covering the destination image entirely (high opacity). An opacity value of 100 (100 percent) means that the pattern is completely opaque; an opacity value of 1 means that the pattern is almost invisible (which is not very useful).

Previewing Tiles

A preview of the current tile appears below the symmetry swatch. The pixel dimensions of the current tile are also displayed below the tile. You are provided with a constant preview of the tile you are creating.

Saving a Tile

One of the benefits of having the Terrazzo filter integrated into Corel PHOTO-PAINT is that saving a tile button becomes a real time saver. The Save Tile feature saves the tile created by Terrazzo as a .BMP file. This way you can quickly use Terrazzo to make a tile, and by saving it as a tile, you can use it immediately as a bitmap fill.

To save a Terrazzo tile:

1. Choose the symmetry, and position the motif where you want it in the source image.

2. Click the Save Tile button in the Terrazzo dialog box. The Save Tile dialog box opens.

3. Name the file and confirm where you want it saved. Click the OK button. When you return to the Terrazzo, click Cancel if you do not want any pattern applied to the image.

The Boss (Emboss) Filter

The Emboss filter, like the Glass filter (which was made by the same company), makes the selected area look as if it is pushed out of the image. The effect is achieved by putting what appears to be a slanted bevel around the selected area. It is called The Boss (to avoid confusion with the original Emboss filter). The Boss filter dialog box is shown here. This filter has a preview window, but it doesn't allow the panning or zoom control found in the other Corel PHOTO-PAINT filters. You must have a mask in place to be able to use this filter.

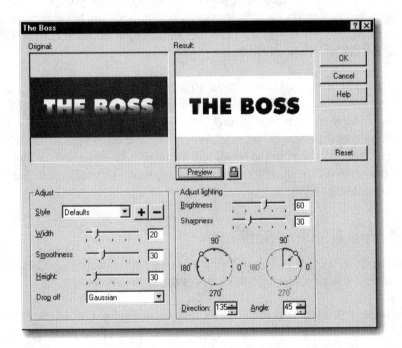

 TIP: *If you are going to apply the filter to the entire image, select All from the Mask menu to quickly mask the image, and then create the mask from it.*

The Boss Dialog Box

The Boss filter and the Glass filter are very similar in operation. That's because they use the same filter engine (program) internally. This is not an uncommon practice.

I only mention it in case you experience a feeling of deja vu. It is the commonality of the programs at work here—you don't need to call the psychic hotline. The controls will be covered in order not of appearance but of use.

THE ADJUST CONTROLS The Adjust controls of the Emboss dialog box affect the shape of the bevel around the selection. The Height slider controls how far the selection pushes out of the screen toward the viewer. This is the primary way to control the amount of the 3D effect. The Width slider controls how much of the image is taken up by the bevel. Be aware that the bevel grows around the area selected by the mask. Therefore, if it gets too wide or the objects selected are too close together, they will begin to merge into one another. Thin bevels appear steeper than wide ones, so this setting also controls the strength of the 3D effect. Drop-off controls the general shape of the bevel.

SMOOTHNESS The basis of the trade-offs with the Smoothness settings is that if there were no "jaggies," there would also be no sharp lines. So instead of deciding how much The Boss filter would "melt" the bevel, they added a smoothing slider, so you can make the decision yourself. When Smoothness is set low, the edges will be sharper, but little steps in the bevel will be more noticeable. When Smoothness is high, the edges will be more rounded, and it will look like your objects are floating on marshmallows.

The Adjust Lighting Settings

Part of the realism of 3D is in how reflections of light are displayed. These controls determine the source point and brightness of the light source.

BRIGHTNESS Brightness is the bright reflection of the light off of the 3D surface. The Brightness slider can make the highlight disappear at the lower settings, or it can wash out part of the image at the higher settings. The Brightness Sharpness slider lets you control how small and crisp the highlight is. Sharper highlights tend to make the surface look shinier or even wet. Dull highlights are more spread out and make the surface look chalky.

The shape of the bevel interacts with the highlights. Sharper bevel corners (low width, high height, low smoothing) will make sharper highlights, so you will have to experiment to see how all these parameters combine to make the final 3D effect.

LIGHTING CONTROLS: DIRECTION AND ANGLE You can control the direction that the sun or light source comes from using the Direction and Angle controls. High light angles light the selection from directly above the surface, which tends to cause bright and even lighting. Low light angles tend to make shadows stronger, thus accentuating the 3D effect. See the previous discussion of this subject under the Glass filter.

Creating a License Plate

Here is a basic hands-on exercise that uses The Boss filter to create a very realistic license plate. You can make almost anything look like a license plate, embossing tape, or whatever else your imagination can dream up. In this exercise we are not going to make an entire plate; instead we will concentrate on the technique for a portion of the plate. You can use any state you want, but since I live in Texas, we are going to make something very similar to our plates in the Lone Star state, y'all.

1. Create a new file with the following settings: 7 × 3 inches, 72 dpi, 24-bit color and white for the Paper color.

2. Select Noise from the Effects menu and choose Add Noise from the drop-down list. When the filter dialog box opens, click the Gaussian in the Type section. Set the Density to 10 and the Level to 30. Click the OK button.

3. Change the Paint color by clicking blue on the palette.

4. Click the Text tool in the Toolbox. Place the cursor in the image area and click with the left mouse button. Type in the word **TEXAS**. On the toolbar, change the Font name to VAGRounded BT with a size of 150 and an inter-character spacing of 8.

5. Select the Object Picker tool. Open the Align command (CTRL+SHIFT+A) and center the text to the page. In the Objects roll-up, click the Single button. Apply noise to the text using (CTRL+F).

6. Click the Create Mask button. Select Feather from the Mask menu. In the Feather dialog box, enter a Width of 5, Direction: Inside, Edges: Curved. Click the OK button.

7. From the Effects menu, select Fancy and choose The Boss... from the drop-down list. This opens The Boss dialog box. In the Style drop-down, select Wet (one of my favorites). We are going to make a few changes to this preset. Reduce the Width to 10. Change the Smoothness setting to 60. Set the Height to 55. This changes the visible steps in the bevel. A high

22

setting make it very smooth, while a low setting makes it look like it's chiseled from metal. Save this setting by clicking the icon of a plus sign and name the new setting License Plate. Click the OK button. Here is the result.

Beyond What the Designer Had In Mind

When Jeff Butterworth of Alien Skin Software originally created this filter, he wanted it to be the best embossing filter available on the market. He put so many controls on it, it can be used to go beyond just plain old embossing. Here are some other things to try with it that even Jeff may not have thought of yet. I really enjoy all of the interesting 3D effects that can be created with CorelDRAW. Here is a technique to produce 3D objects with The Boss filter.

Making a 3D Button

In this hands-on exercise we will create a basic 3D object that can be used on a Web page or made part of a control panel illustration. Once you have made the basic button, before you add the text, you can duplicate the object and make as many as you want.

1. Create a new image. Select 24-bit color; Paper Color: White; Size: 4 × 4 inches; Resolution: 72 dpi.

2. From the Tools menu, select Grid & Ruler Setup. On the Grid tab, enable Show grid and Snap to grid. Click the OK button.

3. Select the Ellipse Mask tool from the Toolbox. Click the cursor in the image area and drag a circle mask in the center of the image made up of four squares. Disable Snap to grid (CTRL+Y). Invert the Mask.

4. From the Edit menu, choose Fill. From the Edit Fill & Transparency dialog box, click the Fountain Fill button and click the Edit button. From the Fountain Fill dialog box, choose the Gold Plated preset. Click OK to close the dialog box and OK again to apply the fill.

5. Invert the mask. Click the color blue in the onscreen palette with the right mouse button. Select the Fill tool from the Toolbox and click inside the circle mask.

6. From the Effects menu, select Fancy and choose The Boss from the drop-down list. From the Style drop-down, select Wet, change the Width to 60, the Smoothness to 100, and the Height to 100. Click the OK button. The result is shown in Figure 22-11.

7. Click the Invert Mask button.

8. Open the Boss filter again. Change the Height to 80, the Width to 15, and the Smoothness to 50. Click the OK button. The finished blank button is shown in Figure 22-12.

9. Click the Text tool and select the VAGrounded BT font at a size of 150. Click the center of the button and type the number **8**.

22

After the
first
application
of The Boss
filter

FIGURE 22-11

The
finished
blank button

FIGURE 22-12

10. Click the Object Picker tool in the Toolbox. Click the Remove Mask button on the Property bar and in the Objects roll-up (CTRL+F7), click the Single button. Use the arrow keys to line up the letter in the center of the image as shown in Figure 22-13. The fill color of your text may be different.

The text
centered on
the button
with the grid

FIGURE 22-13

11. From the Edit menu, choose Fill and click the Fountain Fill button. Click OK. The text is now filled with the Gold Plated fill. Ensure the Preserve Image button is not enabled and click the Create Mask button.

12. Open the Boss filter again. Change the Height to 20, the Width to 3, and the Smoothness to 40. Click the OK button. The button is almost finished, as shown in Figure 22-14. All we need to do now is make it into an object so we can place it. Click the Remove mask button.

13. To remove and place just the button in another location, from the Tools menu, select Grid & Ruler Setup. Enable Show grid and Snap to grid. Click the Frequency button and change both of the settings to 4 per inch. Click the OK button.

14. Select the Circle mask tool. Beginning in the upper-left corner at the intersection of the grid two squares down and to the right, drag a circle mask that covers the entire button. A small fringe at the edge will remain outside of the mask. Click the Preserve Image button. Click the Create Object button. Drag the object out of the image and onto the desktop and it becomes a new image. In Figure 22-15 I have added a drop shadow for that extra touch.

22

The almost finished button

FIGURE 22-14

The
finished
button

FIGURE 22-15

There are many more things that can be done, but space is limited. I hope I have given you enough material to arouse your interest. Happy filtering!

23

The Color
Transform Filters

This chapter presents a collection of eight filters that run the gamut of usefulness from the essential to the goofy. The first four filters listed here are located in the Color Transform category of the Effects menu. The remaining four are in the Transform category of the Image menu.

- Bit Planes filter
- Halftone filter (available with grayscale, too)
- Psychedelic filter (available with grayscale, too)
- Solarize filter
- DeInterlace filter
- Invert filter
- Posterize filter
- Threshold filter

The Bit Planes Filter

This filter, available with grayscale, Paletted, 24-bit, and 32-bit color images, applies a posterization-style effect to each channel individually. The Bit Planes effect can be a powerful tool for analyzing gradients in images. The effect reduces the image to basic RGB color components and emphasizes tone changes. For example, different areas would appear as solid blocks since there is little change in tone. Since gradient fills have a high degree of color tone change, the Bit Planes effect is very useful for analyzing the number of steps in gradients.

The Color Plane sliders control the sensitivity of the effect. Higher settings display fewer tone changes and gradient steps. At the highest setting, the image contains a large amount of black-and-white area, since the effect is displaying only extreme tone changes. Lower Color plane settings display more tone changes and gradations. At the lowest setting, a photographic image will appear like color noise, as subtle changes are virtually random. A graphic or computer-generated image will show salient contours of change in tone.

The Color Plane sliders can be used separately to see the tone changes in a specific component color, or together to see all tone changes. The Bit Planes filter is used to provide unusual color effects to an image.

The Bit Planes Dialog Box

The Bit Planes dialog box with an RGB file, shown here, controls the effects of this filter.

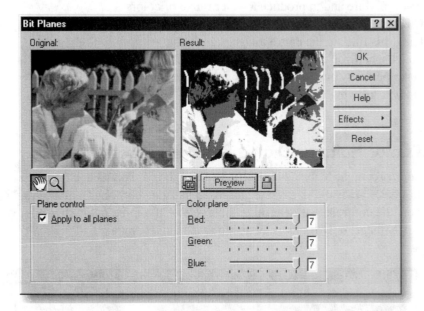

When Apply to All Planes is enabled, all of the color plane values change so that all of the plane values are identical. Adjust the Color Plane sliders (Red-Green-Blue) to set the sensitivity of the color effect. Higher values display more coarse changes in tone. At the highest settings, the image will show large, flat areas with or without color, where the image is brightest and darkest. At the lowest settings, the image will show the finest level of tone variation. The result depends on the type of image to which you are applying the effect. With a grayscale file, there is only one Color Plane slider, gray, and the Plane Control option is unavailable.

The Halftone Filter

The Color Halftone filter, only available with grayscale, 24- and 32-bit color images, simulates the effect of using an enlarged halftone screen on each channel of the image. For each channel, the filter divides the image into rectangles and replaces each rectangle with a circle. The circle size is proportional to the brightness of the rectangle.

23

The Halftone filter converts color images into color halftone images. Use the Max Radius slider to control the maximum radius of a halftone dot, and the Cyan, Magenta, and Yellow slider bars to control the channel angle in order to determine the color mixture and to produce a wider range of colors.

Click the Preview button to display the effects of the current filter settings before applying this filter to the entire image.

So what can you do with the Halftone filter? The best I have been able to figure is to take perfectly good art and make it look like the DC Comics that were around when I was growing up.

The Color Halftone Dialog Box

The controls unique to the Color Halftone dialog box are divided into two areas. Dot Control determines the size of the simulated halftone dot. The Channel Angle area contains the controls that determine the angle of the three color channels. With a grayscale image, only Black is available as a channel angle.

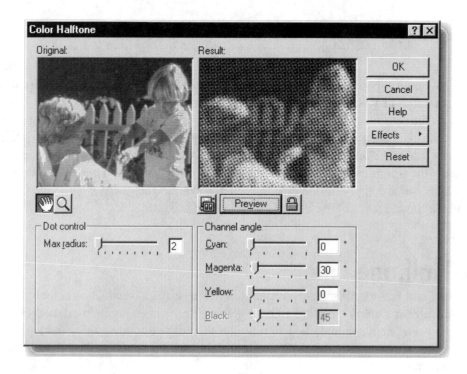

Using the Color Halftone Filter

- Select Color Transform from the Effects menu, and choose Color Halftone from the drop-down list. The Color Halftone dialog box will appear.

- Enter a value in the Dot Control section from 2 to 10, for the maximum radius of a halftone dot.

- Enter a screen-angle value for each available channel. Click Reset to return all the screen angles to their default values. The values indicate the angle of the dot from true horizontal.

The Psychedelic Filter

If it isn't bad enough that the '60s are showing up in the fashion world, we now have this filter in the Corel PHOTO-PAINT program. (It has been said that if you clearly remember the '60s, you weren't really there. Perhaps this filter will bring them back to you.) The Psychedelic filter, only available with grayscale, 24- and 32-bit color images, changes the colors in selected areas of an image to bright, electric shades such as orange, hot pink, electric-banana yellow, cyan, lime green, and so on. If the image is a grayscale, the replacements are limited to shades of gray.

The Adjust level, shown here, spans a range of 256 shades (0-255). Use in large doses and it can induce flashbacks. Use in small amounts to achieve the best effects.

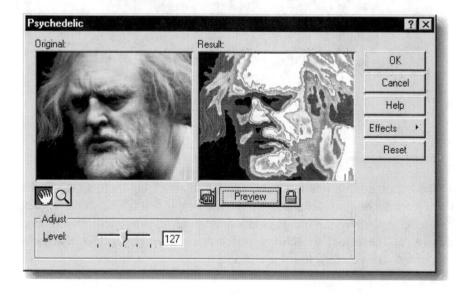

The Solarize Filter

The Solarize filter, only available with grayscale, Paletted, 24-, and 32-bit color images, enables you to make an image look like a photographic negative. The effect will be more pronounced in color images. Solarize is an effect that, when applied to its maximum (255 shades), results in a negative or inverted image. It simulates an old photographic technique that required the photographic plate to be briefly exposed to sunlight outside of the camera. This resulted in the darkest areas being washed out. How washed out they were was determined by how long the plate was exposed. (The emulsions they had in the old days were very low speed and very, very slow.)

The Corel PHOTO-PAINT Solarize filter operates in a similar fashion, except that instead of entering in the time the image is in the sun, you can control the shades of color that will be affected by the filter (0 through 255). In the dialog box, shown here, a setting of zero has no effect on the image. A maximum setting of 255 shades makes the image a complete negative.

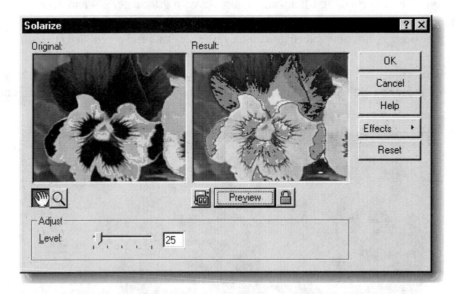

The Solarize filter, like the Invert filter, transforms colors to appear like those of a negative photographic image. Unlike with the Invert filter (which produces an absolute effect where the image colors are completely inverted), you control the intensity of the effect to achieve different results. This effect will be more pronounced when applied to color images.

So what can you do with the Solarize filter? Not much. This is one of the filters that begs the question, "Why is it here?" That said, its best use is to apply a partial inverted effect to an image. This limits its application to special effects and backgrounds on color images. Although it can be applied to grayscale images, I only recommend its use with color images unless you are trying to create a special effect.

The DeInterlace Filter

This filter, new to PHOTO-PAINT 7, removes even or odd horizontal lines from scanned or interlaced video images. You can fill the spaces left by the discarded lines using either *duplication* or *interpolation,* which have a total of four options as shown in the dialog box. Duplication fills in the spaces with copies of the adjacent lines of pixels, while interpolation fills them in with colors created by averaging the surrounding pixels.

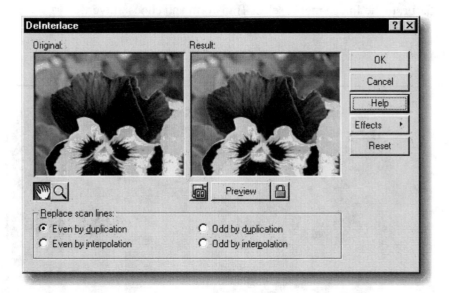

The Invert Filter

This filter, available with all images, is both the simplest and most essential filter. The Invert filter changes the colors in an image so that they appear as a photographic negative. While the ability to make a photographic negative is rarely needed, the

Invert filter can be used to reverse a portion of the image to create interesting effects. There is no dialog box for the Invert filter. Clicking on the command displays the effects.

Making Day out of Night with the Invert Filter

 Many times you will have an image that will not reproduce well in either grayscale or photocopy reproduction. While it won't work with many images, the following little trick might sometime help you out of a bind and convince everyone else you're an artistic genius.

1. Locate the image \PHOTOS\LANDMARK\555069.WI. Load the image and Resample it to 6 inches wide. Click the OK button. The original image is shown in Figure 23-1.

2. From the Image menu, select Transform and choose Invert.

The original photograph is too dark to be used

FIGURE 23-1

3. From the Image menu, choose Convert To and choose Grayscale (8-bit). The result is shown in Figure 23-2.

4. Close the file and don't save the changes.

Other uses of the Invert filter are demonstrated throughout this book.

The Posterize Filter

This is the second most useful filter in this group. The Posterize filter, which only works on grayscale, Paletted, 24-bit, and 32-bit color images, removes gradations, creating areas of solid colors or gray shades. This is useful when there is a need to simplify a complex color image without converting it to 256- or 16-color mode.

Another way to use this filter is to apply the Posterize effect selectively to individual channels through the Channels roll-up. Please note that individual color channels are grayscale images. Posterizing an image with a setting of three and four shades is a standard use of this filter. The Posterize filter removes gradations,

One of the times that Inverting a photograph works

FIGURE 23-2

creating areas of solid colors or gray shades. This is useful when there is a need to simplify a complex color or grayscale image for use as a background. Figure 23-3 is the original photograph of the Golden Gate Bridge. In Figure 23-4 I have applied the Posterize filter at the default setting.

To Reduce Color Gradations in an Image

■ Choose Color Transform in the Effects menu and choose Posterize from the drop-down list. The dialog box opens as shown here.

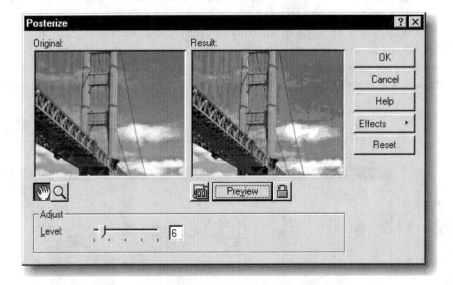

■ Adjust the Level slider to specify the number of gray or color channels. The lower the value, the more pronounced the poster effect will be.

The Threshold Filter

One of the uses of the Threshold filter is to convert grayscale or color images into high-contrast line-art images. When scanning images that are high-resolution black-and-white (not grayscale), it is sometimes advantageous to scan them in as grayscale and then use the Threshold filter to remove the light gray background. See

Original photograph has lots of shades and smooth transitions

FIGURE 23-3

After the Posterize filter is applied, the levels of colors are greatly reduced

FIGURE 23-4

23

Chapter 5 for more details about how this is done. Another use is to convert specific colors in an image to black or white or both through multiple applications.

Operation of the filter is simple although the filter dialog box, shown here, at first appearance seems very complicated. Corel has put a wealth of information about this filter in their online help and I recommend that you review it. Open the Help file (F1) in PHOTO-PAINT 7. Click the Index tab and enter Threshold.

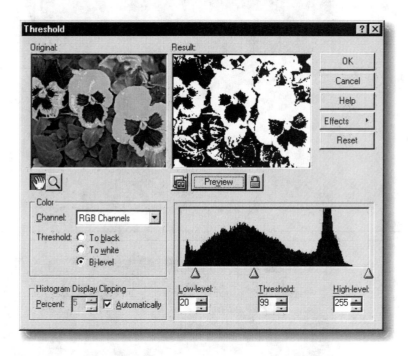

24

Off the Beaten Path

T his chapter was originally titled "Advanced Topics." I changed the name because the material covered isn't necessarily advanced, and I don't want you to overlook it because you might not feel that you are an "advanced" user. This chapter contains information about applications that may be important but are not often used by many PHOTO-PAINT users. With that explanation behind us, let's move on to the Corel Command Recorder.

The Command Recorder

One of the features that is buried in Corel PHOTO-PAINT is the Command Recorder. It is a powerful tool that allows you to produce some effects that might otherwise be considered too labor intensive. If you haven't used the Command Recorder before, it may have been because the documentation borders on being vague. I had a different reason for not using it. I believed that the gains made by using the Command Recorder were outweighed by the time it took to use it. Was I ever wrong.

The Corel Recorder acts like a macro recorder. You press the Record button and go through the steps of the task that you want to accomplish. The Recorder records each step until you click the Stop button. You open the Command Recorder by selecting Roll-ups in the View menu and choosing Recorder from the list of roll-ups, or by using the keyboard combination CTRL+F3. Here you see what the Recorder looks like when it is first opened.

The VCR-style buttons at the top provide the following functions (from left to right): return to first command; play; step forward, which plays one command at a time; fast forward, which advances to last command; stop; and record. Operation is like a VCR. When you have a sequence of events you want to record, you click the Record button, perform the steps, and then click the Stop button. The resulting list of commands are a script, which can be saved, reloaded, and replayed at a later date.

To save your recorded commands as a script file, click the small right-facing arrow just below the red Record button, which opens a selection drop-down list, as shown here.

There are several new options on the drop-down list with the PHOTO-PAINT 7 release. One of these is Scale on Playback. When this is enabled, the commands that are applied to images are scaled as a function of the image size. For example, using the Resample command with Scale on Playback enabled will produce the same final image size each time it is played, regardless of the original image size. I discovered this when making all of the illustrations for the buttons in this book. I created a script with the Command Recorder that would resample the screen shot to a size of .75 inches. Because many of the buttons are different sizes, when I ran the script, it produced buttons of varying sizes because the Scale on Playback feature wasn't enabled. Therefore, if the button was a smaller size than the one I used for the original script, it would produce a button smaller than .75 inches. This feature is important because there are many operations that require the user to ensure the image to which the script is applied is the same size as the original when the action was recorded.

The commands can be saved as Corel Scripts. The previous version of PHOTO-PAINT had a format called QuickScript (.QSC), which was the native format of the Command Recorder. The Corel Script file (.CSC) is now the native format. If you made QuickScripts with Corel PHOTO-PAINT 6, you can convert them to Corel Script files in Corel Editor. When you save the file, you can open it in the Corel Script editor and add all kinds of functionality to it. It becomes a real programming type of task at that point. The .CSC file can now be run from the Command Recorder or from the Corel Script editor.

24

What got me working with this Command Recorder to begin with was a need to produce a woven mat style of background. After I figured out a way to do it, I began to look for ways to make it easier. That is when I remembered and uncovered the Corel Command Recorder. Now, follow along and we will enter the world of PHOTO-PAINT automation.

Creating a Script

The first six steps of this hands-on exercise produce the base image and will not use the Command Recorder. After you have created the initial script in this exercise, you can use any fill you want to create the base object to get different effects.

1. First we need to create a working area. From the File menu select New. When the Create A New Image dialog box opens, choose the following: Color Mode: 24-bit color; Image size: 400 × 400 pixels; Resolution: 96 dpi.

2. Select the Rectangle Mask tool from the Toolbox, and from the Property bar change the Mask Style setting from Normal to Fixed Size. Make the Width and Height settings both 200 pixels.

3. Click the cursor in the middle of the image area, and a square mask will appear. The position of the mask in the image is not critical, but it must be far enough away from the edge to prevent the mask from being resized. Even though the mask is a fixed size, the program will stop the mask boundaries at the edge of the image regardless of the size requested. If you cannot see the mask, make sure that Mask Marquee in the Mask menu is checked.

4. Select Fill in the Edit menu. When the Edit Fill & Transparency dialog box opens, click the Fountain Fill button. Now click the Edit button, which opens the Fountain Fill dialog box. At the bottom of the dialog box, locate the Presets area and click the down-facing arrow to open the Preset list. Locate the Cylinder-Green 04 preset and click the OK button. Click the OK button again to apply the fill.

5. To make this pattern look more real, we are going to add some edge shadow using the Stroke Mask command. From the Mask menu select Stroke Mask method and keep the Middle of the Mask setting, which opens the Stroke Mask dialog box. From the Brush tab select the Airbrush. Click the down-facing arrow and choose Medium cover from the list. Click the OK button, and the entire mask border will be painted with the

current Paint (foreground) color. If your Paint color is not black, Undo the action (CTRL+Z), change the Paint color, and reapply. Don't be concerned about the paint on the image area. The result is shown in Figure 24-1.

6. We will now make the masked area into an image. First ensure the Preserve Image button on the toolbar is not depressed (if it is depressed, tell it a few jokes and cheer it up—sorry). Now click the Create Object (from mask) button on the toolbar or select Create From Mask in the Object menu. The masked area becomes an object, and the Object Picker (at the top of the Toolbox) becomes selected.

7. Finally, open the Command Recorder (CTRL+F3). It should not have any commands visible when it opens. If it does, click the right-facing arrow below the Record button, select New, and don't save any changes. Click the Record button and follow along carefully.

8. Open the Align dialog box (CTRL+SHIFT+A). Choose Vertically: Top, Horizontally: Left. Click the OK button. The result should look like Figure 24-2. As a reminder, don't worry about the mess we left with the airgun.

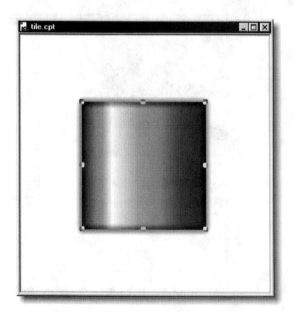

The basic building block for our script

FIGURE 24-1

9. Duplicate the object (CTRL+SHIFT+D). Another image appears and is automatically selected.

10. Select Align (CTRL+SHIFT+A) and choose Bottom, Right. Click OK.

11. Duplicate this object (CTRL+SHIFT+D). Don't be concerned that the object went outside of the image area—unlike masks, objects don't change their sizes.

12. Select Align (CTRL+SHIFT+A) and choose Top, Right. Click OK.

13. Select Rotate from the Object menu and choose 90° Clockwise.

14. Because Rotation slightly resizes objects, we need to apply a minor correction to the tile we just rotated. Select Scale Mode from the drop-down list on the far left of the Property bar. Ensure the Maintain Aspect button is enabled and enter a value of **101 percent** in either of the H or V value boxes. Click the Transform button. Click the Apply button.

15. Duplicate this object (CTRL+SHIFT+D).

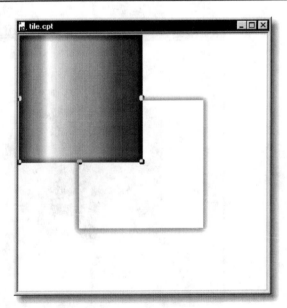

After the first Align command, the image looks like this

FIGURE 24-2

16. Select Align (CTRL+SHIFT+A) and choose Bottom, Left. Click OK. Your image should look like Figure 24-3.

17. From the Object menu, select Combine and choose All Objects With Background.

18. From the Mask menu choose Select All.

19. From the Object menu select Create From Mask.

20. For the last step we are going to scale the image down to size. Select Scale Mode in the Property bar. Ensure the Maintain Aspect button is enabled and enter a value of 50 percent in either of the H or V value boxes. Click the Transform button. Click the Apply button.

21. Stop the Recorder by clicking the Stop button (the one to the left of the Record button).

22. Click the left-facing arrow below the Record button and save the script in the \Corel\Draw7\Scripts folder as TILE START.CSC.

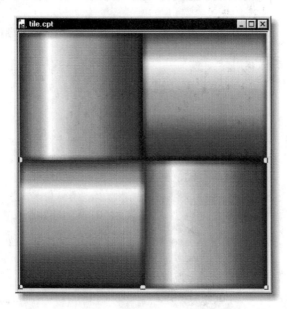

The completed background before scaling

FIGURE 24-3

Testing the Script

At this point your image should look like Figure 24-4. Now comes the fun part. Before we play the script the first time, we need to have a safety net. From the Edit menu select Checkpoint. Now, we have a temporary copy of the file to go back to if a mistake was made during the procedure. On the Command Recorder, click the Play button. You should have a figure as shown in Figure 24-5. If not, select Restore from Checkpoint and click through the script in the Command Recorder one step at a time with the Single Step button (to the immediate right of the Play button). Use the Delete button or the Insert new Commands checkbox to correct the script.

Modifying a Script and Making a Toolbar Button

Because the script we just made always ends with a small tile object in the corner, we need to modify the script so that it doesn't apply the 50 percent scale. Then we will save it and create buttons that launch these two scripts.

1. Click the Forward To Last Record button (to the right of the Stop button), and select the last command by clicking it.

The image looks like this after you record the first script

FIGURE 24-4

The image
should look
like this
after you
play the
script again

FIGURE 24-5

2. Click the Delete button at the bottom of the roll-up. The script will return to the first command.

3. Save this script as TILE END.CSC.

4. From the <u>T</u>ools menu select <u>C</u>ustomize. Click the Toolbars tab. Move to the bottom of the <u>C</u>ommand Categories and click the + next to General Scripts.

5. Find the script you just created, TILE END.CSC, and highlight it. Its name appears as a button along with all of the other icons. Click and drag the named button onto the desktop.

6. Click on TILE END.CSC and drag its button on top of the first button. The cursor will turn into a + sign when it is ready to be added to the first toolbar we created. Release the mouse button, and we have a new toolbar with our two script buttons on it.

7. Rename the toolbar by selecting Toolbars in the View menu. In the list, click on the new toolbar with the right mouse button and choose Rename. Name the toolbar Tile Tools. The result is shown next.

24

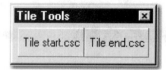

8. Close the Toolbar dialog box by clicking the OK button.

9. Test the new button by clicking TILE END.CSC. The result should look like Figure 24-6.

The advantage of these scripts is their ability to do the "grunt" work and let you be creative. Now on to a completely different subject.

Duotones

A duotone is a grayscale image printed with two inks. This technique expands the depth of the image by allowing additional shades for highlights, shadows, and midtones. Duotones are great attention-getters, and they take less ink. The duotone feature is ideal for adding an accent color to a photograph or for extending the tonal ranges of inks.

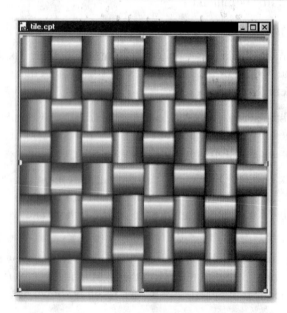

The finished product using the Tile End script

FIGURE 24-6

The Duotone Dialog Box

The Duotone dialog box, shown here, is accessed by selecting Convert To and choosing Duotone (8-bit). It may appear complex, but it offers you complete control over the process of creating duotones.

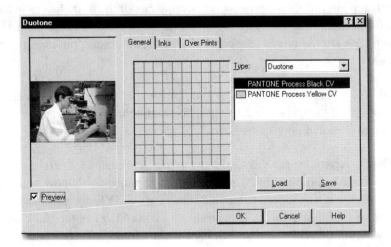

The Duotone dialog box lets you convert grayscale images to monotone, duotone, tritone, and quadtone images. It features three tabbed property sheets that display a grid area with a single, diagonal, unedited curve cutting across its surface. The curve indicates the distribution and density of each ink from the shadow, through the midtone, to the highlighted areas of the image.

By manipulating curves on the Inks tab, you control how each ink is used in the highlights, midtones, and shadows. The highlights and shadows run from left to right across the horizontal plane of the grid. The ink density runs vertically from bottom to top. Each ink curve is edited separately by clicking the desired ink icon located to the right of the grid. By default, each curve is straight; they run diagonally across the grid from bottom left to top right, indicating that the grayscale value of each pixel composing the image is presently identical to the value of the selected ink. To adjust the curve, click a point along the curve and drag the node to the desired position. You can also click on an area of the grid; a node is instantly created and positioned.

The major options for the dialog box are described in the following sections. Not all of the options are described due to their complex nature relating to the duotone printing process. For information on options not described in this chapter, click the option in question with the right mouse button. A message bar appears that reads

"What's this?" Click the message box with the left mouse button, and a very detailed explanation of the option will appear.

Choosing Types

The first step in the duotone process is selecting one of the four choices in the Type list on the General tab. Clicking the down arrow displays a drop-down list from which you can choose one of four types of images: monotone, duotone, tritone, and quadtone.

MONOTONE A monotone is a grayscale image that is printed with a single ink, that produces all the shadows, midtones, and highlights in the image. A monotone is like a conventional grayscale image.

DUOTONE A duotone is a grayscale image that is printed with two inks, typically a black ink and a colored ink. The black ink is applied to shadow areas and the colored ink (usually a Pantone color, and sometimes CMYK process inks) is applied to midtone and highlight areas. This produces a colored tint on the black-and-white image, which is effective in establishing a warm or cool effect, depending on the colored ink.

TRITONE A tritone is a grayscale image that is printed with three inks. The advantage of either tritones or quadtones for general printing is limited.

QUADTONE A quadtone is a grayscale image that is printed with four inks.

Ink Display

The display to the right of the grid shows the currently selected ink colors. The default ink used in a duotone is a Pantone Process color. To select a different color than the one shown, double-click the ink, and the Select Color dialog box opens, in which you can select a new color.

When creating duotones, tritones, and quadtones, prioritize your inks from the darkest at the top to the lightest at the bottom of this display. Because Corel PHOTO-PAINT prints inks in the order they appear in the dialog box, the inks will then print from the darkest to the lightest. This ensures rich highlights and shadows and a uniform color range.

Load/Save Buttons

The functionality of the Load and Save buttons depends on the duotone property sheet currently selected. When the General tab is selected, the Load button opens the Load Duotone File dialog box, where you access one of the 31 preset duotone (.CPD) files provided with PHOTO-PAINT. The Save button allows you to save custom .CPD files. When the Inks tab is selected, the Load button opens the Load Ink File dialog box, where you access ink (.CIK) files; and the Save button allows you to save custom settings. These files are the same as those found in the Tone Curve area. They control the curves of the applied ink.

 TIP: *To convert an image to a duotone, it must first be in grayscale format.*

Converting an Image into a Duotone

Here are the basic steps involved in converting an image into a duotone. The same procedure applies to converting them to tritones and quadtones.

1. Click Image, Convert To, Duotone.

2. In the Type list box, click Duotone.

3. To choose different colors for the duotone than those displayed, double-click a color's icon and select a different color from the dialog box.

4. Repeat step 3 to choose a second color if desired.

5. Click the Inks tab and adjust the duotone curve for each ink by clicking a color swatch. By moving the curve, you can adjust how much color is applied to the highlights, midtones, and shadows in the image. Having the Preview option checked displays the changes immediately.

6. If you want to specify how the overprint colors display onscreen, click the Over Prints tab, click Edit, and adjust the settings.

7. Enable the Preview checkbox to see what the image will look like.

8. Click OK. The image displays as a duotone.

Be careful about your choice of ink colors. Duotones can become very dark very quickly if you choose a darker ink without compensating by adjusting the Tone Curve. Other than that, you need to find out from the printer who will be producing your duotone, tritone, or other image, what format he or she requires for the separation files. Most printers want Encapsulated PostScript (.EPS) files.

Late-Breaking
News

No sooner had I finished this book and put my metaphorical feet up on the desk than had my friendly Federal Express man shown up with a beta copy of the Rev. B Maintenance Release for CorelDRAW7. Here is the latest information about the changes that have occurred in CorelDRAW7 as a result of the Maintenance Release. This information has been extracted from the documentation that came with the release.

New for DRAW 7

If your copy of PHOTO-PAINT came with a version of the DRAW7 suite that is a build earlier than 433, you will receive a Maintenance Release update CD-ROM after you have registered your product. If you have PHOTO-PAINT 7, which came with the DRAW7 suite, you can upgrade to the Plus version for $49.00. If you have PHOTO-PAINT 7 Plus, you have all of the items mentioned in this update. While the Maintenance Release covers all of the products in the DRAW7 suite, it is only appropriate that PHOTO-PAINT 7 items be mentioned first.

PHOTO-PAINT 7 Plus Only

The big news for PHOTO-PAINT 7 users has already been covered in the book. It is the inclusion of the Lens object into PHOTO-PAINT 7 Plus.

Another new feature being included in PHOTO-PAINT 7 Plus is the Squizz 1.5 plug-in filter. It appears in the Effects menu under HSoft. It is a turbo-powered version of the Mesh Warp filter. When you open the filter you are presented with a dialog box, shown here, which gives you the choices Brush, Grid, and Quit.

Grid Mode

Selecting Grid gives you an operation very similar to the Mesh Warp filter. You use the Select button to choose more than one grid point. With the Select button enabled, you can marquee select a large number of nodes and then choose one of the actions that you wish to apply, such as Pinch, Expand, Reduce, or Enlarge, and apply it by dragging one of the selected nodes. You can restrict the movement of the effect to horizontal, vertical, or both by clicking the appropriate check boxes.

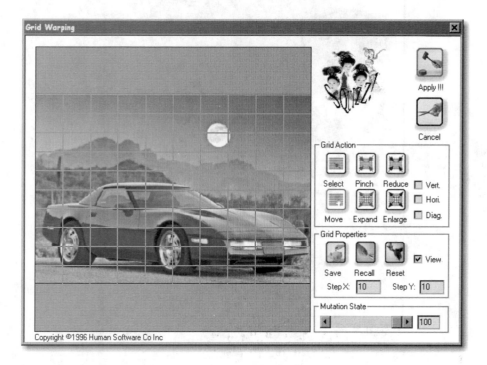

Warp Brush Mode

Choosing the Brush button opens the Brush warping mode. Rather than move grids to cause the changes to be effected in specific areas, there are two effects that can be applied with a brush tool within the dialog box: Squizz and Storm. Squizz effectively warps the area under the brush, and an example of this effect is shown in the preview window of the display box shown next. The Storm option, if enabled, scatters the pixels underneath the brush in a random pattern.

As I write this appendix, Corel is trying to make available a copy of the Squizz Users Manual on the PHOTO-PAINT 7 Plus CD. Look for it.

Maintenance Changes to PHOTO-PAINT 7

The following changes occurred to the PHOTO-PAINT 7 program with the addition of the Maintenance Release.

Rearrangement of Command Items

Command items appearing in the Object menu have been somewhat rearranged to facilitate the inclusion of commands associated with the new Lens object feature. While the items that existed in the original DRAW7 suite release have not been removed, this drop-down menu is now shorter. You can still customize your menus any way you want via the Customize dialog box in the Tools menu.

Close Scan Dialog After Acquire

A new check box called "Close scan dialog after acquire" has been added to the Advanced tab in the Options dialog box (accessed through the Tools menu). Enabling this check box causes the TWAIN dialog box to be closed after each successful scan. If the check box is not enabled, the TWAIN dialog box remains open until you close it. This is very handy when scanning in multiple images.

Selectable Default Object Mode

Users can now determine the default Object Editing Mode setting. This setting used to default to Multi mode. Now, using a setting in the General tab of the Options dialog box (accessed through the Tools menu), you can choose which of the Object modes is the default mode.

Show CMYK in Percentages

By enabling the Show CMYK in percentages check box in the Display tab of the Options dialog box (accessed through the Tools menu), you can force CMYK color values displayed in the Color Roll-Up and the status bar to be displayed in percentage values (0–100 percent) instead of grayscale values (0–255).

Import and Export of PSD Images

Corel PHOTO-PAINT 7 and PHOTO-PAINT 7 Plus now support both the import and export of PSD format images, including *adjustment layers*, the Photoshop version of *lens objects* in PHOTO-PAINT 7. In some cases you may be asked to verify the PHOTO-PAINT lenses created from the existing adjustment layers contained within the PSD. This is due, in part, to the unique nature of the implementation of these technologies in both PHOTO-PAINT and Photoshop.

Import and Export to FlashPix

Importing and exporting to the new FlashPix format are now supported in PHOTO-PAINT. Because FlashPix may be new to some of you, I have included some excerpts I extracted from various Web sources about the subject. Most of it will sound like an advertisement, but the information is beneficial.

How FlashPix Technology Works

FlashPix technology supports images of any size, captured at any resolution. Images in FlashPix files are stored at multiple independent resolutions, and each resolution is subdivided into square tiles. These features allow applications to select the appropriate resolution a user needs for a selected procedure and to directly access the specific areas of an image needed for the operation being performed. No longer do applications have to process the entire image in order to view a small section, nor process a high-resolution image to produce a low-resolution display. Edits are applied to high-resolution images only when necessary—usually when users want high-quality output, have clicked the print button, and are done interacting with their image.

An edit, a layout choice, or another use of an image called an *image view* is stored as a small script separate from the image data itself. The script and image data are wrapped inside a structured storage "container." Microsoft's structured OLE storage enables software to easily store a variety of information types, such as scripts, image data, ownership information, color management data, etc.—all in one convenient single file. This file is interoperable with existing structured storage architectures such as OLE II and OpenDoc, as well as Java and Netscape Navigator plug-ins.

To display or print the edited version, a FlashPix-optimized application applies the changes described in the image view script to the appropriate resolution of the original image data. In FlashPix architecture, you can use and modify an image in any number of ways but store the original high-resolution image data in only one place. Computers don't process the complete file to display an image, and they employ only the resolution level required for the selected view and monitor size. Software applications don't have to convert between *interchange* formats (such as TIFF) used outside the application and proprietary *representation* formats used within. They can use the FlashPix format exclusively as the application workspace, as well as the interchange format. Also, changes to images take place faster, because only affected tiles have to be adjusted before processing.

For more information on the subject, open your Internet browser and search on FlashPix.

CorelTUTOR

There have been several internal improvements to CorelTUTOR that make it operate much faster than the original release, and it now supports large fonts and small and medium-sized toolbars.

CorelSCAN

The image enhancement process has been modified to give more control to the user. It no longer requires the use of the Intellihance filter. The post-processing options now allow selection of more destinations.

Color Management

Performing a Typical installation only installs generic color management device profiles. To install the color profiles for your devices, launch the Color Manager from the Tools menu or from the Windows 95 Start menu (under Programs) and choose "Get Profile from disk..." or "Install profiles" in the list. The instructions will guide you through the process of loading specific device profiles. This new procedure allows you to install only the drivers you wish to use. Color profiles may also be installed via the Custom installation.

Bibliography

The following is a short, opinionated list of books that I think will help you, either with using PHOTO-PAINT or with photo-editing in general.

- *Real World Photoshop 3: Industrial Strength Production Techniques* by David Blatner, Bruce Fraser, and Stephen Roth

  This is the best book to help you learn everything from getting the finest-looking output from scanning clear through correcting problems with your printer. Even though it is written for Photoshop 3, I have used it very successfully with PHOTO-PAINT 7.

  Peachpit Press, 1995
  ISBN: 1-56609-169-1

- *Professional Photoshop: Color Correction, Retouching, and Image Manipulation with Adobe Photoshop* by Dan Margulis

  Everything you ever wanted to know—and a lot that you didn't know you wanted to know—about color correction is in this book. Dan Margulis jumps into the subject of color correction with great depth, but he usually explains the terms and techniques he presents, making this a very readable book. The only problems you may have with this book are the rather steep price (around $50.00 new) and finding it at all.

  John Wiley & Sons, 1994
  ISBN: 0-471-01873-2

- *Looking Good in Color: The Desktop Publisher's Design Guide* by Gary W. Priester

  This book is a must for anyone venturing into color design work for the first time. Gary (the Mook) writes in a very readable style, and even if you don't like to read, it's great because there are lots and lots of pictures.

  Ventana Press, 1995
  ISBN: 1-56604-219-4

- *The Color Scanning Book* by Jerry Day

  If you own a Hewlett-Packard scanner (and statistically, 70 percent of you do), ALL you need to know about using it is here. This book covers the device itself, its software, and other scanning software. It's simple: if you have an HP scanner, you should have this book. At press time the book had not gone to the printer and the title was still up in the air, so if you cannot find this title, use the ISBN number which is correct.

  Prentice-Hall
  ISBN: 0-13-357-211-0

- *Photoshop in Black and White: An Illustrated Guide to Reproducing Black-and-White Images, Second Edition* by Jim Rich and Sandy Bozek

  If you are working with grayscale rather than color, you should pick up this little gem. Even though it is only 44 pages long, it contains a wealth of information about getting the most out of your black-and-white (grayscale) images.

  Peachpit Press, 1995
  ISBN: 1-56609-189-6

I warned you this was a short list. There are at least 20 other Photoshop titles (I have them all) that I didn't reference because they were either too Photoshop-specific to be a benefit to PHOTO-PAINT users or they just weren't all that good. I also warned you this list was opinionated.

INDEX

C

S

V

W

X

Y

Z

FUTURE CLASSICS FROM

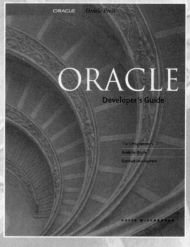

THE WEB SERVER HANDBOOK

by Cynthia Chin-Lee and Comet

Learn how to set up and maintain a dynamic and effective Web site with this comprehensive guide that focuses on Oracle's new Web solutions.

ISBN: 0-07-882215-7
Price: $39.95 U.S.A.
Includes One CD-ROM

ORACLE MEDIA OBJECTS HANDBOOK

by Dan Shafer

The power, flexibility, and ease of Oracle Media Objects (the cross-platform multimedia authoring tools) are within your reach with this definitive handbook.

ISBN: 0-07-882214-9
Price: $39.95 U.S.A.
Includes One CD-ROM

ORACLE DEVELOPER'S GUIDE

by David McClanahan

Loaded with code for common tasks, developers will find all the information they need to create applications and build a fast, powerful, and secure Oracle database.

ISBN: 0-07-882087-1
Price: $34.95 U.S.A.

ORACLE: THE COMPLETE REFERENCE

Third Edition

by George Koch and Kevin Loney

ISBN: 0-07-882097-9
Price: $34.95 U.S.A.

ORACLE DBA HANDBOOK

by Kevin Loney

ISBN: 0-07-881182-1
Price: $34.95 U.S.A.

ORACLE: A BEGINNER'S GUIDE

by Michael Abbey and Michael J. Corey

ISBN: 0-07-882122-3
Price: $29.95 U.S.A.

TUNING ORACLE

by Michael J. Corey, Michael Abbey, and Daniel J. Dechichio, Jr.

ISBN: 0-07-881181-3
Price: $29.95 U.S.A.

ORDER BOOKS DIRECTLY FROM OSBORNE/McGRAW-HILL

For a complete catalog of Osborne's books, call 510-549-6600 or write to us at 2600 Tenth Street, Berkeley, CA 94710

Call Toll-Free, 24 hours a day, 7 days a week, in the U.S.A.
U.S.A.: 1-800-262-4729   **Canada: 1-800-565-5758**

Mail *in the U.S.A. to:*   *Canada*
McGraw-Hill, Inc.   McGraw-Hill Ryerson
Customer Service Dept.   Customer Service
P.O. Box 182607   300 Water Street
Columbus, OH 43218-2607   Whitby, Ontario L1N 9B6

Fax *in the U.S.A. to:*   *Canada*
1-614-759-3644   1-800-463-5885
          Canada
          orders@mcgrawhill.ca

SHIP TO:

Name

Company

Address

City / State / Zip

Daytime Telephone *(We'll contact you if there's a question about your order.)*

ISBN #	BOOK TITLE	Quantity	Price	Total
0-07-88				
0-07-88				
0-07-88				
0-07-88				
0-07-88				
0-07088				
0-07-88				
0-07-88				
0-07-88				
0-07-88				
0-07-88				
0-07-88				
0-07-88				

Shipping & Handling Charge from Chart Below		
Subtotal		
Please Add Applicable State & Local Sales Tax		
TOTAL		

Shipping & Handling Charges

Order Amount	U.S.	Outside U.S.
$15.00 - $24.99	$4.00	$6.00
$25.00 - $49.99	$5.00	$7.00
$50.00 - $74.99	$6.00	$8.00
$75.00 - and up	$7.00	$9.00
$100.00 - and up	$8.00	$10.00

Occasionally we allow other selected companies to use our mailing list. If you would prefer that we not include you in these extra mailings, please check here: ❑

METHOD OF PAYMENT

❑ Check or money order enclosed (payable to Osborne/McGraw-Hill)

❑ AMERICAN EXPRESS   ❑ DISCOVER   ❑ MasterCard   ❑ VISA

Account No.

Expiration Date

Signature

In a hurry? Call with your order anytime, day or night, or visit your local bookstore.

Thank you for your order   Code BC640SL

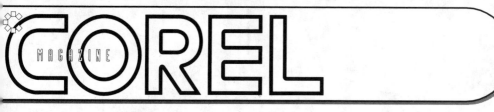